Gross Misbehavior
and Wickedness

Gross Misbehavior and Wickedness

*A Notorious Divorce in
Early Twentieth-Century America*

JEAN ELSON

TEMPLE UNIVERSITY PRESS
Philadelphia • Rome • Tokyo

TEMPLE UNIVERSITY PRESS
Philadelphia, Pennsylvania 19122
www.temple.edu/tempress

Copyright © 2017 by Temple University—Of The Commonwealth System
of Higher Education
All rights reserved
Published 2017

Library of Congress Cataloging-in-Publication Data

Names: Elson, Jean, 1948– author.
Title: Gross misbehavior and wickedness : a notorious divorce in early
 twentieth-century America / Jean Elson.
Description: Philadelphia, Pennsylvania : Temple University Press, [2017] |
 Includes bibliographical references and index.
Identifiers: LCCN 2016050529 (print) | LCCN 2017009867 (ebook) |
 ISBN 9781439913925 (ebook) | ISBN 9781439913901 (hardback : alk. paper) |
 ISBN 9781439913918 (paper : alk. paper)
Subjects: LCSH: Walker, Nina Chinn, 1873–1947—Trials, litigation, etc. |
 Walker, J. W. G. (James Wilson Grimes), 1868–1950—Trials, litigation,
 etc. | Trials (Divorce)—Rhode Island. | Trials (Adultery)—Rhode Island.
 | Divorce suits—Rhode Island. | Divorce—Law and legislation—United
 States—History—20th century. | Women—Social conditions—United
 States—History—20th century. | BISAC: SOCIAL SCIENCE / Women's Studies.
 | LAW / Gender & the Law.
Classification: LCC KF228.W285 (ebook) | LCC KF228.W285 E47 2017 (print) |
 DDC 346.74501/66—dc23
LC record available at https://lccn.loc.gov/2016050529

9 8 7 6 5 4 3 2 1

To

my mother, Edith, who is a strong woman;

my late father, Matt, who appreciated strong women;

my late grandmother Bessie, who said,

"Nothing but trying";

and

all people who continue the struggle

for justice

Contents

	Prologue	*1*
1	Coming Together and Coming Apart	*7*
2	The Perfect Couple? A Dissenting Note	*13*
3	Early Days: Winter 1897 to Summer 1905	*27*
4	A Series of Temporary Truces: Summer 1905 to Summer 1909	*49*
5	The Beginning of the End: Summer 1909 to February 1911	*71*
6	Some Cases Are Simple; This One Is Not: March 1911	*97*
7	Conflicting Testimonies: March 1911	*121*
8	A Baffling Piece of New Evidence: Spring 1911 to December 1912	*143*
9	More Trials and Tribulations: January 1913 to November 12, 1913	*165*
10	A Question of Virginity: November 13–21, 1913	*195*
11	"Gross Misbehavior and Wickedness": December 4, 1913, to December 4, 1916	*225*
	Epilogue: The Rest of Their Lives	*241*
	Author's Notes	*277*
	Notes	*283*
	Index	*315*

Photographs appear on pages 157–164

Gross Misbehavior and Wickedness

Prologue

> The sociological imagination enables us to grasp history and biography and the relations between the two within society. That is its task and its promise.
>
> —C. Wright Mills, *The Sociological Imagination*

Nina and James Walker wed as American Victorianism was yielding to new cultural values. Writing half a century later, historian William L. O'Neill notes that the Progressive Era from the late nineteenth through the early twentieth centuries produced "a new sense of what the family was and where it fitted into the social structure."[1] In particular, "divorce came to be the principal issue over which the old and new sets of ideas about family clashed."[2] Indeed, American cultural attitudes toward divorce changed considerably between 1880 and 1919,[3] and the protracted divorce proceedings between Nina and James Walker clearly illustrate this shift. From 1909 to 1916, the two waged a bitter and public court battle that repudiated the affections that had led them to marry eagerly and hastily in February 1897.

Contemporary Americans are generally familiar with the rising divorce rates of the 1970s and 1980s, but the divorce mini-revolution of the early twentieth century is little discussed. In 1870, the United States recorded 10,962 divorces, equating to just 1.5 per 1,000 marriages, but by 1900, the absolute number had risen to 55,751 (4.0 per 1,000 marriages), and by 1920, there were 167,105 divorces (7.7 per 1,000 marriages).[4] Although the 1920 rate was a small fraction of the 50 percent figure seen for first marriages at the end of the twentieth century,[5] this increase during the Progressive Era was dramatic, particularly when compared to earlier periods.

The Statistical Survey of Marriage and Divorce, published by the U.S. Census Bureau in 1909, found that the American divorce rate was increasing by 30 percent every five years and concluded that rates were headed "almost without exception upward."[6] Social historian Elaine Tyler May observes, "During the late 19th and early 20th centuries, American marriages began to collapse at an unprecedented rate."[7] Despite this, George E. Howard, a well-known early twentieth-century historian and sociologist at the University of Chicago, viewed divorce as "a remedy, not a disease."[8] In William Graham Sumner's 1908 keynote address at the third annual meeting of the American Sociological Society (now the American Sociological Association), he noted that the family "had lost its position as a conservative institution and become a field for social change."[9] Sociologists Herbert Spencer and Lester Ward recommended reducing obstacles to divorce, and many other social scientists saw doing so as a strategy to save the institution of marriage.

Changes in the economy placed greater stress on individual urban family units, which could no longer rely on the extended family support prevalent when most families participated in an agricultural economy. This shift meant that love and understanding between marriage partners became the basis for marriage, even in the upper class, where family alliances simultaneously persisted as a rationale. This transition was not without peril. According to one legal scholar, "The greater emotional content of family relations elevated the stakes in marriage, making domestic life delightful when it succeeded and devastating when it failed, as was [then] more likely to happen."[10]

Despite the greater emphasis on intimacy between husbands and wives, sexual disagreements often arose. With limited reliable birth control, conflict "often took the form of a struggle between men's desire for sex and women's concerns about health and maternity."[11] A frequent outcome of this conflict was for men to engage in extramarital relationships, often with poor young women who were moving to the cities in large numbers, seeking work and living apart from their families for the first time in history. This trend led to an epidemic of sexually transmitted infections (then called "venereal diseases"); a Boston physician found that more than one-third of his male patients admitted to having been infected with gonorrhea,[12] and New York physician Dr. Prince Morrow claimed that at least 60 percent of the male population had contracted syphilis or gonorrhea. Unfortunately, when unfaithful men contracted these diseases, they often infected their wives. In his 1904 medical text, *Social Disease and Marriage*, Morrow claims, "There is more venereal infection among virtuous wives than among professional prostitutes."[13] This circumstance became a problem in many marriages, including the Walkers', and adultery was a leading ground for divorce.

The increasing divorce rate was often associated with women's aspirations for independence, and the 1909 Bureau of the Census Report recorded that women initiated two-thirds of American divorces.[14] However, fervent disagreement over the issue split the suffragist movement. Elizabeth Cady Stanton and Charlotte Perkins Gilman favored liberalizing divorce laws, but other women's rights leaders, including Susan B. Anthony and Frances Willard, strongly opposed doing so. Despite the decreasing barriers, divorce remained unavailable to those who could not afford it. Lawyers were expensive, and the 1909 census report found that alimony was awarded in just one of eleven divorces.[15] In an era before women could support themselves, most women needed husbands for economic support.

Newspaper readers of the time were particularly interested in the often lurid accounts of high-society divorces. The public was extremely curious about this phenomenon that had been quite rare until the mid-nineteenth century. The Walker divorce hearings took place in Newport, Rhode Island, but newspaper reports and gossip about their marital troubles created a sensation throughout the nation, and their divorce case is an interesting example of the many private divorces that became public issues during the Progressive Era.[16]

An article on page seven of the December 9, 1913, *New York Herald* details recent developments in the Walker case that had "interested all New England,"[17] and news elsewhere on the page provides fitting historical context. A piece titled "President Denies Women's Request for Suffrage" relays Woodrow Wilson's message to a delegation of eighty-five representatives of the National Woman Suffrage Association that he could not "use the power of the administration to bring about the organization of a special committee in the House to take up the suffrage question" because the Democratic Party (which he represented) had not endorsed the issue.[18] American women were thereby informed that the federal government would not consider granting them the most fundamental democratic right.

Although their attempts to achieve justice in the public sphere were largely thwarted, many women sought change in the domestic sphere through the courts. Several other articles on that same page of the *New York Herald* illustrate women's use of the legal system to settle domestic disputes. According to one article, a Mrs. Griffin sought to divorce Dr. Edward Harrison Griffin, whose patients included famous opera stars, actors, and members of some of the wealthiest families in New York City. Mrs. Griffin claimed her husband's income to be $80,000 a year, "greater than the President of the United States." His office was "furnished with costly marbles, bronzes, and tapestries," and he owned real estate valued at $150,000. However, Mrs. Griffin testified that, despite this wealth, after dismissing several servants, her husband had cut off her $40 weekly allowance and refused to continue supporting her. In response, Mrs. Griffin separated from her husband and filed for divorce,[19] an option that may have been unavailable to her not long before.

Another article on the same page of the December 9, 1913, *Herald* describes the case of a Mrs. Annetta Slocum, who sought to divorce her husband, Dr. William H. Slocum. She alleged that he drank to excess, neglected his practice, and permitted her just seventy-five cents per day for food. In addition, he compelled her to wash his car and to do heavy labor. Moreover, he "showed an unusual interest in Mrs. Frieda Schmidt, wife of a chauffeur." The Slocums continued to live in the same house, but they were not on speaking terms. Her mother lived with them and was incensed that the doctor forced her to chop the wood she bought from him.[20]

This newspaper page also presents the stories of several other women seeking to divorce their often prominent husbands on grounds of cruelty, lack of cohabitation, and physical abuse. One unfortunate woman, a Mrs. Justine Sutton Gray, "broke down and became hysterical" upon learning that, yet again, her husband had failed to appear at the New York Supreme Court, and his lawyer was requesting a sixth postponement.[21]

Prior to the advent of "no-fault" divorce laws in the mid- to late twentieth century, divorce was an even more adversarial process than it is now. Divorces could be awarded only if one spouse proved that the other was guilty of wrongdoing in breach of the marriage contract, with common grounds for divorce including adultery, desertion, failure to provide, and extreme cruelty. However, states differed as to which grounds were legally acceptable justifications. Marriage in the United States has always been a civil contract regulated by individual states, and the dissolution of marriage is controlled at the state level. That said, the "full faith and credit" provision of the U.S. Constitution (Article IV, Section 1) requires states to accept marriages and divorces granted in other states.

State legislatures, particularly in the eastern United States, attempted to reverse the rise in the divorce rate by passing more than one hundred pieces of marriage and divorce legislation between 1889 and 1906.[22] By 1909, when the Walker case began, legal grounds for divorce varied widely among the states, as did residency requirements for filing. Of all the places the Walkers had lived during their marriage, Rhode Island provided the best opportunity for Nina Walker to pursue her divorce. In that state alone, a divorce could be obtained for "gross misbehavior and wickedness in either of the parties repugnant to and inconsistent with the marriage contract."[23] These vague terms left room for broad interpretation, and "gross misbehavior and wickedness" became an important allegation in her case, as other legal grounds were more difficult to prove. Nina Walker cited several shocking charges that fit into this broad category.

The events leading up to and taking place throughout the Walker divorce hearings raised issues that were not solely individual matters; they signified social changes evolving in American culture at the time. Acrimonious testimony often focused on incompatible views of gender, family, and class—ideas that characterized broader cultural debates of the Progressive Era. The trials raised many questions including the following:

- Must a wife obey her husband's orders?
- Is a wife required to submit to her husband's sexual desires?
- Are children the property of their father?
- Should fathers provide their children with emotional as well as financial support?
- Is corporal punishment of children to be condoned?
- Must a husband be faithful to his wife?
- Must a wife remain with her husband when doing so endangers her physical or mental health?
- Is a wife obliged to be more loyal to her husband and his family than to her own?
- Should a feminist always support the woman when a husband and wife argue?
- How involved should parents be in a grown child's marriage?
- Is it proper for a married upper-class man to befriend a single working-class woman?
- Is divorce the appropriate solution for a troubled marriage?

We continue to grapple with most of these questions in contemporary American society.

I

Coming Together and Coming Apart

Wednesday, February 24, 1897

THE BRIDE WAS BEAUTIFUL; the groom was elegant. At four in the afternoon, Miss Nina Chinn and Mr. James Wilson Grimes Walker were united in marriage. Both were descendants of prominent American families whose lineages predated the American Revolution. The bride was twenty-four, the younger daughter of Mrs. Virginia Serrellina Chinn, and the groom was twenty-nine, the elder son of Admiral John Grimes Walker and Rebecca White Pickering Walker. The *Washington Post* society editor declared the Chinn-Walker nuptials "one of the prettiest afternoon weddings of the season"[1] and featured the story as the first item in the following day's column. The wedding was important society news not only in the nation's capital but also in other parts of the country. Details of the event were reported across the nation, from New York to California.

The Chinn-Walker wedding took place at historic Rock Creek Church in Washington, DC, with the Reverend Reese L. Alsop, of St. Ann's Church, Brooklyn, officiating. This was a traditional ceremony; the bride's parents had been married at the same church by the same minister. The bride, slender and approximately six feet tall,[2] wore her mother's wedding dress of ivory white silk with a richly trimmed bodice of family point lace.[3] A long veil "enveloped her figure."[4] It was a "family heirloom, and was made of point applique, being the same worn years ago by her aunt, Mrs. Beech, who was considered one of the beauties of Washington."[5] Miss Nina Chinn gracefully carried a large bouquet of bride roses as she made her way down the aisle.

Nina's bridesmaids included her sister, Bertha; the groom's sisters, Frances and Susan Walker; and Elsie Ripley, Nina's cousin from Brooklyn. They wore identical corn-colored iridescent silk gowns, with collars sewn of jeweled gilt braid and skirts individually trimmed with three carefully pinked ruffles. Their silk jackets revealed chiffon ruffles underneath. To complete their outfits, the bridesmaids also wore large black Gainsborough hats, each highlighted with a black plume and a single red rose. They carried baskets of red roses.[6] The admiring guests agreed these ensembles were very effective.[7] A distinguished physician and family friend, Dr. Joseph R. Bromwell, escorted the bride down the aisle and gave her away.[8]

James Wilson Grimes Walker had chosen his younger brother, Henry Pickering Walker, as best man. The ushers included Henry Goddard Pickering (his uncle) and Mr. Edward W. Green (his cousin), both from Boston, as well as Charles Cooley, of Hartford, and John Parker, of Baltimore. The church was attractively decorated with a green and white theme and "was filled with friends of the families of the bride and groom, among whom diplomatic and official circles were well represented."[9] Guests included noted political figures, military dignitaries, and various socialites prominent in the DC area and beyond.[10]

Following the ceremony, a private reception was held for relatives and intimate friends from 5:00 to 7:00 P.M. at the Connecticut Avenue home of the bride's mother, Mrs. Virginia Serrellina Chinn. Mrs. Chinn received her guests in an elegant mauve velvet gown. Lilies and bride roses decorated the drawing rooms, while "graceful festoons of ivy and asparagus plumosa adorned the walls and draped windows and doorways." The bride and groom "stood in a bower of green arranged in the recess of the bay window to receive the congratulations of their friends." A gracious wedding feast was laid out on the dining room table for the guests to enjoy. There was a rather large bride's cake, which "formed a conspicuous adornment." In addition, four miniature bridesmaid's cakes were provided, "in one of which reposed the ring which was to predict which of the four young ladies would be the first bride."[11] The newspapers do not reveal who was the lucky bridesmaid to win the prize.

A sizeable room was required to display the large number of "elegant and useful presents" given to the newlyweds by friends, relatives, and associates. One of the most magnificent was an exquisite Burmese bowl that had been sent by the bride's uncle, Major Wood, who was stationed in Quetta, India. Unfortunately, he and his wife were unable to attend the wedding, a situation greatly lamented by the family.[12]

Following the reception, the newlyweds left for a wedding journey to a secret destination.[13] The bride's friends caught "the last glimpse of her in a stylish traveling costume of brown cloth with hat and wrap to match."[14] The newly married couple planned to set up house in Saint Louis, where the groom had recently worked for the railroad.

Aside from the absence of the bride's uncle, nothing seemed to be amiss in the nuptial celebration of Nina Chinn and James Wilson Grimes Walker. Even the weather cooperated. Although the day was a cool forty-three degrees Fahrenheit with northerly winds at the time of the wedding, there were fair skies.[15] The couple married on a Wednesday—according to tradition, the luckiest day for weddings.[16] It seemed that fortune would surely smile on the young husband and wife. And yet, only a dozen years later, a vastly different set of events would take place.

Tuesday, October 19, 1909

Lieutenant James Walker lived at Cottage #5 at the Newport Naval Training Station on Coaster's Island with his wife, Nina, and four children. As was his habit, James returned to the cottage a little after noon. Nina and Mary, the housemaid, had luncheon ready for him. He did not see the children, who usually joined them for the midday meal. A car regularly brought them home from school at just about the time their father arrived. James remarked to his wife that they were late today. Nina replied, "It's such a pleasant day, they are probably walking home." The children did not return while their parents lunched, and Nina was even more quiet than usual. James assumed she must still be feeling unwell. After all, she continued to sleep in a separate room from him, as she had done since returning from her vacation at Mrs. Batcheler's house in Newport. Or, perhaps her lack of conversation was to demonstrate that she was still angry at him regarding their disagreement about schooling arrangements for their sons and daughter. James finished his meal, and, although the children had not yet appeared, it was time for him to get back to his office on the other side of the naval base. James said good-bye to Nina, who averted her face. Bright autumn sunlight burst through the cottage door as James pulled it open. "Tell the boys and Elizabeth I will see them at supper," he remarked as he walked out the front door, brusquely kicking aside fallen leaves in his way.

Nina watched her husband walk down the path until he reached the road to his office. She was suddenly distracted by the realization that the leaves on the maple tree in their front yard had turned bright crimson overnight. Nina closed the front door and handed Mary a long list of items to pick up at the other end of the training station. "Please keep the pots on the stove; I will feed the children," she murmured.

Nina was well aware that she and James had not said much over the midday meal—merely the formalities of "please pass the [whatever it was James wanted at the moment]." She had slept only fitfully the night before in her own room—the room separate from James she had claimed as hers since she came back from staying at Mrs. Batcheler's. Was lack of sleep the reason she felt dazed, or was it what she was planning?

Nina forced herself to concentrate. She had lots to do. She tried to stay calm as she walked quickly through the cottage, throwing whatever she could into trunks and a hamper. The children finally returned from school, rosy cheeked and boisterous from their long walk. They looked like a happy little troop: Elizabeth was almost twelve years old; Grahame was ten; Serrell was almost nine; and Herbert, the youngest, was not quite eight years old. Grahame came through the door first and looked expectantly at the dining table. "Where's Father?" he asked. "He had to return to work," Nina told him quietly. She served the children their food as quickly as possible without revealing her impatience. When they were finally finished, Nina sent them to play. She went back to the table and, out of habit, cleared the dishes and the crumbs, even though doing so didn't matter anymore.

Thankfully, the children were in the habit of amusing each other and therefore paid little attention to her furious movements throughout the cottage. Belatedly, Elizabeth took notice of her mother's packing. "Where are you going?" she asked. Nina guessed that Elizabeth was worried that her mother was again leaving without her and her brothers. "We are all going on an adventure," Nina told the children, "and you must be very good and help Mama and come with me quickly." Elizabeth liked adventures, and since she was the eldest, the younger three would follow agreeably. "Where are *we* going?" she responded. "To see Grandma Chinn and Auntie Bertha," her mother explained. Nina dreaded what she would say if the children asked whether their father was joining them, but they were accustomed to his busy work schedule and did not inquire. By 2:00 P.M., one and all were ready to go. As she looked around the cottage for what she prayed would be the last time, Nina sucked in her breath, lifted the telephone, and rang up her husband. "A man called who would like to see you at your office," she informed James. "I told him you would be there until at least three this afternoon." Nina was already replacing the receiver as James replied that he would wait for the man to come.

Nina needed a pass for her, the children, and their belongings to leave the naval training station. She had a blank one saved especially for this occasion. Having signed her husband's name many times before as a matter of convenience, she knew just how to do it. She smiled sweetly, and the guard handled the parade of Mrs. Walker, her children, Trixie (their black cat), and the baggage as just one more routine daily chore. He even called some of the men to help the lieutenant's wife through the gate with the three trunks and a hamper.

It was about fifty degrees, not too cool for an October day in Newport, and she and the children were dressed warmly. In spite of this, Nina felt a shiver that began in her shoulders as she shepherded her brood aboard the boat from Coaster's Island. The shiver traveled down her spine just as she had everything and everyone transferred to the hired car waiting at the dock in Newport. Nina did not stop shivering until her bags and children were unloaded at the house on the mainland. Her mother and her sister welcomed them to 67 Rhode Island Avenue. This was to be their refuge for now.

James glanced at the wall clock in his office. Nina had called almost an hour before and told him a man was coming to see him by 3:00 P.M. It was nearly three now, and James wondered who this man could be and whether he wanted to see him on naval or personal business, but Nina had hung up at her end before he could ask. Probably just wants to sell me something, he thought. James continued to work on the specifications for dock repairs. After a while, he looked up and noticed that three had passed, yet the man Nina had mentioned had not yet come to call. James busied himself with some paperwork, expecting his visitor to appear at any moment. "I will have to admonish him that, whatever he wants, tardiness is not a good way to begin," he reflected. By 4:15 P.M., James was more than a little displeased, and by 4:40 P.M., he was actively annoyed. He could not imagine what had delayed the mystery man and decided that he would read a discarded copy of the *Newport Daily News* until precisely 5:00 P.M. When no visitor had arrived by that time, James stood up, put on his coat, and locked his office door. It was getting dark by then, and there was an autumn chill in the air. He took the long walk down the road to the family cottage.

When James reached home, the sky was almost completely dark and, with the sun gone, it was cold and damp. He barely noted the silence that was unusual for a household with several children. His first impression upon opening the front door was that the cottage had been looted and the rest of his family kidnapped. The front room and the bedrooms were nearly bare. Nina's clothes and other personal articles were gone, as were the children's clothing, toys, and school books. A shock went through him, and, when he searched the cottage in the eerie quiet, he could find no trace of the Walker family silver. James sat down heavily on a greenish slipper chair in his bedroom. He put his hands on his temples, closed his eyes, and dropped his head into his lap. He remained in this position for the amount of time it took to realize what had actually taken place. When James sat up and opened his eyes again, he noticed a scrap of paper stuck in the mirror of his bureau. Torn between rage and grief, he picked at the corner to release what turned out to be a ragged piece of old wrapping paper with a note scribbled on it. It read:

> If you love me you would love my mother.
> seigned, [sic]
> Elizabeth Walker
> Graham [sic] Walker
> Herbert Walker
> Serrell Walker

Each child's name was penned in a distinct childish scrawl.

The following day, James Wilson Grimes Walker was served with divorce papers charging that he "hath violated his marriage oath in this: that he hath been guilty of adultery and hath been guilty of extreme cruelty to your petitioner, his said wife, and of other gross misbehavior and wickedness in violation of his marriage covenant."[17] Specific charges by Nina Chinn Walker included the accusation that her husband had carried on a lengthy affair with a former Boston waitress, who had also been a housekeeper and governess for the Walker family. In addition, Nina charged James with extreme cruelty toward her and the children. In turn, James accused Nina of desertion and of being an unfit mother.

The protracted and acrimonious Walker divorce battle would take place over more than seven years. In excess of sixty witnesses, including many of the Walker wedding guests, would testify for one side or the other. In the early twentieth century, newspaper reports and gossip about the Walkers' marital troubles created a sensation throughout the nation. This book tells the story of how Nina and James Walker came together as husband and wife, of what drove them apart, and of the arguments for and against dissolving their marriage. It is a story of sociohistorical significance that sheds light on a critical period in the evolution of American culture.

2

The Perfect Couple?

A Dissenting Note

At the time of Nina Chinn and James Wilson Grimes Walker's wedding, most people agreed that they were eminently suited for each other. After all, they were both descended from prominent American families. Not just their last names but the first and middle names of their parents and their siblings—and, in Mr. Walker's case, his own name—were reminders of their distinguished lineages.

James Wilson Grimes Walker could trace his father's family in North America to the Widow Walker, who emigrated from England to Rehoboth, Massachusetts, before 1643. Among his illustrious paternal forbears was a lieutenant in the colonial army. His paternal grandmother, Susan Grimes, was the sister of James Wilson Grimes, an Iowa governor and U.S. senator.[1] John Grimes Walker, James's father, was born in Hillsborough, New Hampshire, on March 20, 1835, and had a promising naval career at the time he married Rebecca White Pickering on September 12, 1866.

Rebecca White Pickering, James's mother, descended from another venerable American family, the Pickerings of Salem, Massachusetts, who had first emigrated from England to North America in the middle of the seventeenth century. Her family line included John Pickering, a distinguished soldier in King Philip's War, and Timothy Pickering, who had been a member of President George Washington's staff, U.S. postmaster general, secretary of war, secretary of state, and a U.S. senator from Massachusetts. More recent forbears included an eminent philologist and several lawyers. Henry White Pickering, Rebecca's father, was president of the Old Boston Bank.[2] His wife, Frances Dana Goddard, from yet another distinguished New England family, gave birth to Rebecca in Boston on September 12, 1836.[3]

With his impressive family background, James Wilson Grimes Walker must have seemed an excellent marriage candidate to Nina Chinn and her mother. Nina's older sister had not succeeded in finding a suitable husband, and it was now up to Nina to find a partner worthy of her family's lineage. In common with James Walker, Nina Chinn's paternal forebears came from England (where the name was spelled "Chynn") to North America prior to the Revolutionary War. They settled in Virginia and then moved to Kentucky. The Chinn family was proud to have not just one but two ancestors who were related by marriage to President Washington. Nina's paternal grandfather, Richard Henry Chinn, was future U.S. Secretary of State Henry Clay's law partner and served in the Kentucky House of Representatives and in the U.S. Senate. Nina's father, also named Richard Henry Chinn, was born in Scott County, Kentucky, the seventh of fourteen children of his namesake and his mother, Elizabeth Holmes Chinn, whose father had migrated from New Hampshire to Kentucky.[4]

Nina Chinn's maternal grandfather was Robert Serrell Wood, an Englishman who kept the title to his English estate when he immigrated to the United States in the early nineteenth century. A prodigious traveler, he reportedly came to the United States to pursue his avid interest in studying Native Americans. Nina's maternal grandmother, Elizabeth Davis, was descended from the Davis family and the Thomas families, with long Quaker lineages in Pennsylvania.[5] She met her husband when he boarded at her parents' home in Philadelphia while attending medical school. Virginia Serrellina Wood, Nina's mother, was born on May 29, 1843, the second child of several daughters and a son. Two of the daughters died in childhood. Virginia and her siblings grew up in Washington, DC, where their father owned forty acres of land named Mount Hermon, in honor of "the mountain in Palestine where a holy light transfigured the land the Diciples [sic] beheld the assent of their Lord." The Chinns impressed their neighbors by having English rather than black servants, and they had a pet peacock.[6] Robert Serrell Wood also wrote one of the first books on electricity. He died of yellow fever on a voyage back to Philadelphia from Haiti in 1853 and was buried at sea. Virginia, nine years old, and her sister Emily, twelve years old, were on that voyage with their father and had to return alone. Their mother, Elizabeth Davis Wood, raised the two girls and a younger daughter and son by herself from that time on. During the Civil War, the family fled to Europe, where they waited out the war by meeting distinguished relatives and royalty and enjoying continental culture.[7]

After General Robert E. Lee surrendered in 1865, Nina's grandmother returned to their Mount Hermon home with her three daughters, leaving her son, Jefferson Serrell Wood, in England to be educated by his paternal uncle. The beautiful Wood sisters had many admirers. In 1868, Virginia was introduced to Richard Henry Chinn at White Sulphur Springs in West Virginia, which happened to be General Lee's favorite resort. Richard, a plantation owner, had graduated with honors from Transylvania College and "was popular in New Orleans society, a beautiful dancer and an habitue of the French Opera."[8] Virginia and Richard Henry Chinn married on October 27, 1870.[9]

James Wilson Grimes Walker and Nina Chinn grew up in privileged families. By the time James's parents married in 1866, his father, John Grimes Walker, had already begun a distinguished naval career. Following the death of his mother in 1846, young John Walker moved to Iowa to live with his uncle, U.S. Senator James Wilson Grimes.[10] No doubt benefiting from his relationship with his politically connected uncle, John was appointed as a U.S. Naval Academy cadet in 1850. Only fifteen years old at the time of his appointment, he graduated at the top of his class in 1856. That same year, John Grimes Walker was assigned to the warship *Portsmouth*, the first ship to fly the American flag in San Francisco harbor. With his promotion to master, young John served on several ships from 1858 to 1861, including the *Falmouth*, the *St. Lawrence*, the *Susquehanna*, and the *Connecticut*.[11]

The Civil War presented John Grimes Walker with the opportunity to distinguish himself. As a first lieutenant, he was cited for bravery on the warship *Winona* during its attacks on Forts Jackson and Phillip as well as for the capture of New Orleans from 1861 to 1862. Under Admiral David Farragut's leadership, Walker never missed a battle in the Mississippi Campaign. Commander-in-Chief David Dixon Porter reported that Lieutenant Commander John Walker exhibited "heroic conduct" at the helm of the *Baron de Kalb* in its assaults on Vicksburg in 1862 and 1863.[12] John Walker then commanded the gunboats *Saco* and *Shawmut* from 1864 to 1865, culminating in the capture of Wilmington, North Carolina. His naval superiors were again duly impressed.[13] In 1866, the year he married Rebecca White Pickering, John Grimes Walker was officially promoted to the position of commander and began his term as assistant superintendent of the Naval Academy in Annapolis, where he served until 1869.

James was the second child of John Grimes Walker and Rebecca White Pickering Walker. Their first child was a daughter, Frances Pickering

Walker, born on August 16, 1867, in Roxbury, Massachusetts. In the fall of 1868, Rebecca Walker stayed behind in Salem, Massachusetts, with her Pickering relatives while her husband resumed his duties for the academic year at Annapolis. On September 22, 1868, her brother, Henry Goddard Pickering, sent a telegram to John Grimes Walker with the news that a "nice boy" had been born and that mother and son were doing well.[14] Rebecca and John Walker had hoped to name their first son "James Grimes Walker" in honor of John's uncle and mentor, Senator James Wilson Grimes. However, there seems to have been a misunderstanding, which is how James came to have two middle names: "Rebecca wrote asking the senator's permission to name the baby after him. Before the parents could say James Grimes Walker, a baby cup arrived engraved 'James Wilson Grimes Walker.'"[15] Hence, James would bear the full name of his famous and politically connected great-uncle.

James's sister Susan Grimes Walker was born in Cambridge, Massachusetts, on May 9, 1871, followed by his only brother, Henry Pickering Walker, also born in Cambridge, on July 15, 1872. Rebecca White Pickering Walker then gave birth to two sisters. The first of these unfortunate siblings was Alice Pickering Walker, born on June 25, 1874, in Rye Beach, New Hampshire, and deceased within two months, on August 10, 1874. Her sister, Elizabeth Grimes Walker, was born on January 2, 1876, in Washington, DC, and died only four years after, in 1880. The youngest child, who did survive into adulthood, was Sarah Cochrane Walker, often called Sallie, joining the family on July 16, 1878, in Salem, Massachusetts.[16]

While his children grew, John Grimes Walker moved up in the naval hierarchy. At the close of his term as assistant superintendent of the U.S. Naval Academy, he led a training mission to Europe and was then appointed to other prominent naval positions, including secretary of the Lighthouse Board and chief of the Bureau of Navigation, reporting directly to the secretary of the navy.[17] John Walker remained in Washington, DC, while Rebecca and their children moved to Boston in October 1876.[18]

Rebecca had difficulty raising her children, particularly James (whom his family called "Jamie"). Her father, Henry White Pickering, secretly wrote to her husband that "she was breaking down 'under a too heavy load of responsibility & anxiety. Nine-year-old Jamie was giving his mother much trouble by 'disobedience ending often in violence.' It seemed that it might be necessary to send the boy away to a good school."[19] Rebecca's desperate father asked, "Cannot you do or suggest something to alleviate & lighten this burden?" and pleaded with John throughout three more pages of his letter.[20] James was placed in a school in Beverly, Massachusetts, where it appears that he continued to have trouble. In a letter to his friend Henry F. Woodman on March 31, 1878, John stated that he would soon visit Salem for a week and then return about mid-May to spend most of the summer there. "I shall hope next week to see and talk with you about Jamie," John Walker wrote. "Thank you for your interest in his welfare."[21]

John Grimes Walker took a two-year leave from the navy in 1879 to 1881 to work with the Chicago, Burlington, and Quincy Railroad and then returned to serve as chief of the Bureau of Navigation. In 1889, he was appointed rear admiral and put in command of the famous "White Squadron" (also known as the "Squadron of Evolution"), which traveled to Europe and South America. Rear Admiral Walker then became commander-in-chief of the Pacific squadron in 1894, receiving commendation for representing American interests in Honolulu in the wake of a coup d'état. He was appointed to full admiral in 1894 and returned to shore duty in 1896, again as head of the Lighthouse Board. John Grimes Walker was described as "politically the most powerful man in the service" and "one of the ablest administrators and executives the Department has ever had."[22] Admiral Walker reached mandatory retirement age in 1897, the same year his son married Nina Chinn. Two U.S. Navy destroyers would be named USS *Walker* in his honor.[23] John Grimes Walker was a formidable role model for his sons to emulate.

As the elder son of a distinguished admiral and the namesake of an illustrious senator, there were undoubtedly expectations that James Wilson Grimes Walker would have a brilliant future. After attending school in Beverly, Massachusetts, and graduating from the prestigious St. Paul's School in Concord, New Hampshire, James was also educated in Neuchâtel, Switzerland; Pontlevoy, France; and Heidelberg, Germany. He was an undergraduate at the Massachusetts Institute of Technology from September 1887 to June 1891, where his areas of study were Civil and Sanitary Engineering, although he never received a degree.[24]

Admiral Walker's distant relationship with his son James was apparent even to strangers. A family story told how, on the Walker family's voyage home from Europe, their fellow passengers assumed that James, then a young adult, was his father's valet rather than a family member.[25] Despite, or perhaps due to, his father's connection with the naval academy, James did not attend Annapolis. Neither did his brother Henry, who graduated from Harvard University in 1895. However, Henry Pickering Walker did serve as a second and then first lieutenant in Puerto Rico with the First U.S. Volunteers during the Spanish American War.[26] James never served in combat.

At the time of his wedding to Nina, James was living with his parents in Washington, DC, teaching mathematics at a girl's school and tutoring private students.²⁷ According to his own account, he was "out of employment"²⁸ just prior to his marriage, after having worked a short time for the railroad in St. Louis, until his position was abolished.²⁹ Despite his illustrious pedigree, James Walker's professional prospects certainly did not match those of his father at the same age.

Living up to Admiral Walker would be a difficult task for any son. Not only was Admiral John Grimes Walker a renowned naval hero; he looked the part. In his book on the creation of the Panama Canal, historian David McCullough describes the admiral's appearance as follows:

> At age sixty-six Rear Admiral John Grimes Walker was still a majestic figure. Even in his dark civilian suit and string tie he looked like the Old Man of the Sea, as he was sometimes known in Washington. Large and handsome, he carried himself, especially on public occasions, in grand military fashion. The gray hair was smartly parted in the exact center of his head. The complexion was ruddy, the brows heavy and beautifully arched, and from the sides of his face grew magnificent muttonchop whiskers that reached to his lapels and that were several decades out of style.³⁰

Admiral Walker carries the same distinguished look in a family portrait photographed at about the same time. The picture includes the admiral, his wife, his three living daughters, and two sons, then young adults. His younger son, Henry Pickering Walker, who would soon become a war hero, faces his father in the portrait, looking like a dashing young man. The older son, James Wilson Grimes Walker, stands behind Henry and his father. He looks pale, already quite bald, with spectacles and a slight body frame. The contrast in appearances is notable (see the Walker family photographs on page 157).³¹

Nina Chinn spent most of her youth living down the street from the Walker home in Washington, DC. Her sister, Elizabeth Bertha Chinn (known as Bertha), born on September 1, 1871, was the first child of Richard Henry Chinn and Virginia Serrellina Wood Chinn. On January 28, 1873, Nina was born.³² While Admiral Walker was often absent during James's childhood, his father was a major presence in his life by way of example. Nina Chinn had almost no contact with her father. Richard Chinn's family had run a prosperous plantation prior to the Civil War, and during that conflict, he had arranged for a convoy of cotton from the southern states across Mexico to foreign markets.³³ In the aftermath of the war, the Chinn family faced financial ruin, since they could no longer run their plantation, and Richard and his brother went to Cuba to operate plantations there. Virginia detested life on her new husband's isolated, hot, and bug-infested plantation, so different from the sophisticated life she had imagined. By mutual agreement, she left Richard and moved back to her family's estate in Washington when her daughters were very young. Her own widowed mother, Elizabeth Davis Wood, lived with her and the two young Chinn daughters to help raise them.

Although they never legally divorced, Nina's parents never again lived together. When Richard Chinn finally sold the plantation in Cuba, instead of joining his wife and daughters in Washington, he moved to California to work with his cousin and later bought a large fruit tree ranch. However, he frequently provided money to help support his daughters and sent them boxes of dried apricots, prunes, and raisins grown on his ranch. Richard paid for their education and kept informed about them through his sister, Eliza Ripley, who was close to the girls and their mother.[34]

Richard Chinn often wrote of his wish to have his daughters visit him. During the summer that Nina was seventeen and Bertha was eighteen years of age, they took a train trip to California (with a chaperone) and had an enjoyable six-week visit with their father, who regaled them with tales about his youth in New Orleans and his time as a planter in Cuba. He was "reluctant to see [his daughters] leave," gave them funds for their return trip, but told them that, due to his large financial losses, he would not be able to continue to send money for their support. Richard had bought a life insurance policy that he hoped would take care of his girls after his death.[35]

Richard Henry Chinn reported to the 1900 U.S. Census that he lived in Vacaville and was "widowed," although Virginia was his only wife, and she was very much alive at the time. On December 15 of that year, Richard Henry Chinn died of apoplexy. His body was cremated, but his ashes were retrieved and buried with a headstone in the Lexington Cemetery in Kentucky, on March 2, 1908. His older daughter, Bertha, provided the details of his life and death on the official Bureau of Vital Statistics record[36] and probably saw to his burial as well.

As children, Nina and her sister were raised in "a large square house facing on G Street in the City of Washington, with a generous yard at the side and extending far back of the house, enclosed by a high wooden fence with a solid gate opening on Twentieth Street." They had servants, including an English butler supplied by their maternal uncle, a laundress who was the wife of the president's coachman, and a "faithful Newfoundland dog" named Carlo. Their yard was filled with flowers and fruit trees. Inside the house were "large square rooms with high ceilings, and open fire places in the front and back parlors" as well as coal stoves in the dining room and the rooms upstairs. Nina first became aware of the danger of hot stoves when she caught her foot in the zinc mat under the one in her bedroom and her nurse saved her at the last minute. Due to this accident, for the rest of her life, Nina had a scar just below her left knee.[37]

"We were a household of three generations of women," Nina would write many years later. She believed that she and her sister missed out by not having a male figure in their lives.[38] Then, while suffering from a severe illness as a child, Nina was cared for by Dr. Joseph R. Bromwell, a distinguished Washington physician who was a friend of her uncle Serrell. This encounter began a lifelong friendship between the Chinns and the Bromwells. One summer, Nina, Bertha, and their mother sailed to Scotland with the physician and his wife and traveled with them for six weeks.[39] Nina would write later that Dr. Bromwell treated her as his own daughter and "took a father's place in my heart."[40] He served in that capacity when he walked her down the aisle at her wedding.[41]

Their mother dressed Nina and her sister alike until Bertha entered high school. According to Nina, "My sister selected pink for her sashes and shoulder ribbons and I always wore blue. Our stiffly starched sheer white dresses and natural color leghorn hats with pink ribbon and streamers for my sister, and blue for me, I remember as being distinctly pretty." Both girls had light hair and blue eyes, although Bertha's hair was straight and Nina's was curly. Nina was slim and Bertha was plump, and she grew taller than her older sister when they were in their teens.[42] For four years during their adolescence, the girls lived with their mother and grandmother in Hartford, Connecticut, where their Aunt Emily, who had married a wealthy man, had a large house.[43]

Nina would write, "My sister and I in our impressionable years were sadly ignorant of young men, their struggles in the world of business, and the masculine point of view."[44] They had only minimal exposure to social relations with young men, and Nina would recount how, as adolescents, she and Bertha were "mortified" when they dressed for a party in high-necked dresses with long sleeves, while the other girls, wearing "fluffy party dresses," received all the male attention. Nina's "first experience of delicate attention from a young boy" was in Hartford, when the brother of a friend presented her with a bunch of lilies of the valley, which she called "the sweetest of all flowers." She did not see herself as naturally sociable, later writing, "Through[out] my life I have been painfully shy; at intervals I overcame it, but invariably the shyness returns[,] and I struggle again to conquer it."[45]

As was proper for a young lady of the upper class, Nina Chinn made her social debut on Tuesday, December 30, 1890, when her mother, Mrs.

Virginia Serrellina Wood Chinn, held a tea in her honor from 4:00 to 6:00 P.M. Mrs. Chinn wore black silk, while the seventeen-year-old debutante wore a dress of "white mouselin de sole, with a low neck and short sleeves," and "carried a bunch of La France roses."[46] Nina presided in the tearoom, assisted by three young women of suitable social rank, at a party attended by many prominent guests.[47] With this introduction to Washingtonian society, could an elegant wedding to a promising suitor be far off?

The next public mention of Nina is in an account of "a very largely attended tea" given by her sister, Bertha, on December 29, 1892. In "the pleasant duty of hospitality caring for their guests, Mrs. Chinn was agreeably assisted by her daughter, Miss Nina Chinn," as well as a few other select young women. The guest list for the tea included several daughters of socially prominent Washingtonians.[48] The Chinn sisters not only entertained fashionable visitors; they also did some visiting of their own. On October 21, 1893, the social column in the *Evening Star* notes, "Mrs. and Miss Nina Chinn have returned from a visit to Chicago."[49] The *Washington Post* reports on January 21, 1894, that Miss Chinn was among "a bevy of pretty girls . . . entertained by Mrs. John de Tolley Chesley, on Thursday afternoon, at a small euchre party."[50] Euchre was a card game, and parties of this sort were quite popular in the late nineteenth century for fashionable young ladies. Nina Walker is again mentioned in the *Washington Post* on February 12, 1895, in the account of an elegant afternoon tea party given by Mrs. Chauncy A. Reynolds and her daughters at their home in the Capital. The "Misses Chinn" were among the privileged young women who "assisted in the pleasing duties of receiving."[51] On May 30 of the same year, an item in the *Washington Times* notes that the Misses Bertha and Nina Chinn were making a social call in Brooklyn, New York, on May 30, 1895, after visiting friends in Philadelphia, Pennsylvania. From there, they were going to Hartford, Connecticut, "as guests of Mrs. Beech" (their maternal aunt).[52]

Nina Chinn and James Wilson Grimes Walker had comparable pedigrees, traveled in the same social circles, and knew all the "right" people in Washington, DC. The Chinn's home was located near many military residences and close to the Naval Observatory and the new State War and Navy Department.[53] It was probably only a matter of time until these young socialites got to know each other. Mrs. Chinn actively promoted the relationship between her younger daughter and the elder son of Admiral Walker. However, James Walker's mother was not as enthusiastic.

Rebecca White Pickering Walker was skeptical about the precipitous pace of the wedding preparations and dubious regarding her son's readiness for marriage. In a letter to James dated November 15, 1896, she expressed her doubts, anger, and trepidation. Mrs. Walker was particularly annoyed that she had heard about the accelerated marriage plans secondhand, and she intimated that Mrs. Chinn and her daughter were pushing her eligible son into a hasty commitment. Throughout, there are echoes of Rebecca's difficulties with James when he was a boy. She began her letter in an irritable tone:

> I want you to tell me what to think of the various things which I have come to see since Sat. 9 morning.
> Mrs. Chinn came over early & told me that you and Nina wanted to be married soon, that N. had written to you of her willingness & you had replied warmly thanking her, saying that you approved her plan, but had not liked to suggest it, that business was looking up & you thought it would be best to marry even if you had to encroach upon your principal [on his legacy] a little "for the first year." Mrs. C. said she agreed . . . & had given her consent—came over to see what we thought, supposing that we had heard from you, as Nina said you meant to write to me proposing the plan.[54]

Although this was obviously the first time Mrs. Walker had heard of the "plan," she acted quickly to save face in front of Mrs. Chinn:

> I said I should be delighted to have you marry if it could be arranged & was ready to help, but must talk it over with Papa & see what could be done.[55]

One can well imagine what Rebecca White Pickering Walker thought about being the last one to know her son had agreed to marry Mrs. Chinn's daughter in the near future. Her fury increased when she received a letter from James *after* she had been informed by Mrs. Chinn. Unfortunately, James's original letter to his mother has not been found. However, its contents may be surmised from the tone of Mrs. Walker's response:

> She [Mrs. Chinn] had but just left when I received from you the letter of which the enclosed is a portion. What to make of it I did not—and do not know. Not to speak now of the tone in which you wrote, what can I think of your inconsistencies? Why do you talk to Nina of being married—within three months, & to me of breaking your engagement? Why do you write to her of breaking into your

principal "for the first year," as if you expected to get on well after that, & tell me that you have no hope whatever of promotion?[56]

Mrs. Walker then accused her son of trying to bully her into going along with his whims, questioned his manhood for doing so, and informed him that, as far as she was concerned, he was acting against his own best interests:

> Frankly—if I were to be called upon as an impartial outsider to judge such a letter sent by a young man to his mother, I should say that it looked amazingly like a threat, reminding one of Grandpapa's story "Skunks in the chamber or on the top of the house!" But I can hardly imagine *you* to be so unmanly as to resort to such a device, or so unwise as to take a tone so well elicited to defeat your own hopes.[57]

James's mother warned him in no uncertain terms that his letter had the opposite of the effect he might have hoped for:

> If anything could discourage me from making most earnest efforts for your advancement it would be any doubt that might arise in my mind as to the happiness to come to you and Nina from your marriage; and nothing could tend more directly to produce such a doubt than your writing to me in this fashion.[58]

Not content to reprimand her son for his behavior toward her, James's mother then predicted his potential bad behavior toward his future wife:

> If you have so little patience that the prospect of having to wait or work a few months longer before marrying makes you talk of taking a step which would ruin for life the happiness of her whom you profess to love better than yourself, how are you going to bear the greater trials which will come to you and be Nina's stay and comfort "in sickness and in health, in joy & in sorrow"?[59]

As she continued the letter to her son, Rebecca Walker administered a moral lecture:

> You say that under certain circumstances you "prefer to live as you see fit." My son, there is but one way of living which you will ever

"be fit"[;] that is the right way,—the way of a clean, honest, unselfish kind of life. It is often hard, but its' [sic] hardness is sweet and blessed in comparison with the hardness that comes from any swerving from the right path. You *must* come back to it in the end, happily there is that in you which will not be satisfied else, and every wrong step makes that coming the more painful.[60]

James's mother then embarked on a discussion of the dangers of temptation and the need for resistance in facing crises. Throughout her cautionary discourse, Mrs. Walker employed a number of nautical and military analogies, which she perhaps thought befit her position as the wife of a naval officer:

You speak indefinitely—one might almost say mysteriously—but beneath the surface I think I can see evidences of some struggle, and therefore instead of the reproaches which I might seem justified in writing I will send encouragement. If you are tried, you *can* hear; if you are tempted you *can*, *must* and *will* resist and stand firm. God knows all & he gives you strength enough, but he leaves it to you to *use* the strength. Knowing so little of the circumstances I can say nothing more definite, but this is enough. We all pass at times through crises when we feel as if we could not hold out much longer, but happily we have only to hold out one day, one hour, at a time, and we can always do that; and when we do that firmly for a time—suddenly the crisis is over & we have plain sailing again. As soon as we brace ourselves for a fight our opponent weakens & often disappears altogether.

Instead of thinking that at some special time you will be ready to give in, letting your opponent know your intention (and when you are fighting your lower tendencies of course they do know of your plans)[,] just say to yourself 'No flinching ever' and battle—the campaign is half over.[61]

Rebecca Walker did not specify the temptation with which her son was struggling. It must have been powerful if he needed strength from God to combat it. What was the crisis James faced? Who was the opponent he must battle? Was it another person? Was it a situation? Or was it a struggle within himself? Mrs. Walker did her best to discuss the problem while simultaneously refusing to name it. A number of possible vices might have remained unspoken, including sexual temptation, drink, and sloth. How would each of these have affected James's plans to marry and his future family life?

In the next part of her letter, Mrs. Walker abruptly switched to a more mundane topic. She urged her shy son to be more affable and aggressive, fearing, it seems, that he had a tendency to be too reserved and isolated. Perhaps Mrs. Walker was connecting the previously mentioned struggle with his solitary manner. Although reiterating her faith in him, she also implied doubt regarding his ability to act rationally. Her tone was one a mother might take when speaking to a child much younger than her twenty-eight-year-old son:

> Now enough of all this—you will be a reasonable, strong sensible man, & act like one. Make every effort to find a more satisfactory place of business & push your acquaintance with business men [*sic*] and with all friends, ever on the alert for a chance—Talk with Mr. Lewis and ask his advice, and whether there is any business prospect or not, go about among people—*Do not stay by yourself.* Visit, ride your wheel [his bicycle]. Keep out & about, do your gymnastics, and—as Grandmamma would have quoted from a friend of hers who was addressing her husband—"Don't be such a fool, Peter!"[62]

Mrs. Walker informed her son that his father, the admiral, backed her position:

> Well! Papa and I talked over the matter & it seemed to us that there must be some improvement in the business outlook before ... with the help that we shall be glad to give—it would be safe for you to take the risk of marrying—But that improvement we must try to get at as quickly as possible. You must remember that only two days have passed since the result of the election was known, though it seems much longer ... not even to find out what there is to try for, but if we are diligent in our inquiries for a few weeks we may hope for a good result.[63]

Although the Walkers had political influence with the incoming William McKinley administration, Mrs. Walker cautioned that it might be too soon to use it. However, she instructed James to promptly answer a previous note in which she had requested information relevant to finding him a position. Mrs. Walker then returned to the subject of the marriage:

> I will attend to the matter of the wedding present. Papa has already spoken about arranging for your premium. I have seen Mrs. Chinn today and talked with her of your affairs.

> She told me about the arrival of the Leighton twins and your dinner.⁶⁴

Mrs. Walker left the term "affairs" ambiguous. Did she mean his business affairs or his social affairs? Why did she insert a mention of dinner with the twins? Was she offended that she had to hear about her son's social life secondhand? There is no way to know the answers to these questions.

Mrs. Walker then magnanimously offered to pretend that James had never sent the letter to which she was replying, said she would conceal its very existence from his father, and advised him to destroy any evidence of it:

> Of course I did not show your letter to Papa and I return to you all but the [part] about Mr. Freeman, that you may destroy it yourself, after wondering at it & regretting (as I know you will) that you ever sent it.⁶⁵

She concluded:

> With faith in your good sense & principle and in the hope that the clouds will clear from your skies before long.
> Always lovingly,
> Mamma⁶⁶

The foremost emotion conveyed in Mrs. Walker's letter to James was angry disappointment in her son. A major matter of contention was James's lack of a suitable livelihood. Another was the temptation that she feared had compelled him to surrender. James probably did destroy the original letter to his mother, since no trace of it survives. In any case, Mrs. Walker apparently relented on her misgivings regarding a marriage to Nina Chinn in the near future; the wedding between James and Nina took place a little more than three months later. But Rebecca Walker's words to her son would come back to haunt them both when her letter would be presented as evidence by Nina's lawyers during a divorce trial.

3

Early Days

Winter 1897 to Summer 1905

THE CHINN-WALKER MARRIAGE began serenely, although it did not take long for marital troubles to develop. Right after their wedding on February 24, 1897, the newlyweds took a trip to Baltimore and then returned to Washington, DC. James was still unemployed, and the couple lived at Nina's mother's home in Washington. That summer, Nina went on a vacation with her sister, Bertha, and mother, Virginia, to Atlantic City, New Jersey. James stayed in Washington to prepare for the competitive entrance examination for the U.S. Navy. Later in the summer, James joined Nina and her family in Atlantic City for a few days.[1]

As James's mother had hoped, the newly elected William McKinley administration considerably improved prospects for the Walker family. Admiral Walker's political network was impressive. According to David McCullough, "For more than forty years, Admiral Walker had been a special favorite in the capital, enjoying, it was said, more political influence than any officer in the Navy. He was direct, unaffected in manner, and if a bit self-important, he plainly meant well. His reputation for integrity was second to none."[2] In 1897, President McKinley established the Nicaragua Canal Commission, with the purpose of determining the best route for a canal in Central America.[3] He appointed Admiral John Grimes Walker as chairman, with several important military and civil engineers as additional members of the group later known as the "Walker Commission."[4] The admiral's new position meant his son James would not be unemployed much longer. He was promptly appointed to work on the engineering staff to study whether a canal in Nicaragua was feasible.

Nina gave birth to the couple's first child, Elizabeth Grimes Walker, in Washington, DC, on November 30, 1897, approximately nine months after her wedding to James. Her husband was not with her at the time, and he would not see his wife and daughter until almost a year later. James subsequently explained that he was not present for his daughter's birth because "he was in New York preparing to go to Nicaragua and too busy to get to Washington."[5] According to Nina, her husband did not even attempt to contact her for several days following the birth. James's mother believed she had to intervene. Rebecca Walker sent a telegram to "J. W. G. Walker, care of the Nicaragua Canal Commission, Army Building, Whitehall, New York" on December 2, 1897, stating, "No response from you. Nina disappointed. Unless letter nearly here telegraph your pleasure. Daughter charming."[6] James's lapse in attention at this time damaged his relationship with his wife. In response to James's absence, Nina became more dependent on her mother and sister, with whom she and the baby were living.

The Walker Commission members and staff left the United States on December 5, 1897, aboard the gunboat *Newport*, allocated by the secretary of the navy for transportation and offshore surveys.[7] Admiral John Grimes Walker, his crew, his commission members, and his son, James Wilson Grimes Walker, were bound for Greytown (San Juan del Norte), Nicaragua.[8] The boat had no heating system, so the passengers were very cold during the first part of the journey, and the strong winter winds and waves bounced them around. James "was thought particularly fortunate in being quartered in the Captain's office"[9] but still suffered from sea sickness. He later reported that, although he had a difficult time at the beginning of the trip, toward the end he recovered, participated in the social life of the boat crew, and enjoyed the water views.[10] On December 17, 1897, the *Newport* arrived in Greytown.

Upon their arrival, Admiral Walker immediately sent a letter to his wife (whom he called "Betty"), telling her that there were difficulties pulling the boat to shore, and the passengers could not disembark until the next day. "I am only writing this to let you know that Jamie and I are both well," John Grimes Walker wrote. "We are lying here rolling and tumbling around in a very uncomfortable way." He discussed the ship's arrival plans, promised to write his wife "a more respectable letter"[11] when he was able, and guessed she was probably writing him a letter to send on the next steamer. The admiral closed by saying, "Hope all is well with you. Love to all in which J. joins. Tell Nina that he is too sickly and the ship is tumbling about too much for him to write. Goodbye with a kiss."[12]

The admiral's wife forwarded his letter to her daughter-in-law, after she appended her own message. In this note, Rebecca attempted to reassure Nina about James's condition and at the same time made excuses for her son's lack of communication with her. "This looks to me as if Papa himself found it pretty hard to write, 'Old Salt' as he is!" Rebecca wrote. "But he evidently had to do duty for two. But seasickness stops quickly and leaves one none the worse and by this time—and long ago—they are doubtless as chipper as possible. Lots of love and I hope to see you very soon."[13]

James would later write a memoir about his experiences in Nicaragua, in which he describes his work and talks about his many adventures, including coming into close contact with an insurrection. He found life in Nicaragua exciting and even briefly contemplated the possibility of buying a plantation and moving there.[14] Although he recognized that he could not live permanently in Nicaragua, James's work with the commission must have been a welcome break from his previous unemployed status and comparatively dull domestic life. On July 29, 1898, President McKinley appointed him as a civil engineer, junior grade, with the rank of lieutenant in the U.S. Navy. This promotion meant that James now had an official status and therefore a direction for his career. The Walker Commission officials and staff, including the new lieutenant and his father, departed Nicaragua on October 7, 1888. James would later write, "The purple hills and sunny plains of Nicaragua became a memory of the past; our hardships were all forgotten, our pleasures magnified an hundredfold. Around us was the sleeping ocean, ahead the Bay of Panama, beyond that, home!"[15] James had been away for ten months and undoubtedly returned a different and more experienced man. He reunited with his wife and infant daughter at his mother-in-law's home in Washington, DC. For the next six months, the young family stayed there, while James worked on Commission reports.[16]

On April 19, 1899, James Walker was officially detached from the Nicaragua Canal Commission and assigned to work as a civil engineer at the Boston Navy Yard.[17] Admiral Walker sought to ensure James's reception there. He wrote a letter to Rear Admiral H. F. Picking, commander of the Boston Navy Yard, stating that he hoped his son would do well and "be entirely satisfactory to you."[18] The young Walker family of three moved into a house on Brinton Road in Brookline, Massachusetts,[19] a suburb of Boston. James's mother offered to help with furnishing the house. On April 28, she wrote to Nina:

> Buy good, nice things & don't be afraid about the money; there will be plenty of it without the least inconvenience to me, for it is

an extra & in fact the gift is half Uncle Harry's [Henry G. Pickering, Rebecca's brother] so to speak—.

It happened in this way; there was some money to which I had *no claim at all,* but which he wished to divide with me because it had once been Father's. He knew that I should somewhat demur at accepting what was really an outright gift from him & utterly unexpected, & he also knew that I was wishing that I could provide furniture for you—and it was *his* suggestion that a part of the money—(or all, if necessary) should be used in furnishing your house. It is quite a windfall, you see, & I can furnish your house nicely without any inconvenience with other plans. Really your gratitude should be to Uncle H., though he was not willing that I should put it in that way—.[20]

Rebecca Walker then wrote that she was not certain how much a dining table would cost but that she wanted Nina and James "to have a thoroughly good one, handsome one—[i]t is an important piece of furniture" and "[a]lso good chairs, that will last." She suggested that Uncle Harry might help Nina look for furniture if James was too busy working. Mrs. Walker also informed Nina that she supposed "there will be $2,000 or more, if needed, to spend on furniture."[21] Years later, Rebecca Walker would claim that her daughter-in-law had spent far too much money on home furnishings.

By this time, Nina was pregnant with the Walkers' second child. James's older sister, Frances (called Fanny), was engaged to marry Dr. John Jenks Thomas, a graduate of Williams College and Harvard Medical School who was descended from a distinguished American family who had come over on the *Mayflower.* Although originally from Columbus, Ohio, he now worked on the staff of the Boston Dispensary, and the two young couples socialized.[22] Nina gave birth to a son, John Grahame Walker (who would be referred to thereafter as Grahame), in Brookline, on October 2, 1899. She would later complain that, because he did not return home until the evening, her husband was absent for the birth of this child as well.

Fanny and John married in Washington, DC, on Saturday, October 21, 1899. The *New York Times* describes the wedding of Admiral Walker's oldest daughter as "the first of the autumn fashionable weddings."[23] Fanny was escorted down the aisle by the admiral, and her sisters, Susan and Sarah (called Sallie), were her attendants. Dr. Thomas's best man was Mr. Charles Cheney Hyde of Chicago, and several distinguished young men served as ushers, including Theodore M. Taft and Henry Pickering Walker, Fanny's younger brother. James, the bride's other brother, did not participate in the ceremony. However, he is mentioned in the detailed *Times* description of the guest list, which included, among many others, Admiral George Dewey and Secretary John Davis Long of the navy, Mr. and Mrs. Henry Pickering, various Pickering relatives, and guests representing other eminent families.[24] Upon returning from a wedding trip, Dr. and Mrs. Thomas moved to a fashionable address in Boston.[25]

Nina apparently did not attend Fanny and John's wedding; she had so recently given birth. It must have been difficult for her to maintain a social life while undergoing several pregnancies in quick succession, but Nina endeavored to do so. In late October 1900, she entertained Mrs. Charles G. Summers, who was on her way to the general executive meeting of the Women's Foreign Missionary Society in Worcester.[26] Shortly afterward, on November 16, 1900, Nina gave birth to her third child and second son, Robert Serrell Wood Walker, who would be referred to thereafter as Serrell. He was a sickly baby who needed the care of a special nurse.

There were in-law problems. While James believed that Nina spent too much time with her family, it was not easy for Nina to get along with her husband's relatives. Apparently, everyone who knew him was expected to acknowledge that Admiral Walker was not only correct but also infallible. James was not consulted in his father's plans for him and simply followed them dutifully.[27] Nina would later observe that the admiral also bullied Rebecca, using a subtle form of mockery that hurt her intensely; Nina believed that this humiliation provoked James's mother to control him and his family. Her meddlesome sister, Bertha, also created difficulties between her and her husband's family.

Soon after Serrell's birth, Bertha purportedly wrote a letter to James's mother that, although superficially polite, was clearly irate in its content. This letter would be offered as evidence by James's attorneys in a later divorce hearing, but the judge would not allow it to be read because the original had been destroyed and only an alleged copy remained. According to the letter, a woman named Mrs. Long had been hired as a nurse for Serrell while the baby stayed with Mrs. Chinn and Bertha in Washington, DC. Although Rebecca Walker had agreed to pay Mrs. Long's expenses through December 1, Bertha complained that she had abruptly decided to stop sending money. Bertha felt obligated to pay for the nurse herself and wrote the following:

> You cannot think 3 babies cost less than 2, which you will pardon me for saying, was an unnecessary charity. Now I am outraged at it and shall keep Mrs. Long as long as I see fit at my own expense.[28]

The tone of the purported letter became increasingly hostile as it continued. Bertha accused James of financial incompetence and bad behavior toward Nina and implied that his mother had made things worse:

> James has no business head and no one should know it better than you[;] he is in debt and stopping his allowance does not help him get out. You know what my sister has to endure from your son and why do you want to make it harder for her too[?][29]

Bertha blamed James not only for the family's inadequate finances but also for the very fact that Nina had another baby so soon after the previous one. She provided explicit details:

> Do you think that she [Nina] minded her own suffering in the coming of another baby? If you do you do not know her. There was *every* reason she should not have another now but James said if she did not let him come to her he would go elsewhere. No other argument would have prevailed.[30]

This account insinuated that Nina had become pregnant again because her husband had threatened to have an affair if she did not give in to his demands for sex. At a time of unreliable birth control, which was often illegal even to married women, pregnancy was an expected result of sexual relations.

After having made her point, Bertha ended her letter to Mrs. Walker with a demand stated as a request: "Will you do me the favor of starting up James' allowance and oblige[?]"[31] Mrs. Walker would later maintain that she had stopped her son's allowance "at the special request of his wife."[32] She would allege that Nina had begged her not to continue giving James money, because doing so only encouraged him to go further into debt. Nina, on the other hand, would claim that she had not known that the money for the nurse came from her husband's mother.[33]

There is no written evidence of Rebecca Walker's response to Bertha. However, it can be assumed that a proud and domineering older woman would not have reacted positively to accusations and demands, particularly from a younger woman who was her daughter-in-law's sister. An unambiguous consequence was that the lukewarm relations between the senior Walkers and the Chinns became much chillier. Rebecca Walker would later state that from that point on, her husband forbade her from having contact with Nina's family. Following the letter from Bertha to Mrs. Walker, James brought baby Serrell and his nurse to stay with his sister

Fanny and her husband in Boston for several months. Whether this arrangement was with Nina's agreement would later be disputed, when she would claim that she had begged to have her child back but that Dr. and Mrs. Thomas had refused to give him up.[34]

Nina Walker gave birth to their fourth and last child only thirteen months after Serrell. Herbert Wood Walker was born in Brookline on December 18, 1901. Nina's mother-in-law would later accuse her of saying during that final pregnancy that if she became pregnant again, she would leave James.[35] This young woman, having had four pregnancies in as many years beginning right after her marriage, with a husband who had financial problems, probably felt overwhelmed. Nina might have found that the only way to limit the further growth of her family was to cease having sexual relations with her husband, despite his alleged threats to find someone else. According to Nina, the couple did not "live together as man and wife" for several years prior to the breakup of the marriage in 1909.[36]

The Walkers no longer had an intimate relationship, but their sexless marriage did not necessarily mean that James was abstinent. While working at the Boston Navy Yard, James often had his lunch at a restaurant in North Station and received attention from some of the young waitresses there. Nina would state at a divorce hearing that, during that time, her husband thought constantly about "questionable women," often told her about them, and repeated his experiences with them in front of guests in their home.[37] She also would later charge that James kept "constant companionship with lewd persons and [made] constant conversation and expression of preference for lewd and loose females."[38] There was an additional reason for Nina to avoid sexual relations with her husband, as he "was suffering from a venereal disease [sexually transmitted infection] or from the effects thereof from November 1901 so as to render co-habitation dangerous" to her health,[39] but it is not certain whether she knew that at this time.

During his three years at the Boston Navy Yard, James met a pretty young woman named Mabel Cochrane, who waited tables in the restaurant at North Station where James took his lunch and lived in nearby Roxbury.[40] Later, James and Nina Walker would strongly disagree about the nature of James's relationship with Miss Cochrane. James would acknowledge that Mabel was a friend who had given her photograph to a number of restaurant patrons, including him. However, he would contend that when his wife objected to his having the picture, he returned it to Mabel.[41] According to Nina, beginning in 1901 and continuing for several years, James had an "undue, improper indecorous and licentious" relationship with Mabel Cochrane, who was "much younger" than James and "of questionable character and immoral habits."[42] Nina would claim that James secretly visited Mabel at her apartment in Boston behind locked doors with no one else present and while "she was immodestly and improperly clad." He also "bestowed upon and received [from her] marked and improper attention" and indulged in "undue and improper familiarity and intimacy" with her.[43] When Nina finally brought a suit for divorce against her husband, Mabel Cochrane would be named as a co-respondent. Confronted with testimony from a witness who had seen him enter Mabel Cochrane's apartment, James would admit that he had called on Miss Cochrane in Boston. The first time was a business visit, he would claim, and the second time was while she was busy cleaning her apartment.[44] In later testimony, James would admit that he had gone to see Mabel at her place in Boston at least five times and that the visits continued as late as 1909.[45] Further information about those visits would become the basis for testimony during the divorce trials.

While James and Nina both came from well-to-do families, the young couple was beset by money troubles. James's salary from the Navy was $2,400 a year, which was well above the average income at the time,[46] and he received an additional annual income from his family of about $600. However, the Walkers had expectations, based on their family backgrounds, of living a more privileged life. James would later acknowledge that his house in Brookline "was furnished by his uncle and his mother, but there were three servants to be paid, and Navy uniforms and entertaining proved costly, so that expenses exceeded income."[47]

James's work, family, and extracurricular activities did not interfere with his plans to write a book about Nicaragua. Upon his return in 1900, he began working on a memoir, which recounts his adventures there and includes some historical perspective and a description of the canal commission's work. Admiral Walker advised him that the book would probably be popular if he finished it while the canal was still a current topic.[48] Titled *Ocean to Ocean: An Account, Personal and Historical, of Nicaragua and Its People,* James's book was published by A. C. McClurg and Company early in 1902. By that time, a second Walker Commission, also known as the Isthmian Canal Commission, had already determined that it would be more advantageous to build the canal in Panama rather than in Nicaragua. Even the chairman of the Commission, Admiral Walker, who had at first staunchly supported the Nicaraguan route, backed the Panama plan.[49]

James writes well, including lots of descriptive detail. Although his book is mainly about his activities in connection with the Walker Commission, readers were amused by a chapter devoted to the adventures of William Walker (no relation), the American lawyer, journalist, and adventurer who made himself the president of Nicaragua in 1856 and was executed in Honduras by a firing squad in 1860. Another chapter that drew public interest includes a political critique in which James boldly refers to the Nicaraguan government as a "military despotism masquerading as a republic."[50] He also discusses the merits of building a canal in Nicaragua, while acknowledging that Panama was probably a better choice.

James's book received favorable reviews. The critical consensus was that, in *Ocean to Ocean,* James demonstrates a genuine interest in and an attempt to understand the people, history, and culture of Nicaragua. The *Buffalo Express* states it is "a good book for one who wishes to study the interoceanic canal question" and concludes that "the most valuable chapters are those in which Lieutenant Walker sums up the history and physical conditions of Nicaragua. His personal narrative of experiences is, however, entertaining and picturesque."[51] A positive book review in the *Outlook* states that *Ocean to Ocean* includes information that "is hardly to be had elsewhere."[52]

A probably unintentional but recurring theme throughout his book is James's detailed descriptions of Nicaraguan women. He is attentive to the scantiness of their dress, disclosing that "women do their washing clad only in skirts, whose wet, transparent folds accentuate rather than conceal their forms."[53] Another book passage depicts "women clad in garments both diaphanous and scanty, bath[ing], sublimely indifferent to the proximity of men."[54] There was apparently an abundance of women in the countryside; James writes enthusiastically that "women [were] vastly in the majority.... [T]here were women galore ... bare-footed, black-eyed, brown-armed, olive-cheeked women."[55] He also recounts long rides along the riverbed, passing clearings and cottages "where groups of half nude, sunbrowned women stood knee-deep in water, washing clothes, gossiping and lazily puffing wreaths of blue smoke from puros of domestic make. Few men were to be seen."[56]

James Walker's appreciative summation of Nicaraguan women is as follows: "Although rather below our standard of height they [the indigenous people] were extremely well-formed, particularly the women, graceful figures, erect carriage, clear, dark complexions and liquid black eyes made them far from unattractive."[57] *Ocean to Ocean* includes several photographs taken by James. Although most are of local scenery, a full page is devoted to a photograph of a lovely dark-skinned woman with beautiful eyes. The caption under the photograph identifies her as "A Native Belle."[58]

James published a briefer account of his Nicaraguan adventures as "Journey through Central America," in the *Chautauquan Magazine*.[59] In this article, Walker summarizes his accounts of the history, geography, and culture of Nicaragua as well as his own activities there. As in his book, James mentions his admiration for the women of the region, stating, "The people of the interior and the west coast[,] where the Indian blood predominates, are rather small, but are well formed and good looking, particularly the women, many of whom are really beautiful."[60] Photographs taken by the author accompany the article in the *Chautauquan*, several of which portray attractive indigenous women.

These beautiful young Nicaraguan women must have seemed very different from the much more conservative ladies James knew at home, including his wife. No wonder they aroused his interest. There is no certain evidence that James acted on his attraction for the local women. However, if he did, it would not be the first time a young man far from home indulged his desires with a member of the indigenous population. It is possible that Nicaragua was where James first became infected with venereal disease.

On March 25, 1902, the *Boston Daily Globe* reports that Lieutenant James W. G. Walker, USN, who had been the assistant civil engineering officer at the Boston Navy Yard in Charlestown for the past three years, would move to the new navy yard station in Charleston, South Carolina. He would be charged with "laying out and construction of the necessary improvements at that point." The *Globe* article notes that James was the son of Admiral John G. Walker, USN, retired, and had "become quite generally known by reason of his book, writings, lectures and information relative to the Panama and Nicaragua canals, on both of which he had been professionally engaged." James is credited with planning and overseeing the construction of several buildings at the Boston Navy Yard and described as respected and liked by his associates. The article concludes, "Lieut. Walker's departure will be regretted by every man at the yard, for his geniality won hosts of friends, while his professional abilities were recognized by all."[61] James Walker believed he had finally found his career.

James arrived at the Charleston, South Carolina, Navy Yard in the spring of 1902, where he would stay for approximately four years.[62] He would explain later that he asked for this assignment to be farther away from his mother-in-law and sister-in-law. Nina was not as pleased with this assignment as her husband. When she and the children moved to South Carolina, the amount of money appropriated to her by the government for furnishing their residence was not enough to make the rooms comfortable, and she "could not make them look snug during the cold months." In her unpublished autobiography, Nina complained, "There was no cellar, and no central heat[;] we depended on open grate coal fires and a stove in the hall to keep us warm."[63] The lack of a telephone made Nina anxious, because it would be difficult to call a doctor if one of the children became ill. In addition, she found, "I could not keep the children in the Yard during the summer, the intense heat, mosquitos, the largest I have ever seen, and the swamps around us filled with typhoid and malarial germs."[64] Therefore, Nina and the children left Charleston during the summers.[65]

While staying alone in Charleston during his first summer, James received two visitors from Boston. He would later recount that, upon returning home from the yacht club one afternoon, he was quite surprised to find his old friend from Boston, Mabel Cochrane, and her brother sitting on the steps of his house on Gamball Street. James had obtained a position for Mabel's brother, John (Jack) E. W. Cochrane (who later took to spelling his last name without the final "e"), at the Charleston Navy Yard. However, he had not invited Miss Cochrane and was "genuinely astonished" to see her there. James would later admit that she stayed in his house for three weeks while his wife and children were away, explaining, "I suggested that as the house was practically vacant, the Cochranes might stay there. I took meals at Mrs. Frost's and the Cochranes elsewhere. During this time I occupied the northeast room and Miss Cochrane the southeast."[66]

During the following summer of 1903, with Nina and the children away again, James hired Mabel Cochrane as a housekeeper to supervise the "negro [sic] servants." He would later claim that he had notified Nina about this decision, implying her consent, but Nina would argue that James had allowed Miss Cochrane to live in the Charleston house for long periods of time during her absence and entirely without her knowledge.[67] She would further assert that Mabel Cochrane had stayed in a room adjoining her husband's "so that they were constantly in each other's company, and improperly familiar and unduly intimate."[68]

Mabel enjoyed living in Charleston for the summer. Just before July 4, 1903, she wrote a letter to her sister that implied things were going well there and described her plans for the Fourth of July:

> The niggers [sic] are the only people that celebrate down here. But I am going to do a little celebrating all by myself. Yesterday I bought a big package of Joss-sticks [incense] to keep away the misquitoes [sic], and I am going to make Eddie and Mr. Walker buy a string of Chinese lanterns to string along the piazza; and a couple of red lights and a few fire crackers. I expect to scare the devil out of the natives; I may have a little *pink Lemonade* on the side with a *stick* in it. For there is a full quart of Club Whiskey in the wine closet, and I hold the key. I guess I will be able to make things hum for a little while.[69]

This letter suggested that Mabel believed she had full control over the house and, perhaps, over the husband, while his wife was away.

During that same summer of 1903, Nina and James corresponded with each other. In a letter dated August 22, 1903, James explained that he had not written for almost three weeks because he had been "exceedingly busy with my annual report and other things." He told Nina he had appealed to the Navy Department about a problem he had with the Commandant but had been betrayed by the skipper and might get "'turned down' good and hard." James wrote that work at the navy yard was proceeding slowly because several of the inspectors had malarial fever and another coworker had appendicitis surgery. With several absent staff and medical problems among those remaining, James told Nina, "We might as well shut up the office as try to run it with our present force."[70]

Later in his letter, James continued his account of local disasters as he wrote about a "negro [sic] girl who had drowned [after falling] from the bridge leading to Burton's mill, just behind our house, and her body floated around for 36 hours, tethered to the bank, until it suited the coroner's convenience to come and hold an inquest." He also told his wife that a few days later, "a good looking mulatto girl was brutally shot down and killed . . . by a negro [sic] who escaped and has not yet been arrested." James complained that, since the murder occurred at noon, the murderer would have been caught within two hours "if we had had a live commandant, who would arm his watchmen." He explained that the commandant was afraid that "someone might get hurt" if his men were armed. "Our force of watchmen," James grumbled, "is therefore as efficient as if it were composed of young children,—and the yard is close to one of the worst negro [sic] settlements in the United States."[71] James concluded his letter by telling Nina that their house would be finished by November 1, and he sent "love to the babies and yourself."[72]

The negative tone permeating the main part of this letter to Nina may have been merely a typical outlet for a husband expressing frustration to his wife. However, it could be seen as strange that James would scare Nina with detailed descriptions of violent episodes that had taken place close to where she and the children would live when they returned to Charleston. Whether he did this to deliberately frighten her or was unaware of the effect it might have is not clear. However, Nina became fearful about living in Charleston.

When she and the children returned to Charleston, Nina began to enjoy life in their new house. "We had a large vegetable garden that more than supplied our wants," she would later write. "My husband got the benefit of the cantaloups [sic] and watermelons while we were away[;] he said they compensated him for having to endure the intense summer heat. Our

Alderney cow was a beauty; when her calf arrived, the children laughed at its long insecure legs and frisky behavior and took it to their hearts at once." The children also had a small donkey that drew a "rather crude wooden cart." Nina often walked to James's office to meet her husband and look at the work on the dry dock. "I knew nothing about cooking," she wrote, "so I purchased the *Boston Cook Book* and studied that." At night, Nina tucked the children into bed and went downstairs to the library, where she discovered the pleasure of reading, because "our evenings were long and we were thrown upon our own resources. My husband heartily disliked games and declined to learn with the exception of solitaire."[73]

Nina was charmed by Charleston yet afraid of the "gangs of colored prisoners" and the loud noise at night, "for the Yard was in the immediate vicinity of Hell's Half Acre," a dangerous neighborhood." Nina would later write, "The nights became a terror to me. I spoke of it to the admiral when in Washington, [and] he readily understood the need of some protection for us, so he kindly went to the Navy Department and asked that a squad of Marines be detailed to guard our home. The Department complied at once."[74]

After the children's governess left to go back to her family, Nina hired a new governess referred to as "Fraulein," who she believed was far too strict and mistreated the children. Nina had engaged "a good colored nurse," but, then she explained,

> my husband brought into our home a young woman who he said would help me in the care of the children and give Elizabeth and Grahame lessons. Time and sentences dropped here and there disclosed that my husband had known her as a waitress in the North Station in Boston where he frequently went for his lunch when working at the Boston Navy Yard. His infatuation led to his bringing her and her younger brother to Charleston where they lived with him without my knowledge during the children's' [sic] and my absence and giving the brother work in his office.[75]

Nina would later insist that at that time, she had not been aware that James and Mabel were previously acquainted and that she would not have agreed to employ her if she had known. It took a while, she would say, for her to become suspicious of the relationship between her husband and Mabel.[76] During a divorce hearing, Nina would describe an episode in which Mabel "was getting ready to go to the most exclusive ball given in Charleston during the season and expressed a desire to wear Mr. Walker's cape, which was part of his Navy uniform." James agreed to let her wear the cape, although, Nina complained bitterly, "He never, under any circumstances, would let me wear that cape."[77]

Nina's jealousy over what she considered to be her husband's inappropriate attention to the family governess only flourished. In the spring of 1904, James was called to Washington, DC, on naval business and stayed with his parents, while Nina's sister, Bertha, came to Charleston for a visit. During this time, Mrs. Walker suggested that James invite Mabel Cochrane to spend a week as a guest at her Washington home. Mrs. Walker would later say that she did this to give Mabel a rest from the tension while Bertha was visiting, because she was afraid that Mabel might quit. In response to the invitation, Mabel wrote the following to James:

> My dear Mr. Walker,
> Your letter just received with the money O.K. I want to thank you very much for your kind invitation up to Washington. I would start on the first train if I were certain that Miss Chinn [Bertha] could stay. I heard her tell Mrs. W. [Nina] she could not stay any longer than two weeks. I feel very enthusiastic at the thought of going to Washington for I really think I need a change. . . . I will probably hear something from Mrs. W. tonight, but I have my plans all arranged and will let you know immediately how soon I can start.[78]

Anticipating that she would again spend the summer in Charleston with James while his wife and children were away, Mabel informed James that she was arranging things with her sister and had spoken to Mrs. Harris (probably a reference to the wife of James's assistant at the navy yard, Frederic R. Harris; the couple shared living quarters with James for a while), who "said she would love to come and live out at the navy yard this summer." "I am looking forward to this summer when we will have some good old times again," Mabel wrote wistfully. She complained that Nina and her sister were giving her too much responsibility with the children and concluded her letter by again referring to the invitation to visit Washington: "I wish you would thank your mother for me."[79]

While he was away, Nina wrote to her husband that she was frightened of the violence near the Charleston Navy Yard. Although James told her it was too early in the season for her to leave, Nina decided that she and the children would pay her husband and in-laws a visit. She would later write:

> In the late Spring James went to Washington on business, while there I followed within a few days with the anticipation of once

more endeavoring to make some arrangement with him and his family, to keep my little household sacred without an unwelcome intruder. To my utter amazement I found Admiral Walker had left for a meeting of the Commission in Panama and Mrs. Walker had invited James' "friend" to pay her a visit at that very time. She arrived the [day after James' arrival] and was accepted as a friend of the family. Such a move on the part of my mother-in-law was indeed "a riddle wrapped in a mystery inside an enigma." Be that as it may, the "friend" was taken sightseeing by my husband.[80]

Upon Nina's arrival at the admiral's home, she and James had a loud argument and slept that night in separate bedrooms. Nina's jealousy of Mabel increased even further. She believed the other woman was given special treatment, while she, the wife, was treated poorly. Nina protested to James's mother about the presence of "this woman" as a guest in the house and confided her suspicions of an improper relationship. However, Nina would later claim, "So far from sending her from the house, Miss Cochrane was made the guest of honor at a theatre party, and she [the] wife, was not invited, although her husband went."[81] James's mother would deny this was so, saying the entire household was expected to go to the theater, where her youngest daughter was appearing in an amateur play for charity.[82] Nina pondered:

> Was it bravado that activated Mrs. Walker, or did she in her conceit think she was throwing dust in my eyes? I cannot believe the Admiral would have permitted such a gross blunder. The strain of the past years was taking its toll, my nerves centered in my weak stomach, and I could not digest even a glass of water, and I lost weight rapidly.[83]

According to Nina, only when she later reported her suspicions to James's father was Mabel asked to leave the Walker household.[84]

After she returned to Boston, Mabel Cochrane and her former employer exchanged letters. Nina's attorneys would later charge that James "carried on a correspondence with said Mabel Cochrane, has received from her a letter or letters reflecting upon [Nina], as well as letters of an improper and lascivious nature, and which show improper and lascivious relations between [James] and Mabel Cochrane."[85] The letters from Mabel to James, quoted below, would be offered as proof that they had carried on an extramarital relationship. James's attorneys would contend that they were not true copies of Mabel's letters but had been altered by

Nina. This debate would play a major role in the court battles waged between the Walkers.

Mabel began one purported letter by stating that she had received previous letters from James and protested, "You are entirely mistaken if you think I am trying to start a quarrel with you. If I never answered some of your letters I guess I had good reasons for not doing so." Mabel then shared the news that she had taken a flat with five rooms and had been busy since her arrival in Boston. Obviously still assuming that she might again go to Charleston the next summer, she discussed a letter from her brother, Jack, wherein the cook had asked whether Mabel was returning to Charleston. Mabel suggested that, since the cook "seemed to be rather discouraged," James should write her an encouraging note or she might not stay. Regarding the events that had taken place in Washington, DC, Mabel wrote:

> It seems to me it all depends on Mrs. W. [Nina] as to when you start for Charleston. I thought it was business that detained you so long. You say I ought to have stayed in Washington a week or two longer, but I think I stayed there just a week two [sic] long. I put up with a great many insults for that one week, but I stood it all for your sake. Now I am sorry that I did not act different. Every time I think of how Mrs. W. treated me, my blood just boils. If I should ever by chance happen to meet her, I will know just how to treat her too. I hope you will excuse me for writing just what I think, but I cannot help it, and I will never forget the way she treated me.

Mabel wrote that she had bumped into a previous employer, who had told her he would give her a job any time she felt like coming back. However, she had told him she had "forgotten how to work." "There is no place like Boston after all," she continued. "I feel like a different person all together." Mabel was in a hurry to mail the letter to James and told him this was "one of the days that I have the blues even if I am in Boston," but if she ran into one of her friends, she would cheer up.[86]

If the previous letter was not what would be expected to be written by a servant to a former employer, the next purported letter from Mabel to James seemed even more inappropriate. It began:

> My Dear Mr. Walker:
> Yours of the sixth received today. I am very angry with you for not answering my letter sooner. I did not intend to answer yours for two or three weeks; but I felt to [sic] cross[;] I could not wait—"Out

of sight—out of mind"—but I won't tell you what I dreamed of[;] I am going to try and dream of some body else now. If you had only written a line[,] I would not of [*sic*] felt so bad, But I know you were glad to get rid of me. I have been watching the mail every day expecting to get a letter from you. If you don't think it will hurt you to write[,] you may write to me 107 Bower st. [*sic*] Roxbury Mass.
 Very Sincerely
 Miss Cochrane[87]

Another alleged letter from Mabel to James was the most shocking of all, both in tone and content. Dated January 9, 1905, and reportedly sent to James at the Charleston Navy Yard, it read as follows:

My dear Mr. Walker
 I told you I would wait to hear from my brother before I could decide what to do. I had a letter from him a few days ago; he told me, he was under the impression you wanted me down there; [b]ut he thinks I ought to stay with Clara; [b]ut that he would not interfere with me, if I should decide to go. For you know dear that I love only you; and I would do most anything for you. But to tell you the truth I feel a little nervous about going down. Have you been reading about Nan Paterson[?]I would not want anything like that to happen to me. Well darling it is a long time since I have been *loved* and I think I could almost kill you with kindness. Oh! If you were only here in Boston: it is a large place. I really do not see much sense in my going down there for a few months, I will certainly have to come home when Mand gets here which will be sometime in March or April. Now it is imitirial [*sic*] to me whether I go south or stay in Boston. But I must decide this week for the month is up here and I must get out right away. If I stay I must take a furnished room, for trying to keep house for two of us is too much of a proposition.
 Your old friend Lillian is sick in bed & I go over to Somerville every day and stay there for four hours with her. She wants me to stay with her all together. Have you dreamed of me lately? I dreamed of you last night. That is why I am writing to you tonight. Well I am still true to you. But I feel pretty nervous sometimes, and wish you were here with me. I never used to feel that way—[b]ut I guess it is because I love you. Have you heard the new song? "I want to tell you babe how much I love you"[;] it is very pretty. I would sing it to you tonight if I only had you here. Well I hope you

are as true to me, as I am to you. I guess I shall have to look you over to see if you have been jollied[;] do you think you would bear inspection? No—Yes?

Well it is a shame to tease you. But—this is just the way I feel. I must go to bed now and see if I can have another dream like last night.

Write to me as soon as you receive this and let me know what you think in regards to my plans? I am not asking you for *advise* [*sic*] *this time.*

If you can let me have an answer this week, I shall thank you very much.

Yours as ever.[88]

This appeared to be a blatant love letter alluding to not only a romantic relationship between Mabel and James but a sexual one.

Mabel's query to James in the alleged letter "Have you been reading about Nan Paterson[?]" and her comment "I would not want anything like that to happen to me" are provocative. Nan Patterson, the young daughter of a prominent family, had gained notoriety by becoming a chorus girl. In June 1904, she was charged with the fatal shooting of her married lover, Francis Thomas ("Caesar") Young, a New York bookmaker. The prosecution accused Nan of killing Caesar because he planned to leave her and go away with his wife.[89]

This infamous case was sensationalized in the newspapers and drew widespread attention (including from Mabel Cochrane). It is unlikely that Mabel's mention of the Nan Patterson affair was a threat to kill James. Perhaps when Mabel said that she "would not like that to happen to [her]," she meant that she would not want James to leave her. Or possibly she meant that she would not want to become infamous, as Nan had. Whatever Mabel implied by her reference to Nan Patterson, it is evident that in this letter, she associated her own situation with a possible scandal. If she actually wrote the letter, Mabel may have felt both frightened and thrilled to compare herself with a glamorous woman who had an affair with a prominent married man. If Nina, in fact, altered the letter (as James claimed), then she had cleverly inserted a disreputable reference to support her claim that Mabel and James had carried on an illicit relationship.

The letters from Mabel to James, quoted above, would be used as evidence in court. How did Nina get them? Throughout the Walker divorce trials, different explanations would be suggested. One account was that Nina intercepted the postman, recognized the return address on a letter from Mabel, opened and copied it, resealed it, and then gave James the letter.⁹⁰ At another time, according to Nina, she picked torn letters out of her husband's wastebasket, pieced them together, and copied them exactly in her own handwriting.⁹¹ In rebuttal, James would claim Nina had indeed copied some of the letters but that she had made changes to them in doing so.⁹² In the courtroom, he would reportedly "[cause] a stir by testifying that these letters, as introduced into the case, had been 'doctored' by his wife, and that she had opened and tampered with his personal mail."⁹³ Originals do survive of the letter written in July 1903 to Mabel's sister, the 1904 letter discussing James's invitation for Mabel to visit Washington, and the first letter written after Mabel's return to Boston, so there is less doubt regarding their contents than that of the copied letters.

James's personal problems were not his only worries while stationed at the Charleston Navy Yard. Although he was popular and respected at the Boston Navy Yard, he encountered work problems in South Carolina. James was the civil engineer in command of the $1,250,000 dry dock construction project in Charleston, which the Jewell Filtration Company was contracted to build. This project turned into a Navy scandal widely reported in newspapers throughout the country. According to the *Boston Daily Globe*, in the spring of 1904, Lieutenant Walker charged that the concrete used to build the dock did not meet the terms of the company's contract; therefore, he removed two inspectors on the project, whom he suspected of "being too lenient," and then "ordered [that] no more of the unsatisfactory concrete be used."⁹⁴ The *New York Times* states that Lieutenant Walker "admitted he was unable to prove such suspicions, but the men were removed under the civil service regulations for other misdemeanors.⁹⁵ John Dougherty, the president of the Jewell Filtration Company, allegedly threatened to go to a "higher authority" to have James Walker removed from the project if he were not more lenient in enforcing the terms of the contract.⁹⁶

On June 17, 1905, Paul Morton, then secretary of the navy under President Theodore Roosevelt, determined, "On account of the constant friction between Walker and the filtration company, the construction of the dry dock might proceed more rapidly if a new officer were placed in charge."⁹⁷ Therefore, he announced that he would move Lieutenant L. E. Gregory from the Portsmouth, New Hampshire, Navy Yard to replace Lieutenant James Walker in Charleston, who would then be transferred to the navy yard in Norfolk, Virginia. Lieutenant Frederic R. Harris, Lieutenant Walker's chief assistant, who had "also been a thorn in the side of the contractors by his insistence on strict compliance with specifications," was to be sent to the Key West, Florida, Navy Yard.⁹⁸

Several newspaper articles describe Lieutenants Walker and Harris as champions of the public interest, who had been greatly wronged. According to the *New York Times*, "The action of the Secretary of the Navy in overriding Rear Admiral Endicott . . . caused something of a sensation in navy circles." The *Times* states, "[Walker] was most strenuous in his inspection to such an extent that he watched the concrete work day after day, and when he believed the contractors had used crushed stone in any degree larger than the size called for in the specifications, he made them take it out and do the work over again."⁹⁹

On June 20, 1905, the *State*, a prominent South Carolina newspaper, ran several articles about the Charleston Navy Yard dispute. John Dougherty, the president of the Jewell Filtration Company, gave the following statement to that newspaper:

> Mr. Walker held up our work 90 days altogether. In every case his decision was found to be wrong. When he condemned concrete, experts showed that the material was all right; when he disapproved stone, experts made thorough tests that made him "take water."

Dougherty maintained that "[Walker's] unwarranted criticisms and hold-ups were delaying the job beyond all reason." In defending Walker, an editorial in the *State* retorts, "[Walker's] order was unheeded, though the contract expressly provides that 'the civil engineer in charge of the work shall at all times have full direction and control of the work under contract.'" The editorial also points out that no other contractors had complained about Walker's oversight and that it was unusual for a naval civil engineer to be transferred prior to the completion of a project.¹⁰⁰

A letter to the editor from Andrew J. Riley, a prominent Charleston contractor, appears in the *State* the same day. He supported Walker and his assistant, confirming, "Having done considerable work for the government in Charleston I have intimately known Lieut. Walker and Lieut. Harris, and can freely say that I have never met two men who impressed me more favorably for fairness and ability." Along with many others, Riley charged that the Jewell Filtration Company had used political influence, commenting, "It looks as though a great government was being pulled about by the nose by a few politicians." Riley urged, "[Charleston] Mayor Rhett should at once call the attention of our representatives in congress to this matter."¹⁰¹

The depiction of Walker and Harris as victims of political intrigue is prevalent in several national newspaper articles, all of which support the civil engineers. Some go further, urging corrective action. On June 21, 1905, the *Syracuse Journal* ran a front-page story headlined, "South Anxious for

Square Deal." This upstate New York paper reports, "Responding to a plea for a 'square deal' from citizens of Charleston, S.C., President Theodore Roosevelt directed suspension of the orders transferring Civil Engineers J.W.G. Walker and F.R. Harris, who have been at loggerheads with the New York Continental Filtration Company." The article explains that President Roosevelt had received a telegram that day from Representative George Swinton Legaré of South Carolina, "alleging that undue political influence was being urged against the engineers and insisting, 'Give Charleston a Square Deal.'" Mr. William Loeb, the president's secretary, "replied that the President had suspended operation of the transfer orders and would make a thorough investigation."[102] Another New York paper, the *Evening Post*, also reports this event.[103]

Shortly afterward, Secretary of the Navy Paul Morton resigned from Roosevelt's cabinet. Morton had been implicated in the widely publicized financial improprieties while he was the vice president of the Santa Fe Railroad. The Charleston Navy Yard crisis may have been the last straw prompting his removal, or perhaps the problems at the Charleston Navy Yard became a scandal because they involved an already denounced secretary of the navy. In Morton's place, President Roosevelt appointed Charles Joseph Bonaparte. An American descendant of Napoleon's family, Bonaparte was a legal advocate for progressive causes in the United States. He permanently halted the Walker and Harris transfers as one of his first acts in office. Following a prompt investigation, the new secretary of the navy concluded, "Consideration of the facts developed convinces me that, under all attendant circumstances, a mistake was made when these orders [to transfer Walker and Harris] were issued. The mistake I deem it my duty to correct."[104] In reversing his predecessor's actions by reappointing Walker and Harris to the Charleston Navy Yard, Secretary Bonaparte affirmed that they had been "vigilant and conscientious" in holding the contractor to the required specifications. He claimed that their dismissal at the urging of the contractors would have an undesirable "moral effect" on other government contractors and supervising officers.[105]

In a laudatory profile of the new secretary, the *New York Times* praises Bonaparte for his "disregard of political influence." His speech reinstating Walker and Harris is described as "old-fashioned, sound, straight-forward talk." The *Times* slyly suggests, "To men with a 'pull,' a Secretary of the Navy who behaves in that way must be a highly objectionable thing."[106] The *State* claims, "The action of Secretary of the Navy Bonaparte in revoking the transfer orders for Lieuts. J.W.G. Walker and F.R. Harris from the Charleston navy yard has saved the administration from the development of a new scandal." With regard to the Jewell Filtration Company's request for the removal of Walker and Harris, the *State* asks, "Was there ever a document of more astounding impudence?"[107]

A progressive political wave was sweeping the United States, and this was only one example of many alleged incidences of political influence that were prominently featured in the popular press. Lieutenant Walker and his assistant were excellent candidates to play out the media drama of public protectors who were wrongly threatened with punishment for standing up to industrial bullies. In the newspapers, charges of political influence were presented as one-sided. The press did not discuss the possible influence of Admiral Walker, who had important political connections in the navy and in the president's cabinet. John Grimes Walker had helped his son professionally in the past, so why would he not do so in this case as well? The elder Walker's status as an admiral is only briefly mentioned in some articles about the Charleston affair. The president of Jewell Filtration Company, John Dougherty, used political pull to support his son, who was the company's resident engineer. It is quite possible that Admiral Walker, another prominent father, may have exerted his own influence, but that angle might have ruined the David and Goliath aspect of the Charleston narrative.

Also not mentioned in the newspapers is the fact that James's wife and children were boarding for the summer (in Watch Hill, Rhode Island) with a close friend of James's mother, who just happened to be the cousin of Charles Joseph Bonaparte, the new secretary of the navy. The story of a young naval officer who had defied corporate interests suited the progressive climate of the time. James Walker's ultimate triumph in the Charleston Navy Yard affair made him a champion of public reform. As an unintended consequence, his marital relationship entered a period of tranquility.

4

A Series of Temporary Truces

Summer 1905 to Summer 1909

Nina Walker was furious at her husband during the late spring of 1904. A year later, her anger had abated, and a marital truce had developed between the couple. James's public popularity as a hero may have persuaded Nina that, despite his flaws, he was worthy of her respect and affection. It would certainly have been an awkward moment to expose their domestic quarrels. After all, how could a wife renounce such a widely admired husband?

During the summer of 1905, Nina and the children went for their second season to the seaside town of Watch Hill, Rhode Island. On July 4, 1905, she wrote a letter to James, in South Carolina, that was congenial and supportive. Nina began, "My dear James," and she gave news about the family's health: "Our sick ones are ever so much better and are running about once more. My poor stomach is still very miserable, but I have hopes of better days."[1] After lamenting the very recent death of Secretary of State John Hays, Nina interjected, "Please tell me if Miss Radcliff has done anything to help you in the packing."[2] Nina's mention of "packing" is probably a reference to James's then impending move to the Norfolk Naval Station, where he was ordered prior to his reinstatement in Charleston.

In her letter, Nina told her husband a little about their children's friends at the beach, that the weather had become warm enough to feel comfortable wearing white, and that the owners would like to sell the cottage where she and the children had stayed the previous summer. She commented, "I hear your sister has another boy[;] I know she is disappointed not having a daughter." Nina was probably referring to the birth of Alfred Thomas, the third son in three years for Frances Walker Thomas and Dr. John Jenks Thomas.³ About their own daughter, then seven, Nina wrote, "Elizabeth has lost an upper front tooth, and looks very funny[;] this age is such a trying one[;] she will not get her beauty again for some time." She reported about their three-year-old son and youngest child, "Grandma loves dearly to play with Herbert[;] she laughs at him and enjoys his sweet little ways immensely[;] his rosy cheeks have returned and he seems very well."⁴ "Grandma" most likely referred to Nina's mother, Virginia Chinn, who, with Nina's sister, Bertha, was staying with Nina and the children at the beach. After chatting about summer friends, Nina made a request:

> I have written a short story which I would like to have typewritten[;] it is only of about 300 words[;] could you have it done for me when you go to Norfolk[;] I want to send it to St. Nicholas or the Youth's Companion. Please tell me what to say when I send the story to them and when shall I send it to you to be type-written.⁵

Nina aspired to have her writing published. She hoped to submit her story to two magazines that were very popular at the time and had launched the careers of several well-known writers.⁶ Since her husband was successful in getting his book published, she asked his advice. There is no record that Nina's story ever appears in either *St. Nicholas* or the *Youth's Companion.*⁷ However, she continued to write stories and poems.

While requesting James's help with her writing, Nina mentioned his move from Charleston as only a side note. Later in her letter, she returned to the subject of his impending move, making apologies for not assisting:

> How I wish I could help you with the packing. Sometimes I feel I have been of very little use, and at this time I would like to be two places at once. Yet if I were in Charleston my usefulness would be very limited on account of my horrid stomach giving out. What week [sic] mortals we are after all, and I was *so* proud to have kept well all winter. Dr. Lewis says a mother of four active children cannot expect to be well all the time[;] she has great responsibilities!⁸

When Nina wrote of her regret at not helping her husband pack, it may have been her way of apologizing for not returning to support him during this difficult time. It was not until the fifth and last page of her letter that Nina finally referred to the reason James was packing to move to another post— his conflict with the construction company at the Charleston Navy Yard:

> I really have been very much troubled for you over this move and the horrid mixup with the [d]ry dock people, and so much injustice shown in the matter, but I am proud of the stand you have taken all the way through and very glad you are my husband[;] I have not seen a better yet[;] are you not surprised[?][9]

It seems strange that Nina would wait until after she had discussed more trivial matters to finally broach the topic that was probably foremost in her husband's mind. However, although occurring late in the letter, her affirmations of pride and affection appeared sincere. She seemed to reassure her husband that she had forgiven him for past disagreements. Although this sentiment might have served as an appropriate closing to her letter, Nina went on to talk of other things:

> I bought the most *beautiful* necklace when in Washington with the money you gave me two Christmases ago. You will have to see it to appreciate it's [sic] beauty—I wear it over my dresses which is the style now and I value it above everything except my pearl watch.[10]

This abrupt change of topic seemed incongruous at first. Why did Nina abruptly shift her tone from affectionate support to express her pleasure with a piece of jewelry? In view of the couple's previous financial and personal difficulties, telling James she had finally bought herself a gift with money he had previously given her might have been an additional message that all was forgiven. Nina signed her letter: "Kisses from the little ones, Nina."[11]

At the end of that summer, James and Nina went on a trip by themselves to New Hampshire, stopping for the night in Boston on the way. Nina would later report that this trip was a very happy one, and she felt determined to mend her relationship with her husband. She would say that since it was the first time they had spent together alone and "free from cares," she would refer to this trip as their "honeymoon."[12]

That fall, Nina and the children stayed at her mother's Connecticut Avenue house in Washington, DC. James wrote to her on October 5, 1905, from the St. John, a hotel in Charleston:

> I arrived here safely this morning, three and a half hours late, and came at once to the hotel, which I have hardly left since. The trip shook me up considerably and I passed a large quantity of blood this morning, so I thought it wise to call in [Dr.] Plummer, who broke the record by appearing promptly. He seems to think that

he can fix me up, and I know enough of the subject to be sure that his proposed course of treatment is a good one for the present. I may perhaps need a little surgical manipulation from a specialist sometime in the future.[13]

James's manner for the rest of the October 5 letter was congenial. He told Nina he would go to the navy yard the next day and try to move there permanently in the next few days. James finished by stating, "I trust that all goes well with you, and that Herbert is becoming more contented. I am looking for a letter from you tomorrow or next day." He signed, "With much love to you and the children, Affectionately, James."[14]

Two days later, on October 7, 1905, James again wrote to Nina from Charleston. In his brief note, he mentioned receiving her most recent letter and again told her that he was glad things were going well with the family. After stating that he was very busy, he informed her that he was moving out to their house at the navy yard that very day. Regarding his health condition, he wrote, "My trouble seems to be yielding somewhat to Plummer's treatment, although it will probably take some time to get into good shape. Fortunately there is very little discomfort, although I am still passing blood." He concluded, "No time to write more. Love to all. Affectionately, J. W. Walker."[15]

The letter James wrote to Nina two days later, on October 9, 1905, began with more news about his medical ailment:

> Yesterday being Sunday, I slept until eleven o'clock and spent the rest of the day nursing myself. As a result I am much better today. Neither blood nor pus is visible, and the urine is comparatively clear. A week or ten days ought to see me cured—for this time.[16]

In these letters, James seemed to refer to a chronic condition, with recurring difficulties, but he did not name it. The manner in which James referred to his health problem suggested that his wife was already familiar with it. Whether she knew the full nature of his condition was doubtful. Several years later, Nina's lawyers would claim that Nina was "ignorant of the cause and nature of the disease up to the time she left him."[17]

During divorce hearings, a physician who testified on James's behalf would claim that he suffered from a condition called "oxaluria" rather than a venereal disease. James might have explained his condition that way to his wife during their marriage. However, his medical records from December 7, 1901, clearly noted a "diagnosis of chronic gonorrhea; explanation in the notes slight discharge; previous history of gonorrhea." This diagnosis would later be confirmed in court by a physician who testified for Nina.[18] The symptoms described in the medical record were said to be a more appropriate match for gonorrhea than for oxaluria, which is a very rare condition.[19] Would Nina have responded so compassionately if she had known that James suffered from a sexually transmitted disease? Would the truce between them have prevailed during this period? It is not possible to know for certain. For the time being, at least on paper, all seemed well with their relationship.

In his October 9 letter, James also responded to a servant problem on which Nina had consulted him. Regarding "Miss Radcliffe," James advised Nina to write a short note stating that she had received her letter and "will give it attention upon your return to Charleston, as you are now very much occupied with other things." He counseled, "Be careful to say nothing to indicate what you propose to do about it. When you get down here I will look after it." In the meantime, he advised Nina to find out how much notice this woman had given Nina's mother and sister regarding her intended departure and the completion of her travel arrangements. It is not clear from James's letter what was the specific problem with Miss Radcliffe, although he stated, "I was at first inclined to help her out financially, but her attitude is one I do not fancy and I think we had better let her pay nearly, if not all, her expenses." He commented, "Her methods are typically Charlestonian" and cautioned Nina to "keep any letters of hers which you may have."[20] This last piece of advice was important, since James's father gave him similar advice regarding letters from his wife. Both James and Nina would present letters from their own correspondence as evidence at trial.

After discussing the Miss Radcliffe matter, James wrote, "I am glad you have found a nursery governess who seems promising. Be sure that *she* understands what she is to do."[21] This comment was most directly a reference to the problem with Miss Radcliffe currently under discussion in the letter. Yet, considering the difficulties caused by a previous governess, it could also have resonated with Nina as a reference to Mabel Cochrane.

The balance of James's October 9 letter read like typical correspondence from husband to wife. James expressed his pleasure that Herbert was doing well and described various cows at the yard, commenting, "We shall have quite a dairy in operation." He also reassured Nina, "Frazier and his wife are in the house and they say that they will stay after your arrival, so the cook problem is probably solved." James then told his wife that he had not yet been to see their garden but had heard it was doing well and would produce vegetables by the time she returned. He told Nina, "Do not hurry your trip down here. I am getting along very comfortably," and then he warned her to reserve Pullman accommodations several days in advance before she did come to Charleston.[22]

In closing this letter, James complained that the dentist's bill he had received seemed high, sent "love to the children and much to yourself," and signed, "Affectionately, J. W. Walker." A postscript informed Nina that it was still warm in Charleston, although not uncomfortable, and that most of the mosquitoes were gone.[23] These reassurances would support James's later denial that he had discouraged his wife and children from joining him that fall.

Nina's letter from Washington, DC, on October 10, 1905, to James at the Charleston Navy Yard probably crossed in the mail with James's letter from the day before. Nina started her letter with this update:

> I am writing from the hospital again[;] Herbert boy is as gay as a cricket. Dr. Shamus left word for me to call and see him this afternoon, so I went around at once and found he wanted to talk about Herbert's leaving the hospital[;] he says the boy could not be doing better, but he feels a week longer under Miss Haggard's care would be advisable, as Herbert is still on his back and ought to be about the room a week before leaving. He thinks as soon as he leaves the hospital he will be perfectly strong and ready to travel, so he advises keeping him at the hospital until he is ready to go to Charleston[;] that means he thinks it safe for us to travel a week from Friday[;] do you not think by the 20th it will be cool enough[?] [Y]ou see that is almost a month's [sic] later than last year. Please say we can come then.[24]

Besides cooler weather, there had been a good reason for Nina and the children to stay in Washington that fall. Herbert, three years old and the baby of the family, was under medical care. He had suffered from a hernia since he was a month old that was surgically corrected in Washington. Nina would later write, "The dear baby suffered often and keeping a homemade woolen brace on was difficult."[25] Shared concern for Herbert's welfare offered an additional explanation for Nina's now conciliatory manner toward her husband, despite his suspected previous transgressions. Nina pleaded with James to allow the rest of the family to join him as soon as possible, an unambiguous message that she yearned to be with her husband.

Nina wrote that the new governess was doing very nicely and requested that James ask the cook in Charleston to find a housemaid for the family. She informed her husband that his father had visited Herbert and her that afternoon. The admiral told her that Fanny's cook had taken "French leave" by departing the day she and her young children had returned to Boston and that he was disappointed that his own butler would not be returning. The Walkers were not the only prosperous family to suffer from servant problems during this time period, when better jobs became available to working-class people. "Enough of the trials and tribulations!" Nina declared and continued her letter in a very affectionate tone:

> Dearest—I sent you this morning from Galt a charm for your watch chain[;] it is your birthday present, but especially to commemorate our honeymoon[;] the latter dearest you remember is to last forever and all the love that is in me goes with the little charm to you, [so] please don't take it off or cease to wear it—even when you get your second wife my advise [*sic*] is to marry a northern girl the next time. The man at Galt's told me the gold ring I have belonging to your chain is not worth doing anything with as it is quite worn and it is better to get a new one, so please have that done at Allen's as soon as possible so you can wear the charm. I hope you will like it Jamsie dear[;] it suddenly occurred to me you might not, [so] I can change it if you would like a different kind.[26]

Nina had written in a previous letter that she had recently purchased a necklace with the money James had given her for Christmas two years before; now she affectionately wrote that she had bought a piece of jewelry for him as well. The language and sentiments expressed would certainly give James the impression that everything was forgiven and that conjugal bliss was restored.

Not yet having received James's letter from the previous day, Nina ended this letter by asking about his health:

> The most important part comes last, and that is how are you[?] I expected a letter from you today. I know you have your hands more than full, but I feel most anxious to hear how you are, and I hourly wish I could be with you, yet that is taking undo flattery unto myself, for I cannot cure you[;] how I wish that I could. Is your treatment proving still beneficial, and has the flow of blood stopped[?][27]

These words of solicitude were further evidence that Nina was probably unaware that James's suffering was due to a sexually transmitted disease. At the end of her letter, Nina told James that Herbert's nurse had returned and that it was time for her to finish. She signed, "Worlds of love from us all and especially, Nina."[28]

Nina's next letter to James, on Friday, October 13, 1905, was most likely written as a reply to his letter of October 9 and shortly before she and the children made their trip back to Charleston. Nina began, "It was a great relief to get your letter saying you were really improving under treatment and that you felt you would be over your difficulty shortly." There was still no hint that Nina recognized James's "difficulty" as a venereal disease. In an intimately conspiratorial manner, she continued, "I wrote a short note to Miss Radcliffe and said just what you advised, so we will have an amusing time in store for us. What strange freeks [sic] inhabit this world." She then again assured him that the new governess, Miss Baldwin, was satisfactory.[29]

Nina informed James that his mother had come home from a trip and looked well and that she and the children had all gone over to see her. She then notified him that she was shipping a large box of provisions down to Charleston, including canned goods and preserves that would keep the family supplied during the winter. Finally, Nina commented, "Really my life is very much occupied and I shall be glad to get home again and have the little ones start their lessons." She signed, "Fondest love and kisses from us all and Nina."[30]

When Nina and the children returned to Charleston, family life was placid for a while. Many years later, Nina and James's daughter, Elizabeth, would recount to her own daughter how happy and safe she felt as an officer's child on a naval base. She would also tell her "some delightful stories," including "the time she and her brothers snuck downstairs before a party, carefully keeping out of the sight of all adults, and drank greedily from the punchbowl. Then they snuck away, only to become horridly, vomitously sick from the liquor." Elizabeth's daughter believes that this problem was "all taken care of by the nursemaids, not by my lady grandmother."[31]

According to Nina, at some point after she returned to Charleston in 1905, she found Mabel Cochrane's earlier letters in James's wastebasket.[32] It is baffling that James would have left these notes, although torn, in a wastebasket in his home where his wife could easily find them; he would later insist that Nina had actually found the letters in a wastebasket in his office rather than in the house. In her unpublished autobiography, many years later, Nina wrote:

> The following winter . . . I experienced one of life's tragedies [sic]. A letter came to my husband[;] it fell into my hands and stabbed my heart like a poisoned arrow. The dark days, months, and even years that followed seemed to me more poignant with sorrow than

that of the separation through death of a loved one. I was rudely shaken in my implicit faith of my husband's love for me, consequently also in my youthful confidence generally in mankind.[33]

Nina decided she had to take action:

> In my perplexity I sent a copy of *the letter* I made to Cousin Reese asking his advice[;] his reply was kindly and sympathetically worded[;] he gave me three alternatives, engage a lawyer to acquaint me with the law of SC in obtaining a divorce, go and talk the problem over with my husband's father[,] or accept the conditions as they were. I preferred to go to the Admiral. I mailed him a copy of the letter from Boston and in mine I said I would arrive in Washington the day after he received them. To my husband I made the excuse for my absence that my grandmother had a severe cold and my mother was anxious about her[,] considering her advanced age. In the end I did not see my family at all, for they would question why I left my children for an expensive trip when mother had written me my grandmother was improving. The Admiral wished his wife to be included in our conference[;] they tossed the letter aside as being of no import, just the reflection of a young man's peccadillos. My inexperience could not cope with or comprehend their cold calculated worldly perspicacity. I left with a heavy heart yet with a determination to keep my family together as long as possible.[34]

Nina was not yet ready to leave her husband. She was also distracted by the death of her beloved grandmother, Elizabeth Davis Wood, who passed away at ninety-two years of age on January 14, 1906. This was a great loss to Nina, who said that her grandmother "had always made [us] feel her home was ours" and that "her room was invariably the center of our home and the gathering place for friends." Nina took the children to their great-grandmother's funeral at the family plot in Rock Creek Cemetery, in Washington, DC, where she said, "My grandparents were the founders of our family. . . . [T]hey left a priceless inheritance in their noble characters, straight living and purposeful lives."[35]

On their way home to Charleston from the funeral, Nina and the children were unexpectedly delayed. They were told that there was an epidemic of small pox and the city was quarantined; all passengers for Charleston would be let off at a "way station." Nina was baffled about what to do, until, as she later wrote:

To my great relief before the crucial time came my husband stood before us in his uniform[;] how or when he boarded the train I did not ask[;] it was enough to know Uncle Sam was taking care of us and all was well. It was my first experience of the power of my husband's office[;] having the Navy back of us felt mighty good.[36]

For Nina, there were definite advantages to having a husband who was an officer in the Navy, which may have balanced the drawbacks of being married to him.

In April 1906, James W. G. Walker was promoted to civil engineer, with the rank of lieutenant in the U.S. Navy.[37] Having completed four years in Charleston as an assistant civil engineer, James was ordered to temporary duty at the New York Navy Yard in Brooklyn, where he was assigned as first assistant to Civil Engineer R. C. Hollyday.[38] On April 27, 1906, James wrote a long letter to Nina from Brooklyn. She and the children were again staying at her mother's house in Washington, DC. He mentioned that he had received a letter that she had sent the day before and was pleased that she had a conversation with his father. James then told Nina that there was no special news but wrote the following account:

> Tuesday night one of the men gave a birthday party which was rather a riotous affair. There were seventeen or eighteen present, several of them being women—actresses and other lively individuals. It was considered a highly successful affair, although three of us remained sober. I hid several of the preliminary cocktails, and successfully exchanged my full glass for my neighbor's empty one over and over again. The neighbor succumbed, but I escaped with about three drinks instead of thirty. One of the women went under for a time, but was revived with aromatic spirits of ammonia, and one of the men died bravely after attempting to empty, unaided, a huge loving cup of champagne. He was put to bed, after attempting to thrash the assembled multitude, and the next day he had no recollection of the events of the evening. We supplied his lack of memory, however, making him guilty of all sorts of horrible deeds. The guests departed at three in the morning, escorted by most of the mess, one of the girls coming back to kiss me a tender goodnight. I have advised Ferguson, the host of the occasion, not to have another birthday for at least three months. I think he appreciated the advice when he counted the empty bottles and figured up the cost.[39]

James may have thought that he was simply entertaining Nina with an amusing story. He may have also believed that she would appreciate the fact that he had shown restraint in remaining sober. Possibly, James told the story as a way of bragging that women were attracted to him or to induce his wife to join him in Brooklyn. However, it was perplexing, knowing that his wife was jealous of his previous attention to other women, that he would mention the "tender kiss goodnight."

After recounting the birthday party escapade, James told his wife about attending a vaudeville performance in support of the San Francisco earthquake victims and how some of the actresses came into the audience to sell tickets. With good humor, he told his wife that he had declined to give any more aid to the San Franciscans but had "purchased and smoked a couple of cigars for the benefit of a certain veteran of the St. Louis cyclone, remembering that charity begins at home."[40] James was undoubtedly referring to himself as that "veteran," since he had been in Saint Louis when an epic cyclone struck there on May 27, 1896.

James attempted another note of humor at the end of his letter, when he told Nina that he was waiting for needle and thread with which to repair his clothes. "I believe," he joked, "that darning socks is more in my line than birthday parties. I must be lacking in sporting blood." He closed his letter, "With much love to you and the children, from James."[41] It is unknown whether Nina found James's letter amusing when she first read it. However, during the divorce hearings, her attorneys would refer several times to the drinking that had taken place at the birthday party as well as to James's consorting with actresses.

In the summer of 1906, Nina's poor health prompted her physician to advise "a complete rest and freedom from all care." Her mother also needed rest after caring for her invalid mother for many years. Together, they rented a cottage in the Blue Ridge Mountains at Charmian, Pennsylvania. "In a spirit of true kindness," according to Nina, Mrs. Walker offered to take Elizabeth and Grahame to spend the summer with her in Wilton, New Hampshire, where the admiral had spent his early childhood: "It was a safe locality where they could run loose." Nina's two youngest sons, Serrell and Herbert, joined her and her mother in the mountains.[42]

On September 22, Rebecca Walker wrote a letter responding to her daughter-in-law's request that she keep the two older children through the fall. She told Nina that, at her age, she could not possibly care for them in Washington. Since Nina had declined another alternative that her mother-in-law proposed for Elizabeth and Grahame's care, she asked Nina where she should send them and warned that she and the admiral were leaving Wilton on October 5.[43]

Then, Mrs. Walker informed her daughter-in-law that she was aware that Nina had covertly written to request further financial assistance from Rebecca's brother Henry Goddard Pickering, who had furnished Nina and James's Brookline house. Henry had discussed her letter when he had visited his sister the previous evening. She wrote:

> We were surprised at your request as when we last talked of these matters you insisted that such pecuniary aid as I had given had done more harm than good, that no such help was needed, and you particularly preferred that it should not be given in future. The Admiral and I do not feel that it is best for us to make any agreement about an allowance.⁴⁴

Mrs. Walker stated that Elizabeth and Grahame were well and looking forward to seeing their parents and younger brothers. She closed, "Affectionately yours, Rebecca W. Walker."⁴⁵

According to Nina, her health and her mother's improved in the mountains, and when they went back to Washington later in the summer, they "welcomed Elizabeth and Grahame with open arms." Nina said, "I had missed them far more than I anticipated and they must have missed me for I was shocked to find them thinner and pathetic looking." Although her mother-in-law blamed their condition on homesickness for their little brothers, Nina would later write, "It was hard on the little mites. Elizabeth was nine and Grahame was seven[;] they could not read my letters or write to me to express their feelings, and were compelled to rely on their grandmother for the mother love they missed. Hers was cold and austere, a product of her New England ancestry." Nina was upset to find that Grahame had been lonely, isolated in a bedroom away from the rest of the family, and that when Elizabeth did not pay attention while Mrs. Walker was teaching her to read, the old woman had locked her in "a dark closet for many hours."⁴⁶

By the fall of 1906, whatever truce had temporarily existed between Nina and James was ended. They fought over domestic matters, and Nina refused to bring the children to join her husband in Brooklyn. Nina would later explain that she and the children had been staying at her mother's home in Washington while her husband had temporary orders for Brooklyn because she did not want to disrupt the family until he received final orders. After several weeks, when Nina and the children still did not come down, James became irate. He wrote his father a letter in which he threatened to seize the children and take them back to the Brooklyn Naval Base. On Tuesday, October 16, 1906, Admiral John Grimes Walker wrote a cautionary letter to his son, beginning as follows:

> My dear Jamie,
>
> I have your note of yesterday. Of course you cannot come home and carry off the children. That would be a very false move & likely to fall to your great prejudice. All that you can do just now is to write Nina repeating your questions, saying that you have a right to replies & expect them, that you are very desirous of having her and the children with you, the hot season now passed, and want to make the necessary arrangements at the earliest possible day.[47]

It was evident that the admiral sensed that a legal separation or divorce might be possible, and he warned his son to prepare to defend himself in case the worst should happen:

> Make the letters pleasant to bear reading later in case of need. Keep copies and keep Nina's replies.
>
> Be able to show that your conduct in the matter has been kind and considerate from the beginning.
>
> I don't understand her conduct, it is so absurdly wrong. But keep quiet and don't be drawn into saying or doing anything that would put you in the wrong.[48]

James's father then indicated his suspicions that Nina's mother and sister might be influencing her behavior and again warned him to be careful:

> I think she must be very badly advised but you can't prevent that now. If you ever get your family together you must take care to keep her from such influences in the future.
>
> You are in a very unpleasant and unfortunate position but you must make no mistake that will prejudice your position.[49]

John Grimes Walker then assured his son that he was well and signed:

> Much love
> >Your affectionate father,
> >J. G. Walker[50]

Admiral Walker's advice to his son would prove prescient. However, he would die within a year and would not witness Nina's suit for divorce.

James's anger at Nina and his determination to have his wife and children join him did not abate. According to Nina, James's mother was the instigator of further trouble:

> Our domestic arrangement did not meet with my mother-in-law's approval, so there followed another upheaval for us. She sent for my husband who was then in Brooklyn and with her persuasion he tried to induce me and the children to accompany him back, where we would have to board for the few months interim. My argument in favor of our remaining where we were until final orders came was futile. I was still under Dr. Morgan's care and treatment, and the children comfortably provided for, whereas in Brooklyn they would be restricted in a boarding house, confined in a large city and a new nurse engaged, but all that was chaff against the wind.[51]

James traveled to Nina's mother's house in Washington to speak with his wife and demand that she bring the family to Brooklyn. When told she was too ill to travel, James warned Nina that he would take their four children to a boardinghouse in Brooklyn the very next morning. If she did not allow the children to go with him, he would instigate legal proceedings to take them from her. Evidently, Admiral and Mrs. Walker had also lost their patience with Nina's refusal to give in. The next morning, escorted by his father, James came and demanded the children. Mrs. Walker was in the carriage to accompany them to Brooklyn. Nina would later write:

> My mother-in-law, to carry her point, left her home, and with traveling bag in hand, accompanied by my husband, forcefully took our four little children from me out of my mother's home with just the cloths [sic] on their backs, to a boarding house in the Heights in Brooklyn. She hired an Irish nurse who took them to [a store] to get new clothes. I followed within the week. To my surprise Mrs. Walker[,] being advised of my coming, left for Washington an hour before my arrival.[52]

Nina wondered why it all could not have been worked out with more kindness toward her and the children.

On November 27, 1906, a letter was sent to James in Brooklyn from the office of Dr. William Gerry Morgan at the Rochambeau in Washington, DC. Dr. Morgan was a specialist in diseases of the stomach and lectured at Georgetown University Medical School on that subject. He was treating Nina in Washington and wrote in reply to James's November 24 letter requesting information about his wife's medical condition. He stated that Mrs. Walker was in the same condition as when he had last written James and that "her present troubles seems to have pulled her down a trifle in flesh and well being." While Dr. Morgan considered her physically able to join her husband in New York, he thought that "she should lead as quiet a life, and be as free from worry as it is possible under the circumstances." He further recommended, "I think in order for her to make a complete recovery, her present condition makes it necessary to suspend for the present the usual relations between husband and wife." This was a clear medical order for James to avoid engaging his wife in sexual activity. Dr. Morgan then advised that Nina should continue treatment with a competent specialist in diseases of the stomach.[53]

Nina complained of stomach problems for several years, as mentioned in previous correspondence with her husband. Almost certainly, the ailment she suffered from was pelvic inflammatory disease (PID), caused by transmission of her husband's infectious gonorrhea. PID is a chronic infection of the uterus, fallopian tubes, and other reproductive organs that causes symptoms including chronic lower abdominal pain. Antibiotics, the current treatment for this problem, was not yet available in the early twentieth century; untreated, PID can lead to internal abscesses, long-lasting pelvic pain, and infertility. It may be through Dr. Morgan that Nina discovered the true nature of James's medical problems, and how they related to her own.

In the meantime, hostilities between the Central American republics of Nicaragua and Honduras heated up. On February 14, 1907, the *Brooklyn Daily Eagle* interviewed James Walker, a civil engineer at the local navy yard, about his experiences in Nicaragua as part of the Walker Commission. The article includes many direct quotations from James's book, *Ocean to Ocean*, particularly regarding his confrontation by a rebel group while in the country, and a story about the career of the famous filibuster William Walker, who is misidentified as a relative.[54] A little more than a month later, on March 28, 1907, James W. G. Walker was ordered to report for duty at the Portsmouth, New Hampshire, Navy Yard.[55]

Nina would later say that the children hated being confined in a Brooklyn boardinghouse or shuttled around the cobblestone streets by the "incompetent nurse Mrs. Walker had engaged." She actually found it a relief when they broke out with chicken pox, because then she had the excuse to rent an additional room where they could play and to hire a trained nurse, who told them stories. Nina believed, "That was a waisted [*sic*] winter from an educational standpoint," and, "With a sigh of relief I welcomed my husband's news in the blustering month of March that he had received his orders, and we were to go to Portsmouth, New Hampshire, where we would have a house in the Yard and could remain the year round."[56] Nina's mother and sister left on a trip to Europe, originally scheduled to see Mrs. Chinn's brother Serrell at his Osmington Estate. When he died shortly before they left, they went anyway to attend the funeral, meet other relatives, and travel.

"Portsmouth was one of the choice stations," according to Nina, and "it was familiar ground to my husband, as many of his boyhood holidays were spent there."[57] The Treaty of Portsmouth, ending the Russo-Japanese War, had been signed recently, and the Walkers were given a tour of important sites of the event. They had "very comfortable quarters" that "overlooked the bay." Nina wrote, "It was there that I experienced the fullness of a woman's life in the service. The officers and their families, and also the people of Portsmouth[,] I found friendly and gracious[;] they accepted me as one of them with true hospitality and sincerity."[58] She was happy with her domestic life at the time:

> I had well trained servants, a large kitchen garden, a fine cow that gave us all the rich milk we needed, and a man detailed to do the outdoor work. And, above all, I had four lovely and devoted children who made the house merry. Elizabeth and Grahame, I sent them to the public school, in a fine building with cultivated teachers.[59]

Nina found "the town of Portsmouth [to be] unique and especially satisfying to a lover of the beautiful," and she enjoyed the "bracing climate and happy surroundings." The people on the Portsmouth Naval Base felt to her like "the congeniality of one large family." There were many receptions and luncheons, card parties, and launch parties. However, James's temperament stood in the way of her full enjoyment:

> I was denied the frequent dinners given, for my husband declined all invitations to them and the dances. I could not go alone[; n]or would I go without him. Early in our married life I accepted that, and gave myself more to my children and the afternoon pleasures.[60]

Admiral and Mrs. Walker spent a day with Nina and James on September 16, 1907. They were on their way to visit Mrs. Walker's cousins, Mary and Sally Pickering of Salem, at their summer cottage in Ogunquit, Maine, very close to the Portsmouth Navy Yard. Nina noted that "the Admiral seemed happy at being with his grandchildren, and expressed his satisfaction in our comfortable home, and of our being in a northern climate so beneficial to us all."[61]

James and Nina joined his parents for dinner at the cousins' cottage. Nina observed, "The Admiral was inclined to be quiet, as he told us he was suffering a bit of indigestion, saying it was brought on by the tempting seafood of which he had indulged." Just after Nina and James returned home and sat down to supper with the children, "the maid announced a telephone call for my husband," which, said Nina, "brought the sad news of his father's death." The admiral was reportedly looking out at the sea and listening to his cousin play harp music when he died of heart failure. "The shock was too great for my husband to accept or realize how much it would influence his future," Nina wrote. "His father had been the rock on which he leant during his life in the Navy, and suddenly that was taken from him. The deep affection between father and son was not felt by either man, but the strong support of an able officer left a void never to be filled."[62]

The family patriarch was seventy-two at the time of his death, and, as befitting a naval hero, after his body was cremated, the admiral's ashes were interred in Arlington National Cemetery. Battalions of marines, infantry, and artillery participated in one of the largest escorts of the time.[63] John Grimes Walker left an estate worth approximately $300,000. Personal property was estimated at $250,000 and his real estate and securities at more than $30,000. He bequeathed half of his estate to his wife, Rebecca. As executrix, Mrs. Walker was directed to provide $120,000 in trust to the Massachusetts Hospital Life Insurance Company of Boston to pay income to four of his children, including Frances Pickering Walker Thomas, Susan Grimes Walker FitzGerald, Henry Pickering Walker, and Sarah Cochrane Walker. With regard to his oldest son, James Wilson Grimes Walker, Admiral Walker directed his wife to invest the remaining $30,000 for his benefit, with her as trustee. The life estate bequeathed to Rebecca Walker was to be distributed evenly to their children after her death.[64]

Why was James's inheritance treated differently from bequests to the rest of the admiral's children? One reason might be James's record of poor money management. Another possible explanation is the correspondence between James and his father the previous year. Admiral John Grimes Walker suspected that the trouble between his son and Nina might continue, even leading to a legal separation or divorce. By directing Rebecca to invest the legacy for James's benefit, she would be able to retain legal control and therefore be better able to protect it from either her son's squandering or from a lawsuit by her daughter-in-law. James's brother Henry's new wife would later testify that Nina had complained about the terms of the will.[65]

Perhaps mourning brought Nina closer to her husband directly following his father's death. Early in her marriage, she had had personal conversations with the admiral and had sought his advice. He may have been a substitute for her own father, who had not been a part of her life since she was a child. Shared feelings of loss may have prompted Nina's renewed commitment to James. Or, perhaps the possibility of a legacy gave her hope that their financial situation would improve. Regardless, Nina planned to live with her husband and their children at his next posting. "Through the Admiral's influence my husband was ordered to Portsmouth," Nina would recall. "Now that he had passed on, we too, were to pass, and orders came for us to move to Newport, Rhode Island."[66] "Portsmouth," she declared, "proved to be the calm before the storm!"[67]

James arrived at the Naval Training Station on Coasters Harbor Island, Newport, Rhode Island, on May 12, 1908. Nina and their four children followed him there on May 16. The family settled into life in Cottage #5 at the station.[68] According to Nina:

> Our cottage at the Training Station was one of eight standing on a narrow pinnacle, where the winds never ceased. The houses were built in twos, back to back like the Siamese twins[;] there was very little space between the fronts of each of the four groups [and] therefore the private life of our neighbors was quite evident[,] especially in the summer months, when our evenings were spent on the front porch.[69]

The Walkers were apparently popular at the station and held several social gatherings during their first year there. Friends were not aware of any difficulties between the couple.[70]

Elizabeth attended Mrs. March's school in Newport, and Grahame and Serrell went to Miss Sayer's school. Mrs. Chinn and Bertha returned from one of their trips around the world in the autumn of 1908, bringing many exotic gifts for Nina, James, and the children. The next spring, Nina was still feeling ill, and her physician, Dr. Easton, decided she needed some rest. She asked her sister and a friend, Annie Townsend, to accompany her on a trip. On Saturday, April 3, 1909, they left from New York Harbor aboard the Hamburg-American Lines steamship for a two-week cruise to Bermuda, St. Thomas, San Juan, Puerto Rico, and Havana.[71] Nina would recall, "I brought back boxes of Cuba's renowned cigars, and heartily wished my husband could have been with me on that memorable cruise. We neither had a honeymoon nor a pleasant trip together to share our pleasures; it was a grave mistake[,] for life must have its pleasures as well as duties, and shared together cements the bond."[72]

While she was away on her cruise, her daughter Elizabeth suffered an attack of appendicitis and had emergency surgery. James's sister Susan

Grimes Walker FitzGerald came to Newport from her home in Hyde Park, Massachusetts, to help care for her niece. Susan had married a young lawyer, Richard Y. FitzGerald, in 1901, and they already had three children of their own. Anne, the eldest, was seven years old. Rebecca, who had been very ill as an infant, was three years old, and their youngest daughter, Susan, was only six months old at the time.[73] Susan was very different from her sister-in-law in several ways. She had left home to attend Bryn Mawr, an excellent women's college, while her sister-in-law never received higher education or lived away from home prior to her marriage. Like Nina, she was married and had several children. But unlike Nina, Susan worked outside the home, first as an administrator at Bryn Mawr and then as head worker at the Richmond Settlement House in New York City, and she had also been a prominent member of the first New York Child Labor Committee. Susan provided the main financial support for her family while her husband was ill, and she still held a paid position directing social work in Boston.[74]

On Saturday, April 17, Susan sent a letter from the Naval Training Station to let her husband know that she "had a very comfortable trip down and found Jay [James] just starting for the hospital." They were able to see Elizabeth "for a few moments but she was rather nervous and inclined to be excitable," so they did not stay, but Susan intended to go over to the hospital again that afternoon "to try to get a word with the nurse."[75] She and James were told Elizabeth was doing well, but she was in pain and restless. "She had quite a hysterical time this morning a little before our visit,"[76] Susan explained to Richard. It must have been very disturbing for young Elizabeth to undergo such an ordeal, particularly while her mother was away, and she was fortunate to have her aunt Susan with her, in addition to her father. The next day, Susan wrote that, when she went to see her niece in the afternoon, "I found her better and happier and very glad to see me and I stayed about an hour." The next morning, Susan and James visited Elizabeth again for an hour, and he went back in the afternoon.[77] On Monday evening, Susan, not wanting to stay away from her own children too long, returned to Boston. Nina came home from her trip the following afternoon.[78]

This is how Nina described her return to Newport in her unpublished autobiography:

> I left my children in the care of a semi-trained nurse. She was capable and my servants also. Upon my return my husband met me at the station in Newport, where the dusk had fallen, and I was anticipating relating my adventures as we gathered about our din-

ner table, but, when seated in the carriage[,] James said, "We will see Elizabeth first." "Where?" I said with a lump in my throat, for I knew of no reason why she should not be at home. We drove directly to the Newport hospital and there I found my dear daughter was recovering from an appendicitis operation[;] she was still very miserable but stretched out her arms towards me, and gave her sincerest smile to reassure me that she was on the mend. I struggled to keep back my tears and smiled in response, but then and there I made a silent vow that I never would put the ocean or even a corner of it between my children and me again.[79]

While staying in Newport during her niece's hospitalization, Susan FitzGerald formed a connection with her nephews and a particularly strong bond with Elizabeth, whom she described as "an interesting child."[80] Her niece apparently returned her aunt's affection. On April 30, 1909, Elizabeth wrote her the following note:

My Dear Aunt Susan,
    I thank you very much for the satin ball you sent Trixie. Mother put the package on my desk for me when I came home from the hospital. Trixie smelt the catnip, and she jumped up on my desk, knocked down the package, and ate a lot of the cat nip. I am going to give a party this summer, and I have thought of twenty one people to ask to it. Aunt Bertha gave me a pretty little pansy in a pot. I have got ever so many flowers from it. I have three buds now that are all most out. A friend of mother's sent me two cute little nigro [sic] dolls. One was a girl and the other was a boy. Mother sends her love and says she will write to you soon to thank you for coming to me when I was sick. We hope you and Uncle Richard will come to see us in the automobile this summer.
    With love from your niece,
    Elizabeth Grimes Walker.[81]

Nina followed up with a letter to her sister-in-law dated May 5, 1909. She wrote first to thank her for helping while she was away and to apprise her of Elizabeth's recovery:

My dear Susan:
    Ever since you left and I returned home the same day, I have wanted to write and thank you for your kindness in coming to our little girl so promptly and cheering her when she most needed love

and cheer. She seems so well now and happy, filling our hearts with gratitude at her recovery.

In keeping with a renewed marital truce, Nina praised her husband and expressed gratitude to him:

> James was so noble in his care of her and promptness of action that I feel my absence made little difference[;] it was a great shock to me, but seeing Elizabeth so comfortable the night of my arrival, I was saved the greater anxiety that James passed through.

Her time away at sea had mellowed Nina's outlook, as she described:

> My trip did me a world of good. The charms and beauty of the various islands will never be forgotten, all so different and wonderfully picturesque.

Nina closed her letter to Susan by reaffirming their familial bond, including the children and James in the affection she sent:

> We trust your little people are enjoying the unfolding of Spring as we are[;] the trees need one more sunny day to induce them to open their leaves. Our little people are out all day long, baseball and Elizabeth with her doll.
> James and the children join me in love to the little cousins, Richard and yourself.
> Affectionately
> Nina[82]

Nina and James's relationship was peaceful through the early spring of 1909. At some point later in the spring or early that summer, the couple quarreled, including about arrangements for the children's schooling.[83] According to Nina, Grahame was growing rapidly and would turn ten in October. She believed that his progress was limited at the "Dame's school" he was attending and that the boys at the government facility were too young for him. Nina strongly believed that Grahame needed "wider scope both for mind and body." At their Sunday dinners, the Walkers entertained an officer's son who went to Cloyne House School, "a small boarding school directly across the causeway," and Nina thought that it would be a good environment for Grahame. She spoke to James about this and asked him to go with her to see Dr. Oliver W. Huntington, the head of the school, to try to persuade him to take Grahame as a day student. According to Nina:

> My husband was suprising [sic] firm in his objections, and declined to discuss the matter. His visits to Boston were more and more frequent since our move to Newport, and his purchase of a motor cycle enabled him to travel freely to reach the section of the city where his inamorata lived. The slow inevitable widening of the breach between us culminated that autumn of 1909. It was inhanced [sic] and finally forced into the open by my mother-in-law through her determination to controle [sic] our family. Again a letter preceded a tragedy.[84]

Nina's mother and sister decided to spend the summer of 1909 at a boardinghouse on Washington Street in Newport. The house was part of a group of rental houses owned by a Mrs. Batcheler.[85] In the middle of August, Mrs. Chinn and Bertha offered to switch places with Nina to relieve her of some stress; they moved temporarily to the naval training station cottage to care for the children, while Nina stayed at their boardinghouse in Newport to rest.[86] Nina would later state that she stayed there for five days, while James would claim that she stayed for two or three weeks.[87] Also, according to James, *he* had suggested that Nina get some rest and relief from the children.[88] Regardless, what is clear is that by the time Nina returned to their cottage at the naval training station, she was ready to end her marriage. Many years later, she would write, "I do not wish to criticize my husband, [but] his code of ethics and mine were not the same, his education and home surroundings radically differed from mine[,] and he was unable or unwilling to face facts with an open mind and talk our problems over together. His emphatically repeated answer 'It's after thinking hours' was insurmountable."[89]

5

The Beginning of the End

Summer 1909 to February 1911

Nina could scarcely believe that a house could be as quiet as the one on Washington Street. Although there were moments when she missed her children, her main response to living apart from her husband was relief. Whereas her cruise the previous spring had been an escape, her current solitude was not just a respite but a time to contemplate her future options. Nina marveled that she had choices to consider. Until fairly recently, she had assumed that life would go on the way it had for the past several years. She and James would continue living in the same house, eating at the same table, sleeping in the same room, and enduring the discomfort between them. Previously this dreariness had alternated with short intervals of contentment, followed by episodes of renewed antagonism. Lately, only animosity had prevailed between them. Leaving James was not something that Nina had once thought possible, but if she could do so and still keep her children, it would be better for them as well as for her. Still, if James agreed to change his behavior, if he told her how much he loved and needed her and agreed to listen to her proposals for the children, maybe they could have the family life that she had imagined on her wedding day.

One afternoon, Mrs. Batcheler came to Nina's room and announced that James was at the front door, asking to speak with her. Nina, her heart racing, ran downstairs and saw her husband standing at the doorstep. She suggested that they talk outside so as not to disturb the other boarders. He stiffly handed her a bouquet of delphiniums—the first time she could remember that he had given her flowers since their early courting days. Nina immediately speculated that James's sister Susan had suggested that he bring them. As usual, though, James had gotten it wrong, failing to remember that Nina detested the gaudy purplish-blue of delphiniums. The thought crossed her mind that if James had come to suggest a reconciliation, it would have improved his position if he had brought the lilies she loved and had chosen to decorate their wedding feast.

James, oblivious to the fact that his wife was not won over by the delphiniums, told her that she appeared well and that the children were looking forward to her return. This information was not what Nina wanted to hear. There were no declarations of love from James, nor indications that he missed her or apologies. Instead, he abruptly switched to the officious manner that she hated so much and ordered her to come home immediately. "My mother has written to say she will arrange for the care and education of the children," James announced, waving a letter in front of her nose. "My mother will take Grahame and Serrell in her apartment on Commonwealth Avenue in Boston, Frances will take Elizabeth, and Susan will care for Herbert!" he shouted triumphantly at his wife. Without waiting for a word from her, and presumably seeing her utter dismay, he said, "This is what I intend to do!" To Nina, it was obvious that this plan was absurd, but past experiences had shown her all too forcefully that her husband's family was capable of what, in her opinion, was "extreme arrogance." She thought they were ill advised to come between her and her children.

Nina was determined not to continue her pattern of ending an argument by capitulating to her husband's demands. This time, she resolved to let him know they were at a serious impasse. After a few moments of silence, she inhaled and spoke. "James," she began, "It would be far better for us both, as well as for the children, that we live apart." James looked dumfounded, but Nina could not imagine why this opinion would be a surprise to him. She continued, "As I told you years ago, we are not fit to bring up children in the way we live." Nina purposely spoke in a soft tone, so that passersby would not overhear and with the hope of keeping things calm so that James would not erupt into one of his fits of temper. Her efforts were in vain.

When her husband responded, it was to shout abusively at her. He screamed a number of things in quick succession, including that he knew he should never have let her mother and sister get near her and that she was an unfit mother. Finally, he snarled, "I will have you committed to an insane asylum!" Nina could not listen any further. She was shaking as she ran back into the Batcheler house, flinging the gruesome delphinium bouquet to the ground. Later, when she would reflect on the incident throughout the tedious courtroom proceedings, she would realize that this was the moment when she had irrevocably determined to divorce her husband. Her memory of her humiliation, fury, and revulsion at that instant would carry her through the prolonged quest to free herself from this man.[1]

Shortly after that incident, Nina returned to Cottage #5 on Coasters Harbor Island. She spoke briefly and civilly to James only when she needed to speak at all. Nina said nothing to him about her intent to begin divorce proceedings, because she knew that her husband and his family would obstruct her plans if they got wind of them.[2] For the first time in their marriage, she slept in a separate room from James and moved her belongings in there without consulting him.[3] James may have imagined that he had prevailed once again simply because his wife had returned to his home and that before long all would be restored to normal and she would return to his bed as well. Conversely, Nina believed it should have been obvious that the conflicts between them were not resolved, and she endeavored to make that point. "My married life had begun with illusions," Nina would later write in her unpublished autobiography; "then came the time of disillusions and now stark reality. My mother and sister urged me to consult a lawyer."[4]

Virginia Chinn was determined that her daughter should extricate herself from this disastrous marital situation, as she had done from her own unfortunate union. She contacted the Wrightington Agency, a reliable real-estate firm in Newport, and through it made plans to rent a furnished house from a Mrs. Lieber at 67 Rhode Island Avenue. Mrs. Chinn advised Nina to say nothing to James and, through her contacts, engaged the eminent Newport law firm of Sheffield, Levy and Harvey to handle her daughter's petition for divorce. Nina would later recall that from the moment she entered Mr. William Sheffield's office, she was convinced that she "had put [her] problem before a man of broad outlook, sound judgment[,] and keen insight—[h]is voice, the kindly expression of his eyes[,] and direct speech gave me confidence[,] and I felt that come what may, he would give the best that was in him to my interests."[5]

On October 19, 1909, notified by Mr. Sheffield that the time was right, Nina took her children and her possessions and left Cottage #5 at the Naval Training Station. The same day, Virginia Chinn and Bertha, Nina's sister, took the train from Washington, DC up to Newport. They secured the keys to the 67 Rhode Island Avenue house and were there no more than half an hour when Nina arrived with her children and her belongings (see Chapter 1). It was a large Queen Anne–style house "with a garden enclosed by a superb English privet hedge," Nina would later remember, adding, "I have never seen its equal, except in Virginia[;] over eight feet tall and four feet thick, the sweet blossoms filled the air of fragrance."⁶ Was it simply the sweet smell of freedom she recalled?

Nina waited until after the children and baggage had been unloaded and then went to the telephone just installed in the parlor. She called James to confirm that she had left him and gave him twenty-four hours to come and talk over their difficulties.⁷ Even at that point, Nina hoped that they could resolve their marital problems. She assumed that James had already been served with her divorce petition earlier in the afternoon. Unfortunately, she was mistaken. The papers were not delivered to him until the following day, so his first inkling about the impending divorce was when he arrived home to a nearly empty cottage. He was still sitting in shocked disbelief when the telephone's ring broke his contemplation. Nina did not understand why her husband was surprised that she was asking for a separation from him and custody of their children. "My husband was incapable of differentiating between cause and effect, [and] he had driven me to a step I believe far beyond his expectations," she would later write. "What outcome of his conduct he may have anticipated remains a secret with him."⁸

James had been sitting in silence until Nina's call and resumed doing so after she delivered her terse message. He could not sleep that night, and in the morning he called his mother to report the news that Nina had left him and had taken the children and the family silver. Mrs. Rebecca Walker had suspected that something of this nature might come to pass and wasted no time in martialing her forces. She called Richard Y. FitzGerald, her daughter Susan's husband, for legal advice.

Richard FitzGerald had married Susan Walker on August 3, 1901. He was the son of a Nevada Supreme Court justice and practiced law in Boston. His family owned silver mines in Nevada and a large ranch in California. After graduating from the University of California in 1895, he had received his law degree from Harvard in 1898. Richard, Susan, and their three daughters first lived in New York City and then on the Clear Creek Ranch in Redding, California, from 1904 to 1906. When Richard developed a serious case of typhoid fever in 1906, the family moved back to the East Coast to live with the admiral and Mrs. Walker at their home in Washington, DC. Richard became a close adviser to Rebecca Walker about trust matters connected with the admiral's estate.⁹ Once he had recovered from his illness, Richard set up a law practice in Boston. When his mother-in-law called to tell him about James's troubles, he probably offered to speak with his contacts to locate a legal team in Rhode Island. The attorneys on both sides of the case would become key figures in the divorce disputes.

Nina's attorneys, Sheffield, Levy, and Harvey, were intimidating opponents. William Paine Sheffield Jr., who filed Nina's divorce petition, had an outstanding family background, education, and reputation. He was the son of a U.S. representative from Rhode Island, had graduated from Brown University, and had studied law at the University of Paris and at Harvard before practicing law in Newport, Rhode Island. Between 1885 and 1901, he served several terms as a member of the Rhode Island House of Representatives and during that time was a member of the commission to revise the state constitution. Like his father, William Sheffield was elected to the U.S. Congress as a Republican, and he served in that office from March 1909 until March 3, 1911. His congressional term coincided with the initial hearings in the Walker divorce case, and he traveled back and forth from Washington to Newport.[10] William Sheffield's law partner, William R. Harvey, was also active in the Walker case. Harvey was an older man who also had considerable political influence, having served as a Newport city official, a director of the Rhode Island Hospital Trust, and the president of the Newport Bar Association.[11] Max Levy, the firm's third partner, did not play an active role in the Walker case and left the firm in 1913, but he also had political connections.[12]

Prior to divorce reform in the late twentieth century, divorce hearings were conducted similar to criminal trials. To break a marriage contract, one spouse had to charge the other spouse with a legal violation of that contract. Article IV, Section 1 of the U.S. Constitution requires that each state recognize the laws, records, and court rulings of the other states. However, although this "full faith and credit" provision requires states to accept marriages and divorces legalized in other states, each state retains the right to regulate the marriages and divorces of its own citizens. In 1909, acceptable justifications for divorce varied widely between the states, as did residency requirements.

Nina and James had lived in South Carolina for several years, and the alleged infidelity with Mabel Cochrane had occurred there. Unfortunately for Nina, divorce had never been legal in that state, except for a brief period during Reconstruction. Since 1895, the South Carolina constitution had specifically banned divorce.[13] Nina and James had also resided in Massachusetts for several years, but not since 1902, and Massachusetts required a five-year residency just prior to filing for divorce.[14] Washington, DC was where the couple had lived when first married and to where they returned frequently. Until recently, that might have been a good location for Nina to file for divorce. However, in 1901, declaring that the national capital should set a good example, Congress had established the District of Columbia Code, which allowed divorce only on the basis of adultery.[15] Likewise, in

New York State, where the Walkers had lived at the Brooklyn Navy Yard, the only ground for divorce was adultery. Although Nina's main charge was adultery, it could be very difficult to prove in court, often requiring eye witnesses to the actual acts, so she needed to make supplementary charges.

Among all the places the Walkers had lived during their marriage, Rhode Island provided the best opportunity for Nina to obtain a divorce. In 1909, Rhode Island divorce law was considered fairly liberal. Specific grounds included impotency, willful desertion for five years, a husband's neglect or refusal to provide, as well as those grounds most likely verifiable in Nina's case, adultery and extreme cruelty. "Extreme cruelty" had begun to be interpreted by some judges to include not just physical but also emotional harm.[16] If they could not prove adultery or extreme cruelty, Nina's attorneys had an alternate strategy available, for Rhode Island was unique in allowing divorce based on another, more ambiguous ground. As far back as 1798, an omnibus clause in the state's legal code had authorized divorce based on "gross misbehavior and wickedness in either of the parties, repugnant to the marriage covenant."[17] In the early twentieth century, that legal basis for divorce was stated as "gross misbehavior and wickedness in either of the parties repugnant to and inconsistent with the marriage contract." As determined by Rhode Island case law, this was defined as follows:

> Rev. St c. 139, § 2, authorizing a divorce for "gross misbehavior and wickedness" repugnant to and inconsistent with the marriage contract, should be construed as including two distinct moral elements or qualities; that is, it must be of such a character as in the first place to amount to gross misbehavior and wickedness, and in the second place to be repugnant to and in violation of the marriage contract. There are consequently many kinds of gross misbehavior and wickedness which are not, under the clause, grounds for divorce, such as embezzlement or forgery; and so, on the other hand, there are doubtless many violations of marital duty and much conduct repugnant to and in violation of the marriage contract which are nevertheless not sufficient as grounds of divorce, for the reason that they do not take, in the statutory sense, the form of gross misbehavior and wickedness. The statute authorizes a divorce only where there is a concurrence of both elements.[18]

Despite these stipulations, the relative vagueness of the terms "gross misbehavior" and "wickedness" left room for interpretation by Rhode Island judges. Therefore, it was crucial that Nina's attorneys prove she had legitimate legal standing to file for divorce in Rhode Island. The obstacle was Rhode Island's two-year residency requirement, which they hoped to circumvent.

Mr. Sheffield presented Nina Walker's divorce petition to the Rhode Island Superior Court in Newport on October 19, the day Nina left her husband's cottage.[19] She asked the court for "divorce from bed, board, and future cohabitation with said James W. G. Walker until the parties shall be reconciled."[20] The phrase *divorce from bed, board, and future cohabitation* meant legal separation rather than absolute divorce. At the time, this approach was often preferred by wives as a more reliable way to secure financial support from their husbands rather than risking whether alimony would be awarded in a suit for absolute divorce.[21] In addition, Nina's attorneys probably hoped that by not pursuing an absolute divorce, it might be easier to overcome the jurisdictional issue. For a divorce from bed and board, a judge could use greater discretion in considering a residence shorter than the two years required for absolute divorce.

In her petition, Nina first swore that she currently resided in the county of Newport and had been a domiciled inhabitant of Rhode Island for upwards of a year and a half. She further asserted that she had upheld her part of the marriage contract and had "demeaned herself as a faithful wife and hath performed all the obligations of the marriage covenant." Conversely, she claimed, her husband, who she also stated was a resident of Newport, "hath violated the same in this: that he hath been guilty of adultery and hath been guilty of extreme cruelty to your petitioner, his said wife, and of other gross misbehavior, and wickedness in violation of his marriage covenant."[22] The petition further asked that the Walker children "now in the care and custody of your petitioner" remain in Nina's custody.[23] Finally, Nina requested that since her husband was "possessed of an ample salary and income from certain funds and has property," she "may be awarded sufficient alimony and support for herself and her said children to be paid her by said respondent, or charged on his property in such manner as the court may order."[24] The petition was signed by Nina and notarized by William Paine Sheffield on "the 16th day of October, A.D., 1909."[25]

Nina, who had initiated the divorce action, was known legally as "the petitioner." James, known legally as "the respondent," would have to answer the charges made by his wife. Through his contacts, Richard FitzGerald arranged for not one but two highly regarded Rhode Island firms to represent his brother-in-law. These were Barney and Lee, of Providence, and Burdick and Macleod, located closer to the scene on Thames Street in Newport. FitzGerald could hardly have found a more impressive legal team. Walter Hammond Barney was the senior partner in the firm of Barney and Lee. A descendant of eminent pre-Revolutionary families, Walter Barney had achieved Phi Beta Kappa at Brown University, graduated as valedictorian in 1876, and gone on to earn a law degree. After his admission to the Rhode Island bar in 1879, Barney had first practiced law alone and then from 1882 to 1892 was in partnership with Francis Colwell, his mentor and a city solicitor. He had eventually become the senior partner of Barney and Lee, the firm he had established with Judge Thomas Z. Lee in 1900 and to which they had added Francis I. McCann as a partner in 1903.

In common with Nina's legal team, Walter Barney was very active in Republican politics. He had represented Providence in the Rhode Island House of Representatives in 1889 and 1890 and had been elected a member and then president of the Providence School Committee from 1889 to 1904. Barney also had been a member of the Providence Common Council and the chairman of several special committees. He was married to Sarah Lydia Walker (no known relation to James),[26] and both were organizers of the American Whist League and the Women's Whist League.[27] Of note, Mrs. Barney had declared publicly that she was opposed to women's suffrage.[28] The Barneys' only child was Walter Howard Barney, born in 1883. At the time that Nina Walker filed her divorce petition, Walter Hammond Barney was fifty-four and balding, sporting a mustache, full beard, and wire-rim spectacles.[29]

The co-counsel for James Walker was Clark Burdick, of the Newport firm Burdick and Macleod, and his legal and political pedigree was almost as strong as Mr. Barney's. Burdick was somewhat younger, born in January 1868, was a native of Newport, and had attended public schools in that city prior to attending Harvard Law School. He also had a naval history, having served in the Rhode Island Naval Militia in 1896 and 1897. Along with Mr. Barney, Mr. Burdick had been a member of the Newport school board from 1899 to 1901, and from there he went on to hold higher political office. He had been the city solicitor of Newport in 1901, 1902, and again in 1907 and 1908, and had served as a member of the Rhode Island House of Representatives from 1906 to 1908.[30] Clark Burdick was forty-one at the time of the first Walker trial, his hair was beginning to turn gray, and his most notable feature was his large piercing eyes.[31]

In response to Nina Walker's divorce petition, James Walker's attorneys first sought to recover custody of the children. On November 5, they brought a habeas corpus proceeding, and several witnesses, including family members, appeared before the court to support either James or his wife. Nina charged that James had been cruel and abusive to the children. At the end of the hearing, Judge Charles Falconer Stearns concluded, "The children would be perfectly safe in the care of the mother until the main issue is tried later." This ruling did not imply that James would not be a good guardian for the children—only that there was no reason to take them away from Nina for the time being. The court ordered attorneys for both sides to draw up an agreement that would allow James ample opportunity to see his children, pending the divorce hearing.[32]

Although he was not a member of the Rhode Island bar, Richard FitzGerald had undoubtedly assured his mother-in-law and his wife that he would consult with Walter Barney and Clark Burdick to ensure that James would have the best legal defense possible. He took an active interest in James's case and included his name on many court documents. On December 6, 1909, he sent a letter to his wife, James's sister Susan, who was staying with her brother at the Newport Naval Training Station. Susan and Richard teasingly referred to each other as "Old Lady" and "Old Man" in their correspondence, and Richard wrote, "Dear Old Lady, I enclose a letter to you from me, with a more formal address and ending as you may want to show it to J. [James] and Burdick."[33] Richard said that he was enclosing a letter sent previously from Nina and told his wife to "be sure to preserve the envelope in which Nina's letter came."[34] This comment may have referred to the letter written to Susan the previous May in which she had thanked her sister-in-law and praised her husband, as it would later be used as evidence for the defense.

In his letter, Richard advised his wife that "Uncle Harry" (Henry Pickering, the prominent Boston attorney) was of the opinion that "the case on the other side is apt to crumble away at any time now, that their counsel are apt to feel that they have nothing to go on and give up the case. "In that event," he instructed, "Uncle Harry thinks it likely the Chinns would disregard the court order and skip with the children and that it might be difficult to trace them. This strikes me as probable and if an eye can be kept on them it should be done." Richard wrote that he believed "Mrs. Chinn is on her way to Washington to open up the house there and have them all go right down." Admitting that this belief was "a guess," he suggested that the hunch could "readily be verified by telegraphing Worthington to ascertain whether she is there and whether she is opening the house." If he was correct, Richard surmised, Mrs. Chinn would probably take the federal express train that very night and reach Washington by 10:00 A.M. the next day. He suggested that "J" give this information to his attorney, Mr. Burdick, and that "some watch be kept on the Newport house to see if they are planning to leave." Richard thought it might be possible that Bertha had already left with the children "to anticipate any adverse decision." Although he admitted "that seems almost too unlikely to speculate on," he also thought it was "not impossible."[35]

Richard was concerned with the question of jurisdiction and that the issue was raised only to determine whether Nina and James had lived long enough in Rhode Island to try the case there. If that were so, he explained, Nina's attorneys could state that the Walkers had residence there for eighteen months, just short of the two-year requirement, and therefore "the question of jurisdiction would not be an absolute one but merely a question of the court's discretion." "Our strong point on jurisdiction," Richard claimed, "is that J., and therefore Nina, up to the time she left him was not a resident of Rhode Island, neither of them had ever been for one single minute up to the time petition was filed. Therefore, the question of jurisdiction is not one of discretion but [that] there is no jurisdiction." He asked Susan to see or telephone Mr. Burdick to talk with him about this opinion. "It seems to me," Richard wrote, "very important that the question of jurisdiction be put to the court in such fashion that it will not be a question of discretion but of an absolute lack of jurisdiction." If James's attorneys did not agree with that perspective, Richard wanted to discuss it with them further.[36]

This letter from Richard FitzGerald to his wife made it clear that Nina's petition for divorce signified more than just a fight between husband and wife. The extended Walker family, including James's sister, his brother-in-law, and even Uncle Harry (Henry) Pickering, interpreted it as a declaration of war. The battle plan required an organized strategy, including the deployment of a "spy" network to combat possible subterfuge by the Chinn family. Richard seemed excited by the opportunity to contribute to the intrigue. His preferred approach to the jurisdictional question—claiming that James had not ever had legal residence in Rhode Island, since he had lived on a government facility—was the tactic that James's defense attorneys did decide to adopt. If they could prove that James had at no time been a legal resident of Rhode Island, it would mean that Nina had never been one either, since, officially, a wife's residence was with her husband. Therefore, success on both sides of the case rested on the jurisdictional issue.

In theory, Susan Grimes Walker FitzGerald might have faced a conflict in loyalties between her brother and his wife. She had helped Nina plan their wedding and had been one of her bridesmaids. Moreover, Susan was a well-known women's rights advocate and suffragist. She had served as the executive secretary of the Boston Equal Suffrage Association for Good Government in 1907, and, shortly before Nina filed her divorce petition, Susan Walker FitzGerald was a principal organizer for the 1909 women's suffrage campaign in Boston.[37] She was well regarded among other women's rights advocates and would become the executive secretary of the Massachusetts Woman Suffrage Association in 1911 and then the recording secretary for the National American Woman Suffrage Association from 1911 to 1915. Susan wrote several pamphlets promoting women's rights, including, "Women in the Home" in 1908, "What is a Democracy?" in 1910, and "Have We a Democracy in 1913?"[38] In one of these, she forcefully argues the following:

> Therefore, so long as the men alone are the source of power of the government, it is not a government *of* the people, *for* the people and *by* the people. It is merely a country under class rule, the *class* being *men*, who, after all, represent but half of the population, half of those that live under the laws they make.[39]

However, despite her feminist sentiments, Susan did not connect women's general lack of political power with her sister-in-law's weak position in her own home. Although another leading suffragist, Elizabeth Cady Stanton, had advocated for divorce, asserting, "States which have liberal divorce laws are to women what Canada was to the slaves before Emancipation,"[40] not all women's rights advocates supported a woman's right to divorce her husband. In fact, the women's suffrage movement was split apart by this issue in the late nineteenth century. Susan Walker FitzGerald did not identify with Nina's situation as a purportedly wronged wife but felt a greater pull toward family. She stood steadfastly behind her older brother James. Nina's mother and sister came to Newport to support her fight against her husband; the Walkers marshalled their forces as well.

On December 15, Nina Walker's attorneys filed a bill of particulars relating to her divorce petition. This bill was a detailed, formal, written statement of the specific charges against her husband. On December 28, James Walker, as the respondent, filed a motion to dismiss her petition. In his motion, James Walker claimed that the Rhode Island Court did not have jurisdiction in the case. He stated that for several years prior to his appointment to the US Navy on July 29, 1898, he had been a "domiciled inhabitant" of the city of Washington, in the District of Columbia, and that "he had never since said appointment, changed his said domicile nor acquired any domicile other than said Washington; that his present domicile [wa]s in the city of Washington; and that he [wa]s not [then] and never ha[d] been domiciled in the State of Rhode Island."[41] Furthermore, James maintained that his wife, the petitioner in the case, had resided with him since their marriage and had never, up until the filing of the divorce petition, acquired a separate domicile. Nina Walker, he stated, had lived with him as his wife at the Naval Training Station on the day she executed and swore out the divorce petition and on the day the petition was filed in court. Therefore, neither the respondent nor the petitioner had any bona fide domicile in the state of Rhode Island; consequently, "this honorable court [wa]s without jurisdiction to proceed to pass upon the subject-matter of said petition or to grant the relief therein and thereby prayed."[42] James Walker's motion concluded, "Wherefore, this defendant respectfully moves that this honorable court dismiss said petition for want of jurisdiction."[43] A hearing on the motion to dismiss was set by the court for January 3, 1910.

Nina Walker filed her petition for divorce from bed and board only a few years after Rhode Island had introduced a new court system, developed by the recently founded Rhode Island Bar Association. In 1903, the twelfth amendment to the Rhode Island Constitution gave the state's supreme court final jurisdiction to revise decisions and determine appeals. In addition, the lengthy Court and Practice Act of 1905 created a state superior court, which now had jurisdiction over, among other types of cases, petitions for divorce, separate maintenance, alimony, and custody of children. It included a presiding justice and five associate judges designated by the general assembly in Grand Committee, and each associate justice had the authority to rule on the cases over which he presided.[44] This was the court to which Nina Walker brought the suit against her husband.

Judge Elmer J. Rathbun was the superior court associate justice assigned to preside over this first Walker divorce hearing. He was a native of Rhode Island, who graduated from Brown University and then from Boston University with an LL.B. summa cum laude. He was active in politics, had been elected to the Rhode Island General Assembly while still in law school, and had since been reelected several times. Rathbun had served as clerk and assistant justice of the Rhode Island Fourth District Court from 1900 until 1909, when he was elected justice of the Rhode Island Superior Court. Judge Rathbun's wife was Virginia S. Pollock, who was descended from a distinguished southern family, and her brother had been a U.S. senator from South Carolina.[45]

Due to the Walker family's high social profile, local papers covered the story of the upcoming Walker divorce trial, as did newspapers in Washington, DC, and even New York City.[46] The press reported that friends found the couple's disagreement unexpected. Also surprising was the story that an unknown officer had signed the pass authorizing the removal of Walker family household items from the Naval Training Station on October 19. Lieutenant James Walker, who had the authority to sign the pass, claimed that he had not done so. Newspaper accounts state that neither Lieutenant Walker nor his wife would discuss the case with the press and that efforts to reunite them had been unsuccessful. It was reported that, in her petition, Nina had made a "serious charge" in addition to extreme cruelty, although the press politely withheld that specific charge.

On the morning of Monday, January 3, 1910, Justice Elmer Rathbun officiated at the Walker divorce hearing in the Rhode Island Superior Court. This was the judge's first superior court case, and although he had been a district court judge for some time, he was undoubtedly determined to make his mark in this new position. He looked over Nina's petition, which asked for a partial divorce from bed and board. He knew the newspapers had reported the filing of this case, which promised to be contentious. As Judge Rathbun looked out at the courtroom, he could see that a large group of spectators had turned out. An elderly man, who had grabbed a second-row seat, was currently testing his large, four-barreled hearing apparatus to make certain it was working properly.

William Sheffield was in court to represent Nina Walker and asked for a full hearing on the merits of the case. Walter Barney and Clark Burdick, counsel for her husband, argued that in a public case such as this, details should not be discussed until the court first took up the question of jurisdiction. Mr. Sheffield then claimed that the city of Newport, Rhode Island, had been Nina Walker's legal residence for nearly two years. James had "cruelly kept his wife with him while he drifted about the country to various posts," Sheffield argued, and Nina was entitled to live separately from him. She had left James previously several times, he claimed, and finally had "left her husband under advice of her physician that her health was imperiled by association with him." It was within the court's discretion to consider her petition based on a Rhode Island residence of under two years, Mr. Sheffield contended, and Judge Rathbun could consider exercising this discretion only after hearing the entire case. He further argued that Rhode Island was Nina's only hope, as her case would be dismissed on technical grounds in another state.[47]

Walter Barney, representing James, argued that Nina had not acquired legal domicile in the state of Rhode Island until the day she had filed her petition, which certainly did not meet the two-year requirement by law to bring the case forward. "From the Supreme Court of the United States down," proclaimed Mr. Barney, "the courts have held that domicile is essential. The court cannot hear such charges unless it can act in the case."[48] Judge Rathbun inquired about the status of domicile on a government reservation, as Nina had lived at the Newport Naval Training Station when she signed her petition for divorce. Mr. Sheffield responded that a good many people voted from such a domicile and that Nina had previously left her husband to live in the city of Newport. "A wife has the right to a separate domicile," he maintained. Mr. Barney quickly interrupted to state that was true but that the wife could not acquire a separate domicile while living in the same house with her husband. He argued that the parties had been separated for only a few hours when the divorce petition was filed and that Nina's previous residence at the Naval Training Station did not allow the court jurisdiction in this case. Judge Rathbun seemed lost in thought. "This is a rather unusual case," he remarked aloud. "I have certainly never previously had a case like it." He then stated that he would first hear the arguments by counsel on both sides regarding jurisdiction to determine the propriety of trying the case on the merits. Sheffield filed his objection to this statement, preparing the way for a future appeal.

Lieutenant James Wilson Grimes Walker was then called to testify by Mr. Burdick. He entered the raised witness box and leaned against the rail provided for support, as was the traditional practice for court testimony. James stated for the record that he had been appointed as a civil engineer in the U.S. Navy on July 29, 1898, while he was in Nicaragua working for the canal commission, and that prior to that he had always returned to Washington, DC, as his home. He discussed his ensuing appointments to navy yards in Boston, Charleston, Brooklyn, and Portsmouth. James stated that he was appointed to the Newport Training Station in 1908 and had lived there in Cottage #5 since May 12 of that year. He testified that the only other time he had stepped foot in Rhode Island prior to then was when he was doing some special duty while stationed in Boston. He had married Nina Chinn Walker on February 24, 1897, and, except for his time in Nicaragua, she had shared a residence with him, "up to the time she ran away."[49]

Mr. Burdick asked James what time of day his wife had left their home on October 19, 1909. "She telephoned me at the office, presumably from the house, shortly before three o'clock in the afternoon, saying a man wished to see me on business, and would I be at the office," James recounted. He paused and then continued, "I said yes, I expected to be there all the afternoon and stayed there waiting the individual who never came—'til somewhere in the neighborhood of five o' clock."[50] Mr. Burdick asked who was at home when he returned to his cottage that day, and James stated, "Mrs. Walker had left, the children were gone and pretty much all their personal belongings and some of my property had gone." Mr. Burdick asked whether his wife had given him any notice that she was planning to leave. "None whatever," James answered, as he stared down at his hands.[51]

Under further questioning by his attorney, James stated that he had never taken legal residence in any of the places he had been stationed since 1898 and had never intended to do so. Washington, DC, was his current residence, he claimed, and his official address with the navy.[52] During cross-examination, Mr. Sheffield asked whether James could be more specific about when he had lived in Washington since his marriage. James replied that he had lived there for six months shortly after his marriage, staying with his mother-in-law, and had not been there for more than a few weeks at a time since then. "But naturally I have to go where I am ordered," James stated; "I have no choice in the matter."[53]

Mr. Sheffield then established that James, along with his wife and children, had lived in a house in Brookline, Massachusetts, for approximately three years. When questioned further, James admitted to paying a voluntary poll tax in Brookline but said he could not remember for which year he did so, and then he claimed that the assessors had offered to remit it, since he was not a legal resident. After running through the locations where James had been stationed, Mr. Sheffield asked whether it was a fact that he and Nina had not lived together "as man and wife" for a number of years. James inhaled and then replied, "I don't know what you mean. We have occupied the same room." "Having the ordinary relations a husband and wife have?" asked Mr. Sheffield, his voice rising slightly at the end of his question. "Not for some little time past," James answered softly. Mr. Sheffield then asked how far back that time went, and James stated that the last occasion he could fix definitely was in the autumn of 1905. Sheffield asked James to confirm that he and Nina had an understanding this circumstance was on account of his health. "It was on account of *her* health," James quickly asserted. When Mr. Sheffield asked whether he remembered his wife's consulting Dr. James Foster Scott about his condition, James claimed that to his knowledge, she had consulted with the doctor only about her own health.[54]

"Didn't you at that time make certain statements to Dr. Scott about your condition and health?" Mr. Sheffield inquired, adding, "That it was said that no wife ought to have any intercourse with you?" "No, it was not!" James protested. Mr. Sheffield asked whether he would swear to that statement, and James agreed, "Yes, I swear to that." After confirming that James also agreed that his wife had boarded in Newport for several weeks the previous summer due to her health, Mr. Sheffield asked James who had the principal care of their four children. "Well," stammered James, "Mrs. Walker—supervision." Mr. Sheffield quickly interjected, "She has been a devoted mother to those children?" "According to her ideas. She is fond of them undoubtedly," James admitted grudgingly.[55]

James's maternal uncle, Henry Goddard Pickering, a Boston lawyer for thirty-five years, was then called to the stand by Mr. Burdick. He testified that he had known James since he was a baby and that James had lived in Washington, DC, with his parents while growing up, except when he lived abroad with his parents and one winter he had stayed in Boston with the witness. On cross-examination, Mr. Sheffield asked Mr. Pickering what Admiral Walker's legal residence had been when he was appointed to the navy. Mr. Pickering thought that the admiral had been appointed from Iowa but did not know whether he had had a residence there. When asked whether the admiral had been appointed to the Isthmian Canal Commission through the personal influence of the Iowa senator William Boyd Allison, Mr. Pickering denied that was so and further stated that the admiral had lived in Washington for twenty-five or thirty years, so he would not have claimed his legal residence in Iowa.[56]

The star witnesses in this hearing were the mothers of the petitioner and the respondent. Rebecca White Pickering Walker, James's mother, took the witness stand and stated that her son's residence was Washington, DC, as was his father's. Although as a boy James was away at boarding school, Washington had been, and remained, his legal residence.[57] During cross-examination, Mr. Sheffield asked Mrs. Walker when her son had last lived in Washington. She seemed to be taken off guard and sputtered, "It is a little difficult, taken unexpectedly that way, to say the last residence was—he was—."[58] Under further questioning, she testified that before he was married, he had taught mathematics at a school for "young ladies" and had private pupils. He had lived at his father's home in Washington for a year or more and had paid part of the expenses, although she could not give the exact dates. Mrs. Walker agreed that her husband's appointment to the navy was from Iowa. However, when Mr. Sheffield asked her to confirm that therefore Iowa was the admiral's legal residence, Mrs. Walker denied that her husband had ever claimed his legal residence there. "He was a native of New Hampshire," she stated. When Mr. Sheffield again tried to discuss the admiral's original naval appointment, Mrs. Walker quickly interrupted him to state emphatically, "He had nothing to do with Senator Allison; he was a nephew of [Iowa] Governor Grimes and was living with him when he was appointed!"[59] Mr. Sheffield then attempted to get Mrs. Walker to agree the admiral's subsequent naval appointments had been obtained through political influence from Iowa. Rebecca Walker glared at him and responded heatedly, "I don't remember anything of the kind! I think simply by regular promotion, except at the end of the war, when he was promoted for distinguished gallantry and services!"[60] This assertion silenced Mr. Sheffield for the moment, and Mr. Burdick quickly recalled James Walker to testify that his father had owned a house in Washington, DC, and that his will was probated there.[61]

At that point, it was Nina Walker's turn to give evidence. As her attorney explained, she was in frail health, so she was allowed to testify sitting down. When questioned by her lawyer, Mr. Sheffield, she responded that she did not know of any Washington residence her husband had, but she understood that he had voted in Massachusetts while living there. Of course, there was no question regarding where Nina voted, since women had not yet won the right to vote. Nina testified that for several years, her husband and she had not lived together "as man and wife" and that she had left him every summer to protect her children and herself from the heat. Sheffield asked whether she intended to live in Newport, and she replied that she did. Under further questioning, Nina stated that she had been advised that she had good grounds to live separately from her husband and that this court should hear her request to do so. When asked whether she had a residence other than Rhode Island, she replied plainly, "None that I know of."[62]

Mr. Burdick cross-examined Nina, and she agreed that her home was with her husband until she left him but added that she had been anticipating leaving him for eight years. When Mr. Burdick asked whether she had gone to Mrs. Batcheler's the previous summer to secure a residence in Newport, Nina replied that she had come to see what arrangements could be made. She had given her husband every reason to suspect that matters were very serious, and when he came to see her in Newport, he had been very abusive to her. Nina had told him that they were not fit to bring up children the way they were living and that it would be better for them to be apart "because of the continual abuse of me and the home friction."[63] After returning to the cottage at the naval station from Newport, Nina had occupied a separate room for the first time. When Mr. Burdick asked whether she had done this with her husband's consent, Nina stated, with a steady voice, "I never asked him, or he me, never spoke of it at all." She admitted that she had not told her husband she was leaving him but explained that she could not have gotten away had she done so. She had expected he would be served with the divorce papers on the afternoon she had left.[64]

Nina testified that she had departed her husband's home at about 2:00 P.M. on October 19, had come to Newport, had telephoned her husband, had given him her address, and had told him that he could come to see her and the children. Regarding the mystery as to who had signed the pass to leave the base, she admitted that she had signed his name, explaining that wives often did so and that her husband knew that she had signed his name previously. When Mr. Burdick asked Nina whether she had given James any indication at luncheon that she was leaving that day, she replied that she had not but added, "I must admit that if he had not been intensely blind he would have known; a woman's actions generally speak louder than words."[65] After a moment of silence, Mr. Burdick asked Nina where she had gone when she left her husband. She testified about the furnished house at 67 Rhode Island Avenue, stating that it had been rented under her mother's name but partially belonged to her. When asked whether her mother had rented the house so that Nina could divorce her husband, Nina replied, "Certainly."⁶⁶

Mr. Sheffield rose for a redirect examination of the petitioner. He again established that she had gone to Mrs. Batcheler's on the advice of her physician, because her husband's condition was negatively affecting her health. Sheffield then asked whether she had finally left her husband on October 19 for the protection of her health, to which Nina replied, "Yes, to enable me to live and bring up my children."⁶⁷ When asked whether she was fond of her children, she replied without hesitation, "Devoted to them, give my life for them."⁶⁸ Nina further testified that she had always cared for her children and that they had been very frail and nervous. "Was that the reason you have lived with Mr. Walker all these years, not as man and wife, in the same house, because of the children?" asked her attorney. "It was indeed," she replied softly. Mr. Burdick then approached Nina for a re-cross-examination. "Why, at this time have you made a change?" he inquired. Nina let out a great sigh, stared unwaveringly at her husband's attorney, and responded, "Because of my doctor's, lawyer's[,] and clergyman's advice that I should keep my health and live to bring up my children."⁶⁹

Nina's mother, Mrs. Virginia Chinn, was then called to the stand by Mr. Sheffield. When he asked why it had been necessary for her daughter to come to live with her in Newport, the older woman stated sorrowfully, "So much unhappiness and friction that I was not willing that she should continue that life."⁷⁰ Mrs. Chinn also stated that she certainly could not tell whether her daughter and husband had actually "lived together as man and wife" for the past few years, but it was necessary that a change be made to save her daughter's life. When questioned about what she had observed regarding Nina's care of the children, Mrs. Chinn readjusted her posture and replied, "She has been too faithful. She has sacrificed her own life to them."⁷¹

During cross-examination, Mrs. Chinn stated that she had two residences—one in Washington, DC, and one in Newport. She agreed that she owned the house at 1145 Connecticut Avenue in Washington and paid property tax to the district. Mr. Burdick asked for what period of time Mrs. Chinn had taken the house in Newport. "Oh, just as long as I choose to keep it," was her reply. Mr. Burdick then got Mrs. Chinn to confirm that she had rented the house for a year. He stepped closer to Mrs. Chinn, looked directly into her eyes, and gently inquired, "Are you going to live here right along?" The elderly woman glared back at him and stated curtly,

"If I feel like it." "Well, you haven't given up your residence in Washington?" Mr. Burdick asked, and Mrs. Chinn replied that she had not. "Aren't you intending to leave for Washington with the family when this is over?" the attorney probed. "I couldn't tell," Mrs. Chinn retorted. "It depends on what we all consider best for the family."[72] The following heated exchange then ensued between Mr. Burdick and Mrs. Chinn:

> Mr. Burdick: You and Mrs. Walker hadn't made up your mind to stay here, had you?
> Mrs. Chinn: If we want to.
> Mr. Burdick: Well, you haven't decided to give up your residence in Washington and make this your home?
> Mrs. Chinn: I am not going to answer that—[d]epends on circumstance.
> Mr. Burdick: But you haven't already decided that you will make use of your home?
> Mrs. Chinn: Haven't decided anything.
> Mr. Burdick: Haven't you planned to take the children away from Newport to Washington?
> Mrs. Chinn: Why should we?
> Mr. Burdick: I ask you if you hadn't.
> Mrs. Chinn: No.
> Mr. Burdick: Haven't you had that in mind?
> Mrs. Chinn: No.
> Mr. Burdick: Never? Haven't talked it over amongst yourselves?
> Mrs. Chinn: Oh, well, it wouldn't do for me to say what we talked over, it wouldn't do.
> Mr. Burdick: I understand you and Mrs. Walker haven't yet decided you will stay here in Rhode Island or what you will do?[73]

This was obviously a cat-and-mouse game. James Walker's attorney was attempting to force Mrs. Chinn to admit that Newport was not really a permanent residence for Nina and the children, whereas Mrs. Chinn was struggling to keep the impression that it might be. At this point, Mr. Sheffield interrupted by stating, "What this lady has decided is immaterial. Mrs. Nina Walker has stated her intentions."[74] Undeterred, Mr. Burdick continued to question Nina's mother about whether she and her daughter had discussed the matter of living in Newport or Washington. It was clear that Mrs. Chinn had had enough of this inquisition, and she responded, "I don't choose to answer such a vague question. You would suppose mother and daughter talked over things generally." When pushed further as to whether Newport would be a permanent residence, Mrs. Chinn glared at her son-in-law's attorney and replied, "I couldn't tell you."[75] Mr. Sheffield again objected to this line of questioning and protested that what Mrs. Chinn thought made no difference. Judge Rathbun agreed, stating that he did not suppose it was strictly material to the case. Mr. Burdick continued, ready to pounce, as he attempted to force Mrs. Chinn to agree that she had discussed the matter of residence with her daughter in front of the children, meaning that there would be witnesses to their conversation. Virginia Serrellina Chinn was tougher than she looked and with her silence refused to capitulate. Mr. Burdick had nowhere to go with his questions after that last effort and stepped aside.[76]

Mr. Sheffield offered a deposition from Dr. Scott, to which Mr. Burdick objected, stating that it did not bear on the question of jurisdiction. Mr. Sheffield stated that the deposition was to contradict James's statement that Nina had left on account of her own health rather than her husband's health. The attorneys argued back and forth, with Mr. Burdick contending that Mr. Walker had said no such thing and Mr. Sheffield retorting that he had indeed. Judge Rathbun read the deposition silently and then directed the attorneys to continue arguing the case solely on the basis of jurisdiction.[77]

Although he admitted that Nina's residence in the state of Rhode Island was shorter than the two-year requirement, Mr. Sheffield asked Judge Rathbun to admit the case as an act of justice in a meritorious cause. "There is a residence here," Mr. Sheffield pleaded, "and none elsewhere."[78] Mr. Barney again contended that legal domicile of two years was required by Rhode Island statute. "The necessary travel of a naval officer," he stated, "should not deprive him of the right of a home in Washington. He has none in Rhode Island and his wife's home was his while she was in the same house with him."[79] Judge Rathbun then terminated arguments in the case and announced that a decision would be forthcoming. The courtroom emptied of the attorneys, the petitioner, the respondent, the relatives, and most of the spectators. The judge turned his attention to a brief hearing on another legal matter but found it difficult to concentrate, as the various jurisdictional arguments in the Walker case circled his brain.

On January 9, 1910, the Department of the Navy in Washington, DC, announced what was described as "the biggest shake-up in the civil engineer corps in the Navy." A number of officers were ordered to report to new locations, including Lieutenant James W. G. Walker, who was to go from the Newport Training Station to the Pensacola Naval Station in Florida. Transfers were ordered particularly for those men who had been at their current stations for more than the usual navy limit of three years. Although the time limit did not apply to Lieutenant Walker's situation, he was still ordered to move.[80] Both sides were aware that a change in location might affect the jurisdictional issue in the Walker divorce case.

February 7, 1910, was motion day in the Rhode Island Superior Court in Newport, with Judge Rathbun presiding. As was customary, Judge James G. Topham, the veteran crier, was due to announce the orders of the court. He arrived at the courthouse early, hoping to take a long walk "up on the Point," but, due to the wind and cold, he determined that doing so would not be a good idea, and he occupied himself by reviewing the court calendar while waiting for court to open. Although he had performed his role for many years, Topham still took great pleasure in it, believing that he was doing his part to preserve the dignity of the legal system. He noted that many members of the local bar were attending court that day, and several bar members from Providence were present as well.[81]

William Harvey, Walter Barney, and Clark Burdick were in court, as expected, to hear Judge Rathbun's ruling regarding whether the court had jurisdiction in the Walker divorce case. Judge Rathbun entered the courtroom, all present rose, and he curtly announced his decision: "Mrs. Walker's residence in the State of Rhode Island is not sufficient and therefore the Rhode Island Superior Court will not hear her divorce case." Rathbun had chosen not to use his jurisdictional discretion on this, his first superior court case. In addition, the judge refused to grant Nina's request for an allowance of $300 and fees for legal counsel. James's attorneys entered a decree to dismiss the case, but Mr. Harvey filed an exception to Judge Rathbun's decision, leaving open the possibility that the jurisdictional matter could be appealed to the Rhode Island Supreme Court. He undoubtedly knew that the higher court was currently reviewing whether it should allow appeals in divorce cases and hoped that the matter would be settled in time to affect Nina's case.[82]

Judge Rathbun quickly turned his attention from the Walkers' troubles to the next item on the docket, *Newport Water Works v. William N. McVicker*.[83] James W. G. Walker was free to return to navy business, "staking off ground at the naval coaling station for the erection of fifteen immense storage tanks for oil fuel to be used for torpedo boat destroyers and submarines."[84] Gossip about the Walkers' private life subsided for the moment.

Then, on February 22, the Walker case took a most unusual turn when Lieutenant James Walker filed two lawsuits for "alienation of affection" in Newport Superior Court. The first suit named Mrs. Virginia Serrellina Chinn, his mother-in-law; the second named Miss Elizabeth Bertha Chinn, his sister-in-law. In each case, James asked for $25,000 in damages.[85] A legal definition of *alienation of affection* includes "the robbing of husband or wife of the conjugal affection, society, fellowship, and comfort which inheres in the normal marriage relationship."[86] In 1910, alienation of affection was a recognized tort offense in many states, including Rhode Island.[87] Actions alleging alienation of affection could be brought by deserted spouses against outside parties who were said to interfere with the marriage relationship. Typically, this outside party was an adulterous spouse's lover, and one might wonder why Nina Walker did not accuse Mabel Cochrane of alienation of affection. To charge a spouse's relatives with alienation of affection, as James did, was very uncommon. Although there were reports that James's alienation of affection cases were scheduled for a hearing in superior court the following June, it appears that nothing further developed.[88] However, the fact that he brought suit against his wife's mother and sister indicates how acrimonious the relationship between James and the entire Chinn family had become.

James continued to live in Newport during that year. The 1910 U.S. Census reports that he was head of his household, living in Newport Ward 2, Newport, Rhode Island. He was designated as "married," but no other members of his family were listed as residing with him. Included as household members were Mary A. Mahon, Julia Oleary, both from Ireland, and Clara W. Mawin, from Michigan, all described as servants and designated as "White." Strangely, James himself was first listed in this census as "Black." Although his racial designation was later corrected to "White," the reason for the error was not recorded.[89]

James persuaded naval officials to revoke his orders to go to Pensacola, pending the divorce proceedings, and he continued to fulfill his naval duties in Newport. A conference at the Naval War College in that city was convened from June through October, and naval officers, marine corps officers, and army officers attended. James was one of the few officers selected to deliver lectures to this group.[90] On June 11, Susan Walker FitzGerald came down to Newport with her three daughters and her nanny to help care for the Walker children, who were visiting at the training station. She wrote a letter to her husband, Richard, on James's official stationery, telling him that they had arrived safely and that her brother had "gone off for the night[,] which will be good for him, but will be back tomorrow noon." The cousins apparently enjoyed each other's company, had already been all over the house, including the cellar, and were happily playing with a cat while Susan was writing.[91] She wrote to Richard that James had taken her to the "moving picture show."[92] Susan and her children again stayed at her brother's cottage in late August, both to help and to keep him company. The plan was for James's older sister, Fanny, and her husband, John, to relieve Susan and stay in Newport over Labor Day weekend.[93] The Walker troops were continuing to rally around James.

It took many months for the Rhode Island Supreme Court to hear Nina's appeal. On Wednesday, November 9, 1910, the case was finally tried in Providence. Mr. Sheffield and Mr. Harvey argued that the superior court had erred in hearing the motion to dismiss the case on jurisdictional grounds before hearing the petition on its merits.[94] Then, on December 30, the state supreme court sustained Judge Rathbun's decision to dismiss the case. Chief Justice Edward C. Dubois explained, "The only question involved was that of jurisdiction," and therefore, the superior court "did not err in entertaining the motion to dismiss the petition for want of jurisdiction."[95]

Nina Walker had signed her divorce petition on October 16, 1909, while she was still living with her husband; she did not leave him until October 19, 1909, and "did not attempt to gain a residence separate and apart from him until that day." From the date of their marriage up to October 19, 1909, Nina's "residence and domicile was merged in that of her husband." Therefore, the Rhode Island Superior Court "had no alternative other than to grant the motion to dismiss the petition." The ruling made it known that in the case of "urgent necessity," a wife could become a domiciled inhabitant of the Rhode Island by living apart from her husband for only one day or even "a fractional part thereof." However, she must acquire the separate residence prior to filing her divorce petition.[96] Whereas Nina had believed she was exercising caution by executing her petition for divorce prior to physically leaving James, by doing so she had in fact helped invalidate it.

Nina and her attorneys were not deterred; they simply waited. Nina determined to establish a residence in Rhode Island. She took part in the social life of Newport, both within the naval community and generally. Dr. Huntington, the founder and headmaster of the Cloyne House School, which Nina had fought with James about, came to see her and offered to take Grahame as a day student at "a surprisingly moderate rate." Eventually, all three sons attended the school, either as day students or as boarders. Nina believed this situation provided stability for them, and "both masters and pupils showed understanding and consideration for the sensitive feelings of my sons during the years of court proceedings."[97] In the summers, Nina took her children to Easton's beach in Newport, a public beach, where they learned to swim and play tennis.

The court had ordered that the Walker children visit their father at the training station every Sunday afternoon. Nina wrote in her unpublished autobiography that facilitating these visits was complicated. She explained, "Mrs. Walker [James's mother] left her home in Boston, accompanied by her housekeeper Miss Bangs, a maiden lady of uncertain age, to be with her son, who frequently went out of town on those days. It was Miss Bang[s]'s duty to entertain my four active children for three hours." The children had a busy Sunday, Nina said, since "Trinity Church Sunday School was at half past nine, then came our [c]hurch service, and walk home to dinner, another walk back again for the children past the church to the Government Wharf where they took a small launch to the Naval Station landing, where they climbed a steep hill to reach the house." Nina wrote that "in severe winter months, the Sunday schedule was a trial of endurance for the children, especially little Herbert, yet during one entire year they did not miss a day at Sunday school or the visit to their father."[98]

On January 12, 1911, Nina filed another petition with the Rhode Island Superior Court, again asking for a divorce from bed, board, and future cohabitation with James W. G. Walker. The grounds were adultery and cruelty on James's part. In addition, Nina asked for custody of the four Walker children and sufficient alimony to support her and them. Her new divorce petition included her claim that she had resided in the state of Rhode Island since May 16, 1908, first at the Naval Training Station at Coasters Harbor Island and, since October 19, 1909, at 67 Rhode Island Avenue, both in the city of Newport. She claimed that she had therefore been a legally domiciled inhabitant of the state for more than two years prior to the filing of this new petition.[99] Concurrently, her attorneys filed an additional petition stating that Nina was "a proper and suitable person to have the care and custody" of her minor children, that James was "an unfit and improper person to have custody," and that for the "best interests and welfare of the children[,] they should remain in the care and custody of [their mother]."[100] A hearing on February 6 established that the four Walker children would remain in their mother's custody, pending the divorce trial.[101]

In a bill of particulars filed on February 18, Nina Walker specified her charges of adultery and cruelty. She claimed that her husband had suffered from a venereal disease from November 1901 to December 1905, or for some part of that time. James had committed adultery, she charged, with one Mabel Cochrane in Boston in the fall of 1901; at James's home in Charleston between July 1 and September 30, 1902, and in the summer of 1903; and in Boston during the winter of 1905–1906. Details included for the charge of cruelty were that James had a venereal disease and "kept constant companionship with lewd persons, as well as making constant conversation and expression of preference for lewd and loose females." In addition, Nina accused her husband of "constant neglect, a violent temper, the use of abusive language[,] and threats so as to endanger her health." Finally, she alleged that James had endangered his wife's health from the effects of his venereal disease, dating back to November 1901.[102]

Nina Walker's attorneys amended the original petition they had filed in January. In addition to the charges that James was guilty of adultery and extreme cruelty, they again added the unique Rhode Island ground of "other gross misbehavior and wickedness, repugnant to and in violation of the marriage covenant."[103] As a hedge against possible failure to prove adultery, the particulars for this charge were "that for a period of time from 1901 and continuing thereafter he [had] kept up and continued an undue, improper, indecorous and licentious association and intimacy with a woman, named Mabel Cochrane, many years his junior, and of questionable character and immoral habits."[104] Furthermore, Nina's attorneys accused James of "bestowing upon and receiving marked and improper attention beginning in the fall of 1901[;] indulging in undue and improper familiarity and intimacy" with Mabel Cochrane; and "in the absence of his wife, and without her knowledge (and all of the time without her knowing who Mabel Cochrane was), ha[ving] Mabel Cochrane stay in his home for long periods of time and ha[ving] her occupy a room or rooms adjoining or connecting with his so that they were constantly in each other's company, and improperly familiar and unduly intimate."

Nina's amended petition further supported the charge of gross misbehavior and wickedness by stating that "at other times while respondent was in the city of Charleston, South Carolina, he has boarded the said Mabel Cochrane in a hotel in said city" and that "during said period from 1901 the respondent has carried on a correspondence with said Mabel Cochrane, has received from her a letter or letters reflecting upon your petitioner, as well as letters of an improper and lascivious nature, and which show improper and lascivious relations between the said respondent and said Mabel Cochrane." The petition stated that James "ha[d] from time to time visited her [Mabel Cochrane] clandestinely in her apartments in Boston and elsewhere, and ha[d] been received by her alone, and with locked doors, when she was immodestly and improperly clad." In conclusion, Nina's amended petition charged that her husband was guilty of "licentious and lascivious conduct with one Mabel Cochrane."[105]

Both sides prepared for *Walker v. Walker*, to be heard in full before the Rhode Island Superior Court in March 1911. Attorneys Burdick and Barney spent several weeks at the end of February deposing witnesses who could not appear in person on behalf of the respondent. Testimony was taken in a variety of locations, including Macon, Georgia; Boston, Massachusetts; New York City; Schenectady, New York; and Washington, DC.[106] Judge Darius Baker was the associate justice of the Rhode Island Superior Court now charged with hearing the case. Born in Yarmouth, Massachusetts, in 1845, as a young man he had served in the Civil War with the Fifth Regiment, Massachusetts Volunteer Militia. Baker had graduated from Wesleyan University in 1870 as the salutatorian of his class and had spent two years teaching while studying law. He began practicing law in Newport in 1876 and became a prominent attorney there. Baker had already had a long and distinguished career as a judge at the time of the Walker trial. He had served as a judge of probate from 1877 to 1898 and as a justice of the First Judicial District Court of Rhode Island from 1886 until his appointment as associate justice of the superior court.[107] Among other legal decisions, Judge Darius Baker is attributed with the dubious distinction of imposing the first ever jail sentence issued for speeding in an automobile, which he carried out in Newport on August 28, 1904. The driver had been going fifteen miles per hour, probably considered an outrageous speed at the time.[108] Judge Baker obviously took the law seriously; the press and its loyal readers were poised for a very interesting trial.

6

Some Cases Are Simple; This One Is Not

March 1911

Rhode Island Superior Court Hearing, Tuesday Afternoon, March 7, 1911[1]

It was the afternoon of Tuesday, March 7, 1911. Judge Darius Baker, associate justice of the Rhode Island Superior Court, looked down at his court calendar and noted that he would have another busy session. He first heard arguments in the divorce case of *Bessie W. Manchester v. Jonathan G. Manchester*, with Judge Franklin as counsel for Mrs. Manchester, the petitioner, and William Sheffield representing Mr. Manchester, the respondent. This was a simple one—no contest—and Judge Baker ruled quickly for the petitioner on the ground of nonsupport.

The next case up was not so simple. It was a divorce action brought by Nina Chinn Walker against her husband, Lieutenant James Wilson Grimes Walker. The case had drawn plenty of popular attention the previous week, including an article in the *Washington Post* promising "testimony of a sensational nature."[2] The courtroom was filled with a large number of Walker relatives and friends, many prepared to testify for either side. The lawyers' table was also full, with William Sheffield and William Harvey present for the petitioner, Nina Walker, and Clark Burdick and Walter Barney ready to argue for the respondent, James Walker. The Walkers had previously appeared before the court on this matter; an earlier petition by Mrs. Nina Walker had been dismissed due to lack of legal residence. Judge Baker noted that legal residence might also be a problem in the case at hand and that a habeas corpus petition by Mr. James Walker to gain custody of the children had already been denied. He expected that this case would take at least three days.³

Nina Walker took the stand first and was examined and cross-examined for the entire afternoon. Nina answered a number of questions about where the Walkers had lived, and she gave a history of their changing residences. She testified that James had never had a permanent home so far as she knew and that when she left him on October 19, 1909, she had intended to make Newport her permanent home.

At this point, Nina's testimony got grittier. She claimed that James was completely uninterested in family life; he was "irascible" with her, although shy and retiring with other people. "The morning after our wedding," Nina stated, "James suggested that we take only two meals a day in order to save money." "He stayed constantly in the house," she said, "and would not go out to walk with me." After three weeks of marriage, the young couple had gone to live with Nina's mother. At one point, Nina claimed, her husband had worn a shirt for ten days straight until she put it in the wash, after which he had stayed in bed all day. James had never taken her to the theater or any other entertainment, Nina complained; "I could never please him and he was constantly irritable."

Nina described how James had sailed for Nicaragua five days after their first child was born, without first seeing her or their baby. Although she had been very anxious to hear from him, her husband had not written until five or six weeks afterward. Subsequently, when they had been reunited in Washington, James had stayed out in the evenings, leaving her alone. Nina claimed that when they had first moved to Brookline, Massachusetts, she had been 'very weak, but her husband had continued to go out alone. Although she had begged him to take walks with her, he had gone bicycling alone instead.

Nina stated that when James was first transferred to Charleston, she had not thought it would be wise to bring the children there that spring because it would be too hot. However, based on James's reassurance, she had taken the children down and found that, although there had been snow when the family left Boston, the weather in Charleston had been very hot. When Nina and the children had arrived in Charleston, "There was no room for [us] in the hotel and [we] were left in the gentlemen's smoking and waiting room for the entire day." "The babies were very sick in Charleston," she complained, "and there was no milk if you did not have your own cow." Nina explained that her mother had kindly paid expenses for the children and her to stay in the mountains that summer and that, after doing so, their health had improved. Nina and the children had lived in Washington with her mother the following year and had gone to Watch Hill, a seacoast town in Rhode Island, the next summer. "James would not take responsibility for the children and me, and seemed not to care about us," she commented.

Her attorney asked Nina about what life was like after the family had moved to the training station in Newport. Nina stated that she had been very nervous and run down, with four children to care for and an irritable husband. She claimed that James had not shown any affection for the children or for her. Nina's doctor had told her, for the sake of her health, that she should go away for three months. Although she had tried to talk to her husband about this suggestion, he would not discuss it. Nina told how, in August 1909, when her mother and sister had switched places with her, James at first had said that he thought it was a good plan, but then he had later brought her a letter in which his mother and sisters offered to take over care for the children while Nina rested. Nina had not thought the children would be happy in that situation and would not consent to it. "James then told me he would do as he pleased and if I objected, he would place me in an insane asylum," she stated. He had demanded that she return to the cottage at the training station, and she had complied because she had feared that if she did not, he would take away the children.

Nina continued her accusations from the witness stand. While stationed in Charleston, she stated, James had not gone to the mountains with her and the children but had "stayed in a furnished house with colored servants." He had told Nina about a young girl from Boston and her brother and had said that he was interested in helping the brother, who seemed very intelligent. The girl, Mabel Cochrane, had stayed at the Walker house in Charleston for the summer and part of the winter, and Nina had not met her until later. When she had returned to Charleston, Nina had been shocked to recognize Mabel Cochrane as the girl who had previously mailed a photograph to her husband. She had been further appalled when James had informed her that Miss Cochrane was to stay on as a governess for their children. When they were all in Washington, DC, James had paid Miss Cochrane a lot of attention, Nina stated angrily. He had taken her to the theater and on walks, and he had planned a day at Mount Vernon for just the two of them.

At that moment, Mr. Sheffield produced a copy of the first letter that Mabel Cochrane had sent to James Walker, in 1904. Nina stated that, when the postman had delivered this letter, she had recognized the return address on the envelope. She had thought it proper to know what Mabel was corresponding about with her husband, so she had opened it, copied it, and resealed it. When James had rushed in and demanded Miss Cochrane's letter, she had given it to him. At this point, Mr. Barney, counsel for James, objected to presentation of the letter. He stated that, according to the decision in *Razor v. Razor*, a letter from a third party was not admissible as evidence. Judge Baker considered this objection for a few minutes before admitting the copy of the letter as evidence *de bene*,[4] which meant that it was accepted provisionally, and marking it "Petitioner's Exhibit B," although he did not allow it to be read aloud. Mr. Barney and Mr. Burdick silently read the letter, with James reading it over their shoulder, his face turning an unbecoming shade of scarlet.

Mr. Sheffield continued to examine the defendant. "What did your husband tell you about some of his experiences, in Boston, with fast women?" he asked her. Mr. Burdick quickly objected but was overruled by Judge Baker. Nina explained that her husband had told her about "a flirtation" at a room at a small hotel in Boston with a waitress he had met. She also commented that, while James had been stationed in Brooklyn, the officers had parties with actresses, who he had admitted had "kissed him goodnight."

Mr. Sheffield introduced the topic of James's intimate health problem. Nina stated that her husband had undergone treatment for this problem, had expected to have surgery, and also had treated it himself. Her attorneys produced some of the letters James had written to her about this condition, and parts of the letters were read aloud to the court, no doubt causing great embarrassment to her husband. Mr. Sheffield also presented a paper that Nina stated was "a prescription" she had found in James's pocket right before she left him. The paper was accepted as evidence but not read aloud. Nina testified that she and her husband had visited Dr. James Forster Scott in Washington to discuss James's health problem.

Under further questioning, Nina explained that she had four children, from nine to fourteen years of age, and gave all of her time to them. "They are delicate children," she said, "but are doing well." Nina claimed the children had not had a day of illness since she left James. "My husband," she said, "had always wanted them to be kept away from him, and complained that they were a nuisance." According to Nina, the children were "perfect." She stated that their father had frequently thrashed them violently with a double-thonged whip and that since they had been away from their father, they had been completely happy. "I could not live without them!" Nina declared dramatically. "And I fear that they would not live if they were taken from me!"

Mr. Sheffield asked about James's financial situation. Nina stated that he had been unemployed when they had married, but he had told her that he had $10,000. At the time of the trial, he was receiving a commander's pay as well as money from his family. She did not know the exact amount of his income, because he would not tell her, but she guessed that James received about $7,000 total per year. Nina testified that James had told her previously that his mother had so much money that she was unable to spend it all; after her death, Mrs. Walker's property would be divided among her five children. Nevertheless, Nina claimed, since custody had been awarded to her, James had not supported his own children. She stated that she had a small income and that her mother was assisting her in paying the children's expenses.

When Mr. Burdick cross-examined Nina, he asked about her claim that she had resided in Newport for two years and the circumstances that had prompted her to leave her husband. She repeated her statement that the doctor at the naval training station had told her that no medicine could help her and that she must leave the home situation for at least three months. She had returned to the naval training station only because her husband had threatened to send the children away. Nina said she had made her final decision to leave her husband only a few days before departing, when she had learned that she could do so and legally keep her children.

In response to questioning, Nina testified she had left the naval station on October 19, 1909, after the children had come home from school. She believed that James should have known the situation was serious due to the actions she had already taken, including for the first time staying in a separate bedroom after returning from Mrs. Batcheler's in Newport. Nina said her husband barely spoke to her, was very cold, and was "out of temper" all the time. She admitted that she had mislead James on the day she left, but only because that was the only way she could get away: "I did sign his name to a permit, as the ladies do there, so that I could take my silver, my own personal belongings, and the children's things from the station in trunks." Nina affirmed that she planned to make Newport a permanent home for the children and her. Judge Baker interrupted Nina's testimony at 5:00 P.M. and adjourned the hearing for the day. "The reporter from the *Newport Daily News* declared her "one of the clearest witnesses ever—transparent is the word."[5]

Rhode Island Superior Court Hearing, Thursday Morning, March 9, 1911[6]

Mr. Burdick continued his cross-examination of Nina Walker by asking her questions about what she had done with the original letter sent by Mabel Cochrane to her husband. Nina responded that she had made two or three copies, the first of which was in pencil, which she produced for the court. Nina said she had shown the copy of the letter to Admiral Walker, who had then shown it to his wife. She had wanted to discuss the situation with James's father, who had insisted that his wife be included in the discussion.

In response to a question regarding whether she had objected to having more children, Nina strongly denied that she had ever done so. She then described her husband and herself as "completely separated, mentally as well in every other way," and said that she "knew very little about his life." When Mr. Burdick asked Nina a series of questions about her husband's interest in their children, she responded that James was not fond of them and had never taken care of them. Nina then charged that when their third child was an infant and under the care of an excellent nurse provided by her mother in Washington, DC, James had forcibly removed the child and brought him to Boston so that his sister Frances could care for him in her house. Nina also talked about the incident that had occurred while she was convalescing from an illness at her mother's home in Washington, DC. Her husband had been awaiting orders to another navy yard and had not provided any place for the family to stay temporarily in Brooklyn, she stated. James had come to her mother's house and demanded to take her and the four children to a boardinghouse in Brooklyn the very next morning. Nina had explained that she was not well, they did not have a nurse, and it was physically impossible for her to go to Brooklyn. James had told her that if she did not allow the children to go with him, he would instigate legal proceedings to take them from her. Nina testified that the next morning, James, escorted by Admiral Walker, had taken the children to Brooklyn. She had seen Mrs. Walker waiting for them in the carriage before they left. According to Nina, James had not objected to the children's staying with Nina's mother until his mother had opposed it. Nina explained that she had allowed James to take the children away to avoid further trouble. Mr. Burdick then asked Nina, "Did you ever attempt, by will or otherwise, to give your children to your sister?" Nina gasped and declared, "I never dreamed of doing such a thing—I will never part with them! I suppose if I die, Mr. Walker will have them—so I have tried to keep on living for their sakes!"

Mr. Sheffield then began his redirect examination by asking Nina when Mabel Cochrane had sent her photograph to James in Charleston. "It was about five weeks after I arrived," she replied, "and Mr. Walker was in Washington at the time, so I sent it on to him." Nina explained that when she went to the mountains with the children in summer of 1902, a married couple had lived as servants in the Charleston house. When she had returned home, Miss Cochrane was not there. The next summer,

James had told Nina that she should go away with the children due to the extreme heat. While she had been away, he had written that he had hired young Mr. Cochrane's sister as a housekeeper and "would not allow the children and me to return at all that year." Nina stated that when she had finally arrived back in Charleston in February 1904, "I found Miss Cochrane," she said, "young and pretty and the original of the photograph she had sent." James had made Miss Cochrane the children's governess, although Nina had not found this appointment appropriate. The girl was not very educated herself—"she only read novels," Nina said with a deprecating sigh. In the evenings, Mabel and James had played cards while Nina had gone to bed. Nina then stated that, while in Washington, Miss Cochrane had "received Mr. Walker's special attentions." During the summer of 1904, Nina and the children had gone to Watch Hill, with her mother paying the expenses. Mabel Cochrane had stayed in the Charleston house with James that summer.

Nina explained that when another letter from Miss Cochrane had arrived in January 1905, she had let James know that she had copied it and sent a copy to her cousin, the Reverend Reese Alsop, in Brooklyn. Nina produced the reply she had received from her cousin, but Mr. Burdick objected. Judge Baker considered the objection for a few minutes and then ruled out the cousin's letter as part of Nina's testimony. Mr. Sheffield offered a copy of another letter from Miss Cochrane to James, to which Mr. Barney also objected. As with the first letter from Mabel Cochrane, Judge Baker admitted this one *de bene* (with exceptions).

After this exchange, Nina breathed a sigh of relief and began to step down from the witness box, thinking her testimony was over. At once, both Mr. Barney and Mr. Burdick shouted, "A moment, please!" and Mr. Burdick approached the witness once again. In response to his questioning as to why she had finally left her husband, Nina testified that it was because she had discovered the true nature of his disease. "Even then," she stated, "I gave him twenty-four hours to come and talk it over with me, before I signed the divorce proceedings. And, I would have stopped even then, for the children's sake, if he had come." Nina was finally allowed to leave the witness box and take her seat in the gallery as murmurs of support filled the courtroom.

Mrs. Latham had worked as a nurse for the Walker children at the Newport Naval Training Station. During her testimony, it became clear that she was quite deaf, as she requested that questions be repeated several times. She told the court that, although at times Mr. Walker had treated the children very well, at other times he had not seemed to care for them at all. "Once," she testified, "Mr. Walker lashed the boy so that he carried the marks of it for a week. He did it with what looked like a policeman's billy with two lashes on it. The children were afraid of him." Mrs. Latham said the Walker children were very good and that she had never had any trouble with them. Regarding their relationship with their mother, she stated, "Oh, they were very fond of their mother—very!" Mrs. Latham maintained she had not been as severely deaf when she had worked for the Walkers. When James's lawyer cross-examined her, Mrs. Latham told him that every so often, the children had tried to climb into Mr. Walker's chair, but he had made them get off and sit elsewhere. "He would put their picture puzzles together for them, but would not allow them to touch them," the nurse stated. "He was there hardly any with the children."

It was then time for Virginia Serrellina Chinn, the mother of Nina Chinn Walker, to testify. She approached the witness stand with all the dignity and reserve required for a court appearance by a *grande dame*. Mrs. Chinn spoke clearly and directly to the court as she confirmed for the record that she intended to stay in Newport in the future. In answer to questions from Nina's lawyer, she stated that Nina and James had come to live with her in Washington, DC, for three months after their honeymoon and that she had seen them there continually. Mrs. Chinn gave her frank appraisal of her son-in-law's behavior toward her daughter: "James was the most indifferent husband I ever saw!" Mrs. Chinn declared. "He did not seem at all kind or thoughtful to her."

Nina's mother said that it had been so hot in Charleston during the Walkers' first summer that she had funded the trip to the mountains for her grandchildren and Nina, and the following summers she had paid two-thirds of the expenses for Nina and the children to get away; her son-in-law had paid only one-third. James had seldom written to Nina while she was away, Mrs. Chinn stated, and he had never come to visit. Mrs. Chinn described how Mr. Walker had removed the children from her house in Washington and forcibly taken them to Brooklyn. "Nina was totally unable to make them ready and begged and implored him to wait," she testified. "But Admiral Walker stood in the door to see it properly done."

Mrs. Chinn stated that she and her daughter Bertha had taken a trip around the world in 1909 and then visited her daughter's family at the Newport Naval Training Station. She and Bertha had stayed at the station while Nina had gone to rest at Mrs. Batcheler's. "Mr. Walker seemed to take no interest at all in his children and saw them very little," Mrs. Chinn stated. "He never took them or Nina out. He was always in a grouch—a very disagreeable temper." She testified that previously she had had friendly relations with her son-in-law and admitted that she had never really heard him use profanities in the presence of the children. "Their mother idolizes the children, [but] they don't care a cent for their father," she concluded.

When cross-examined by Mr. Walker's attorneys, Mrs. Chinn testified that she did own a house in Washington on which she paid taxes and that she had not yet been taxed in Newport. She emphatically declared that she had not encouraged Nina to leave her husband. "I intended to take a house in Newport that winter—had decided it while at Mrs. Batcheler's," she explained. "Nina never voluntarily told me of her troubles—I am a close observer and learned more from Mr. Walker's lips than from Mrs. Walker's!" she declared. Her daughter had properly kept matters to herself. "I was spared the knowledge of Nina's troubles, except as I observed them for myself," Mrs. Chinn stated. She reiterated that even right after their honeymoon, Nina and James had not lived together pleasantly, but she had never known what the trouble was. "Mr. Walker was impolite and paid Nina no attention. He neglected her by word and deed," Mrs. Chinn claimed, although she could not provide a specific example of this behavior. She had noticed similar bad behavior from James while she was visiting the naval training station in 1909. "There are certain rules and gentlemanly instincts in the presence of ladies," Mrs. Chinn remarked plainly, "Mr. Walker did not observe them."

Under further questioning, Mrs. Chinn stated, "James and I were always very good friends[;] he was perfectly polite to me and to others; it was only to his wife that he was not polite." She also said, "He was absolutely indifferent to the children—no affection. They had none for him." When questioned once more regarding her permanent residence, Mrs. Chinn claimed that her house in Washington, DC, had been shut up and placed for sale with five or six agents. She again maintained that her permanent residence was on Rhode Island Avenue in Newport.

James's attorney again asked Mrs. Chinn about the letter from Miss Cochrane that her daughter had allegedly found in her husband's wastebasket and whether she had made suggestions to Nina based on seeing that letter. "My daughter was quite competent to attend to her own affairs," she replied haughtily. Upon further questioning, Nina's mother gave more details regarding Nina and James's relationship: "If Nina had an opinion, Mr. Walker always had an opposite one. There was always discord. There was but one opinion to be followed—that was Mr. Walker's. Mr. Walker never yielded; it was his wife, Mrs. Walker, who had to yield." This statement caused several older spectators to ponder for a few minutes. Not so long ago, it would have been considered completely appropriate for a husband to demand that his wife comply with her husband's preferences over her own. However, in the current social climate, Mrs. Chinn felt secure in implying that a wife had a right to her own opinion. Talk in the papers, on the streets, and even in some of the best homes suggested that women might even get the right to vote.

Despite this change in social attitude, Mr. Barney continued to ask Mrs. Chinn whether Nina had disobeyed James's instructions that she and the children could go to the North Carolina mountains only if they were not in contact with the Chinns. Mrs. Chinn hotly refuted this claim, saying, "I paid expenses to send my other daughter to help Nina with the children." She admitted that she had never seen James strike his wife or punish the children. Although her testimony was not expected to be impartial, a host of approving courtroom whispers agreed that Nina's mother had done an excellent job of making her daughter's case.

Mr. Sheffield read the deposition of W. D. Grove, a surgeon in the U.S. Navy who had formerly served at the Newport Naval Training Station. Dr. Grove stated that he had treated Nina Walker in September 1909 and had advised her to leave the station. She had spoken of her troubles and had been in a generally nervous, debilitated condition. He testified that he had seen Mrs. Walker only two or three times and thought that he might have prescribed a tonic for her—probably cod-liver oil. He had recommended that she go somewhere away from her family and take a complete rest. "The idea was for her to go for a short time, understanding that she had been going away [during the] summers. I had no idea there was any disagreement between Mr. and Mrs. Walker," he concluded. Nina was recalled to testify about what she had told Dr. Grove. "I told him I had been on the anxious bench for years, worried by Mr. Walker, and never knowing what was coming," she said in a timorous voice. "Dr. Grove said to me, 'Mrs. Walker, whatever is troubling you, you will never get well until you have a change.'"

Elizabeth Bertha Chinn, Nina's sister, next took the stand. Although a couple of years older than Nina, she seemed several years younger than her sibling, free of the careworn look that Nina conveyed. Bertha stated that she had visited her sister and her sister's husband and that Mr. Walker had always seemed pleased to see her. While the Walkers had lived in Brookline, Bertha and her mother had taken a house there during the summers to be close by. Mr. Walker had asked her to visit in Charleston and take one of the children. Bertha had also visited with the family while they were in Portsmouth, New Hampshire; and while living in Newport for the summer of 1909, she had seen them frequently. She confirmed her mother's assertion that James had not written to Nina often while he had been in Nicaragua, stating, "Others there sent letters oftener."

Rhode Island Superior Court Hearing, Thursday Afternoon, March 9, 1911[7]

Bertha stated that she first noticed that Mr. Walker's conduct was not proper toward his wife in 1899. He had either objected to what she did or was indifferent to her. He had not returned for dinner at a regular hour but had insisted that it be ready whenever he came home. "He arrived looking as if he felt he was going to an unpleasant place[;] he was always upset, very unhappy," stated Bertha. When Nina had told James that she was embarrassed to charge their new furniture to Mr. Pickering, "he snapped at her that it was false delicacy."

Bertha recalled that after one of the children was born, James had at first refused to go see his wife. "She was weeping and I begged him to go to her room," Bertha stated, "[and] he finally consented to go in. He did not care for the baby and we tried to induce him to notice it. The baby was so small [that] it was not expected to live." While James had been away in Washington, Bertha had noticed that other officers' wives in Charleston had received letters from their husbands, but her sister had not. James had treated his wife with what Bertha would classify as "scorn."

When questioned regarding the incident when James took the children away to Brooklyn, Bertha responded, "He came in a very angry way, with Admiral Walker and his wife, and demanded the children. Nina was in a wretched state of health. The children were very miserable at leaving her, but they would go to Hell if their mother told them to—and they went!" Whether Bertha meant to equate living in Brooklyn with the Walkers with living in Hell was not clear, but she certainly made her point.

Bertha further testified that while she had been at the Newport Naval Training Station, the children would run to see their father only because he would give them a few peanuts if they did so. "Mr. Walker talked very little to Mrs. Walker," she said. "She gave him no cause for complaint and was devoted to him. The most thoughtful and delicate attentions from her were received by him merely as her duty. He seemed to regard the children as an insult." Bertha described how she had suggested that her brother-in-law take his little daughter for a walk, but he had refused to "take the responsibility" unless Bertha went with them. She stated that James had used a "broncho whip" on the oldest boy—which had "a handle 18 inches long and two thongs each two feet long."

When asked about Nina's relationship with her children, Bertha replied, "My sister is devoted to the children. She influences them by her slightest thought[,] puts the most beautiful ideas in their minds. They are so happy now, and perfectly well, with their mother." Regarding her sister's attitude toward her husband, Bertha stated, "Nina was very sad over the inattention of Mr. Walker. She constantly tried to please him. The monotony wore on her."

During cross-examination by Mr. Burdick, Bertha testified, "Nina did not confide any of her troubles to me. I did see the torn-up letter from Miss Cochrane and helped her put it back together. But my sister never asked my opinion or complained of the family troubles." Mr. Burdick pursued a line of questioning relevant to James's relationship with the children. "I never saw any evidence of affection from Mr. Walker for his children—absolutely none. I tried to teach them to run to their father—to make them overcome their fear," Bertha stated. She continued, "We [tried] to teach the children not to hate James's mother," she explained, "because that is wicked." Bertha maintained that she knew nothing about any document in which her sister had made plans to dispose of her children, including through her will or any other means.

According to Bertha, James had always acted agreeably toward her. It seemed to her that he had liked having her visit, because Nina had been happier when her sister was with her. She recalled a very pleasant outing with Mr. Walker when had she mentioned that it was too bad that Nina could not have enjoyed it as well. James had responded, "Nina is not pleasant[;] she's morose." Bertha stated, "I told him she is pleasant. I know she is—you don't take her right." "Anybody could see it was an unhappy marriage," she continued, "but Nina never spoke of it. . . . James seemed to be threatening Nina all the time; if she did not do just as he said, he would be very angry. Whatever she thought or desired, he did just the opposite." When Bertha stepped down from the witness stand and walked back into the courtroom gallery, she was pleased to overhear one of the women spectators comment that she would make a good lawyer herself. Another woman agreed, saying that Bertha had responded to Mr. Burdick's questions just as a real lawyer would, asking about the relevancy of certain questions and so forth.

William H. Crapo was an elderly man who had come to testify all the way from Boston, where he owned a boardinghouse on Massachusetts Avenue. He had been an invalid for several years, and his wife now ran the boardinghouse. He stated that Miss Mabel Cochrane had resided in his house from March 1905[8] until January 1, 1910. Mr. James Walker had come to the house a dozen times while Mabel had lived there, going into her room. Mr. Crapo testified that he did not know at the time the man was Mr. Walker, but he now recognized him in court. "Mabel did not usually rise in the morning until 10 or 11 o'clock A.M.," Mr. Crapo harrumphed. "Her door was always locked when she received company."

He testified, "Miss Cochrane referred to Mr. Walker as 'the doctor,' and gave directions to admit him at any time." He could not tell just when Mr. Walker had started visiting Miss Cochrane but was certain that he had seen him there in the past two years. They had many lodgers in the house, Mr. Crapo explained, and he generally tended the door. "Miss Cochrane had the back parlor on the first floor, with a kitchenette," he said and added, "There was an upright piano in the room." Mabel Cochrane was about twenty-four, he stated, and, in a disdainful aside, said that one time she had received Mr. Walker when she had apparently just gotten up, before dressing.

Quite a bit of buzzing erupted in the courtroom following this provocative statement. Judge Baker quieted the court and allowed Mr. Crapo to step down. Dr. George Douglas Ramsay was then called as a witness. He had practiced medicine in Newport for fifteen years and had formerly been an army doctor. Dr. Ramsay was asked to read aloud a crumpled piece of paper that Nina had claimed was a prescription for James's disease. He did so, explaining each item in turn. Nina's attorney then asked the doctor a long hypothetical question:

> Assuming[,] Doctor, that a male person for approximately four months used the above directions daily; and assuming further that during that period he wore on his genital parts a pad of absorbent cotton which he changed constantly night and day and each time burned them after removing and that he frequently had a thick discharge of distinctly yellowish color; that at times he suffered considerable pain so that it hurt him to walk and also at times of emission had a discharge of blood sometimes in considerable quantities; that at times pus was visible and the urine cloudy and at other times clear . . . and that also he used in his genitals a syringe or douche and injected a solution of reddish color, the attributes of which had qualities to stain; from what disease, in your opinion and experience[,] was he suffering?[9]

James's attorneys immediately objected to the wording of these questions and suggested excluding the words "that at times pus was visible and the urine cloudy and at other times clear" and substituting instead the words "at times the urine was comparatively clear . . . from what disease would you say he was suffering?" Judge Baker overruled this objection and allowed the witness to answer the original question. Dr. Ramsay replied that the described symptoms indicated an acute or subacute presence of gonorrhea, which, he agreed, could not have been contracted from a drinking cup and which, had it been communicated to her, could have resulted in Mrs. Walker's death. Gasps arose from the courtroom gallery.

After Judge Baker quieted the court, Mr. Barney attempted to cross-examine Dr. Ramsay regarding the items in the alleged prescription and their possible uses for other diseases. The witness testified that he had never seen any of them used for any other disease. He testified that he had treated five thousand or six thousand cases of gonorrhea, and sometimes it was never cured. "It may disappear and after years reappear," the doctor stated. Although he admitted that other strains of gonorrhea might be contracted from such sources as an infected towel, Dr. Ramsay maintained, "There is practically but one way known of contracting this species of the disease—direct contact." Approximately half of the courtroom gallery erupted in boisterous conversation, while the remainder sat in shocked silence. Judge Baker had enough for the day and adjourned the court until the following morning.

Rhode Island Superior Court Hearing, Friday, March 10, 1911[10]

Nina's lawyers rested their case, for the time being, on the morning of Friday, March 10, 1911. Mr. Walker's attorneys began to present their case for the respondent. After the shocking testimony that had ended the session on Thursday afternoon, all eyes were on James as he took the stand. He stood upright in the witness box and insisted that he had suggested that Nina exchange places with her mother and sister at Mrs. Batcheler's in Newport. James had been concerned about her health, and when she had taken a separate room upon her return to their cottage, he had simply thought that she was still sick. James testified that he and Nina had discussed what should be done with their children and that Nina had insisted that two of them be sent to boarding school and the other two be sent to live with her mother. He had not thought this was a good proposal and suggested several alternative options, but she would not agree to any of them. "It is absurd to say that I threatened to put Nina in an insane asylum!" James declared. "I may have said jokingly, 'You ought to be in an insane asylum,' but I never meant any such thing, and she knew I didn't!"

James told his version of what had happened the day Nina had left the cottage and taken the children. He explained his surprise that the children had not been home for lunch, how Nina had told him that they were probably walking home, and about the phone call from her when he had returned to his office, during which she had told him that a man would be coming to see him. He stated that he had waited all afternoon, but no man had come. Tearfully, James described how, when he had returned to their family cottage that evening, the house had been ransacked and that Nina had taken not only her personal items and those of the children but his family silver and other Walker family property as well. "I did notice that the silverware [had been] disappearing," he commented. "She told me since we were not using it much and it was trouble for the maids to clean it, she had packed it away."

James's attorneys then tried to establish his relationship with his children in contradiction to the negative image presented by his wife's lawyers and several witnesses for her side. James explained that Mrs. Walker had objected to punishing the children herself and had told him that he would have to perform that function. "Nine times out of ten I punished them at her request," he stated. "If I erred, it was in not punishing them enough!" he declared, mentioning that the oldest boy had occasionally come to him and suggested that he should be whipped. The leather on the two-thonged whip mentioned previously in court was old and "punky" and could no longer really cause much harm, James explained. He claimed that his children had always been very affectionate toward him and that he was fond of them. "They never showed the slightest fear or dread of me, and do not show any at present," James testified. He stated the children visited him at the naval training station three times a week, under court order, and that he had not noticed any change in their attitude toward him. "They are stunned, and unable to understand the situation," James commented bitterly.

James stated that after Nina had taken the children, he had found a note the children had left behind. At this point, Lieutenant Walker was visibly overcome with emotion and began to weep. He cried out that he had not given his wife any cause to leave him—"Everything has been done entirely for her and the children—for their best interests!" He bowed his head and looked down at the witness stand. Mr. Burdick stopped speaking and waited several minutes while James regained his composure.

James's attorney then took another approach and began to attack the assertions that Nina had made about "other women." Regarding the "flirtation" with a waitress in a Boston hotel room that his wife had mentioned, James claimed that it had all begun when he had been at a restaurant in Boston. He had several large bills, and the woman cashier had been unable to change them for him. Several days later, the same cashier (who was most definitely not Miss Cochrane) had stopped him on the street and said she wanted to speak with him. He had taken her to a restaurant or hotel—he was not quite sure which it was—and ordered something to drink. The woman unaccountably had begun to talk to him about needing funds to furnish her suite of rooms, and James had suddenly caught on and ended the conversation. After returning home, he had told Nina about the incident, because he had thought it funny that he would be mistaken for the sort of man who would give money to a strange woman. "That was all there was to that episode," James concluded.

Mr. Burdick questioned James about his time in Brooklyn and the officers' parties with actresses, including one of whom, he had admitted to his wife, had kissed him goodnight. James said he realized that this part of Nina's testimony must be referring to his friend Ferguson's party, which he had written about in a letter to her. He had gone to his room to go to bed while the others had gone onto the ship to continue the party. Suddenly, the others had returned, bursting into his room to bid him goodnight, and one of the ladies had insisted on giving him a kiss. "I had been rather a glum figure-head at the party, as I was not much for social functions, and they came in to give me a shock," James explained. He added that the women involved were not, so far as he knew, the "questionable" sort. In fact, one of them had subsequently married a naval officer.

James clarified more details about his medical condition. He testified that he had first told his wife about it while they were in Charleston, describing it as a reoccurrence of an old condition that had begun before he knew her. As for the "prescription" Nina had found in his pocket, it was simply a series of notes he had made from the instructions Dr. Charles M. Whitney had given him in Boston. James testified that he was not sure now what the medical condition in fact was. He denied that he had had any improper relations with anyone since his marriage to Nina.

James disputed his wife's testimony that he had lied to her by saying that the Cochrane boy had worked at the Charlestown Navy Yard and that he had stayed in bed for a whole day after Nina had put his shirt in the laundry. He admitted that he liked to spend almost all of his evenings at home but insisted that he had taken his wife out when there was somewhere to go and when she was able to go out, stating that he could remember only about three times when she had not been busy with the children. James also complained that the children had spent a comparatively small amount of time with his family, based on Nina's preference; however, when his mother could not take them for an entire winter, Nina had been upset.

James gave testimony about his annual income and expenditures for the past several years. He stressed that his expenses had always been greater than his income, although for himself he paid for only clothes and what he smoked. "How were you able to spend more than your income?" Mr. Burdick inquired. James replied that his parents had helped make up the difference.

James's attorneys were no doubt aware that it would be difficult to rebut the evidence given by Mr. Crapo, Mabel Cochrane's landlord. Therefore, Mr. Burdick encouraged James to describe his visits to Miss Cochrane's rooms. He explained that he had indeed visited that lady recently but only to acquire some letters written by Mrs. Walker to use as evidence in the divorce case. He had only been to visit Miss Cochrane maybe twice before, he stated, once to discuss her brother's possible career in the navy and the other time to stop for a few minutes at her place when his motorcycle overheated. James maintained that Miss Cochrane had never received him while she was undressed; on one occasion, she had been wearing a wrapper because she had been in the middle of cleaning her apartment. James disputed Mr. Crapo's identification of him in court, because he had seen him at an inn called the Perry House the previous day and the man had given no indication of knowing him, even though they had looked straight at each other. James explained that he had recently shaved off his mustache, so his appearance had changed, which would make it difficult to identify him. Finally, James asserted that neither Mr. Crapo nor Miss Cochrane had ever called him "doctor."

When cross-examined about his legal residence, James replied that he had always considered Washington, DC, to be his "real residence." He had stayed in Boston when he was a student at "the Tech" (MIT), but he had lived in Washington for several years after that. In response to questions about whether he had been attentive to his wife when their first child was born, James replied that Nina had made the decision to live with her mother at that time, while he had been immersed in work for the canal commission. He did not think his wife's health had deteriorated after giving birth to their third child, although she apparently claimed that it had. Regarding Miss Cochrane's first visit to Charleston with her brother, James reported that he had been greatly surprised at their arrival. He had later hired her to act as a housekeeper while her brother and he were at the navy yard all day, and she had boarded in town. James also insisted that he had never invited Mabel Cochrane to Washington; his mother had done that. Mr. Sheffield read the letter James had written to his wife on August 22, 1903, while she and the children were still in Washington (excerpted in Chapter 3). It described shootings near their home at the Charleston Naval Base. "Not," the attorney commented dryly, "of a nature to reassure a timid woman." The intimation was that perhaps James had been trying to keep his wife from returning to Charleston.

James could not remember whether he had ever taken his wife to the zoo, as he had taken Miss Cochrane. He stated that if there had been trouble between Nina and Miss Cochrane in Charleston, it had only been when Nina's sister was there. When asked whether his wife had previously spoken to him about seeing a lawyer, James replied that she might have done so right after seeing the letter from Miss Cochrane. Mr. Sheffield asked James whether his father had written to him that he should be careful that his letters to Nina gave a good impression to anyone who might see them in the future. James denied that his father had ever given him that advice. Mr. Sheffield produced the letter from Admiral Walker to his son, dated October 16, 1906 (excerpted in Chapter 4), in which he had written that James should make his letters to his wife sound kind, keep copies of them, and also retain his wife's letters. James seemed chagrined at this revelation and was forced to admit that he had received the letter.

James agreed that he had once written a letter stating his refusal to pay his wife's bills. Regarding his disagreement with his wife over what to do with the children, he again stated that he had offered several different plans to provide for their care and reiterated that he had never threatened to put Mrs. Walker in an insane asylum. Cross-examination returned to the subject of James's financial situation. He verified that he had property in Washington that he had inherited from his uncle and namesake, James Wilson Grimes. Senator Grimes had bestowed a gift of $2,000 on James the day he was christened, which had been invested to earn interest, of which he received $500 to $600 a year. James guessed that the fund in total was probably now worth about $10,000 but maintained that his mother was completely in charge of it. James acknowledged that he had given his wife $220 a month for family expenses. He stated that his current pay was $3,300 a year and that he was paying $720 for rent, in addition to charges for heat and light. "My other income is not enough to stay awake nights thinking about," James remarked. His father had left him about $700,000, from which he received interest of $1,200 a year. He stated that he also had a little farm near Conway, New Hampshire, which did not amount to much. "How many acres?" asked Mr. Sheffield. "About 130 acres," replied James.

In response to Mr. Sheffield's questions about Mabel Cochrane, James stated that he had seen her practically every day when she was a waitress at the North Station restaurant where he ate lunch while stationed in Charlestown, Massachusetts. He commented that he had helped a good many employees and some friends from various places and that he had been interested in helping her brother. Miss Cochrane had come to Charleston without any invitation, had at first been a guest, and the next season and following summer and winter had worked at his house there. James acknowledged that he might have authorized her to sign his name to acquire half-price railroad tickets, a deal available to members of his family, when she came down to Charleston.

Mr. Sheffield asked James to identify the letter to him signed "Mabel," which had been torn up and pasted together (excerpted in Chapter 3). James read the letter carefully, and sweat began to form on his brow. "You are entirely mistaken if you think I was trying to start a quarrel with you," it began. James replied that the letter looked like it was in Miss Cochrane's handwriting, but he could not remember ever accusing her of starting a quarrel. "I wrote to her in a friendly way—not affectionately," he maintained. Since it was already 4:45 P.M., court was adjourned.

While Lieutenant James Wilson Grimes Walker was testifying in his divorce trial, a ceremony was held at the Charlestown Navy Yard in honor of Rear Admiral John C. Fremont, who had served in the navy concurrently with Admiral Walker. According to the *Newport Daily News*, Rear Admiral Fremont's funeral was "the most imposing naval funeral held in the vicinity of Boston in many years." It was no doubt attended by several of Lieutenant Walker's former colleagues at the Charlestown Navy Yard, some of whom could not resist asking each other whether James or the deceased had had a worse day.[11]

Rhode Island Superior Court Hearing, Monday Morning, March 13, 1911[12]

Mr. Barney, an attorney for James Walker, was granted permission to interrupt his client's testimony to put two Boston physicians on the stand to rebut the testimonies of Dr. Ramsay and Dr. William A. Sherman for Nina Walker, the petitioner. Barney first called Charles M. Whitney, who was a professor at Tufts Medical College and a surgeon at the Boston dispensary. Dr. Whitney specialized in genitourinary diseases and stated that he had seen several thousand cases at the dispensary, in addition to about twenty-five thousand to thirty thousand in his office practice. His credentials were read for the court record, including that he was a member of the American Urinary Society as well as other professional organizations. Dr. Whitney described the internal examination he had performed on Mr. Walker in October 1903, and court spectators seemed fascinated by his description of the electric light device he had used. The doctor had found a "distinctly chronic condition, but no evidence of gonorrhea." He had treated Mr. Walker for five weeks, but the patient had improved only slightly. Dr. Whitney testified that he had also fully examined Mr. Walker in September 1905 and had performed a brief examination of him at another time.

Mr. Barney then approached Dr. Whitney with what Nina had indicated was the "prescription" she had found in James's pocket right before she left him. Pointedly, James's attorney referred to it not as a "prescription" but as a "memorandum of remedies" recommended by Dr. Whitney to Mr. Walker. In reply to Mr. Barney's questions about the items on the list, the doctor stated, "Some of these would not be prescribed for treatment of gonorrhea; others would not specially indicate it. The patient gave symptoms that showed that he did not have it."

Mr. Barney asked the doctor a long and technical hypothetical question, similar to the one Mrs. Walker's attorney had asked her medical experts and to which Mr. Barney had objected. The difference in the question Mr. Walker's attorney asked was that he substituted the words "at times the urine was comparatively clear" for the words "at times pus was visible and the urine cloudy and at other times clear." The court stenographer stopped Mr. Barney in mid-sentence, pleading that he was unable to follow the wording, and even Dr. Whitney stated that he could not understand what he was being asked. Mr. Barney repeated the question, and the doctor responded that he could not tell from his description what disease was indicated. Dr. Whitney also testified that he may have found some microorganisms in his examination: "They are always present and some resemble others; but I found none which were pathological."

During cross-examination, Mr. Harvey asked Dr. Whitney how many microscopic examinations he had made of Lieutenant Walker. The doctor replied that he had made six or eight microscopic examinations for organisms. Mr. Harvey showed him a copy of the "memorandum of remedies." Dr. Whitney stated that one of the remedies mentioned, permanganate of potassium, had not been used as a cure for gonorrhea for the past ten to fifteen years. He testified that, as in the majority of cases, Mr. Walker's symptoms from a previous infection might recur any time for up to twenty-three years, but he acknowledged that "the presence of pus would indicate fresh contagion." Dr. Whitney confirmed that he had been consulted about Mr. Walker's case a year earlier, as well as recently, with John Jenks Thomas, the physician husband of Mr. Walker's sister, Frances Walker Thomas.

Mr. Harvey called Dr. Charles H. Gwynn as a rebuttal witness. He stated that he had been a physician for twenty-two years and had served for seven years as secretary of the U.S. Examining Surgeons of the Pension Bureau in Boston, and he listed several other impressive credentials. Dr. Gwynn testified that he had seen Mr. Walker as a patient in his office and had also corresponded with him. The second time he had been examined, Mr. Walker had not improved since the first time. "It looked to me," Dr. Gwynn commented, "like a chronic case of gonorrhea." Included in what he had seen on examination of Mr. Walker in summer 1903 was "more or less pus." He had then referred Mr. Walker to Dr. Whitney.

Under cross-examination by Mr. Barney, Dr. Gwynn stated that when Mr. Walker had come to his office, he had given his name as "Paul Jones." He thought Walker's words were "Put down any name; put down Paul Jones if you want to." The witness denied that he had been offered $100 to testify on Mrs. Walker's behalf. Although he had met a William P. Malloy of Boston, he had never told him that Mr. Walker had confided that he had "been up against a woman with a dose and got bitten." Dr. Whitney explained that Mr. Malloy had called on him and offered him $100 to testify for Mrs. Walker but that he had flatly rejected his offer without dickering over price. Dr. Gwynn maintained that he had made no deal regarding his testimony.

After the physicians finished, Mr. Sheffield resumed his cross-examination of the respondent, James Walker. Lieutenant Walker referred to a typewritten list to refresh his memory while undergoing questioning, and when Sheffield asked to see it, he refused to show it to him until Judge Baker directed him to do so. Mr. Sheffield asked whether he had any other similar lists, and Lieutenant Walker stated that he did and agreed to show them to him as well. When asked again about his income, he replied that the figures showed his pay but not his income. James explained that during his first year of marriage, his family had given him about $1,200, and Mrs. Chinn might have helped her daughter directly. Nina had distributed the funds for household expenses, which were about $1,700 that year. When they had lived in Charleston, he had also had a garden and a cow to support, and in Newport his wife had had a monthly allowance of $225.

Mr. Sheffield asked James whether it was true that he had "quite a temper" and that he had had problems with his father in the past. James denied that he had a temper but admitted to some friction between the admiral and him. Sheffield questioned him about having a "gay time" and attending a "riotous affair" while in Brooklyn; James replied that he would not have used those terms. Mr. Sheffield asked whether actresses had been present at social events in Brooklyn and whether he had attended one party that had included only three sober attendees out of seventeen or eighteen guests. Regarding the actresses, James replied that he was unsure, but regarding the number of sober party goers, he replied, "Probably."

When Mr. Sheffield asked James about the part in his letter from Brooklyn where he said a young woman had kissed him (excerpted in Chapter 4). James replied that he had simply tried to make the letter sound "picturesque." When Mr. Sheffield asked him whether he had received a photograph of Mabel Cochrane through the mail, James denied that he had: "I only remember the photograph that I had at my house and returned at Mrs. Walker's desire." Mr. Sheffield read from the letter allegedly written by James to Mabel in May 1902, in which he stated, "Many thanks for the photo, which was an unexpected pleasure. You need not have taken the trouble, however." James testified that he did not remember writing that, although he confirmed that he had written to Miss Cochrane several times. He said she used to write him every now and then, and he had replied to her. He had not considered her to be a "servant"—more like a "housekeeper." James also admitted to having written to Mabel Cochrane since the divorce suit had begun in order to discuss her testimony.

Rhode Island Superior Court Hearing, Monday Afternoon, March 13, 1911[13]

James testified that he did not think that he and Miss Cochrane had corresponded when he had first left the Boston area and moved to Charleston. Mr. Sheffield questioned why Miss Cochrane had stayed in Charleston even though she knew Mrs. Walker was not there. James maintained that he had hired her to look after the "negro" servants, for which she had been paid a salary of $25. Mr. Sheffield wanted to know more about Miss Cochrane's visit to James's parents' home in Washington, DC. Lieutenant Walker stated that he had not expected his wife would be there at the same time, but there had been no trouble between them until after Bertha's arrival. It had gotten so bad at one point, according to James, that Miss Cochrane had accused Nina of throwing her clothing all over the floor.

When Mr. Sheffield asked James about the letter Mabel had written him on January 9, 1905 (excerpted in Chapter 3), James responded that he did recognize some things in the court copy but repudiated the rest. He claimed that he could not imagine why she would have written, "For you know, dear, that I love only you." Other parts of the letter that he claimed he did not remember included Mabel's statements "It's a long time since I've been loved," "Oh, if you were only here I could kill you with kindness," and "Have you dreamed of me lately? I dreamed of you last night and that's the reason I am writing to you." James stated for the record, "I do not see any reason why she should dream of me." When asked whether Miss Cochrane had ever sung songs to him, James replied, "No, never. I never heard Miss Cochrane sing." He particularly denied her written declaration "I am still true to you, I hope you are as true to me as I am to you."

Mr. Sheffield read from the letter Mabel had written to James on May 7, 1904 (excerpted in Chapter 3), and asked why Miss Cochrane had written that she was angry with him, adding "out of sight—out of mind." James guessed it was because he had not written to her sooner. "Why did Miss Cochrane include her address at the end of the letter?" inquired Mr. Sheffield. James replied that she had kept him up to date about her address. Mr. Sheffield then asked Mr. Walker whether he had any of the original letters from Miss Cochrane. James responded that he had destroyed Miss Cochrane's letters directly after receiving them and had thrown the scraps in the wastebasket. However, he was certain that the copies presented in court were not true copies. "Much of the phraseology is Miss Cochrane's; much is not," James commented. He stated that until recently, he had not known that a copy had been sent to his father. He also said that while he was at the Brooklyn Navy Yard, a steam pipe had burst and destroyed some of his letters. One time he had caught his wife going through letters that she herself had sent to him, destroying some, but he had recently found some of her letters in a locked box.

Nina Walker's attorneys were certainly not going to miss an opportunity to cross-examine James Walker on the topic of his visits to Miss Cochrane's rooms. James acknowledged that he had always been let in without delay when he had arrived at her apartment, but "it was never before 11:00 A.M. or after 8:00 P.M. and she never received me in her night dress. Mr. Crapo is wrong about that." About two or three weeks after the divorce case had been filed, he had gone to see her in order to find a letter from her to use as evidence. Unfortunately, he did not get it the first time and therefore had gone back. Much later, he said, he had returned for a third time, looking for anything that might relate to the case.

Cross-examination turned to Mr. Walker's ailment. James admitted that he had not told his wife about his gonorrhea until several years after their marriage, in 1903. He had experienced recurrences of the condition from 1901 through 1905 and had continued to visit Dr. Whitney's office for examinations. James claimed that Dr. Gwynn had suggested that he use the name "Paul Jones." He had been told that he was most likely cured of gonorrhea in 1903 but also had an ailment called "oxaluria" in 1905. When Mr. Sheffield asked James about the children's visits, he explained that the children came to see him on the boat and that he sent them back to their mother in a hack (taxi) or sometimes in a car. He denied knowing that the apprentices in the car used language that "was not fit for children to hear." James stated that he was always ready to receive his children; he was rarely away. James was beginning to look pallid. After a recess, Judge Baker said that he had some questions for Lieutenant Walker, including about Miss Cochrane's age and why he thought she would make a good housekeeper. James responded as best he could. He was exhausted and beginning to think that he would never be able to step down from the witness stand. When he was finally excused, he had to stifle a long sigh of relief.

James's sister Susan Walker FitzGerald testified that she had not noted anything unpleasant between the Walkers during their first year of marriage, but she mentioned that there had been "some friction" at the table another time she had visited. She had observed that her brother and his children were clearly attached to each other. Susan was particularly surprised to see how close James was with his sons, since he was not known as a demonstrative person. Her brother was greatly devoted to his children. "They play and romp with him," Mrs. FitzGerald described, "and give every evidence of wishing to make the most of their time with him." When Judge Baker adjourned court, the crowd of observers in the courtroom poured out into the street. They speculated that Mrs. Rebecca White Pickering Walker, the widow of the venerable admiral, would take the stand next. What would she have to say about her son's behavior?

7

Conflicting Testimonies

March 1911

Rhode Island Superior Court Hearing,
Tuesday Morning, March 14, 1911[1]

ON TUESDAY MORNING, March 14, 1911, Judge Darius Baker again presided over the Walker divorce case. Rebecca White Pickering Walker, the widow of Admiral John Grimes Walker and the mother of James Wilson Grimes Walker, took the stand. She was an elderly woman, with white hair pulled into a bun and a determined-looking face. Although rather short in stature, she made up for her lack of height with a dignified bearing. Walter Barney approached the witness box with great delicacy, and some spectators claimed that he bowed slightly as he reached James's mother.

Mrs. Walker testified that her son had lost his position in Saint Louis just prior to his wedding to Nina Chinn Walker, so she had offered to financially support their first year of marriage. She had seen the newly married couple frequently, and their relationship had been "perfectly satisfactory." Mr. Barney asked about her son's communication with his wife while he was in Nicaragua, and Rebecca Walker replied that James "did the best he could" and that immediately upon returning, he had gone to his wife and child. When asked about the young couple's relationship during the following winter, Mrs. Walker stated, "He bore himself towards his wife as a gentleman and a husband; he was devoted to his child." Under further questioning, Mrs. Walker acknowledged that she had promised to furnish the young couple's house when they moved to Brookline. Since she was not able to leave Washington right away, she had asked her daughter-in-law to be her "agent" to buy what was necessary. Nina had properly asked her the spending limit and had been told that it was $1,000 but, if necessary, could exceed that amount. "When I arrived in Brookline," Mrs. Walker stated haughtily, "I found the house fully and prettily furnished and also found it had cost $2,270!" Later, Nina had been worried about the financial situation: "I advised her to rest while I looked into the accounts. I went over them and found Nina had done very well to cover household expenses on the amount allowed to her." However, Mrs. Walker had determined that the rent was too high and that they had too many servants. They could not reduce the number of servants because Nina was sickly, so Mrs. Walker had agreed to help them financially until the following August.

After allowing her to catch her breath, Mr. Barney asked James's mother to describe the relationship between her son and his wife. Rebecca Walker stated that Nina had constantly been running to her with "babyish complaints" about James. "Once," she stated, "I heard her greet James unpleasantly upon his return. He took it patiently. Afterward I suggested to Nina that was not wise behavior on her part. Nina did not take that advice well, and I said no more." James and his wife had not lowered their expenses, Mrs. Walker said, and she had to send money every so often to help them out. After the third child, Serrell, was born, he had required a special nurse, and she had paid for that expense as well. Serrell and his nurse had gone to live with Nina's mother, and when Mrs. Walker had heard the nurse was to be dismissed, she had sent a message to Mrs. Chinn stating that she would pay the nurse's expenses. At this point, Mr. Barney referred to an "angry letter from Nina's sister," and Mrs. Walker produced a purported copy of that letter, in which Bertha accused Mrs. Walker of stopping James's allowance shortly after Serrell's birth and blamed James for coercing Nina to having sex with him, resulting in this third child (Chapter 3). Mrs. Walker admitted that the letter she presented was not the original; she had destroyed it at a time when she was "optimistic" that the trouble between the families would end. Judge Baker ruled that the letter could not be read aloud.

Mrs. Walker testified that she had invited Serrell and his nurse to stay at her house, but Mrs. Chinn had not allowed it. James had then taken them to his sister Frances's Boston home. Prior to the fourth child's birth, Mrs. Walker claimed, Nina had been very angry and had told her that if she ever again found herself in that "condition," she would leave her husband. "I was, of course, horrified!" stated Mrs. Walker. "I told her, 'Think what you are saying! Take it back!' Far from taking it back, Nina repeated it." Mrs. Walker continued in an indignant tone, "I told her, 'Then go! But you will leave your children behind you.' Nina told me, 'I don't know about that!'" Mrs. Walker then commented that she did "know about that," because her son was devoted to his children.

James's treatment of his wife, according to Mrs. Walker, had been "invariably proper." Since it was difficult to find someone to care for the Charleston house and provide suitable meals for James while Nina and the children were away for the summer, she had offered to pay a young lady, Miss Cochrane, to take care of things. Mrs. Walker did not disagree that she had extended an invitation to Miss Cochrane to visit her in Washington, DC, while James was there and Bertha was with Nina in Charleston. She claimed that she had done so "to avoid friction." "I had no complaint whatsoever about Miss Cochrane," the elderly woman said. "I was teaching her solitaire to make it pleasant for her; she was neither a servant nor a member of the family." When Nina had unexpectedly arrived in Washington, Mrs. Walker had heard her give James a "Caudle lecture" (scolding)[2] that went on for about two hours. As Mrs. Walker described it, "James only spoke three times to reply[,] 'Oh, Nina!'; 'Why Nina!'[;] and 'I suppose I am a perfect brute.'" According to Mrs. Walker, this had not been an argument about Miss Cochrane; it had been about Nina's plans for the summer. "I had James help me make up a vacant room," his mother stated, "hoping he would have a quiet rest by himself." According to Mrs. Walker, Miss Cochrane had stayed in Washington as long as the children were there, and Nina had not complained about that. James had paid no special attention to Miss Cochrane—he had only been civil and kind to her, as he usually was. Mrs. Walker did not understand why Nina had testified about being excluded from a theater party. Nina had not needed to ask to be included; everyone had gone to the theater together as a matter of course.

Mr. Barney produced the purported January 9, 1905, letter from Mabel Cochrane to James in which she referred to Nan Patterson (described in Chapter 3). Mrs. Walker confirmed that she and her daughter Frances had seen a copy of that letter. Mr. Sheffield had read part of the letter as evidence for the petitioner, and now Mr. Barney read the entire letter aloud to the witness. When he finished, Mrs. Walker declared that the copy he had read was not the letter she had seen previously. "This copy is compromising, and would leave no question as to a woman who would write 'I love you' to another woman's husband," Mrs. Walker harrumphed. "The copy I received," she continued, "was foolish, unconventional, but susceptible to an entirely innocent interpretation. This copy has been changed! The admiral and I advised Nina not to be distressed about the letter we saw. If James said it was all right[,] there was nothing to be troubled over."

Mrs. Walker stated that after the situation with Miss Cochrane's letter, her son and daughter-in-law's relationship had seemed fine, except that Nina had become suspicious. She commented, "He always treated her well. He was not demonstrative. She may have desired caressing and things of that kind." Mrs. Walker testified that the children had enjoyed spending the summer with her and still talked about it. They were good children, but, "of course there were occasional little contests, as with all small children." She had been concerned that the oldest child, Elizabeth, then almost nine years old, could not yet read words of three letters and admitted that, while trying to help her learn, this child had been so disobedient that Mrs. Walker had put her in a large closet to teach her a lesson. Mrs. Walker said she had kept near the closet and would tap on the closet door and say, "Are you going to be a good girl?" and Elizabeth would pleasantly say, "Yes," and she had been good afterward. Mrs. Walker added that she had written the child's mother about it and Nina had "replied very sensibly that such occurrences were inevitable and the child would not remember it against me."

Following a recess, Mr. Barney returned to the allegations made by members of the Chinn family about how the Walkers had inappropriately taken the children from Mrs. Chinn's house to Brooklyn, New York. The proper thing to do, Mrs. Walker stated, would have been for Nina to join her husband with the children. When the children had gotten to Brooklyn, Elizabeth had said that her mother should have come with them and that she had tried to convince her to do so. "That little girl was worried and prayed about it," her grandmother said gravely. About her son's relationship with his children, Mrs. Rebecca Walker stated, "It has been touchingly beautiful[;] he has shown tact and particular skill with them. They are devoted to each other and the children show great pleasure when they meet him. I have also been with them during their visits and have helped in their games." Mrs. Walker said the children had put on a "little play" and asked her to be the stage manager.

As Mr. Sheffield approached the witness box to cross-examine Mrs. Walker, she regarded him sternly. He showed her the cautionary letter she had written to James before his marriage (excerpted in Chapter 2). Mr. Sheffield read it aloud, including the passages where she had written of her son's impatience, his declaration that he would live as he pleased, and her warning that "there is but one way to live—the right way." When he had finished reading the letter, Mr. Sheffield commented that it was "a fine piece of advice to a son." Mrs. Walker regarded him with a look that said, "I know what you are up to." After a momentary glance away, Mr. Sheffield looked directly at her and asked about the portion of the letter in which Mrs. Walker wanted to know why James had talked to Nina of marrying in three months but had talked to his mother about breaking the engagement. Mrs. Walker replied firmly that she had received a letter from him that made it seem "as if he was discouraged, ready to throw everything up. I was anxious to hold him up in what seemed to be a crisis for him." Mr. Sheffield read aloud the part of the letter where she had asked, "If you write to your mother so discourteously, what can Nina expect?" Mrs. Walker seemed flustered for a moment but then replied, "My son's bearing toward his wife was that of a gentleman." When Mr. Sheffield asked the witness whether she had telegraphed her son to tell him to send his wife a message about the birth of their first child, Mrs. Walker replied that she did not remember doing so but offered as an excuse for James that, at the time of the child's birth, he had been "five or six hours away by express train." She wondered silently how on earth Nina's attorneys had acquired these messages that she had sent her son.

Mr. Sheffield cross-examined Mrs. Walker about her expressed shock that furnishings for the Brookline house amounted to $2,270. He read from a letter in which Mrs. Walker had written, "Dear Nina—Buy nice things and don't be afraid of the money; there will be plenty of it. I suppose there will be $2,000 or more to spend on furniture."[3] Mrs. Walker let out a sigh and muttered that the money was not the problem—"it was a windfall and she didn't mind parting with it." "But," she clarified, "anything that cannot be paid for within one's income is extravagant." Mr. Sheffield then reviewed various statements that Mrs. Walker had previously made, including that she had advised her son to take his children from Washington to Brooklyn. Mrs. Walker stated brusquely, "My advice to my son was to take his wife and children, not to take his children from his wife," she stated firmly. "It was his own idea to take the children without his wife."

Mrs. Walker testified that she did not know what property her son had, although she did allow him to use her safe and sometimes deposited his stock coupons and sent him the checks. Admiral Walker had left nothing outright to James in his will, although he had left funds for the other children in trust. The remainder of his estate had been left to her for her lifetime, she stated, and she had been directed to pay James as much as the other children received. James's share of the estate was in trust for his lifetime, to go to his children after him, and the trustees were her two married daughters. Mr. Sheffield asked Mrs. Walker for her best estimate of the amount in trust for James. She replied, "I really don't know the income; I had been wishing to figure it up, but with my poor eyes I have not been able to do so," but she guessed that it was about $500,000. At this point, a lunch recess was announced, and even the indomitable Mrs. Walker looked like she could use a rest and some sustenance.

Rhode Island Superior Court Hearing, Tuesday Afternoon, March 14, 1911[4]

Mr. Sheffield continued his cross-examination of Mrs. Walker. He asked her whether she thought her son was a proper person to have the care of his children, and she responded that she thought he was "entirely appropriate." When asked about what arrangements could be made for the Walker children, Mrs. Walker stated emphatically, "Three homes, with welcomes and loving care are open to the children—my own and those of my two daughters!" Mr. Sheffield read a letter Mrs. Walker had written on September 22, 1906, in which she had stated that she could not possibly care for the Walker children in her home (described in Chapter 4). Mrs. Walker explained that circumstances had changed; she now had her youngest daughter with her as well as another young lady who was committed to taking care of the children. The young lady was her secretary but was really like a member of the family, she explained. In answer to Mr. Sheffield's question regarding her poor eyesight, Mrs. Walker replied that she expected to have that problem "entirely taken care of" after the trial. Mr. Sheffield concluded his cross-examination of the witness.

Later that afternoon, James's attorneys called several Walker acquaintances and relations to give testimony in his favor. Mr. Timothy C. O'Leary, the paymaster at the Newport Naval Training Station, testified that James and his children "were real comrades." Mrs. O'Leary corroborated her husband's testimony and added that Mr. Walker had built snow forts for the children and "gave them much more time than the ordinary father gives his children." In a previous generation, the topic of whether James played with his children would not have been an issue. However, during this time period, there were new expectations for fathers to be companions and not just moral educators to their children.[5] Miss Ida R. Bartlett also testified that James and his children "seemed to be fond of each other and good comrades."

Miss Helen E. Hull, a friend of Sallie Walker's and her guest in Washington while Mabel Cochrane was visiting in her parents' home, testified, "Mr. Walker was very polite to Miss Cochrane, that was all. There were no marked attentions—none whatever." She also testified that the children now seemed happy with their father. Miss Alice P. Mullen, James's former housekeeper, testified that she had seen the Walker children happy with their father; "he did everything for them," she stated quietly.

Miss Sallie Cochrane Walker, James's youngest sister, took the stand. Although she had not married, court spectators thought it would be too harsh to call her an "old maid," since, at thirty-three years old, she was still comely, and one never knows. Miss Walker testified that she had not seen any trouble between James and Nina. When asked about the relationship between James and his children, she replied sweetly, "He has shown remarkable devotion to them. They show great confidence towards him." She reported that the children had been happy visiting with the Walker family in Wilton, New Hampshire. Mr. Barney asked Miss Walker about the incident in which her mother punished Elizabeth by putting her in the closet. Miss Walker said that she had the impression the child had believed it was a just punishment and that it had not broken her spirit at all. She also talked about participating in the play the children had put on in Washington. Her main conclusion was that James would be "a very excellent father to the children." When asked about Mabel Cochrane, Sallie Walker declared that her brother had merely treated her with ordinary courtesy.

Dr. John Jenks Thomas was the physician husband of James Walker's oldest sister, Frances, and had lived near James and Nina in the early part of their marriage. He testified that he had seen James and his wife attending dances as well as going to the theater and participating in other activities together. This claim refuted Nina's testimony that James had not taken her anywhere. Dr. Thomas could not recall Mr. Walker's going out without his wife in the evening, which contradicted Nina's testimony that he had done so. He stated that the affection between the Walker children and their father "seemed very strong" and agreed that it would be proper for James to have care of his children.

James's brother, Henry Pickering Walker ("Hank"), had been the best man at James and Nina's wedding but had not seen much of them in recent years. He testified that he had noticed "only one slight friction" between the couple but said that was "likely to occur in any family" and that it was not due to any discourtesy of James toward his wife. Hank Walker stated that James "has been very chummy and given time to the children; they were very affectionate towards him. He is absolutely a proper person to have care of them."

Miss Mary F. Bangs, Mrs. Rebecca Walker's secretary, testified that she thought that Mr. Walker and his children were "on affectionate terms" and that "he [wa]s very anxious for their welfare—mental, moral, physical." The children also showed affection for their paternal grandmother, as she did for them. In answer to Mr. Sheffield's cross-examination, Miss Bangs replied, in turn, that she had never seen Mr. Walker go to the boat to meet the children, that he did not go to church on Sundays, and that it was true that sometimes he went away and did not let the children know he was going. Miss Bangs corroborated that she was not a governess and stated that Mrs. Rebecca Walker was almost always present when she cared for the children.

Mr. Henry Goddard Pickering, Mrs. Walker's brother and a lawyer in Boston, testified that his nephew James's treatment of his wife had seemed "perfectly courteous" and that his relations with his children were very pleasant and "mutually affectionate." Immediately after Nina Walker had left her husband, Mr. Pickering had called on her to try to bring about reconciliation, but she had told him that she "had been considering leaving for twelve years." At the time, he had been surprised to see that she had "show[n] no visible signs of emotion at separating from her husband." Mr. Pickering added to the chorus of testimony from friends and relatives confirming that Mr. Walker was "entirely a proper person to have care of the children."

A Post-hearing Incident, Tuesday, March 14, 1911[6]

The sensational nature of the Walker divorce case meant that not just reporters were present; press photographers were there as well. Judge Baker tried desperately to avoid a carnival atmosphere and gave orders to arrest anyone attempting to use a camera in the courtroom. However, as some witnesses left the courtroom earlier in the day on Tuesday, March 14, one ambitious photographer from Boston, Richard W. Sears, used the opportunity to take their pictures. Forewarned about this incident, at the end of the day, Nina, her mother, and her sister left the courthouse by the west door to avoid an encounter with the press. Mr. Sears was waiting for them to leave by the south door, and when he realized his mistake, he took off after the three women. First one and then several reporters from competing papers intervened by placing themselves between the women and the photographer. Exactly what happened next was not clear, but a physical fight broke out, and Mr. Sears screamed that he would have the others arrested.

Nina, her mother, and Bertha fled into nearby Hassard's Grocery, and a cab was called to take them home safely. Mr. Sears went back to the courthouse, followed by a curious crowd. The onlookers were disappointed when nothing further ensued and assumed that the photographer had left Newport on the 5:13 P.M. train. However, this was not the case; "the real fun" began then in front of the Perry House, where James's friends and relatives were standing and talking. As Mr. Sears tried to catch a picture in his camera finder, Henry Pickering Walker, James's brother, approached him and reportedly kicked the camera. Mr. Sears would later claim that Henry Walker had also punched him, but some observers thought it had only been the camera hitting him in the face. Mr. Sears promptly found a lawyer who swore out a civil warrant, claiming $500 in damages from Henry Pickering Walker. He also swore out a criminal complaint against him, claiming that the camera was broken and the lens, worth $300, was damaged and could not be replaced.

Rhode Island Superior Court Hearing, Wednesday Morning, March 15, 1911[7]

Early in the morning on Wednesday, there was a sudden and severe change in the previously mild Newport weather. The rain poured excessively, and there was profuse thunder and lightning. By the time court resumed, the weather had cleared, but a cold wind blew through the town. Not discouraged by the previous day's confrontations, photographer Richard W. Sears again came to the courthouse, this time with a smaller camera, and desperately tried to snap photographs of people entering. A lot of running around and umbrella raising took place, but no altercation occurred. When the photographer later appeared inside the courtroom, Judge Baker directed a deputy sheriff to inform him that he must leave; although dismayed, Mr. Sears followed orders.

When that had been taken care of, another Walker relative was called to testify. She was Mrs. Frances (Fanny) Walker Thomas, James's oldest sister and the wife of Dr. John Jenks Thomas, who had testified the day before. Mr. Burdick showed Mrs. Thomas the copy of a letter allegedly written by Miss Cochrane to James. Mrs. Thomas stated that she had seen the original and, after reading the copy that had been entered into evidence, maintained that "this [version] was distinctly not the same." "The one I saw was silly," she continued, "but it did not convey the same idea that this exhibit does." When asked for more details, Mrs. Thomas stated that she could not recall the phrasing of the original letter from Miss Cochrane—she had only seen it one time and had paid little attention to it. She did not remember the length of the original, only that it was annoying and silly. Mrs. Thomas testified that she had never had any conversation with her sister-in-law regarding the letter. She also commented that she had tried to locate Miss Cochrane to appear as a witness but had been unsuccessful and had been told that the young lady was "beyond reach." In reply to Mr. Sheffield's cross-examination, Mrs. Thomas agreed that she had made a copy of the angry letter that Bertha had sent to her mother, Rebecca Walker, because she had wished to show it to her husband. "Was that to make things pleasant in the family?" Mr. Sheffield asked, under his breath, but the witness simply stared back at him.

Mr. Clark Burdick introduced depositions taken in support of his client, James Walker. Court spectators noticed this was a very thick book of typewritten testimonies. He offered a deposition from an elderly Boston woman who had been Virginia Chinn's teacher. William Harvey interrupted to object that the whole deposition was absolutely immaterial. After paging through the deposition in silence, Judge Baker agreed, and Mr. Burdick withdrew it. Observers in the gallery began to speculate that it was going to be a long day.

Mr. Burdick offered the deposition taken from Mrs. Eliza Ripley of Brooklyn, New York. She was Nina's father's sister, age seventy-nine, and the mother of one of her bridesmaids. He began to read Mrs. Ripley's statement, in which she discussed the relationship between Nina's parents. Judge Baker interrupted to state that he did not see the relevance. Mr. Burdick replied that his intent was to show that for two or three generations, "the same thing had occurred in the family." Judge Baker then impatiently asked Mr. Burdick, "Do you mean to show that wives have left their husbands in this family for several generations, and therefore if Elizabeth Walker is brought up under the same situation[,] she will also divorce?" In response, Mr. Barney agreed and gave "a brief oration on heredity," in which he attempted to prove that divorce was passed down on the maternal side of Nina's family, from her grandmother to her mother. Following this assertion, Judge Baker stated that there was no opportunity to inquire what the reasons had been for the previous marital separations. "Mr. Sheffield and yourself would have to try all three cases," the judge commented dryly.

Nina's attorneys objected to the admission of Mrs. Ripley's deposition and Mr. Barney's statement about heredity and divorce. Judge Baker agreed that the point was wandering and particularly inappropriate in a case in which not absolute divorce but simply divorce from bed and board was sought. "Judges must hear enough without going into what they are not obliged to deal with," he commented in a tone that conveyed his irritation. Mr. Barney spoke up to claim this issue of heredity was "one of the keynotes; it was a reason why Mr. Walker tried to take his children on two occasions." Judge Baker finally stated that his role was to decide whether the petitioner had affirmatively made her case and that he was ruling out discussions of whether the tendency to divorce could be inherited.

Mr. Barney, obviously annoyed, continued to read from a different part of Mrs. Ripley's deposition. She had been asked, "Do you know the reputation of Mrs. Chinn for veracity?" During the deposition, Mr. Harvey had objected, and the question had been withdrawn, as had similar questions. Finally, the wording "According to the speech of people[,] is Mrs. Chinn known for her veracity?" had been deemed acceptable, along with Mrs. Ripley's response, "No, they say not." She could not specify who had doubted Mrs. Chinn's truthfulness but had stated that the impression was "universal." During cross-examination at the deposition, Mr. Harvey had pressed her to be more specific, but Mrs. Ripley had replied, "I won't tell." She had stated that she was friendly with the Chinn family but admitted that she had been asked to testify by "Mrs. Admiral Walker." The remainder of her deposition was withdrawn, but several other depositions were read that supported James Walker's case.

Mr. Barney read the deposition of William B. Ferguson, USN, who had shared quarters with James at the Brooklyn Navy Yard for about a year while his family was still in Washington. Mr. Ferguson stated that he had become well acquainted with Lieutenant Walker, although he was hard to get to know, and had found him "upright and honorable." Mr. Ferguson further testified, "Lieutenant Walker was very temperate and could not be called a drinking man at all; he only occasionally took a glass of beer." He continued, "Lieutenant Walker's morals were, so far as I saw, above reproach, and his conversation was always gentlemanly." Although Mr. Ferguson had confided in Lieutenant Walker, Walker had not talked about his own family matters. When asked about the infamous party mentioned in James's letter to his wife, Mr. Ferguson said he recalled a birthday party that his best friends had attended, but no one had been intoxicated. In response to questions about the presence of actresses, he replied that he had friends who were actresses and that he held them in as high esteem as he did preachers. As a matter of fact, Mr. Ferguson stated, his wife was a "sort of public performer."

Yet another deposition in support of Mr. Walker was read by his counsel, this time from Dr. Henry M. Cutts, who had attended the birth of the last two Walker children, who were born a year apart. He testified that Nina had become hysterical upon finding that she was pregnant with the fourth child and had told him she did not want the baby. To placate her, he had given her some pills,[8] although he believed they were useless, and had also prescribed that she take hot baths. Dr. Cutts stated that he had hoped that Nina would adapt to the situation of her pregnancy in the meantime. At this comment, a low murmur of whispers filled the courtroom.

Mr. Barney continued his march through the procession of depositions. Dr. Almon Cooper, of Brookline, Massachusetts, stated that he might have told Nina Walker that she would be better off not having another child right away. He thought she "looked a little delicate" following childbirth and could use some rest. Mrs. Alma Child, a former nurse for the Walker children, contributed the information that whenever Miss Bertha Chinn visited the Walker household, there had been "general unpleasantness," resulting in her leaving her position there. Professor Edward C. Pickering, an astronomer at Harvard University, testified that he had known the extended Walker family for many years, as "a sort of cousin." He knew James Walker only slightly and did not know his wife or children. At this point, Mr. Harvey, with a huge sigh, objected to the reading of the deposition any further. Judge Baker agreed that there was "no need to prove the character of so distinguished a family as the Walkers." Even so, Mr. Barney then read his deposition of Mr. George Wigglesworth, an attorney and member of the Harvard Board of Overseers who was Rebecca Walker's cousin. Although Mr. Wigglesworth stated in his deposition that he had never visited Mr. Walker and had not seen him very often, he testified that he considered him "proper to have charge of his children." With a deep sigh, Judge Baker ruled out testimony about the Walker family's reputation as well as that about Mr. Walker's reputation, banged his gavel, remarked that it was 12:45 P.M., and called a recess until 2:00 P.M.

Judge Baker tried desperately to improve his mood over the noontime recess. He generally took his lunches in a restaurant near the courtroom, either alone or with colleagues, and the staff there knew him well. Today, the judge dined alone, and the waitresses could see that he was not in the mood to exchange pleasantries, so they provided prompt and courteous service. The judge was ruminating about the length of the Walker trial and reflecting wearily on the long list of people deposed as character witnesses for Mr. Walker and his family. They were really quite superfluous, he thought.

Rhode Island Superior Court Hearing, Wednesday Afternoon, March 15, 1911[9]

Judge Baker halfheartedly returned to his seat in the superior court just after 2:00 P.M. He found that Mr. Burdick wanted to revisit his seemingly endless collection of statements in support of James Walker. As the depositions dragged on and on, Judge Baker ruled them out as either irrelevant or simply corroborations of previous evidence. When Mr. Burdick announced that he had taken depositions from Mr. Oliver Wendell Holmes, a justice of the U.S. Supreme Court, and from Admiral George W. Dewey regarding James Walker's reputation and that of his family, Judge Baker had to admit to himself that he was impressed. Evidently, James Walker's attorneys hoped his moral character might benefit from basking in the light of testimony from these impressive figures. However, Judge Baker thwarted these expectations when he sustained the opposing attorneys' objections to these depositions. The judge mused silently that if the respondent's attorneys could obtain a posthumous deposition from President Lincoln regarding the high morals of Mr. Walker, they surely would.

When Mr. Burdick recalled Mr. Walker to the stand, James declared that he had not lost his affection for Nina when she left him. He had maintained a home and would continue to do so for his children—and for his wife, if she were to return. His counsel produced a letter "accurately stating his [medical] condition" to Dr. Charles Whitney. Dr. George Ramsay, who had testified for Mrs. Walker, was present in court and went through the letter with Mr. Sheffield, who objected to its submission. Judge Baker ruled that it could not be entered as evidence, but he did allow James to read the letter silently to himself to refresh his memory for testimony on "matters of his own knowledge." Mr. Walker stated that a trip in October 1904 had restarted his health problem and that he had then tried a remedy that improved but did not cure his condition.

Mr. Barney called another medical witness, Dr. Henry Joseph Perry, who had a medical degree from Harvard and an office on Beacon Street in Boston, and who also specialized in "genito-urinal" cases at the Boston Dispensary. Mr. Barney read aloud the same long hypothetical question that he had posed to other defense witnesses, again substituting the words "at times the urine was comparatively clear" for the words "at times pus was visible and the urine cloudy and at other times clear" in the original question asked by Nina Walker's attorney. Dr. Perry replied that the symptoms did not indicate gonorrhea. "There are several different types of cocci which resemble each other," he stated. "Attacks often reoccur without new infection." Under further questioning, Dr. Perry testified that James's condition could result from gonorrhea in most cases but could also be caused by something else.

When recalled to the stand by Mr. Sheffield, George Ramsay, one of his medical experts, explained the differences between gonorrhea and oxaluria. If a patient suffered with oxaluria, the physician would recommend dietary changes. "Oxaluria," he stated, "begins with indigestion. If there was no indigestion[,] it would prove conclusively it was not oxaluria, which is, by the way, a very, very rare disease." Dr. William Sherman, another medical expert for the petitioner, corroborated Dr. Ramsay's medical opinion, adding that certain vegetables, including cabbage, kale, rhubarb, tomatoes, and some kinds of fruit could cause, temporarily, "oxalate of lime," or calcium oxalate poisoning. These medical testimonies presented a final rebuttal to the medical opinion given by Dr. Perry that James Walker had oxaluria rather than gonorrhea. Mr. Walker's attorneys seemed ill at ease but did not continue the debate further.

Miss Bertha Chinn, who many spectators had previously noted was an adept witness, was recalled to the stand by Mr. Harvey. Regarding the nurse who had testified in favor of James, Bertha stated that she probably had ill will toward her sister, Nina, since she had discharged her for staying out too long in the afternoons. Mr. Harvey asked Bertha about Mrs. Eliza Ripley, the paternal aunt who had spoken in her deposition about repeated divorces in the family as well as Mrs. Chinn's lack of veracity. She replied flatly, "I have not been on friendly terms with Mrs. Ripley for at least nine years." Mr. Harvey then showed Miss Chinn the purported copy of the "angry letter" she had sent to Mrs. Rebecca Walker. Bertha took her time reading the letter silently and then stated that she could not say whether it was a true copy. She added that she had been annoyed at the idea of Mrs. Walker's paying someone who was working in her mother's home.

Mrs. Nina Walker once more took the witness stand to respond to testimony given for her husband. Nina affirmed that she had never seen a photograph of Mabel Cochrane in Brookline and that the only photograph of Miss Cochrane she knew about had come in the mail to Mr. Walker in Charleston. In rebuttal to the claim by James and his mother that Nina had not objected to Mabel Cochrane's acting as a housekeeper, Nina testified, "I was completely upset by this[,] and I said I would do anything rather than have that; I would have given up everything if only my husband had let me stay with him at Charleston! He said he had already made the arrangement and it was going to stand. It stood, and the children and I went to Watch Hill." Mr. Harvey gave Nina an opportunity to further discuss how she had dealt with the correspondence between Mabel Cochrane and her husband. She said that after she had spoken with the admiral about the letter, her husband had become very angry and told her he could put her in prison for intercepting his mail, so she had dropped the matter.

Nina's attorneys had to show the court that she had made every effort to reconcile with her husband. She stated that when she had phoned to ask James whether she could send the children by boat to visit him, he had approved but then told her, "You have made a great mistake." When she had responded, "Come over here and talk it over," he had replied, "I can't do that." When Nina had suggested that they meet on the street somewhere to talk, her husband had told her finally, "We are entirely in the hands of our counsel, now."

The most crucial decision to be made in this case concerned which parent should have custody of the Walker children. Nina Walker needed to refute the allegation made by Rebecca Walker and a physician that she had been unhappy to be pregnant. She unequivocally stated to the court, "I never, ever, told Mrs. Rebecca Walker that I did not want another child!" Nina's attorneys sought to make the case that her husband was an irresponsible and disinterested parent. Nina testified that during the children's return from visiting their father in a "shared car," they had heard some "rough language," which was objectionable for a young girl like Elizabeth to hear. Her lawyers had to persuade James to thereafter send the children by private carriage instead. Nina denied that James had ever made any snow forts, despite what a witness had claimed, and stated that he had not been demonstrative with the children prior to her leaving him. Nina said that she had used all of her own income entirely for her children. She declared once again that she had never told anyone she would not want to have more children and had never thought such a thing. "My children are my only riches," she lamented quietly.

Following Nina Walker's testimony, Mr. Sheffield stated, "We rest here," and then he offered a suggestion: "There are four children, making the case a serious one. They are old enough to know their wishes and feelings. I would be glad if it could be arranged for the court to talk with them, entirely apart from their parents." Mr. Burdick spoke on James's behalf, saying that he would also like that, if it were possible under the circumstances; however, he believed that the father would be at a disadvantage, since the children were with him only eight hours a week. Judge Baker agreed that the welfare of the Walker children was of utmost importance in this case and that he would consider conferring with them. Final arguments in the case would be heard the following Saturday at 2:00 P.M. This case had already taken up more than the three days originally expected.

Resolution of *Sears v. Walker*[10]

Following the superior court's adjournment on Wednesday afternoon, the district court clerk's office continued criminal and civil hearings connected with Henry Pickering Walker's alleged harassment of a photographer. Mr. Walker was arraigned on two warrants—the first for criminal physical assault on Richard W. Sears and the other a civil claim for $3,000 in damages to Mr. Sears. Upon hearing the damages claim, Mr. Walker declared, "That photographer is more valuable than he looks!" Admiral Chadwick, a family friend, furnished $200 bail in the criminal case and $2,000 in the civil case, and both cases were continued. Sears also asked for a warrant against the reporter who had clashed with him the previous day, but that warrant was not sworn out.

The case of *Sears v. Walker*, although merely a sidelight to the Walker divorce case, culminated in a precedent-setting decision that guaranteed the rights of future American press photographers. Richard W. Sears's assault case against Henry Pickering Walker finally reached the Rhode Island Superior Court. Judge Charles Stearns presided over a jury trial, during which Mortimer Sullivan, the attorney for Mr. Sears, stated that press photography was one of the most important assets to a modern newspaper and was just as honorable and legitimate as any other profession. On Thursday, June 22, 1911, a jury awarded Mr. Sears $400 in damages for assault and personal injury. Although Henry Walker appealed the decision, he did not win the appeal and was ordered to pay Mr. Sears. Judge Stearns, in his decision, stated that Henry Pickering Walker did not have the right to take the law into his own hands; Sears did have the right to take pictures and a further right to receive damages for the assault and personal injury. Mr. Sears declared that he was gratified by the outcome of the case but was more pleased by the legal status given to his professional work than by the monetary award. He claimed that this was the first time a court had handed down a verdict in favor of a newspaper photographer, which set an important precedent. He asserted, "The verdict cannot fail to have wide influence throughout the country, where wealthy men have often been tried and exonerated on charges of breaking cameras, merely because they objected to having their pictures taken."[11]

In the Interim

Nina Walker was pleased to have the court testimony ended, and Thursday, March 16, passed quietly at her mother's rented house in Newport. Although she had promised herself that she would not do so, she did peek at the newspaper coverage of the trial. As she skimmed the article about the end of the trial in the *Newport News,* she mused that, while it was certainly not her intention to become a public spectacle, sympathy did seem to be on her side. Friday, March 17, was another quiet day, with her mother and Bertha assuring Nina that her attorneys were doing the best that could be asked. The children had gone to school and come back again. Her sons were playing while her daughter read a book. Although the boys were aware that something important was happening, Elizabeth was probably the only one old enough to suspect the full gravity of the situation. As Nina thought apprehensively about the outcome of the court proceedings, she again glanced at the *Newport Daily News.* She was relieved that there was no more news about her case, so she continued to look through the paper. A small article titled "Lowers Divorce Bars" caught her eye. Apparently, both houses of the Nevada state legislature had passed a bill making a residence of only six months the sole requirement in divorce actions.[12] "Oh well," Nina thought wryly, "if Judge Baker does not see my side[,] I can always go west." She certainly hoped it would not come to that.

Rhode Island Superior Court, Closing Arguments, Saturday Afternoon, March 18, 1911[13]

As Judge Baker took his seat in superior court at 2:00 P.M. on Saturday, March 18, 1911, he was startled to see that every seat in the courtroom was occupied. A large segment of Newport's residents had turned out to hear the closing arguments in the Walker case, as had spectators from farther away. Also present were members of the press, who represented not only the local papers but such national papers as the *Washington Post*, the *New York Times*, and the *Boston Daily Globe*. One reporter observed that in the superior court that day, "every inch of space was filled with spectators,"[14] and another described the courtroom as "crowded to suffocation by men, women, doctors, clergymen, lawyers, and others."[15] "Why are people so enthralled with other people's troubles?" Judge Baker asked himself. He, for one, had had a bellyful with this trial.

Mr. Barney, representing James Walker, first spoke, reading dramatically from prepared notes. "Mr. Walker," he stated, "would be a poor specimen of humanity if, with as good a mother as he had, he should minimize the value of a mother." He continued:

> But, there is another relation just as holy, that of a father. A child needs the care of a father. The unpleasantness and the complaining of petty annoyances by the petitioner, Mrs. Nina Walker, are the result of her lack of the care and society of a father or a brother, the consequence of her development in only female surroundings. How many women are enduring far more than Mrs. Walker ever suffered just to protect their children? The law by which the sins of the parents are visited upon the children to the third and fourth generation[s] is the most terrible one![16]

The danger to the children presented by the absence of male figures in her household was a serious charge against Nina. Although precluded from raising the issue of "genetic divorce" during the trial arguments, Mr. Barney made a valiant last attempt in his closing statement to Judge Baker.

Next, Mr. Barney sought to diminish the charges that Nina and her witnesses had made against his client. He first claimed that there was no proof that James's "disease" had been caused by any behavior since his marriage to Nina and therefore did not prove adultery. Mr. Barney stated that opposing counsel had not proven the charge that James had associated with improper persons or that he was guilty of neglect. He argued, "There is not a single scrap of evidence of improper acts with Mabel Cochrane. The letters in her handwriting amount to little. 'We will have some good old times' may be language upon which a misconstruction might be easily put." Two other letters in evidence, Mr. Barney maintained, were copies and "may or may not contain something which Mabel Cochrane wrote." Regarding the fourth letter, with more blatant suggestions of improper conduct, he declared that it was "absolutely stamped as something doctored up for this case." Mr. Barney explained that the Walkers were of a "different class" from Nina and her family. "There was never a whisper of scandal," he stated. "Something more than surmise must be shown. Home, happiness, character, standing in the community, are serious things at stake for Mr. Walker."

According to James's attorneys, Nina had instigated the divorce suit out of "pure selfishness." With regard to testimony that James had been cold to his wife, Mr. Barney claimed that he had been brought up in an "undemonstrative Puritan style of reserve" and therefore did not give his wife "little attentions" that she would have liked. When she had complained that she needed rest, the Walker family had proposed a solution whereby two of the children would stay with James's mother and one each would stay with his sisters, one of whom was a "suffragette," he hastened to point out. "Whether or not Mr. Walker's course in previously taking the children was wise, it was not cruelty," his attorney explained. "He would agree to anything except the taking of the children to her people." Nina had wanted the children to stay only with her family. Mr. Barney declared, "When she was advised that she could go and take the children, she went. She did not mind taking them from their father." The real complainants, Mr. Barney asserted, were the mother and sisters of the named petitioner. He further claimed, "If the parties could be shut up on a desert island for forty-eight hours, the reconciliation so much to be desired would come."

James's counsel knew that the Walker family name was probably the strongest defense available. Mr. Barney therefore claimed, "One of the most unfortunate circumstances of granting this petition would be the separation of the children from the Walker family, so united, of such social standing, education, and diversified interests." Conversely, he argued, "Petitioner's [Nina's] family is a divided one, separated from their relatives, childless and man-less." Although he did not minimize their mother's love and devotion, he contended that the children and James were also attached to each other. It is notable that Mr. Barney did not refer to James's legal and moral right to obtain custody of his children, which would certainly have been enforced by American courts only shortly prior to this time period. Instead, he appealed to the court's discretion based upon the newer understanding of emotional ties between fathers and children. Mr. Barney referred to the note left for James that had been signed by all the children as a "poor, pitiful round robin which nearly broke Mr. Walker's heart." Mr. Barney closed his case with the following plea:

> If the parties cannot resurrect sufficient affection for each other, and if love of children will not bring them together, they should be told that they cannot leave these children homeless, and all proper pressure of the court should be brought to bear to bring them together. A decision granting this petition is the destruction of all hope of a reconciliation![17]

Following Mr. Barney's impassioned closing for his client, Mr. Sheffield rose to speak for the petitioner. He first stated flatly that for years, the Walker marriage had been an unhappy one, and it was clear who was responsible for this state of affairs: "It is impossible to expect happiness or the proper bringing up of children if the past state of affairs were to be resumed." Mr. Sheffield implored Judge Baker, "The court must act much as a surgeon does. The wife has held the bond of affection together all these years; she has stopped now." In common with Mr. Barney's argument for James, Mr. Sheffield appealed to a more modern concept of marriage. He based his argument for dissolution of the marriage upon the understanding that marriage was now seen as an emotional and companionate bond rather than as a religious or moral pact that must not be broken. It is also important that Mr. Sheffield asserted that a woman had the right to dissolve this union, an argument possible only because wives were no longer viewed as their husbands' property.

Mr. Sheffield then asked the court to compare the evidence given by Nina Walker with that given by James Walker. "Mr. Walker's evidence contradicts itself and he has no explanation to offer," he stated, pointing out that James's claim about when Nina had seen Miss Cochrane's picture was evidently false. Mr. Sheffield then declared, "Mr. Walker himself wrote of atrocities at Charleston. What he wrote was either true, supporting Mrs. Walker's contention it was not a fit place for her, or it was false, and written to keep Mrs. Walker away from there." Furthermore, Mr. Sheffield claimed, there was no evidence to disprove the integrity of the copy that Mrs. Walker had made of Mabel Cochrane's letter, and, he exclaimed, "After such a letter[,] he continues to correspond with Miss Cochrane and visits her clandestinely! He went once in three weeks from Newport to Boston. He was continuing his relations with this woman! The kind of housekeeper he had in Charleston has been demonstrated!"

Nina's attorney continued to catalogue her husband's shortcomings. Lieutenant Walker had not revealed his finances, and his relatives were certainly in no condition to give the children proper care. "They would be brought up prejudiced against their mother, who has given her life for them!" he declared. "Mr. Walker is not a hasty-tempered man—he is a mean-tempered man, a bad-tempered man! The leather thongs on the whip were worn on the ends from his beatings." And, Mr. Sheffield stated, James himself had said that he had noticed no change in the children's attitude toward him since they had left his home.

James's treatment of his wife showed that he had no appreciation for her sacrifices, according to Mr. Sheffield. "If he had been any kind of a man," the attorney stated, "she would have kept the home together. His mother's words of reproof in her letter show what he was; had he heeded her words, this case would never have been brought!" Mr. Sheffield continued:

> Mr. Walker's conduct is not that of an average New England father; any wife worth a sou would resent it. She appealed to him not to scatter the children, and he said that if she opposed him[,] he would have her put in an insane asylum. He said on the stand that was a joke. He is not much of a joker! If given the opportunity, Mr. Walker might take the children out of the court's jurisdiction.[18]

Mr. Sheffield then disparaged opposing counsel's assertions that Nina's family was inferior to her husband's. "Family history!" he exclaimed. "I could have asked questions that would have brought tears to the eyes of the other side!" Mr. Sheffield said he had yet to see any evidence that Mrs. Walker had failed to do all a wife could do and maintained that she had held on fast as long as it had been possible for her to do so. Mr. Walker's character had been shown when he had recounted the Ferguson party to his wife, at a time when she had not been well, and particularly after she had seen the Cochrane letter. "These children need moral training and training which will fit them for a different family life," Sheffield stated, and that moral training must come from their mother. They might visit their father to receive "whatever desirable things he might be able to provide them with in other areas."[19]

Arguments in this particular *Walker v. Walker* trial were thus concluded. It was time for Judge Baker to speak. He talked emotionally about how he had been deeply touched when the Walker children had visited and spoken with him. He believed they were bright and attractive children, which added to his great regret that it would be necessary for him to make a decision in the case. Judge Baker asserted with passion, "This conference has only served to add to my feelings in the case[,] and I advise counsel strongly to use every effort to effect a reconciliation. . . . Mr. and Mrs. Walker know their own feelings and how much they can sacrifice of their personal feelings in the divorce case." He then implored, "If there is any reasonable prospect of reconciliation, it would better be brought about before there is a decision. The parties know if it is possible for them to make some arrangement for a *modus vivendi* [accommodation]. If they cannot agree, then the court must act." At this point, there were many moist eyes among the spectators, who listened silently.[20]

Mr. Barney rose to say that Mr. Walker's side was ready to make any sacrifice. To this claim, Mr. Sheffield responded, "Mrs. Walker's side has always been ready, but Mr. Walker has never made any proposition." According to one journalist present, "No more dramatic plea [had] ever been made in [that] ancient courtroom as when Mr. Barney then pleaded to the judge, 'May our Heavenly Father guide you in deciding this case.' Mr. Sheffield added, 'Amen.'"[21] A very weary Judge Baker looked out at two very tired lawyers and an exhausted petitioner and respondent. At 4:12 P.M., he adjourned the court until 9:30 A.M. the following Monday. Only then was the spectators' silence broken, as they erupted in commentary while exiting the courtroom. The Walker divorce case had been pending for eighteen months, and the most recent hearing had entailed a full ten days of testimony.

James's sisters Fanny and Susan were again taking turns keeping their brother company and helping with the Walker children's visits. On April 4, 1911, Susan left her family and her office in Boston and arrived in Newport, right as Fanny was leaving; she wrote to Richard, "[I had] just time to wave my hand at the back door of my train as hers pulled out." Her letter expressed frustration that there as yet was no decision in the case. Susan said she had reached Cottage #5 three or four minutes after the Walker children had arrived and remarked that they "seemed very glad to see me—especially Elizabeth[,] who has grown very affectionate." She told Richard, "We had a happy afternoon, & how I wish I could have them all at home," corroborating her mother's testimony that she would be willing to keep her brother's children. Susan hoped that Fanny and perhaps her husband, John, would come back to Newport on Friday, as she would have to return to her office. As a postscript, Susan humorously asked her husband, "Did Fan confide to you that Mr. Sheffield had told

Mr. Burwick that he 'could tell him things about FitzGerald—he's a bad egg!'?"[22] This was further evidence that antipathy on Nina's side included the extended Walker family.

Judge Darius Baker waited several weeks, ardently hoping for some kind of reconciliation between Nina and James Walker. When it did not come to pass, he knew the weight of the decision fell on him. Judge Baker took his position seriously and had kept up with the large volumes of essays and studies on the topic of divorce published during the past several years. Margaret Deland's article in the *Atlantic Monthly* just a year before had caused a great deal of discussion regarding the negative societal implications of making divorce widely available. "The purpose of marriage is the protection of the family idea," she had written. "Happiness and marriage may go together; God send they do! But if the incident of happiness is lost, duty remains!"[23] Conversely, several sociologists, including George Howard, Robert Dale Owens, and Franklin Giddings, had made compelling arguments defending divorce as a progressive remediation that would actually raise the standards of home life.[24]

The judge's heart was heavy as he worried about the fate of the Walker children. Young Elizabeth, Grahame, Serrell, and Herbert reminded him of his own five children, now almost all grown. His eldest sons, Hugh and George, had known what it was like to have a broken family, although their situation had been prompted by death, not divorce. Judge Baker ached to think of his own dear Annie, who had died as a young mother only eight years after they had married. He thanked the Lord for his beloved second wife, Bertha, who was such a loving mother to Hugh and George as well as to the children born to her, Dorothy, Alfred, and Margaret. From personal experience, he knew how mothers devoted themselves to their children, and he could not imagine how any man could betray such a woman. Judge Baker was committed to the welfare of children—not just his own but all children in the community. He had worked hard for them as the chairman of the Newport School Committee, a trustee of the Newport Hospital, the president of the Newport Charity Organization Society, and, certainly, as a lawyer and a judge. But what was best for the children in this case? This was a very difficult question. Nevertheless, Judge Baker eventually reached a decision on how he should rule.

8

A Baffling Piece of New Evidence

Spring 1911 to December 1912

"We've heard from the court—and it's not good" was the curt phone message Clark Burdick delivered to James Walker on April 25, 1911. The weather had warmed up in Newport, and it was a pleasant spring day, but James did not notice as he rushed to Thames Street and climbed the stairs to the law offices of Burdick and Macleod. It had been agony waiting several weeks to hear this verdict. When James arrived, Mr. Burdick told him bluntly, "Judge Baker has granted Mrs. Walker a divorce for separate maintenance on the grounds of adultery." James felt his stomach plummet. He was almost glad that his father was already dead. What would the old admiral have said? Here was James causing a public scandal again—dragging the family name through the papers, just like the time with that bastard John Dougherty from the Jewell Filtration Company, who had dared to challenge him in Charleston. Well, James had been proven right in that matter, and he would fight to prove himself right in this case as well.

James asked in agitation, "On what basis did he find adultery?" and then impatiently declared, "I must see that!" as he jerked the court document from his attorney's hands, almost tearing it. He scanned to that part of the decision, where he was appalled to read the following:

> The evidence offered as to adultery in this case is as usual circumstantial. Circumstantial evidence of adultery is said to consist of

three elements—the opportunity, the adulterous intent of the defendant[,] and a similar intent on the part of his paramour—and unless all three of those elements are established[,] adultery cannot be inferred from the evidence.

As in the legal test of the sufficiency of such evidence as to adultery, the rule is as follows. The only general rule that can be laid down upon the subject is that the circumstance must be such as to lead the guarded discretion of a reasonable and just man to the conclusion.[1]

"A reasonable and just man," James mused irritably and then scanned what came next. Mr. Burdick decided that his best option at this point was to let James read the words for himself:

In weighing the evidence and consideration of the facts and circumstances reasonably capable of two interpretations into giving them an evil rather than an innocent one . . . [, c]ircumstances must be considered separately and as a whole. The single threads of circumstances may be weak, but united they often lead with assured conviction to the adultery which is the subject of the investigation.

The doctrine is now generally approved that in a civil action where the issue is a criminal offence, the plaintiff is not required to establish the adulterous act beyond a reasonable doubt. It is sufficient to establish the cause of action by preponderance of evidence.[2]

"What is all this legal double talk?" thought James. "Why not just come out with it?" He breathlessly read further:

There can be no doubt that there were numerous opportunities to commit adultery—for example, for two or three weeks in 1902[,] from July 1903 to February 1904, in the summer of 1904, and later on occasional visits by the respondent to Boston down to sometime in 1909.[3]

At this point, James was so inflamed that he was no longer able to read. He threw the official paper on the floor and began pacing around the lawyer's office. Mr. Burdick took this opportunity to retrieve the rescript and continue reading the decision:

The respondent in 1901 was an officer in the Navy, descended on the part of both parents from families of social prominence and public distinction. All that appears as to Miss Cochrane at that time is that she was a waitress in the restaurant in the North Station in Boston. No criticism of her is made on that account. If that was the best way offered for supporting herself, it is to her credit that she accepted it. It is obvious, however, from her employment and from the references to other members of her family in her letters, and from the evidence as to her later employment and mode of life, that her social position was so far removed from that of the respondent as to render any association or intimacy on their part of a personal nature the subject of comment if not of inquiry, particularly in view of the fact of the respondent's marriage.[4]

"I simply befriended her!" James cried out. Mr. Burdick looked askance at James and continued to read:

At that time he was 32 years old; Miss Cochrane was considerably younger and is described as pretty or good looking. Their acquaintance thus casually and informally begun in the restaurant progressed so far that Miss Cochrane enlisted the respondent's sympathy and active effort in securing employment for her younger brother. When ordered to Charleston, S.C.[,] early in 1902, the respondent early obtained a place in his office for said brother. The young man came down in the summer of that year accompanied by his sister, who remained as a guest of the respondent two or three weeks, Mrs. Walker being absent in the mountains in North Carolina.[5]

Mr. Burdick paused to let out a sigh. He hated to agree with Judge Darius Baker, but the circumstantial evidence was damning. While his client continued to pace around the room, silent except for the sound of gnashing his teeth, Mr. Burdick continued to read in search of a basis for appeal:

After Mrs. Walker had gone north with the children, in 1903, the respondent had Miss Cochrane come from Boston to Charleston as his housekeeper, although she had no previous experience as such to his knowledge, and remained until April, 1904, acting, it is said, as his housekeeper in the city in the summer of 1903, being boarded by him in the fall until his house in the Navy yard was ready for occupancy in the winter of 1903 and 1904, when she again acted as housekeeper until the arrival of Mrs. Walker in February, 1904, who then saw her for the first time and recognized her as the original of a photograph sent to her husband, as Mrs. Walker says, [in] the latter part of 1902 or early in 1903.⁶

In another part of town, Nina Walker's attorney was sharing the good news with his client, who had come to his office accompanied by her mother and sister. William Sheffield had just finished reading the first part of the court's decision to the women and had gotten as far as Nina's recognition of Mabel Cochrane's photograph. Reading further, he was pleased to see that considerable space in the rescript was devoted to an appraisal of Miss Cochrane's letters to Mr. Walker and how the judge had determined their authenticity. He looked up and saw all three women staring intently at him. He continued:

> In January 1905, Mrs. Walker intercepted and opened a letter from Miss Cochrane to her husband of which she says Exhibit B is a copy. Exhibit B is similar in some respects to the two original letters of Miss Cochrane, though it is unmistakably more ardent in tone and more compromising. Mrs. Walker testified that she gave a copy of the letter to Dr. Alsop, the clergyman who officiated at her marriage and at the christening of some of her children, and upon the advice of the latter sent a copy to Admiral Walker.⁷

Pausing for breath, Mr. Sheffield read further:

> It is difficult to see how the petitioner could have had time to have made a copy of the original letter if the respondent's account of its delivery by mail orderly is correct. So far as appears the petitioner had no reason at the time of the trial to suppose that the copy sent to Admiral Walker was not in existence, although, as a matter of fact, it is probable that it was destroyed in 1905. It seems to the court that the suggestion that the petitioner has in Exhibit B presented an expanded and embellished copy of Miss Cochrane's letter is an improbable one in the circumstance of the case. It is more reasonable to infer that the mother and sister of the respondent are mistaken in their recollections as to the contents of the copy seen by them, and to accept said exhibit at least as a substantial if not carefully compared copy of the letter in question, than it would be to adopt the suggestion of alteration and fabrication in relation to [E]xhibit B on the part of the petitioner.⁸

Mr. Sheffield glanced up at Nina, whose eyes did not flinch. After a few moments of silence, her sister, Bertha, requested, "Please continue reading." The attorney found his place and went on:

> The evidence further shows that Miss Cochrane had rooms for four years ending January 1, 1910, in the lodging house of Mr. Crapo, in Boston. Mr. Crapo testifies that he admitted the respondent in Miss Cochrane's room in his home from 10 to 15 times, always in the day time, on one occasion at least when Miss Cochrane had just arisen from her bed in her night clothes to receive him; that he knew the respondent from Miss Cochrane's designation of him only as "the doctor." The respondent admits that he called upon Miss Cochrane at Mr. Crapo's three times, twice to get evidence in this case and once as a friendly call. Once he says she was in a wrapper cleaning her room, but was never in her night clothes. He says that Mr. Crapo admitted him on these occasions. In view of this admission, the respondent's testimony that Mr. Crapo saw him at the Perry House in Newport, while the trial was in progress in which he was a witness [yet] gave no sign that he recognized the respondent seems unimportant.[9]

Elated, Mr. Sheffield delivered the judge's opinion:

> Respondent denies the commission of adultery with Miss Cochrane. She was not a witness. The various matters hereinbefore referred to, together with the other evidence in the case showing the relations of the respondent and Miss Cochrane, afford the means of judging as to their adulterous intent, the one as to the other, and lead me to a strong and abiding conviction that they have sustained adulterous relations with each other and that in all probability such relations extended over a long period of time.[10]

Mr. Burdick did not raise his eyes from the trial rescript and stated to James in a tone that was a little too enthusiastic, "Could have been worse. . . . [C]ould have been worse. . . . [T]he judge found no basis for the charge of extreme cruelty and refuses even to discuss the alleged gross misbehavior and wickedness."[11] At this point, Mr. Burdick needed to take a sip from the glass on his desk.

In his office, Mr. Sheffield paused to explain to the women that the judge did not accept the argument of "condonation" in James's defense, which would have meant that Nina had previously forgiven or condoned his acts of infidelity. Even if it had been proven that James had engaged in behavior that justified divorce, if Nina had previously known about it and pardoned it, she might have waived the right to obtain a divorce on that basis. The judge stated that even though the question of condonation of adultery was not raised or discussed by the respondent, he determined that there could be no condonation by the petitioner, because there had been no admission of guilt by the respondent. Furthermore, since it had not been proven that the petitioner had known of her husband's visits to Miss Cochrane, she could not have condoned them.[12]

Mr. Sheffield continued reading the judge's decision aloud to Nina, her mother, and sister. He paused, slowed his pace, and raised his voice as he read the last line:

> My decision is therefore, for the petitioner, on the ground of adultery.[13]

The attorney looked triumphantly up at the three women. Bertha's eyebrows were raised, Nina nodded her head slowly, and her mother, Virginia Chinn, exclaimed, "This calls for some sherry!"

At the same point in his reading of the verdict, Mr. Burdick's voice dropped somewhat as he continued, "Mrs. Walker has been given custody of the children and separate maintenance of three hundred dollars a month—but," the attorney's tone brightened somewhat, "the judge leaves the way open for further discussion on these points upon entering the decree six months hence."[14] Mr. Burdick considerately did not explain that Judge Baker had determined custody partially on the basis of his conversations with the Walker children regarding their feelings for each parent. He also kindly neglected to mention an article he might have read about a New York Supreme Court decision that had stripped a father of all custody rights to his son following his divorced wife's remarriage.[15] Mr. Burdick paused to reflect on the fact that, earlier in his law career, the common-law maxim had usually been followed in custody cases, providing that "the natural right is with the father, unless the father is somehow unfit."[16] Although there had not been much change in legislative custody rights, he had noted an increasing tendency among judges to award custody to mothers.[17]

It was inconceivable to James that Nina could not only leave but also keep the children with her. His mother had assured him that would not happen. Although he had never actually been to war, James considered himself a military man whose passions were aroused by what seemed to him a just cause. He was determined to continue the struggle to get his children back. They were his legacy, and Nina should not win them as bounty. He must also clear his name. Under Rhode Island law, adultery was not just a personal matter between husband and wife—it was also a statutory offense. In addition, it was a military violation. To accuse him of such a crime—and after he had gone to such extremes to be careful! Despite Nina's declarations that she adored and admired him, he had always suspected that she had married him merely to secure her position in society. Adultery! If he had committed adultery, it would have been her fault. Since the birth of little Herbert, she had refused to even lie beside him. He should have had her locked away years earlier! Yet he had learned in recent years that he could not let his emotions get the better of him. He had to control his anger so that he could fight back. A plan began to form in his mind. "What if," James stated slowly and deliberately as he looked his solicitor directly in the eyes, "what if I could prove beyond doubt I did not commit adultery with Mabel Cochrane?"

On Monday, May 8, 1911, the U.S. Navy announced the official birth of naval aviation. It was a great day for the navy, but not for Lieutenant James Walker. On that day, Nina Walker's attorneys filed a support petition on her behalf in the Rhode Island Superior Court in Newport. They asked that James be required to pay a reasonable allowance for his wife's support and for the education, maintenance, and support of their children, pending determination of her request for separate maintenance as terms of her divorce from bed and board. They also requested that Mrs. Walker be granted funds for attorney fees.[18] "They are ordering me to support the enemy!" James furiously remarked to his attorneys. He was certainly not going to take this latest assault lying down. The temerity of Nina's asking for half of his income! If she wanted to live comfortably and send the children to those fancy schools, she could damn well withdraw her petition for divorce. At the support petition hearing on June 10, Lieutenant Walker testified that he was not able to pay the allowance requested by his wife because his expenses were now as high as they had been during his marriage. He stated that, as an officer, "the unwritten law of the Navy" demanded that he maintain a certain social standard. Judge Baker dryly remarked, "The civil law is not concerned with, nor does it recognize[,] any unwritten law"[19] and ordered James Walker to pay $300 per month to Nina Walker, "the first payment to be made before the 5th day of July, 1911, and said sum to be paid on or before the 5th day of every month thereafter."[20]

Meanwhile, the wheels were in motion to lay the foundation for a new trial for James. It was decided that James's two married sisters, Fanny Pickering Walker Thomas and Susan Grimes Walker FitzGerald, would be the most appropriate family members to make arrangements with Mabel Cochrane regarding this sensitive issue. Neither of them had met Mabel previously, but their mother had entertained her as a guest at her house at Washington, DC, and thought that, although her letters to James had proven very unwise, she was an agreeable young woman who was eager to please. She should be willing to testify on James's behalf not only because she was indebted to him for her brother's position in the navy but also because by clearing his name, she would clear her own. The sisters conferred and determined that offering Mabel an examination by a woman physician would be an acceptable option.

Susan was acquainted with a woman physician whom she admired named Sarah Ellen Palmer. Dr. Palmer was from Exeter, New Hampshire, and had graduated from the Woman's Medical College of Pennsylvania in Philadelphia in 1880. She had obtained advanced medical training at Johns Hopkins Hospital and in France and Germany as well. Dr. Palmer was the first woman to be accepted to the Harvard Medical School Laboratory Graduate Course in Bacteriology, and as a result of her successful completion of that program, it was opened to other women. She had inaugurated the surgical service at the New England Hospital for Women and Children in 1900. Dr. Palmer had also worked at the dispensary for the Woman's Charity Club Hospital, where she had probably met Susan Walker FitzGerald through her charity work with women. They shared support for women's suffrage. By the time Susan Walker FitzGerald met her, Dr. Palmer had an established private practice, specializing in medicine for women, on Beacon Street in Boston.[21]

Fanny, James's older sister, might have asked her physician husband, Dr. John Jenks Thomas, about a woman physician, and he had recommended Emma B. Culbertson. Or, Dr. Palmer might have suggested Dr. Culbertson. She had received her A.B. from Vassar in 1877 and had been awarded an M.D. the same year from the Woman's Medical College of Pennsylvania, where she may have first crossed paths with Sarah Ellen Palmer. She was an attending surgeon at the New England Hospital for Women and Children and the Boston Dispensary. Dr. Culbertson was the first woman admitted to the American Academy of Medicine and became vice president of that organization. She was also an outspoken suffragist and reportedly lived in an intimate relationship with her mentor, Dr. Mary Smith.[22] Among her writings is an article in which she describes medicine as a rewarding career for women and the important role of women physicians in "sociological progress." Her final sentence in that essay is "And, when, in addition to easing pain and restoring health, one is constantly able to counteract, or to prevent, moral degradation and error, life becomes gloriously worth living."[23] Dr. Sarah Ellen Palmer and Dr. Emma B. Culbertson probably knew each other well and had worked together in the past. A good plan seemed to be to have first Dr. Palmer and then Dr. Culbertson exam Mabel so that they could corroborate each other's findings.

In the late afternoon of May 23, 1911, Mabel Cochrane arrived at her apartment on Columbus Street in Boston. Susan FitzGerald, James's sister, had come to fetch her, and they had taken a hackney carriage to Dr. Palmer's office downtown. Mrs. FitzGerald had first visited Mabel the week before. Although Mabel could tell she was every inch a lady, Mrs. FitzGerald was down to earth and had told Mabel to call her Susan. She was highly refined, but she knew what it was to work for a living—she had told Mabel that she had to support her family when her husband was sick and that she was still working at a real job. Mrs. FitzGerald had told Mabel she felt bad about the way the newspapers talked about her. She had offered her the opportunity to make everyone, including Mrs. Nina Walker, see that Mabel was a respectable woman. Mabel was not naïve; she knew that Mrs. FitzGerald's real mission was to help her brother James. That was OK with Mabel; she believed in family support, and she had done everything she could to help her own brother Jack get a job with the navy. Mabel also noted appreciatively that Mrs. FitzGerald had excellent taste in hats, marking a woman of good standing.

Dr. Palmer greeted Mrs. FitzGerald and Mabel in her office at 484 Beacon Street in Boston. She was tall, slim, and straight-backed and looked to be in her fifties.[24] Mr. Walker's youngest sister, Sallie, was there with her friend Helen Hull, whom Mabel had met when she stayed at the admiral's house in Washington. They said hello and then left.

It pinched some when Dr. Palmer inserted the instrument into Mabel's lower part, but she could tell that the doctor was trying to be gentle. Dr. Palmer kept asking softly whether Mabel felt any pain, and she tried to make it hurt less if Mabel answered that she did. At the end of the examination, Dr. Palmer said to Mabel, "I knew you were a decent girl," and that made Mabel feel good. When Dr. Culbertson came into the room, Mabel knew more what to expect. Dr. Culbertson was also fairly gentle, considering what she had to do, and she patted Mabel's shoulder when it was over. After Mabel left the examination room, Mrs. FitzGerald was right outside the door and put her arm around her. The hackney carriage was waiting on Beacon Street, and Mrs. FitzGerald put her into it with what felt like might have been a hug. Only later, when Mabel was back in her apartment on Columbus Street, did she ponder, "I wonder whether Mrs. FitzGerald would have asked her younger sister, Sallie, to have that exam."

By the deadline of December 15, 1911, Lieutenant Walker's attorneys had filed their full bill of exceptions to Judge Baker's decision that James was guilty of adultery. This written statement described and objected to certain points of law determined by the judge. It began with general statements that Judge Darius Baker's decision was "against the law" and "against the evidence."[25] Walker's attorneys then made more specific objections, including that the judge had erred in admitting, without qualification, letters from Mabel Cochrane that he had at first admitted *de bene* (provisionally).[26]

As they had done at trial, James's attorneys again objected to the wording of the question that had been posed to two of the physician experts, George Ramsay and William A. Sherman, which had included the phrase "that at times pus was visible and the urine cloudy and at other times clear." The attorneys again insisted that the phrase "at times the urine was comparatively clear" should have been substituted before asking the doctors, "From what disease would you say he was suffering?" This objection had been overruled at trial, and the witnesses had been instructed to answer the original question. The precise wording of this question posed to the medical witnesses was a crucial point, since one phrasing might point to a diagnosis of gonorrhea, while the other might imply a more benign condition. It was important for James's attorneys to prove that he had not knowingly communicated a sexually transmitted disease to his wife. Opposing counsel had undoubtedly read an article in the *American Law Review* indicating that a defendant in a divorce case who had knowingly communicated a venereal disease to an unsuspecting spouse could be found guilty of cruelty.[27]

Following several other points covered in the bill of exceptions, James's attorneys objected to the judge's exclusion of Mrs. Eliza Ripley's deposition regarding Nina Walker's family history. They had hoped to use evidence from her testimony as proof of a hereditary tendency to divorce. The last several exceptions, numbers 14, 15, and 16, related to the judge's exclusion of testimony regarding Lieutenant Walker's personal reputation and that of the Walker family, which his attorneys had attempted to insert into evidence to prove his integrity.[28]

In addition to filing a bill of exceptions to Judge Baker's decision against their client, James's attorneys also took more aggressive action. On Wednesday, March 13, 1912, as their client looked on, they appeared before the Rhode Island Supreme Court in Providence and petitioned to completely reopen the divorce case that had been decided against him the previous April. The chief ground for a retrial was that Lieutenant Walker had new evidence to present. Nina's counsel argued that any evidence should have been included in the original hearing of the case.[29] However, the following day, the Rhode Island Supreme Court announced that James would be allowed to file a motion for a new trial with the superior court.

Wasting little time, James's attorney Walter H. Barney appeared in Newport Superior Court on March 21 to file the formal motion for a retrial. In it, James's attorneys claimed, "He has discovered new and material evidence . . . which he had not discovered at the time of the trial . . . and which he could not, with reasonable diligence, have discovered at any time previous to the trial."[30] The respondent's defense team presented affidavits taken from Mabel B. Cochrane, Sarah E. Palmer, and Emma B. Culbertson.[31] Mabel Cochrane, of course, was the woman named as a corespondent in the divorce case brought by Nina Walker, as Mr. Sheffield and Mr. Harvey knew well. But who on earth, they wondered, were the other two women?

They soon found out that the unexpected witnesses were women who had obtained medical degrees at a time when it was an extraordinary accomplishment for persons of their sex. The supreme court's opinion referred to the "affidavits of two physicians, apparently of good standing in their profession and having extensive experience in the surgical and medical questions involved," who "had made a physical examination of the genital organ of said Mabel Cochrane and as a result of said examination they were of the opinion that the said Mabel Cochrane had never had sexual intercourse or suffered from any disease, inflammation[,] or infection of the genitourinary organ." Furthermore, "the decision of the Superior Court to grant Nina Walker a divorce based on her husband's adultery was based entirely on circumstantial evidence, whereas the affidavits of the physicians are based on a physical examination of the person of said Mabel Cochrane." The supreme court's decision concluded, "[If] said Mabel Cochrane is a virgin[,] it is manifest that justice requires a revision of the case; that is, that the judge who tried the case and reached a certain conclusion upon the evidence then submitted to him, should have the opportunity to reexamine the same with the additional light that may be thrown thereon by the newly discovered evidence."[32]

As soon as Mr. Sheffield and Mr. Harvey recovered from their astonishment, they filed their own legal motion to oppose a new trial on grounds that proof of Miss Cochrane's virginity should have been produced at the time of the previous trial. Lieutenant James W. G. Walker requested, and in April 1912 was granted, four months' leave from the naval training station at Narragansett Bay, Rhode Island.[33] His main occupation for that period of time was a campaign to reverse the previous divorce decision and to clear his name and gain custody of his children.

Since the Rhode Island Supreme Court had ruled that James Walker was entitled to a new trial with the same judge, on May 12, his attorneys appeared before Superior Court Judge Darius Baker with their petition to reopen the divorce proceedings that had been decided more than a year before in favor of Nina Walker.[34] On May 29, Judge Baker responded in writing. Notwithstanding Nina's objections that there was "lack of due diligence on the part of the respondent in procuring at the trial the evidence relating to the virginity of Mabel Cochrane,"[35] the judge decided in favor of reopening the case. Whatever his own opinion, he stated, the supreme court had passed on the question of due diligence by granting the motion for a new trial in superior court. However, Judge Baker imposed "certain conditions and restrictions."[36]

The judge explained that, although she had known before the trial that she was named as a co-respondent, Miss Cochrane had refused to give testimony. Then, inexplicably, only four weeks after the decision in that trial, she had "submitted herself to a physical examination by two physicians, apparently selected by herself or by the respondent, to determine whether or not she be a virgin."[37] Consequently, justice would not be done to both sides to reopen the case and limit the determination of Mabel Cochrane's virginity to rely solely on the testimony of Dr. Palmer and Dr. Culbertson. Whether Judge Baker was dubious regarding the skill of the women doctors or suspicious of their motives was not stated. To reopen the case, he insisted on receiving evidence from additional physicians. As a preliminary condition for retrial, the judge required that, within thirty days, Mabel Cochrane must submit to a physical examination by two additional physicians—gynecologists "of recognized standing and experience in the profession."[38] These medical experts would be selected by or for Nina Walker, the petitioner. If this condition were met, the case would be assigned for retrial. However, the only evidence to be presented at a new trial would be proof of whether Miss Cochrane was a virgin. Furthermore, the judge would require oral testimony from all the physicians involved as well as from Mabel Cochrane herself.

James Walker notified the court on June 5, 1912, that he would contest Judge Baker's conditions for retrial by prosecuting yet another bill of exceptions to the Supreme Court of Rhode Island.[39] Walker's attorneys hoped the supreme court would once more rule in his favor. The new bill of exceptions, filed by the July 15 deadline, argued that Judge Baker's most recent decision "was contrary to the law and the evidence."[40] It specified that the precondition for retrial of further physical examination of Mabel Cochrane was contrary to the law, because "the conditions and restrictions imposed were not reasonable conditions and restrictions."[41] This bill of exceptions furthermore stated that Judge Baker's decision on the motion for a new trial was "contrary to the law in that it does not lie in the power of the respondent to comply with the conditions imposed."[42] The original December 11, 1911, bill of exceptions to the divorce case was attached to the new bill and filed once again. In a handwritten note, Judge Baker stated that he would allow both bills of exceptions to be heard.[43]

On June 27, 1912, James's attorneys again put forth a motion for reduction of the allowance that he had been ordered to be paid to his estranged wife and their children. They claimed that, since the court had ordered James to pay Nina a monthly allowance of $300, his economic circumstances had changed, and his income was so reduced due to his leave from the navy that it would be "impossible to comply with said order."[44] His attorneys therefore moved that "said order be modified[,] reducing the amount to be paid in accordance with the reduction in his income."[45] A hearing on the reduction of allowance was held on Friday, August 2, 1912. The following day, Justice George J. Brown issued an "order of the bench" to decrease the respondent's payment to the petitioner from $300 per month to $250 per month for the support of Nina and the children. Those payments were to be paid on the fifth day of each month, beginning on September 5, 1912.[46]

Nina's sister-in-law Susan argued for women's suffrage in her speech on August 15, 1912, in a pavilion on the beach in Newport, at a meeting promoted by society woman Mrs. Alva Belmont, the wife of Oliver Hazard Perry Belmont. It was the largest suffrage meeting held in Newport up until that time. Although there was no contact between Nina and Susan, Nina read about the speech in the paper and found it "interesting but far from convincing."[47] Comparable to how Susan Walker FitzGerald did not see the connection between her sister-in-law's personal plight and women's general lack of power, Nina did not relate her own tenuous marital position to support for the political rights of women. She was adamantly opposed to women's suffrage.

On Friday, November 29, 1912, the Rhode Island Supreme Court heard arguments on Lieutenant Walker's objections to the preconditions imposed on him by Judge Baker for retrial. The principal objection was to the precondition requiring additional physical examinations of Mabel Cochrane, which, his attorneys argued, was "unjust and unreasonable and not according to law." Attorneys for Nina Walker again maintained that the conditions imposed by Judge Baker were indeed just, particularly since it was the respondent who had raised the issue of Miss Cochrane's virginity. The court withheld its decision pending further deliberation.[48]

After his leave from the U.S. Navy ended, Lieutenant James Walker requested to be stationed close to Rhode Island so it would be convenient for him to take part in the divorce proceedings. Instead, he was ordered to report for duty in Guam.[49] Apparently, the deceased admiral's naval connections did not work this time. James resigned his naval commission as of December 2, 1912.[50] Former Lieutenant Commander James W. G. Walker prepared to accelerate the battle against his wife.

John Grimes Walker family. *Front row:* Admiral John Grimes Walker and Rebecca White Pickering Walker. *Middle row:* Susan Grimes Walker (?), Henry Pickering Walker, and Sarah Cochrane Walker (?). *Back row:* James Wilson Grimes Walker and Frances Pickering Walker (?). (From the collection of Henry Pickering Walker Jr.)

Nina Chinn and James Wilson Grimes Walker (holding hands); Bertha Chinn (standing by a tree), 1895. (Scrapbook photograph provided by Cindy Iverson.)

Nina Chinn Walker.
(Scrapbook photograph provided by Cindy Iverson.)

Lieutenant Commander James Wilson Grimes Walker.
(From the collection of Elizabeth Walker Davis.)

Admiral John Grimes Walker. (From the collection of Elizabeth Walker Davis.)

Rebecca White Pickering Walker, May 1898. (From the collection of Henry Pickering Walker Jr.)

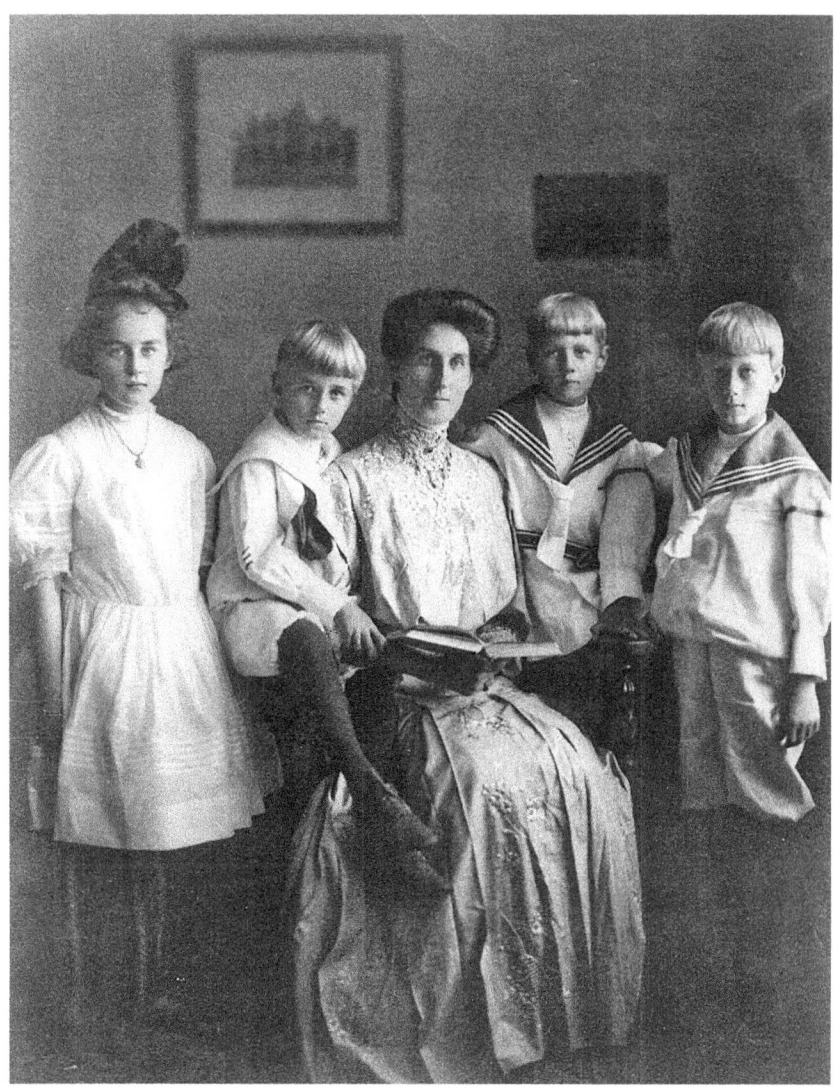

Nina Chinn Walker surrounded by her children: *Left to right:* Elizabeth Grimes Walker, Herbert Wood Walker, Nina Chinn Walker, Robert Serrell Wood Walker, and John Grahame Walker. (From the collections of Elizabeth Walker Davis and Herbert Wood Walker Jr.)

Lieutenant Commander James Wilson Grimes Walker in later life. (Stickney-Barton Collection, Brownfield [Maine] Historical Society.)

James Wilson Grimes Walker on a horse in Brownfield, Maine. (Brownfield [Maine] Historical Society.)

James Wilson Grimes Walker in later life, with one of his dogs. (Brownfield [Maine] Historical Society.)

Side view of James Wilson Grimes Walker's barn in Brownfield, Maine (as it looked in October 2014). (By C. Thomas Arrington.)

Front view of James Wilson Grimes Walker's barn in Brownfield, Maine (as it looked in October 2014). (By C. Thomas Arrington.)

Walker family graves in Mount Auburn Cemetery
in Cambridge, Massachusetts.
Left to right: James Wilson Grimes Walker, Sarah Cochrane Walker,
John Jenks Thomas and Frances Pickering Walker,
Elizabeth ("Bessie") Grimes Walker (who died in childhood),
and Alice Pickering Walker (who died in infancy).
(By C. Thomas Arrington.)

9

More Trials and Tribulations

January 1913 to November 12, 1913

THE YEAR 1913 opened with the Rhode Island Supreme Court still deliberating James Walker's request for a retrial without preconditions. Nina Walker would later write that the years of waiting for one legal decision after another were years of darkness:

> "Darkness is the time for making roots and establishing plants, whether of the soil or of the soul" and during the darkness I grew to full woman hood, accepting the burdens, dedicating my life to my children and God's plan for me as far as I could discern it[;] I groped through the following years dropping one by one my illusions and strove for the real purpose of life. My children were my daily inspiration and they comforted me. Our egotism in youth often leads us to look upon our lot as the hardest, yet God has compassion on us[;] time softens sorrow and we rally the stronger from each lesson learned.[1]

James and his family were also frustrated with the slow-moving Rhode Island court system. They were anxious for him to restore his reputation and gain custody of his children. Finally convinced that his wife would never come back to him, James decided that he would gain the upper hand by turning the tables on her. After moving to Maine, he retained legal counsel with Symonds, Snow, Cook and Hutchinson, a large Portland firm with many railroads and business corporations as clients.[2] On February 11,

1913, Nina opened the door to her new residence on Kay Street in Newport to receive a batch of legal papers addressed to her from the state of Maine. She was served with a divorce complaint charging her with desertion. A hearing was set for the superior court in Paris, Maine, on March 11.[3]

James Wilson Grimes Walker was now a resident of Brownfield, Maine, living on a farm that included the largest barn in the state. The barn had been built in 1908 to breed Jersey cows.[4] Through a series of individual purchases, James's family secured for him an impressive piece of real estate. On August 29, 1910, his mother, Rebecca Walker, had first acquired fifty-five acres and the buildings on them from Herbert E. Cook. This property stretched from Brownfield Center to South Conway on one end and to the New Hampshire state line on the other.[5] Then, Richard Y. FitzGerald had purchased a parcel of land in Brownfield from Albert E. Young on January 14, 1911,[6] which he had then sold to his mother-in-law, Rebecca Walker, on June 12, 1912.[7] On January 8, 1912, Rebecca Walker had purchased more property in Brownfield from Hollis R. Cole,[8] and on January 13, she had bought an adjacent lot from William S. Johnson and Wirt V. Eaton, who had acquired it only the previous June.[9]

Rebecca Walker was living in Hamilton, on the north shore of Massachusetts, at the time. Her son occupied the land she owned in Maine from 1912 until 1942, although he did not officially purchase it from her until December 23, 1919.[10] Consequently, during the course of the divorce hearings, James could truthfully claim that he did not own any property. His status as a Maine resident, however, enabled him to file suit as a petitioner in that state, with his wife as respondent. To his wife, James's resignation of his navy commission and his move to Maine were appalling. She would later write in her unpublished autobiography:

> On December 2, 1912[,] my husband resigned his commission in the Navy after fourteen years of service[;] he bought a farm on the border of New Hampshire and Maine with the purpose of carrying the divorce suit into both states if necessary. To avoid giving alimony he turned his small inheritance of $10,000 (ten thousand) dollars over to his mother and gave up his life insurance policy of another ten thousand. A dreary life on a remote and ill kept farm he exchanged for home and children and a useful life in the Service. . . . [T]he educational advantages given my husband in this country and Europe he let die in embryo.[11]

At the March 11, 1913, hearing in the superior court in Paris, Maine, James Walker's attorneys presented evidence that his wife had lived with him in Kittery, Maine, at the Portsmouth Naval Station. On October 19, 1909, the divorce petition alleged, Nina had "utterly deserted him" and had continued that desertion up to the filing of his Maine divorce petition on January 27, 1913. James Walker also charged Nina with "cruel and abusive treatment" toward him. He claimed that he had resided in Brownfield, in Oxford County, Maine, for more than a year prior to filing his suit and thus had legal standing in the state.

With her family's assistance, Nina retained the politically influential Portland legal firm of Payson and Virgin and an additional Portland attorney, Eben Winthrop Freeman, to represent her in Maine.[12] They filed a motion with the superior court for Oxford County, Maine, arguing to dismiss the case on grounds that the Maine court did not have jurisdiction because neither party had resided in the state during the alleged causes for divorce. They also filed a separate legal motion maintaining that, even if the court did have jurisdiction, there was no legal basis for a divorce suit by Mr. Walker against his wife. No testimony was presented, and the case was sent to the supreme judicial court in Portland, Maine, to determine its legal status.[13]

On March 20, Walter Barney, still representing James Walker in Rhode Island, presented a petition to Judge Chester W. Barrows of the Rhode Island Superior Court, asking for a considerable reduction of the $250-per-month alimony that his client had most recently been ordered to pay for the support of his wife and children. The previous August, this monthly support order had been reduced from $300. Mr. Barney pleaded that the court had originally ordered Mr. Walker to pay his wife [more than] "$3,000 a year, a great deal more than one half the income of the man," which had created financial difficulties for him. "Under the strain of it all," Mr. Barney claimed, Mr. Walker was forced to resign from the navy, which had greatly reduced his income. Claiming that Mr. Walker's current income was less than $1,000 a year, he argued, "Prompt relief is called for." Mr. Barney and his co-counsel, Clark Burdick, proposed to offer depositions in support of their argument and asked for an immediate hearing on the matter.[14]

William Sheffield, one of Nina's Rhode Island attorneys, responded that Mr. Walker "has turned his back on the Rhode Island court, where decision has already been made against him[,] and begun proceedings in Maine." Mr. Barney replied that Mr. Walker was never a legal resident of Rhode Island and believed that he had the right to an absolute divorce rather than simply the divorce from bed and board that had been granted to his wife in that state. Instead of obtaining residence in Rhode Island so that he could bring a case against his wife there, he had gone to Maine, where he intended to live, and filed his case there. Mr. Barney stated that Judge Darius Baker would grant a new trial in Rhode Island only if Mr. Walker met "impossible conditions," and exceptions to this ruling were now being determined by the Rhode Island Supreme Court.[15] Judge Barrows set a hearing on the alimony matter. Since Mr. Barney indicated that Rebecca Walker could not possibly come to court to testify, Sheffield and his partner, William R. Harvey, requested permission from the court to take her deposition.[16]

Judge Barrows announced the Rhode Island Superior Court opinion regarding alimony reduction on May 8. He stated that there was no question that James Walker no longer received $3,900 of his previous aggregate income of $6,800, because he had resigned as an officer in the U.S. Navy. Despite "insinuations" made in the case that this resignation was for the purpose of avoiding the payment of the court-ordered allowance, there was no testimony to that effect. The evidence showed that Walker had resigned "because of certain probabilities of service in foreign lands and conditions of health which he believed made it imperative that he should do so." Judge Barrows noted that, although James Walker was only forty-four years old, his attorneys claimed that, due to his specific naval training and experience, he would be unable to earn a decent income as a civil engineer in civilian life. "He is somewhat broken down nervously by reason of continued and bitter litigation in this case, but other than that his physical health is not shown to have been impaired," wrote Barrows,[17] intimating that perhaps James Walker could find employment in the future.

Judge Barrows found Rebecca Walker's deposition and her son's affidavit "very unsatisfactory," because they failed to make a "full and fair disclosure" of what property he owned. The judge suspected that Mr. Walker, or someone acting on his behalf, must have access to several thousand dollars, because James admitted to receiving a yearly income of at least $800 accrued from his investments. In addition, Mr. Walker received $1,200 a year from his father's estate, and upon the death of his mother, he would receive more. The judge found it "inconceivable that he is ignorant, to the extent that he would have it appear, of what his property consists, and the Court, therefore[,] is not disposed to go to the extent that it might in cutting down this allowance had a full and fair disclosure been made." Despite the fact that James Walker had not fully disclosed his assets, Judge Barrows stated that it was undoubtedly true that his navy income had been "absolutely cut off since the former support order was made, and there was nothing to show what, if any portion, of it can be earned by respondent."

The judge therefore reduced James Walker's support obligation to Nina Walker and her four children from $250 to $150 per month, with the provision that she could ask for a revision of this amount if her husband's property or earnings increased.[18]

At long last, on June 2, 1913, the Rhode Island Supreme Court reached a decision in James Walker's appeal to Judge Baker's preconditions for a retrial in superior court. The most important of these was the requirement for a physical examination of Mabel Cochrane by two physicians chosen by Nina Walker. Attorneys for Mr. Walker had objected that the preconditions were unjust and illegal and that it was not in Mr. Walker's power to comply with them. The court ruled in his favor, announcing, "We are of the opinion that said conditions and restrictions in some particulars were not reasonable and that said exceptions should be sustained." Nina Walker had submitted sworn statements from her own medical witnesses disputing whether a physical examination could determine a woman's virginity. However, the supreme court concluded that this issue could only be decided properly in a trial, with the opportunity for cross-examination. Judge Darius Baker was now a Rhode Island Supreme Court justice and therefore unavailable to retry the Walker case in superior court.[19] Since a new superior court judge would preside over the case to reexamine previous evidence in light of new information, the supreme court ruled that it would be fair to both sides not to restrict the retrial only to the question of adultery. A new trial on all issues in the Walker case would be scheduled for a hearing in the Rhode Island Superior Court.[20]

On July 7, Nina Walker's attorneys entered a motion charging her husband with contempt of court for failure to pay any allowance to her and the children during May and June 1913.[21] While waiting for a hearing on this matter, on August 13, James asked to have care and custody of his four minor children for three weeks.[22] A handwritten order filed on August 21 by Horace G. Bissell, an assistant justice of the Rhode Island Superior Court, ordered that Elizabeth and Serrell Walker be permitted to visit their father in Jamestown, Rhode Island, from August 25 to September 1, 1913. After that visit, they were to be returned to their mother in Newport. Following the first two children's visit, Grahame and Herbert Walker should be allowed to visit their father in Jamestown and then returned to their mother. The order specified, "Neither of said children shall at any time during said visits be taken without the limits of the state of Rhode Island, and in case of illness of either of the children during said visits, their mother shall be forthwith notified and she shall be allowed to see them."[23] Jamestown, Rhode Island, on an island in Narragansett Bay and close to Newport, was a popular summer resort at the time, and James hoped that his children would renew their connections with their father and his family in that tranquil atmosphere.

In October, both sides in the Walker case began preparing for the retrial by deposing witnesses in Washington, DC; South Carolina; and Massachusetts. A possible setback for Nina was the death of William Crapo at age seventy-three from an accidental fall on June 9, 1912.[24] As Mabel Cochrane's former landlord, Mr. Crapo had testified in the previous divorce trial that Mabel had referred to James Walker as "doctor," had told him to admit "the doctor" any time, and had received James while only partially dressed. This testimony had been strong evidence for Judge Baker's decision that adultery had ensued between Mr. Walker and Miss Cochrane. Nina's attorneys therefore requested to take a deposition from Sarah R. Crapo, Mr. Crapo's daughter, and to access a photograph used as evidence in the previous trial.[25]

Charles Falconer Stearns, an associate justice of the superior court, was assigned the task of conducting the new Walker divorce trial. In common with both James and Nina Walker, Judge Stearns was descended from a venerable pre–Revolutionary War family, and his father and brothers were prominent businessmen in Providence. After receiving an A.B. from Amherst College, he had graduated from Harvard Law School in 1893 and had practiced law in Providence. Stearns had served as Rhode Island's assistant attorney general from 1902 to 1905, at which time he had become the Republican Party's nominee for superior court justice, a position he held until 1916, when he was elected by the General Assembly to be an associate justice of the Rhode Island Supreme Court. His wife, the former Amelia F. Lieber, whom he had married in 1904, was from Washington, DC, and the daughter of a U.S. Army general.[26]

Rhode Island Superior Court Retrial, Tuesday, November 4, 1913[27]

The new *Walker v. Walker* retrial began on Tuesday, November 4, 1913, with Judge Charles Falconer Stearns presiding in the superior court in Newport. By this time, Judge Stearns was forty-seven years old and had served as an associate justice for eight years. His main distinguishing physical feature was a bushy mustache that curled up at the sides and partially covered his top lip.[28] This was not Judge Stearns's first connection with the Walker case. As he studied the long record of hearings, Judge Stearns recalled that he had been the initial judge assigned to disentangle the couple's difficulties. On November 5, 1909, he had presided over a custody hearing for the Walker children. At that time, Judge Stearns had determined that the four children should remain in the care of their mother until the divorce was settled but had ordered a visitation agreement for their father (see Chapter 5). Who at that point could have imagined how long it would actually take to resolve the case?

Judge Stearns had dealt with the Walker family again in June 1911, when he had presided over *Sears v. Walker*, in which a jury had awarded Richard W. Sears, a press photographer, $400 in damages for assault and personal injury by James Walker's brother, Henry (see Chapter 7). The judge now realized that it had been almost four years to the day since this unhappy husband and wife had first appeared before him, and they had not yet gotten things settled. His colleague Judge Baker had struggled with this dispute for years, and now it was his turn once again.

Although some of the evidence presented in the second Walker divorce trial was similar to that presented in the first one, there were a number of new surprises for the litigants, witnesses, attorneys, judge, and, especially, for the journalists and other spectators. Nina Walker was the first to testify in the retrial. She elaborated on her allegations that James had neglected her and had subjected her and their children to cruel and abusive treatment. She also charged that her husband had been unfaithful to her with Mabel Cochrane, "a young, good-looking girl, who had destroyed [her] home." Nina tried to follow her attorneys' advice and her own intuition that warned her not to look at her husband during her testimony. However, she could not help but see him out of the corner of her eye, and she was surprised that what she felt was not a rush of emotions but only emptiness. James was now a stranger to her.

Rhode Island Superior Court Retrial, Wednesday Afternoon, November 5, 1913[29]

On the second afternoon of the trial, Nina Walker's testimony was interrupted by Walter Barney, her husband's attorney, who asked that Dr. Sarah Ellen Palmer and Dr. Emma B. Culbertson, two medical witnesses from Boston, be allowed to testify. Dr. Palmer was the first to take the stand, and Mr. Barney asked a number of questions regarding her educational and medical background. She described her medical studies at Johns Hopkins and in Berlin, Paris, and Munich, and she listed the medical associations to which she belonged. Dr. Palmer explained that she had been asked to make a physical examination of a young woman brought to her office by Mrs. Susan FitzGerald and identified as Miss Mabel Cochrane. Mr. Barney's questioning of Dr. Palmer proceeded:[30]

> Mr. Barney: Dr. Palmer, could you please describe for the court your medical examination of Miss Mabel Cochrane on the twenty-third of May, 1911?
> Dr. Palmer: The patient removed her lower outer garments and draped herself with a sheet. She was then instructed to take the Sim's position on my examination table. This requires the patient to lie on her side with the under arm behind her back and her upper thigh bent, which facilitates vaginal examination.
> Mr. Barney: And, Dr. Palmer, did you use any specialized medical instrument to make your examination?
> Dr. Palmer: Yes, indeed. I employed a vaginal speculum.

At this point, Dr. Palmer produced a metal object, consisting of a hollow cylinder with a rounded edge divided into two hinged parts. Courtroom observers were both horrified and fascinated by this device. Mr. Harvey entered the vaginal speculum into evidence as "Exhibit Z."

> Mr. Barney: And, Dr. Palmer, what is the purpose of this speculum device?
> Dr. Palmer: It is inserted into the vagina in order to dilate it for examination.
> Mr. Barney: Is it your routine practice to use this medical device during gynecological examinations?
> Dr. Palmer: Yes, it is my routine practice.
> Mr. Barney: And, did you use this medical device during your examination of Miss Mabel Cochrane?
> Dr. Palmer: I did.
> Mr. Barney: Dr. Palmer, did your examination of Miss Cochrane produce any findings?
> Dr. Palmer: Yes.
> Mr. Barney: And, Dr. Palmer, did you record your findings from the examination?
> Dr. Palmer: Yes.
> Mr. Barney: And what did you find?
> Dr. Palmer: I found a very normal condition for a virgin.
> Mr. Barney: And, could you describe what you mean by the term "normal"?
> Dr. Palmer: I would say that in this case there had never been any sexual intercourse. The hymen had not been ruptured and had the appearance of never having been stretched in any way.

Mr. Barney: Were you able to draw any further conclusions upon examination of Miss Mabel Cochrane?
Dr. Palmer: I felt perfectly convinced that Miss Cochrane was an honest, straight girl and I was absolutely certain that she had never been infected with a venereal disease.
Mr. Barney: So, Dr. Palmer, your findings were that, at the time of your examination, Miss Mabel Cochrane was a virgin?
Dr. Palmer: Yes.
Mr. Barney: And, therefore, Mr. Walker could not possibly have committed adultery, as charged, with said Mabel Cochrane?
Dr. Palmer: Yes, the physical evidence would indicate that.
Mr. Barney: And, furthermore, your evidence indicates that Mabel Cochrane has never been infected with a venereal disease?
Dr. Palmer: Yes.
Mr. Barney: And, therefore, Miss Mabel Cochrane could not have communicated a venereal disease to Mr. James Walker?
Dr. Palmer: Yes, that is correct.

Dr. Palmer stepped down, and Mr. Barney called Dr. Emma B. Culbertson to the stand. She testified that she had been a physician for more than thirty years, had an established practice in Boston, and had examined Mabel Cochrane directly following Dr. Palmer's examination on May 23, 1911. Dr. Culbertson stated, "My findings coincide entirely with Dr. Palmer's; the hymen showed no signs of having been dilated[;] there were no signs of rupture of the hymen and no scar of any former rupture." Furthermore, she testified, "There was no appearance incompatible with absolute chastity and no signs of her ever having suffered infection."[31] Thus, the testimony of these two medical experts disputed Nina Walker's charge of adultery against her husband.

Mr. Harvey, counsel for Nina Walker, attempted to repair the damage to his client's case. He conducted a long cross-examination of Dr. Palmer and Dr. Culbertson, during which he tried to cast doubt on their testimonies. He prompted Dr. Palmer to admit that an intact hymen is not "absolute proof of chastity" and it was possible that "this girl might have had sexual intercourse once or twice." Under similar questioning by Mr. Harvey, Dr. Culbertson stated, "I would not say that it was impossible that intercourse had ever taken place with this woman, but in my opinion, she was a virgin."

When Nina Walker resumed her testimony, she complained that Mabel Cochrane had been appointed governess by her husband without her knowledge and that she had told her mother-in-law, Rebecca Walker, that it was not proper for her to have Mabel Cochrane as a guest; it was, in fact, "extraordinary." Nina reiterated her complaints that Mabel Cochrane had been invited to a theater party although she, the wife, had to ask for a ticket, and that Mabel had worn Mr. Walker's military cloak, which she herself had never been allowed to do. Finally, Nina admitted that she had never witnessed "love making" between her husband and Miss Cochrane. Court was adjourned.

Rhode Island Superior Court Retrial, Thursday, November 6, 1913[32]

Mr. Burdick's cross-examination of Nina Walker included questions regarding Mabel Cochrane's letters to James. Nina stated that she had first opened one of the letters because she had recognized Miss Cochrane's handwriting. She had made copies and sealed the envelope, which had not yet been dry when her husband had seized it. Nina responded to questions regarding other letters she had allegedly copied, including those she had found in her husband's wastebasket and one she had found in his pocket. She testified that, in all cases, her copies were true copies. As explanation for reading her husband's letters, Nina Walker stated that she had believed that "Mr. Walker was living in a strange, odd way" and that she had been "looking for anything which would help put the best appearance on it, for the sake of the children." She had copied the letters because she had been "trying to fathom it out."

Nina's cousin, the Reverend Reese F. Alsop, of Brooklyn, New York, testified that "over and over again," he had been "struck with Mrs. Walker's wisdom and tact with the children." According to Dr. Alsop, the Walker children were "being brought up with high religious and moral training, and with social training; they [were] being brought up to be ladies and gentlemen." "Over and over again," he repeated, he "had been impressed that the children were favored to have a mother so competent to bring them up. The relations were very affectionate. The children were very happy with one another."

Dr. Alsop confirmed that Nina Walker had sent him a copy of a letter said to be from Mabel Cochrane to James Walker. He stated that he could swear that the copy of the letter currently in evidence was exactly the same as the one he had been sent. During cross-examination, Mr. Barney asked, "There may be some endearing terms introduced that were not in your copy?" Dr. Alsop replied, "I particularly remember the endearing terms."

He had kept the copy Nina had sent him in a safe place for several years but did not currently know what had happened to it.

Dr. Alsop stated that he had offered advice to Nina in a letter, which he asked to be entered into evidence. Mr. Burdick objected to this request, but when Mr. Sheffield responded that the court would be "foolish to exclude first hand testimony," Judge Stearns allowed Dr. Alsop to read the letter aloud. Dr. Alsop had presented Nina with four alternatives. The first was to seek absolute divorce with alimony, to which he considered her entitled and believed the court would allow; the second was legal separation with alimony; the third was a separation by mutual agreement, with Mr. Walker contributing to support Nina and the children; the final alternative was "patience and continued endurance, for the children's sake, of an almost intolerable situation." This last alternative, Dr. Alsop explained, "[had been made] to see if an agreement of the parties to live apart could not be reached." He testified that he had particularly advised Nina to consult with Admiral John Grimes Walker, James's father. Following Dr. Alsop's testimony, his wife, Florence R. Alsop, took the stand and declared dramatically that Nina Walker "has the true mother spirit and is a true Christian Woman." Mrs. Alsop said that when she had previously seen Mr. Walker in his home, "his conduct was all right; before that it was. . . ." Mrs. Alsop hesitated, looked at the judge, and, when he nodded for her to continue, concluded her appraisal: "It was scandalous!"

Mr. Sheffield called a new witness, who, he indicated, had come from far away. To the surprise of all present, Mr. Harvey entered the courtroom with a "colored man." He gave his name as Charles Slappy, now living in Savannah, Georgia, but formerly a resident of Charleston, South Carolina. Mr. Slappy had been employed as a cook and butler for Mr. Walker from 1902 to 1903. His wife had also worked in the Walker household during that time. Mr. Slappy stated that in 1903, a young lady and a young man had come to the Walker house in Charleston after Mrs. Walker had gone away for the summer with the children. These two, who had turned out to be Miss Cochrane and her brother, had been at the Walker house all summer, leaving before Mrs. Walker had returned. He added that sometimes the young man had not been in the house. Mr. Slappy testified that one morning, he had gone upstairs to get Mr. Walker's shoes to shine and had seen his employer kissing the young lady in her bedroom. He also stated that he had seen Mr. Walker and Miss Cochrane in "compromising situations, on other occasions." Mr. Slappy testified that Mr. Walker would usually leave the house at about 9:00 A.M. and that Miss Cochrane would always be watching for his return and would rush to open the door for him, so that he never had a chance to open the door. Mr. Walker would kiss the young lady's hand. Mr. Walker and Miss Cochrane had always eaten together, according to this witness, all the while laughing and talking. Mr. Walker and Miss Cochrane had often gone out together, and Mr. Slappy had heard her sing to him. In contrast, he claimed, Mr. Walker typically had not spoken much to Mrs. Walker but had been "cross and rough and short" with her. He had seen Mrs. Walker crying several times, he said.

During cross-examination by Mr. Burdick, Mr. Slappy stated that he was currently a waiter in a hotel and had come to Newport expressly to testify in the trial. He maintained that he was promised nothing but payment for his time and expenses for coming to Newport. He had never talked about the case with either Mr. or Mrs. Walker and had not previously known that there was trouble between them. Mr. Slappy claimed that, during the first summer he had been in Charleston, "Young Mr. Cochrane did nothing—he was out in the street." During the second summer, he said, the young man had worked at the navy yard. Mr. Slappy admitted that Miss Cochrane had not gotten along with Mrs. Slappy. "She wanted to take over the whole house," Mr. Slappy claimed. "There was trouble about it; we had made no arrangements to be 'bossed' by her." The Slappys had left the Walker household because they "couldn't stand the way things were going on." According to this witness, when he had told Mr. Walker they were leaving, Mr. Walker had responded, "You let your wife get the upper hand of you." Mr. Slappy said he had replied, "I love my wife, whether or not you love yours; I would do anything to please my wife."

Following Mr. Slappy's testimony, Nina identified two letters James had sent her about his medical condition, and they were read aloud by Mr. Sheffield and entered into evidence. Mr. Sheffield then called Dr. Hugh Cabot, a forty-one-year-old physician from Boston, to testify. He had been a surgeon for sixteen years, an assistant professor of surgery at the Harvard Medical School, a member of distinguished medical societies, and the founder and chief of the "genito-urinary" department at Massachusetts General Hospital. Mr. Sheffield showed Dr. Cabot a paper that Nina Walker had found in her husband's pocket. This was the document that had been debated during the original trial, with her attorneys referring to it as a "prescription" and his attorneys calling it "the list of remedies." When Mr. Sheffield asked the doctor what disease he thought would require the treatments listed, Dr. Cabot stated that the disease indicated was "undoubtedly gonorrhea" and that it absolutely could not have been contracted except by direct infection. He asserted that the remedies on the list were very commonly prescribed by doctors to treat gonorrhea, including by the doctor who had given the list to Mr. Walker.

Under cross-examination, Dr. Cabot agreed with Mr. Barney that each of the items on the list of remedies could also be used for other diseases. Mr. Barney made several attempts to frame a technical question, but, each time, Dr. Cabot protested that he could not understand what he was being asked and stated, "I don't think that question means anything." When Mr. Barney finally asked whether the list of remedies would be used for a chronic rather than a recent infection with gonorrhea, Dr. Cabot replied, "He did not have a chronic case of gonorrhea[;] it is beyond human belief." He added, "Gonorrhea cannot develop out of a clear sky." Mr. Barney asked whether experts could differ on a diagnosis of gonorrhea, and Dr. Cabot agreed that it was possible.

Dr. William A. Sherman was the next expert witness for Nina Walker's side. He was a bacteriologist with the Newport Board of Health and a former president of the Rhode Island Medical Society. Dr. Sherman concurred with Dr. Cabot that the remedies listed indicated a recent infection with gonorrhea. Following a short recess, Mr. Sheffield recalled Dr. Cabot to ask a version of the hypothetical question he had used with medical witnesses in the previous trial. "Assuming Doctor," he inquired, "that a male person for approximately four months used the directions in the afore mentioned prescription daily; and, assuming further that during that period he wore on his genital parts an absorbent cotton pad, which he changed constantly night and day and each time burned after removing them, and that he frequently had a thick discharge of distinctly yellowish color; from what disease, in your opinion and experience was he suffering?" Dr. Cabot answered sternly, "He must be suffering from gonorrhea. Patients were always told to burn the cotton because gonorrhea is highly infectious." Mr. Sheffield asked the witness whether the man in question could be suffering from oxaluria, instead. "Oxaluria," Dr. Cabot replied impatiently, "is not at all infectious." "And," he added, "it is very rare indeed."

When Nina continued her testimony, she said that, after her discovery of Mabel Cochrane's letters, she had begged her husband not to have anything more to do with that woman. He had replied that he had to answer the letters as a matter of civility: "A man must answer when a woman writes." Nina said she had pleaded, "It would make a great difference to our family life if only he would break off with Miss Cochrane," and James had replied that he would "make no promises." He had told her that the letter was "such as any man might receive." She could not understand his relationship with Miss Cochrane, who was "a servant," particularly his attentions to her when they had been visiting his mother in Washington. "I never, in so many words[,] charged my husband with being unfaithful," Nina said, "but the letter from Miss Cochrane seemed to be a very serious matter. My husband attempted to make me believe that he was surprised to receive the letter, but I could see under his pretense that he was not." Nina testified that her married life had never been good, although she had tried to make it as pleasant as possible.

Rhode Island Superior Court Retrial, Friday, November 6, 1913[33]

During cross-examination, Mr. Burdick suddenly asked Nina, "You talked at one time of giving your children away, did you not?" "Give my children away!" Nina gasped. "No, I never would have done such a thing. I have struggled too hard for them." Mr. Burdick persisted, querying, "Did you not propose that one child should be put in care of your mother and one in care of your sister?" "I never dreamed of giving them to my mother and sister," Nina shot back. "Not even in the contingency of my death did I make such a suggestion!" "Did you discuss your married life with your mother and sister?" Mr. Burdick asked. Nina replied that she had not done so, but his further questioning implied that these women had convinced her to leave her husband. At one point, Mr. Burdick inquired loudly, "Why did you leave your husband?" Nina explained that she could not understand his manner of life. "There was no confidence between us," she stated. Nina testified that while she had been resting at Mrs. Batcheler's on Washington Street in Newport, "Mr. Walker came and threatened to place me in a lunatic asylum if I would not agree to his plan to divide the children among his relatives!" Nina declared, "I knew that he and his family had carried out all the previous threats they had made, and thought that they would carry out this one if I did not act at once!" The last straw, she said, had been when she had learned, from Mr. Sheffield, the true nature of her husband's disease.

Nina Walker testified that her husband had never shown much affection for the children, nor had they shown much for him. James and his family planned to divide the children between her husband's mother and two married sisters, including Susan FitzGerald, a suffragist with her own children, who spent much of her time at her office. Judge Stearns sustained Mr. Burdick's objection to this statement about Mrs. FitzGerald. After she had left Mr. Walker, Nina said, she had made sure her children were watched closely, because "my husband had carried my children away from home in Washington and his sister, Mrs. Thomas, [had] kept my baby for several weeks in Boston and refused to allow me to take him back."

Virginia Serrellina Chinn was called as a witness for her daughter Nina. She gave testimony similar to that she had given during the March

1911 trial. Regarding James Walker's relationship with the children, she noted that she "never knew a more indifferent father; he showed absolutely no interest in the children." The children feared their father, she said, and never went near him. When cross-examined by Mr. Burdick, Mrs. Chinn stated that she had taken a house in Newport to protect her daughter, although she had not given up her home in Washington. When asked, "Do you intend to return there?" Mrs. Chinn replied, as she had in her original deposition in 1909, "If I feel like it."

As Elizabeth Bertha Chinn, Nina's sister, took the stand, habitual court observers recalled that she had been an effective witness at the first Walker trial. With an efficient manner, Nina's sister confirmed that James Walker had been indifferent to the needs of his wife and children. She reported the incident when one of the children had been born, her sister had been very ill, and Mr. Walker had not sent for a physician, saying he thought there was no need for one. "I went out and telephoned and got on my bicycle and hunted up a trained nurse," Bertha maintained. She gave other examples of James Walker's neglect of his wife and again told the story of how he had taken the children by force from her mother's house in Washington to Brooklyn. Bertha testified that, while visiting the Newport Training Station, she had been horrified when she had seen Mr. Walker punishing one of the children with "thongs," leaving marks on the child.

During cross-examination, Bertha stated that she was a resident of both Washington and Newport. She claimed that the Washington house had been listed with a broker for four years. It was up for rent or sale, although the family preferred to sell it. When asked whether the real trouble between the Walkers was that Nina Walker was "fond of society" while her husband was not, Bertha responded that she did not know how anybody could say that, adding, "My sister liked to go out sometimes and I thought Mr. Walker liked to go out, too." Her brother-in-law had been pleasant with her, and she had suggested that he should be agreeable with his wife as well, but he had responded, "Oh, she's so cross." Bertha admitted that it was possible that Nina had been cross at that time; it had been just before she had given birth again, and she "[had been] suffering a great deal."

Mr. Harvey interrupted Miss Chinn's cross-examination to present additional medical testimony for Nina Walker's side of the case. Dr. Edward Reynolds, of Milton, Massachusetts, was called to the stand. He recited the many medical societies of which he was a member, including one for which he had served as president. Dr. Reynolds specialized in women's diseases and had a private hospital on Dartmouth Street in Boston. When Mr. Harvey asked him about the medical evidence given by Dr. Palmer and Dr. Culbertson, Dr. Reynolds read the transcript of their testimonies but stated that he would have to know much more before forming an opinion. Mr. Harvey asked, "Doctor, is it true that the presence of the hymenal membrane proves that a woman is, in fact, a virgin?" This had been the most important assertion made by the women physicians. Dr. Reynolds cleared his throat and then responded, "The condition of an intact hymenal membrane can exist, even in a married woman, if she has not had children. Not infrequently, although it is not common, I have had to have the statement of the woman herself to arrive at the right conclusion. No general rule can be laid down; all depends on the individual case."

Under cross-examination, Dr. Reynolds stated that he had treated at least four thousand women during his career. Court spectators were amused when he commented, "It would be much easier to give an opinion after seeing the actual woman than from a hypothetical question formed by a lawyer." "In my own experience," he stated, "the commonly accepted idea that an examination easily settles the matter of virginity is altogether wrong." Following a recess, additional physicians reported to each of the attorneys, prompting one observer to declare that "the courtroom seemed an arena for medical experts."

When Bertha's cross-examination resumed, she repeated her testimony that her sister's husband was "absolutely indifferent" to the children. "Mr. Walker has been a very busy man, has he not?" inquired his attorney. "Not at all," replied the witness, "he did not take life seriously." "In his demeanor he is very serious, is he not?" the attorney continued. "He is not cheerful in his expressions," stated the witness. Toward the end of this cross-examination, Bertha Chinn stated that she had never spoken to Admiral Walker regarding the frequency of her sister's pregnancies. In fact, the admiral had first broached the subject with her.

Nina Walker's attorneys called a series of witnesses to testify about the Walker children. Captain William McCarty Little, USN, reported that they were friends of his grandson, were very well-behaved, and had shown marked improvement in the past couple of years. Mr. Robert H. P. Thompson, a teacher at the Cloyne School, stated that the boys were "extremely well-behaved and impress one immediately as well-trained and having the instinct of gentlemen." Although they were not physically strong, Mr. Thompson also believed that they had shown marked improvement. "Boys of that age are not demonstrative," he continued, "but these come and go together, help each other, and seem fond of each other." Mr. Alexander O'D Taylor, the father of a friend of the Walker children, stated that he considered them "some of the best brought-up boys" he had ever seen. Mr. Taylor believed that "they must have had careful training and seem attached to each other." He had spent the Fourth of July with the family and had noticed that the Walker daughter was also extremely affectionate with her brothers.

Rhode Island Superior Court Retrial, Monday, November 10, 1913[34]

Nina Walker's attorneys continued to press the point that her husband and Mabel Cochrane had been lovers. Mr. Harvey read a deposition from Mr. W. O. Moore, who had worked at the Charleston Navy Yard and had lived close to the Walker house. He claimed that Miss Cochrane had been living with Mr. Walker while Mrs. Walker had been away with the children and that she would go to Mr. Walker's office and walk with him after dark. A deposition from Mr. John Frazier, a laborer in the Charleston Navy Yard, stated that he had moved Mr. Walker's furniture from a house in the city to a new house in the navy yard in 1902 or early 1903. A woman, whom he had later found out was Miss Cochrane, had moved from the same city house to the same house in the navy yard at the same time as Mr. Walker. Mr. Frazier stated that he had seen the two together at various times and that he "didn't find out Miss Cochrane was not Mrs. Walker until the real Mrs. Walker later returned to Charleston with the children!" Mr. Harvey read the deposition of Mr. C. D. Epting, who had lived at the Walker house with his wife as caretakers. He also verified that Miss Cochrane had lived there while Mr. Walker's wife had been away and confirmed that she had been at his office after dark.

Miss Sarah R. Crapo, of Roxbury, Massachusetts, was deposed in place of her deceased father, who had been Mabel Cochrane's landlord. She testified that during the four years she had lived at the boardinghouse, it had been "Miss Cochrane's habit to rise at 11:00 A.M., but not go out until 3:00 P.M. She would usually return to her room by 10:00 P.M., but stayed up until 3:00 A.M." Miss Cochrane had several male callers, according to Miss Crapo, some of whom had called continually, and one who had called every day. When asked the name of the daily caller, Miss Crapo gave it, and it was not James Walker. This man would call on Miss Cochrane at about 6:00 P.M. and they would go out, returning at about 10:00 P.M. Then they would play cards in her room until about 3:00 A.M. One time a man had left Mabel's room in the morning, according to Miss Crapo. She remembered Miss Cochrane's asking her to close some doors so that he could leave unseen. Miss Cochrane had always locked her door when she had gentlemen callers. Miss Crapo remembered admitting Mr. Walker on two or three occasions: "[Mabel] called him 'the doctor' and said he was to be let in whenever he called." When shown a photograph of Mr. Walker, Miss Crapo testified that it had been found behind a large mirror over the mantel in Mabel's former room, about a year after she had left the house in January 1910.

Miss Crapo further testified that she had liked Miss Cochrane, who was "very lady-like," and there had been no trouble between them. Miss Cochrane had talked with Miss Crapo about her "gentlemen callers" and had told her that she had traveled through Canada with a Mr. Jackson, one of her regular visitors. Another caller had come to the house drunk, and Miss Crapo had told him to leave. "That man often did not leave Miss Cochrane's room until the next forenoon!" she stated indignantly. "The instructions to me were to 'let the doctor in' at any hour, but otherwise not to disturb Miss Cochrane until 11:00 A.M.," Miss Crapo testified, adding, "Mr. Walker did not give his name when he called." Another witness, Miss Gladys Percival, who had lived in the Crapo house with her grandmother, testified that she thought she had seen Mr. Walker enter Miss Cochrane's room. "Perhaps two or three times I saw that gentleman with the glasses with Miss Cochrane at the house," she stated. She had also seen Miss Cochrane coming in or going out with several other men, although not very late at night.

As he had done in the original 1911 trial, Mr. Burdick, arguing for James Walker, objected to admitting into evidence the letters purported to be from Mabel Cochrane. In that previous trial, Judge Baker had at first admitted the letters *de bene* and eventually had admitted them without restriction. Judge Stearns pondered the admission of the Cochrane letters in the current trial and then determined that they might be admissible related to the question of Mrs. Walker's "acting in good faith." The judge stated, "They have been the basis of so much action of the parties that it almost seems that they should go in." He then declared that he would admit all of the letters *de bene*. Mr. Barney asked for an exception if they were admitted. Judge Stearns replied, "The surest way would be to admit them fully and note the exception."

Mr. Burdick opened James Walker's side of the case by calling as a witness Mr. John E. W. Cochran (called Jack), Mabel's younger brother, who had taken to spelling his name without the final "e." Mr. Cochran was currently a draftsman in Charleston and had worked at that trade there since he was seventeen years old. He told the story about how he and his sister had first come to Charleston exactly as James Walker had described it at the original trial. He affirmed that they had gone there without an invitation and had stayed for three or four weeks. Jack had come to Charleston to see about a job, and Mabel had gone with him to keep her brother company. Jack Cochran reported that he and his sister had eaten at a different place from Mr. Walker until the servants had returned, including Mrs. Slappy, who had cooked the meals. After a while, Mabel had returned to Boston, but, at Mr. Walker's request, Jack had written her that there was trouble with the servants, and she had come back down to help out until the family would return. Mr. Cochran stated that he had lived in Mr. Walker's house in the Charleston Navy Yard for the entire time his sister had stayed there. He and Mabel had left the house shortly before Mr. Walker's wife and children had returned. Mr. Cochran claimed that Mrs. Walker must have known that he and his sister had stayed at the house during the summer, because she had referred to it in conversation when he had visited the house the following winter. In response to questions about previous witnesses' testimony that Mabel had visited Mr. Walker at his office, Jack explained that she usually had done that to order supplies. Finally, Jack Cochran stated, "There was absolutely nothing improper between Mabel and Mr. Walker that I ever knew of."

During cross-examination by Mr. Sheffield, Jack Cochran stated that he had contact with Mr. Walker in Boston only once. That was the meeting Mabel had arranged for him to ask Mr. Walker about a possible appointment to the navy. Mr. Sheffield asked the exact date that Jack and his sister had gone to Charleston, but the young man said he would need to refer to his appointment letter, which he had not brought to court. "I had to quickly jump in a taxicab to catch the train, because I didn't know I was coming to Newport today until a half-hour before starting," he explained. Mr. Sheffield asked about Jack and Mabel's habits while in Charleston, and Jack stated that if he had gone out in the evening, his sister usually had gone with him. She had been considered a guest during the first summer they had stayed in Charleston. Mr. Sheffield asked how the rooms had been arranged in the Walker house. Cross-examination of this witness ended when Jack Cochran would not admit that "adjoining rooms" had been occupied by Mabel and Mr. Walker.

Mrs. Helen Kellogg, who had testified at the original 1911 trial when she was Miss Helen Hull, was also a witness at this trial. A close friend of James's sister Sarah (Sallie), she had been a guest at Admiral Walker's Washington home at the same time that Mabel Cochrane had been there in 1904. She stated that she had not noticed that Mr. Walker had paid any special attention to Miss Cochrane; there was nothing at all inappropriate. When Mrs. Kellogg had visited the Newport Training Station in 1910 with Sallie, the children had appeared content with their father, and Herbert had seemed happy when he was with his grandmother. She had also seen the children more recently with the Walker family in New Hampshire, and they had seemed "perfectly happy." Under cross-examination by Mr. Harvey, Mrs. Kellogg said that she thought she and Sallie had gone out once or twice with Miss Cochrane, or maybe more than that. Mrs. Kellogg also confirmed that she and Sallie had helped identify Mabel for the two women doctors in Boston.

Sarah Cochrane Walker (Sallie), James's youngest sister, now living in Boston with her mother, testified that the play in Washington had been an amateur production for charity, which had been "arranged somewhat suddenly." She understood that Miss Cochrane had come to Washington as the children's governess and that the box party had definitely not been organized for her, as Nina had claimed. Sallie and Mabel had gone out together once or twice. Her brother and his children had a good relationship, Sallie stated, and the children could not wait for him to come home from work so that he could play with them. Sallie had gone to the doctor's office with her friend Helen to confirm Mabel Cochrane's identity. "She was the same person," Miss Walker declared decisively.

It was finally the respondent's turn to testify in this retrial. The courtroom was hushed as James Wilson Grimes Walker, now forty-five years old, approached the witness stand. He looked uncomfortable in a suit and tie, and, in fact, he was. James Walker, who previously had been so proud that his naval uniform was always spotless and his shoes polished, had grown accustomed to wearing work clothes that had not been recently washed and work boots caked with mud. That attire was perfectly appropriate for his work on the farm, and he resented every time he had to pull out his old suit from the back of the wardrobe to wear for a courtroom appearance.

On the witness stand, James Walker reviewed the background details of his previous testimony. He considered Washington his home; his job with the railroad had been abolished prior to his marriage, but his mother had agreed to help financially; he had stayed in Washington to take an examination for appointment to the navy while his wife had gone to Atlantic City with her mother; he had not won the first appointment but soon after had been named assistant engineer on the Nicaragua Canal Commission. James stated that, just prior to the birth of his first child, he had been working for the commission in New York, and Nina had stayed with him there until about ten days before he had sailed to Nicaragua, when she had left to go to her mother's house in Washington. At the time of Elizabeth's birth, he had been "extremely busy" and had no time to go see her. He had been away with the commission for ten months before being reunited with his wife and daughter.

Rhode Island Superior Court Retrial, Tuesday, November 11, 1913[35]

James Walker continued to refute charges made by his wife. He again explained why he had not been with Nina at the birth of their first child. As opposed to Nina's contention that they had never gone out, James thought that they had socialized a reasonable amount, going to friends' houses to dine and having friends come to dine with them. They had often visited with family. About the couple's second house in Brookline, James testified, "I came home and found I was moved! This new house cost $200 a year more, it being larger and costing more to heat. I was not in funds[,] and my mother and uncle had to provide assistance to furnish the house." This assertion contradicted Nina's testimony that it had been James's idea to move to that house.

James repeated his denial of Nina's claim that during his time at the Boston Navy Yard, women had left notes under his plate in the restaurant at North Station. He again described his amusement that the cashier at Scollay Square in Boston would think he was the kind of man who would loan her money to furnish her rooms. Relations had been good with his wife, he said, but he had turned down a post in New London, Connecticut, because it was too close to where the Chinns lived, and "things didn't go quite smoothly when they were about." James stated that it was he who had sent Nina and the children to North Carolina to escape the Charleston heat, but with the distinct stipulation that the Chinns were not to join them. He made it clear that he had moved to South Carolina to be away from his in-laws. He had sent Nina money, he said, but he did not know what she had done with it. And she had never sent him a photograph of Miss Cochrane in a letter, as she had claimed.

James's attorney asked him to clarify the circumstances of John and Mabel's first visit to Charleston, while his family had been away and the Slappys had been gone for a month. He reiterated from the previous trial that he had not known they were coming until he had seen them sitting on the steps of his house. Again, he explained that he had invited them to stay because the house had been practically vacant and they had not known where to go. He thought that Miss Cochrane had stayed at the house for two or three weeks, while her brother had been there for a longer period. They had gone to a different place for their meals than he had until the Slappys returned, when they all had meals at the house, and Miss Cochrane had left shortly afterward. James admitted that Miss Cochrane had occupied the room adjoining his, between which there might have been a connecting door, but it had not been used.

The following year, James explained, the Walker family had moved to the "East Battery" house, which Nina had chosen. Jack Cochran and his sister had taken care of the move. That winter, Mr. Cochran had come to the house two or three times a week to receive mathematics instruction from James, and afterward they would talk for a while. Despite Nina's testimony that she had not known that Jack and his sister had been at the house the previous summer, James claimed that they had discussed their activities from that summer while his wife had been present, so she must have known. The summer after that, Nina and the children had gone away to the Chinns' cottage at Woodley Lane, near Washington. James stated, "That was with my knowledge and consent, but hardly with my approval." Immediately after Nina and the children had left, there had been trouble with the servants. "I discovered that the Slappys seemed to be running a negro [*sic*] boarding house at my expense!" James exclaimed. "It was thought [that] some responsible person should be there, as the men were out during the day. Miss Cochrane was sent for and came to be the housekeeper," he explained. His wife had known that she was coming, he claimed, and had even arranged to have her stay. Soon after this, the Slappys had been dismissed.

James's attorney asked questions about the winter that Miss Cochrane had lived at the Walker house as the governess. James stated that his wife had gone to bed at approximately 8:00 P.M. and that he had generally stayed up and read. The house had been built for hot weather and the only heated room was the library, so Miss Cochrane and he might both have been in that same room in the evening. "Is it true that you played solitaire with Miss Cochrane?" asked his lawyer. "No," James replied dryly, "it is not usual to play solitaire with another person." He stated that he had played solitaire but could not recall playing cards with Miss Cochrane, although he acknowledged that he might have done it once or twice. Miss Cochrane had generally retired at 9:30, and James had stayed up later, still reading. According to James, his wife had not complained about his relationship with Miss Cochrane or discussed it with him at that time.

James testified that while he had been in Washington on business and staying at his parents' home, his mother had asked him to invite Miss Cochrane to Washington. Although she had brought two of the children from Charleston with her, Miss Cochrane was not supposed to have any duties while in Washington; she had been his mother's guest. She had stayed for a week in the large front room opposite Admiral and Mrs. Walker's bedroom. Then, Nina had contacted James to say that she was afraid of the "negro" quarter, about three quarters of a mile away, which had a bad reputation. Nina had told him that she had heard shots and had been accosted by a "negro." James had reported the problems to Captain Swift at the navy yard. Although the captain had investigated and reported that everything was fine, Nina still had not wanted to stay there. James had sent her a note or telegram telling her not to come to Washington because it was too early in the season for her to leave Charleston. She had told him that she simply would not return to the navy yard, so James had sent money for tickets for her to come to Washington.

The trouble between his wife and him at the time, James said, had been about her demands to go to her mother's cottage in Virginia with the children during the following summer. James had objected to her doing so and had told her unequivocally that she must go elsewhere. They had quarreled throughout her visit to his mother's house in Washington. One night, his wife had delivered a long monologue (undoubtedly the "Caudle lecture" his mother had referred to in the earlier trial). "My wife finally went to bed and I sat in the library until my mother suggested that I take a room on the floor above," James stated and then commented, "I did."

James Walker's attorney asked him to tell his side of the story about the letter his wife had intercepted and copied. He had been out riding, he said, and the mail messenger had told him that he had given Nina their five letters. When Nina had handed him only four letters, he had asked for the missing one. She had first denied having it but had finally given it to him. He had seen that it was from Miss Cochrane and obviously had been opened. When his attorney showed him "Exhibit B," which was the alleged "true copy" of this letter made by Nina, James stated that it was not a true copy. "It is three times as long as the original. It is padded with a lot of mush and endearing terms," he protested. "The original," he claimed, "while not perhaps in the best form, was perfectly harmless. I objected to my wife's practice of opening my letters. She had done it before!"

"She practically charged me with infidelity!" Walker continued. He then testified that he had told his wife that he could not have been unfaithful because of his medical ailment, which had originated prior to his marriage. He had then explained more about the nature of his ailment, and, he said, "this made my wife very unhappy; she did not like it that I was sick, but I fully persuaded her that my relations with Miss Cochrane were all right. There was not the slightest trouble between Nina and me after this," he said, "and Miss Cochrane did not come again."

James told the court that Nina and the children had gone to Watch Hill the following summer with the Chinns. He had had thirty days' leave and had stopped there for one night, and then he and Nina had gone alone to New Hampshire, where his parents had a house. The trip had been so pleasant for them that afterward his wife had sent him a watch charm and a very affectionate letter (see Chapter 4).

During the next winter at the Charleston Navy Yard, James stated, "relations were perfect." He had then been ordered to the New York Navy Yard in Brooklyn on March 16, 1906, where he had arrived the next day. His salary had then been $3,000 a year. James commented, "I had taken four or five rooms in a good locality in Brooklyn and repeatedly wrote my wife to come. She wrote about everything but that. I finally went to see her." According to James's side of the Brooklyn tale, Nina had said she was unable to go to Brooklyn, although her doctor had "strongly advised" him that she could go. James had then decided that the best course would be to take the children and to let his wife come to Brooklyn when she was ready. At this assertion, Mr. Sheffield jumped to his feet and objected. In response, Mr. Burdick showed James a letter, which he identified as having been written to him by Dr. Gerry Morgan. It was the November 1906 letter (see Chapter 4) in which Dr. Morgan acknowledged that Nina's "troubles" had "pulled her down a trifle in flesh and well being" but that he considered her physically able to join her husband in New York. This letter seemed to confirm James's testimony. Mr. Burdick deliberately failed to read the remainder of the letter, which recommended that Nina "lead a quiet life, as free from worry as it is possible under the circumstances," and that "in order for her to make a complete recovery, her present condition makes it necessary to suspend for the present the usual relations between husband and wife."[36]

Mr. Burdick asked James whether his mother had given him a verbal message from Dr. Morgan, and James replied that she had. As soon as Mr. Burdick asked, "What was that message?" Mr. Sheffield roared, "I object!" and Judge Stearns rapidly sustained the objection. The attorneys began to argue back and forth, and the judge wavered, saying that the testimony was "on the borderland of hearsay." He finally determined that it had bearing on the witness's good faith in taking his children to Brooklyn and allowed the verbal instructions to be entered into evidence. James began by stating, "He advised me as strongly as he could advise." Judge Stearns interrupted to warn Mr. Walker, "Don't put it that way; just give the message!" James replied that was the message—that the doctor had advised him as strongly as he could that Mr. Walker bring his wife and children to Brooklyn. Since his wife would not go, James commented, he had taken the children, hoping his wife would follow, as he had just testified.

James explained that Nina eventually had come down to Brooklyn, and he, his wife, and children had been there together during the winter of 1907. His next assignment had been at the Portsmouth Navy Yard, and his wife and children had also joined him there. In May 1908, he had been ordered to Newport, and Nina and the children had moved there about a week after his arrival. They had lived at the Newport Training Station for more than a year, and James reported that "the relations were excellent." The Chinns had been on a trip around the world that year, and Nina had gone to the West Indies on a yachting trip.

His attorney then questioned James about the incident his wife had described as happening while she had been staying at a boardinghouse in Newport. "I went to see Nina and made all sorts of suggestions as to what could be done to relieve her of the care of the children," he stated. "I had consulted my mother and sisters as to what they could do, showed my wife a letter describing their suggestions, but she would not consent to any of the plans. She was rather angry and put out." James then sat bolt upright and stated unambiguously, "I did not threaten to put my wife in an insane asylum[;] I did not insist upon the propositions in the letter; I told her I would agree to almost anything!"

When she had returned to the Newport Training Station, Nina had taken a separate room for the first time and had seemed "disgruntled." James had assumed that she was not feeling well. She had not mentioned plans for the children after she had returned to the training station. James explained that he was supposed to take lunch at noon, but he had usually delayed it until 1:00 P.M. so that he could eat with the children at the house. On Tuesday, October 19, 1909, he had been at home waiting for them, but when they had not appeared, his wife had told him it was such a nice day that they were probably walking. After he had returned to work, Nina had telephoned and told him he should wait at his office because someone would be coming to see him. She had added that she would be at some address in Newport, but he had not taken notice of that. "That was the last talk I had with her," James commented sourly. "I returned to my house," he continued, "to find it looted of many things, including some family articles and some of my personal jewelry being missing. The next day I was served with divorce papers."

James's attorney led him through testimony on other matters that his wife had previously discussed on the stand. Regarding his alleged harsh punishment of the children, James stated that his wife had generally asked him to take over punishing them. The witness said that he had used a "quirt," a riding whip that had leather thongs on a wooden handle, and that it had become "punky" (rotted) with age. Even after the separation, James claimed, the children did not lose their affection for him. In fact, during visits with him, "Herbert stuck to me like a burr."

James testified that in 1901, he had a recurrence of the "trouble" from which he had previously had minor attacks, beginning in 1893. After not being cured, he had gone to Dr. Charles M. Whitney for daily treatments. Following that, he had been told that he was as cured as he could be but should watch for symptoms for a year. Dr. Dixon had made microscopic tests, but there had been no marked improvement until James had visited a fourth doctor in 1906, who had a "perfect cure for oxaluria," James stated. What his wife's attorney had referred to as the "prescription" and his attorneys had called "the list of remedies" was only a series of notes he had made from what Dr. Whitney told him in 1903. James considered it "simply information, not treatment as such." Regarding the hypothetical question that had been put to several medical experts in the previous trial, James stated that it did not describe any treatment he took. Also, he had never told his wife that he had contracted the disease at a public drinking fountain, as she had stated in her testimony. James claimed that he had not had any trouble since the fourth doctor had treated him.

By late afternoon, Mr. Burdick asked the court to suspend testimony, since Mr. Walker and he needed to catch a boat to take depositions in Macon, Georgia, the next day. Judge Stearns allowed Mr. Sheffield to briefly cross-examine James on some points related to witnesses he planned to question the next day. In response to one question, James disagreed that he had met Dr. James Foster Scott "after dark, on Connecticut Avenue"; he maintained that he had met him only at his own house. James also testified that he had never read Dr. Scott's book and that he had not told the doctor that he had a "fresh case of gonorrhea," despite Mr. Burdick's insinuation.

Rhode Island Superior Court Retrial, Wednesday, November 12, 1913[37]

Despite the absence of Mr. Burdick and their client, Mr. Barney called Dr. Charles H. Gwynn to the stand. Dr. Gwynn had practiced medicine in Boston for twenty-four years and had seen "thousands of cases of gonorrhea." He had testified in the previous trial that James Walker had given his name as "Paul Jones" and that he had had a chronic case of gonorrhea but had also showed pus. Dr. Gwynn now announced that he would like to change his testimony from the original 1911 trial, when he had been given only twenty-four hours' notice to appear. At this time, he wished to testify that Mr. Walker had been treated by him on December 7, 1901, under the name of "Jones," for "a chronic case of gonorrhea." He had again treated James Walker for the same disease for several days in December

1901 and in January, February, and March 1902. Dr. Gwynn stated that although the patient had not given his name, he was certain that the patient had been Mr. Walker. He had called him "Paul Jones" during the appointments, and Mr. Walker had agreed to be treated under that name. The name "Mr. Jones" was in the doctor's record in quotation marks. Dr. Gwynn explained that he had relied on Mr. Walker's statements that the gonorrhea was a chronic case and that his observations and treatment at that time would indicate a chronic case of gonorrhea. Dr. Gwynn had then referred Mr. Walker to Dr. Whitney. The two physicians had discussed the case, and Dr. Whitney had treated "Mr. Jones" for several days in October 1902. Dr. Gwynn's connection with the case had ended at that point. He stated that, from consulting his records, he was certain that it was a chronic case of gonorrhea.

During Dr. Gwynn's direct testimony, Nina Walker's expert witness, Dr. Sherman, arrived in the courtroom and took a seat with her attorneys. Mr. Harvey rose to cross-examine Dr. Gwynn. He first asked whether the doctor had testified at the original trial that Mr. Walker had initially given his name as "Jones." The witness responded that that might have been so and also agreed that Mr. Walker had asked to be referred to a drugstore where he would not be known. In response to another question by Mr. Harvey, Dr. Gwynn stated that his current testimony was taken from notes he assumed were made on the dates indicated. When asked about a record entry written as "chr," Dr. Gwynn explained that it was an abbreviation for "chronic," as in "chronic gonorrhea." Mr. Harvey then announced, "I would like to call the court's attention to the differences in the styles of writing and color ink in which the 'chr' appears in the doctor's record, as opposed to the other entries." Judge Stearns examined the entries in the record and asked Dr. Gwynn whether he was sure they were all written in his handwriting. The witness responded with conviction that he was certain it was his handwriting, but the reason it was in a different ink could be that he might have added the notation "chr" at a later date. Judge Stearns asked Dr. Gwynn whether he was accustomed to going back, after completing treatment, to supplement his records. The doctor, visibly angry, replied sharply that he did sometimes do that. The judge asked him whether he could tell on first examination whether a case of gonorrhea was comparatively new or a recurrence of an old case. Dr. Gwynn stated that he could: "I would define an old case as one existing over a month. If it was a comparatively new case and had been treated before coming to me, I might not be able to tell it from a chronic case." Mr. Barney called Judge Stearns's attention to Dr. Gwynn's medical records for other patients, pointing out that some of the "chr" entries in those records were also written in different ink. The judge examined those records and commented, "That is a fair statement. The entries appear in the midst of other changes."

When asked directly by Mr. Barney, Dr. Gwynn fiercely maintained that he had not made changes to his records after he had been informed of the divorce suit. Judge Stearns asked whether he could leave his records for further examination, but Dr. Gwynn replied that he could not, because his records included charges made to patients, some of which had not yet been paid, and he stated, "I would like to get all that is coming to me." When asked whether "Mr. Jones" had paid his bills on time, Dr. Gwynn agreed that he had, adding, "In cash." Snickering rippled through the courtroom gallery as spectators realized that "Mr. Jones" would not have wanted to sign his real name on a check or to receive incriminating bills in the mail.

Dr. Charles M. Whitney, a physician in Boston and a professor at Tufts Medical School who had also testified at the previous trial, was the next witness to take the stand. He stated that he had specialized in "genito-urinary" diseases for more than twenty years, had examined more than forty thousand patients at the Boston Dispensary alone and more than fifty thousand patients in total, and had written a couple of medical journal articles on the topic of gonorrhea. Dr. Gwynn had referred James Walker to Dr. Whitney on October 9, 1903, stating that Mr. Walker had been complaining about a recurrence of previous symptoms. Dr. Whitney began to discuss details he had found during his examination of Mr. Walker without using his notes, until Judge Stearns instructed that he could look at them. Even then, the doctor only sparingly referred to his notes and discussed his medical examinations in great detail, as though he were giving a medical lecture. Dr. Whitney maintained that James Walker's symptoms had indicated a chronic gonorrhea infection that had dated back five or six years. He had treated Mr. Walker from October 9 to November 14, 1903.

All was quiet in the courtroom as observers attempted to follow Dr. Whitney's fascinating and explicit lecture on medicine and anatomy. They were amazed at the tests and treatments available for "genito-urinary" diseases. Dr. Whitney described Mr. Walker's treatment as "radical," having been administered to him almost daily for about five weeks, which sometimes caused considerable pain and discomfort. Dr. Whitney also explained that a germ usually found in the large intestine could sometimes infect other body parts, producing symptoms just like those of gonorrhea. He stated that when he had again examined James Walker in September 1905 and in April 1906, he had found some of the previous symptoms. "There was no new infection—absolutely none, but his condition indicated that relapses were very probable," Dr. Whitney testified. "Even in the current day," he explained, "it is a matter of absolute impossibility to be sure of the presence of gonorrhea; it may be latent and exist for years without showing noticeable symptoms. Mr. Walker's later symptoms would indicate nothing more than recurrence of the old trouble."

When shown "Exhibit E," James's battered "list of remedies," Dr. Whitney stated it was not in his handwriting. "It is not a prescription," the doctor affirmed. "It covers advice as to what to use in certain situations. Mr. Walker went way beyond my personal treatment, and the listed items are not necessarily indicated for gonorrhea." Judge Stearns called Dr. Whitney's attention to previous medical testimony that this list was a common prescription for gonorrhea, but the doctor strongly disagreed with that assessment. When asked for how long a chronic case of gonorrhea might reoccur, Dr. Whitney stated that he had seen a recurrence of an old case twenty-three years later.

Mr. Harvey began Dr. Whitney's cross-examination by asking him whether he could say with certainty how Mr. Walker had contracted gonorrhea. The doctor replied that he could not. Referring to Exhibit E, Mr. Harvey asked whether it had been a common prescription for gonorrhea ten years earlier. "In part yes, in part decidedly no," Dr. Whitney replied. "A slight case might be cured." He did not specify what would constitute a slight case. Under further cross-examination, the doctor testified that a case of gonorrhea was considered "chronic" three months after infection, thereby contradicting Dr. Wynn's definition that gonorrhea was considered "chronic" after a month.

Under redirect examination, Dr. Whitney stated that he used one of the ingredients on the "prescription" list—permanganate of potash—in certain cases of gonorrhea but not as a general rule. He commented, "It is not good for much." Mr. Barney asked, "Doctor, would you say that any of the other items on Mr. Walker's list of remedies would be appropriately used in the case of gonorrhea?" The witness replied, "I guess that's too much [of] a blanket question for me to answer." When Mr. Harvey resumed his cross-examination, Dr. Whitney acknowledged that Dr. Thomas, James Walker's brother-in-law, was his colleague on the faculty at Tufts Medical School and had spoken to him about testifying at this trial.

Mr. Barney called Dr. Ernest Cushing to the stand. He testified that he had studied medicine in Rome, Paris, Vienna, and Berlin, and that he was an emeritus of the Tufts medical faculty. He had edited and published a journal on women's diseases for many years and ran a private hospital for treating those illnesses. Dr. Cushing was also an associate of Dr. Palmer's. Mr. Harvey objected when Mr. Barney asked the witness to discuss Dr.

Palmer's work, and Mr. Barney shifted to ask him whether he would endorse Dr. Palmer's assessment regarding Mabel Cochrane's virginity. Dr. Cushing stated that he agreed that an intact hymen is the crucial evidence of virginity, but during Mr. Harvey's cross-examination, he stated, "I do not claim to be infallible; I would leave a loophole," noting that he had not examined Mabel Cochrane himself. In response to further questioning, Dr. Cushing explained, "It is in the books that a woman who has followed an immoral life may not show it upon examination, but I have never seen such a case." "There are a great many things in the medical books which I do not believe," he snorted.

The last in the long line of Boston physicians testifying for the defense that afternoon was called forward. Dr. Malcolm Storer stated that he had studied medicine at Harvard, Vienna, and Dublin; had been a gynecologist at the Boston Dispensary for fifteen years; and had taught at the Harvard Medical School for fourteen of those years. He had written fifteen articles on gynecological practice and belonged to a number of professional societies. Dr. Storer told the court that "a competent examiner could tell whether charges of adultery implied against Mabel Cochrane are true." He further testified, "I would say that it is conceivable that charges of adultery against Miss Cochrane could still be true, but they would be very improbable, particularly if it is charged that the acts of adultery had been frequent for over a year or more." Nina Walker's attorneys declined to cross-examine the witness. Judge Stearns granted Mr. Barney's request to adjourn until the next morning. Walker family members had been conspicuously absent from the courtroom during the presentation of medical evidence this afternoon.

10

A Question of Virginity

November 13–21, 1913

Rhode Island Superior Court Retrial, Thursday, November 13, 1913[1]

THE FIRST DEPOSITION that Walter H. Barney, counsel for James Walker, read on Thursday morning was from Dr. Charles M. Green. In common with previous medical experts for the defense, he had attended Harvard Medical School, belonged to a number of professional societies, had a hospital practice in Boston, and taught in the Harvard Medical School. However, Dr. Green's credentials were of no use in assisting James's defense. When presented with Dr. Sarah Palmer's medical assessment regarding Mabel Cochrane's virginity, he stated that there was not enough information to allow him to make an opinion. This comment led onlookers to wonder why Mr. Barney had bothered to read the deposition.

The next deposition entered into evidence was from the Boston physician Dr. Joshua C. Hubbard, a graduate of and now instructor at the Harvard Medical School. Dr. Hubbard agreed with Dr. Palmer's assessment that a woman with an intact, unstretched hymen was a virgin. Mr. Harvey loudly objected that Mr. Barney did not query the witness about Dr. Palmer's subsequent response under cross-examination, which was that it was possible for a woman with an intact hymen to have had sexual intercourse, and, therefore, his testimony did not cover all of her evidence. After an extended discussion, Judge Charles Falconer Stearns agreed to allow Dr. Hubbard's testimony to be included *de bene*.

Dr. Alfred W. Balch's deposition for the defense was intended to shed further light on James Walker's medical problems. This physician had attended the Harvard Medical School and was also a surgeon in the U.S. Navy and the director of the Naval Medical School laboratories in Washington, DC. Dr. Balch testified that he remembered several unusual cases he had seen while serving in the navy, including a man who had certain indications of gonorrhea but not others. Unfortunately, the deponent could not recall that man's name. Judge Stearns interjected, "I should not care to base an opinion on such evidence. Here is a doctor going all over the world, doubtless having many cases, and unless the deponent knew definitively the man in question was Lieutenant Walker, I will not accept this testimony."

Mr. Barney called on Dr. Henry Joseph Perry, yet another Harvard-educated doctor with a hospital practice and affiliation at the Boston Dispensary, who was also currently a senior surgeon at Mount Sinai Hospital. He had been an assistant bacteriologist at the Harvard Medical School for thirteen years and had held the same position for almost as long at the Massachusetts School of Pharmacy. He specialized in "genito-urinary" diseases, seeing from ten to seventy patients a day, and was a member of many medical societies. Mr. Barney carefully led Dr. Perry through a hypothetical question that went like this:

> Suppose a man was treated for gonorrhea, which disappeared after about ten days in 1903, with one recurrence including slight symptoms a few years later, and a more serious recurrence a few years after that, for which he was treated over four months. At that point, the gonorrhea symptoms disappeared, then reappeared once more, but none of the germs specifically associated with gonorrhea had been found in this man in 1903 or subsequently. Would you say that a diagnosis of acute gonorrhea, due to recent exposure, was correct?

All was quiet in the court, as everyone turned to look at the witness, who replied firmly, "He did not have acute gonorrhea."

When asked to explain further, Dr. Perry stated that the man in question had chronic gonorrhea, which commonly relapses or "flares-up." He continued, "Mr. Walker's symptoms would indicate chronic inflammation, and a long-standing process going on." Dr. Perry explained that flare-ups can follow "several inciting causes, including alcohol, ginger ale, horseback or bicycle riding, and violent exercise." "Recurrences are common without new infection," the doctor asserted. He then gave a protracted explanation. "The only positive proof of the presence of acute gonorrhea is finding the particular germ that causes it," Dr. Perry explained. "There are disease germs so similar as to be mistaken, even under testing, for gonorrhea. When 'chronic' is added to the diagnosis of gonorrhea, it indicates a term that is not sharply definable and a condition in which the gonorrhea germ is detected with difficulty, or perhaps not detected at all." Dr. Perry stated that he thought that James Walker's initial attack of gonorrhea had not actually been cured. "It is rather common for the disease to linger after noticeable symptoms have disappeared," he commented.

Seeming quite satisfied with Dr. Perry's testimony so far, Mr. Barney began to question him about Dr. Palmer's evidence. The witness responded cryptically that, on May 23, 1911, he had received a sealed package from Dr. S. E. Palmer, marked "Mabel M. Cochrane." Just as courtroom spectators leaned forward to hear what was in that package, Judge Stearns called for a recess. Only then did Walker family members arrive in the courtroom.

Following the recess, courtroom observers were still in suspense regarding the package Dr. Perry had received from Dr. Palmer, and were disappointed when Mr. Barney called a new witness, Dr. Paul Thorndike, instead of continuing Dr. Perry's testimony. Dr. Thorndike had what was now a familiar compendium of credentials, including being a graduate of and a lecturer at the Harvard Medical School. He had been a specialist in "genito-urinary" diseases for many years and was a member of several medical societies. Dr. Thorndike began his testimony by clarifying that he was a more of a senior associate of Dr. Hugh Cabot's, who testified for Nina Walker's side that her husband's symptoms could only have come from a new gonorrhea infection. When questioned by Mr. Barney, Dr. Thorndike stated that he could not positively say whether the gonorrhea attack suffered by Mr. Walker in 1901 was a new infection. "In most cases it would be due to a fresh infection," he explained. "But, given the details of examination and treatment by Dr. Whitney, it would seem that it was not a new infection."

Mr. Barney asked the witness whether the fact that the Walkers had been able to have several children proved that Mr. Walker had been cured of his previous case of gonorrhea. Dr. Thorndike replied that the ability to father children did not prove conclusively that Mr. Walker had been cured of a previous case of gonorrhea. He commented, "There are not many cases where the trouble continues for years afterwards[;] however, there are some cases in which it does. It is very difficult to find the specific germ in some of those old cases." Dr. Thorndike concluded rather ambiguously, "The recurrence of Mr. Walker's trouble in later years would not necessarily prove fresh infection. Such cases usually are fresh infection but I have known cases when they were not. It may be that the gonorrhea was latent in Mr. Walker from 1897 to 1901, although such cases are not usual."

Mr. Harvey's cross-examination of Dr. Thorndike revealed that there was, in fact, a high probability that a man with Mr. Walker's symptoms had suffered a fresh infection. A case could be considered "chronic" after only two months. This was at least the third definition of "chronic gonorrhea" presented at this trial. "Gonorrhea is usually over in six or eight weeks," Dr. Thorndike explained, "[but] if the infection continues after that it is usually spoken of as chronic. Through some local cause, some little spot of infection might persist—lie dormant." "Nobody knows," he observed, "in these old cases, just when the acute disease ceases to exist—it passes into chronic gonorrhea."

Court spectators fidgeted in their seats until Mr. Barney recalled Dr. Perry to testify about the mystery package he had received from Dr. Palmer. The doctor then slowly opened it and revealed that it contained "smears"—fifteen in all, taken from an examination of Miss Mabel Cochrane. The witness explained that a "vaginal smear" was a way of inspecting vaginal discharge by placing the specimen on a glass slide to view it under a microscope. He stated that two days after he had received the smears, he had spent fourteen to fifteen hours examining them. When Mr. Barney asked Dr. Perry what he had found, the witness replied quietly but clearly, "Not a single infectious germ."

Under cross-examination, Dr. Perry verified that he generally diagnosed gonorrhea assisted by this type of microscopic examination. In response to one of Mr. Harvey's questions, he replied, "Absence of the germs may not prove absence of the disease. Sometimes when not found, one still feels convinced they are there." He also agreed, given the facts in James Walker's situation, that it was probable that he had a new gonorrhea infection. In fact, he said, "it was strongly probable." It was also strongly probable that this statement was disappointing to Mr. Barney, who had hired this witness to testify in his client's favor. Judge Stearns interjected a question that had not yet been covered. "If a woman had gonorrhea in the past, would examination afterwards show it?" the judge asked. Dr. Perry replied that was "outside of my special line." Judge Stearns mused that he would like to have a medical expert answer that question.

John Jenks Thomas, a Boston physician and the brother-in-law of James Walker, came to the witness stand. At this point, courtroom spectators began to wonder whether any doctors had remained in Boston to treat patients during the past two days of medical testimony. Mr. Barney asked Dr. Thomas to testify about family matters rather than as a medical expert.

As he had done at the previous trial, the witness again told a courtroom that James had been an attentive husband and had taken his wife to card parties, dances, dinners, and the theater. James had shown affection for his children, and they had returned it; they had very pleasant relations. He absolutely considered James Walker fit to bring up his children and mentioned an occasion at the Newport Training Station when he had acted out charades with them.

Mr. Sheffield had several questions to ask during his cross-examination. Dr. Thomas confirmed that he had been very interested in the case and had been "instrumental in securing some of the experts to testify." When asked about his claim that James and Nina had attended the theater together, he stated that he had seen them there at least once and would not swear it was more than once, but he believed that possibly it was. Mr. Sheffield asked whether Dr. Thomas remembered an incident in which Nina Walker had come to his house in Boston, begging to be given back the infant her husband had brought there, but had been refused. The witness could not deny that the incident had occurred.

The defendant, James Walker, returned to the stand, and his attorney Clark Burdick took over questioning. Just as he was about to begin, spectators noticed that James's mother, Mrs. Rebecca Walker, swooped into the courtroom, with a rustle of her skirts. She was accompanied by another woman they did not recognize. James, after a slight hesitation, testified nervously that he had confided in Dr. James Foster Scott, a Washington physician, that he had a chronic case of gonorrhea and then had informed his wife about this. Mr. Burdick asked James about the charges of infidelity made against him, and people in the courtroom gallery had to strain their ears to hear his reply. He murmured, "I have never had improper relations with any woman since my marriage." Under further questioning by his attorney, James confirmed that he had certainly never embraced or kissed Miss Cochrane in Charleston. Concerning Mr. Charles Slappy's testimony that he and his wife had left because they could not stand the way Miss Cochrane had been running the house, James stated that Mr. Slappy had been dismissed by Miss Cochrane, had asked to be retained, but had been refused.

Observers in the courtroom paid careful attention to a discussion about how the rooms had been arranged during the summers when Mabel Cochrane had stayed at the Walker house in Charleston. James agreed that a door might have originally connected his room with Miss Cochrane's, but if it had, the head of the bed had been against it. He did not specifically remember anything else about the room arrangements. Mr. Burdick asked his client about his visits to Miss Cochrane in Boston, and James admitted that he had called on her. He had only stayed ten minutes the first time and only a couple of minutes on the second visit, he explained, and then he had gone to see her again solely in connection with this divorce case. When he had gone to Boston, about once a month, it had been to visit his mother and sister. James denied having given Miss Cochrane his photograph, denied he had ever been addressed as "Doctor," and added that he had never been addressed at all by the landlord when calling on Miss Cochrane.

In response to further questioning by Mr. Burdick, James repeated his testimony from the previous trial that his expenses had always exceeded his income. When he had first started his career in the navy, his salary had been $2,400 a year, and he had a supplemental investment income of $600. However, he had a family to support and a house with three servants, so his parents had made up the deficit. James stated that his current annual income was $970, which was derived from bond income with a face value of $13,000. Mr. Burdick showed James the photograph that Miss Sarah Crapo had testified that she had found behind a mirror in Mabel Cochrane's former room. The witness recognized it as one of several copies he had made in 1900 and had given to various people. He said that he had last seen copies of that photograph shortly before his wife left him; afterward, they were missing. James stated, with great emphasis, "I never gave that photograph to Miss Cochrane."

During cross-examination, William Sheffield, Nina's counsel, asked James whether he had been absent during the births of his children. He replied that, at the time of his first child's birth, he had not been with his wife because it would have taken five-and-a-half hours to get to Washington from his job in New York. When another child had been born in Brookline, he had not returned home until 9:00 P.M., because he had not known the child would be born that day. Mr. Sheffield brought up Bertha Chinn's testimony that James had refused to call for a doctor earlier on the day of the child's birth, and therefore she had to get on her bicycle to find a nurse. James stated that he did not remember being asked to telephone a doctor.

Mr. Sheffield continued his cross-examination by asking James why his wife and children had not been in Charleston during the summer of 1902, while Miss Cochrane had been living in the house as his guest. "September is one of the worst months for weather in Charleston," James testified, "and that was probably why I wrote to my wife not to come before October." "And, how long was Miss Cochrane there?" asked Mr. Sheffield. "No way to tell for certain," replied the witness. "I would say about three weeks." James testified that his wife and children had not stayed in Charleston during the following summer of 1903 because their new house had been under construction. The furniture had been stored in a navy yard building until the house was finished. "Did your wife keep writing to you about coming down?" her attorney asked. She might have, according to James, but he was not sure, because his letters had been destroyed. He remembered that his wife and children had returned to Charleston in February 1903. "But, wasn't the house finished at about Christmas?" asked Mr. Sheffield. James replied, "That might have been practically so, but we had trouble with the hardware, so I wrote my wife to come down in February." He then confirmed that, when she had finally come down to Charleston, his wife had met Miss Cochrane for the first time.

Mr. Sheffield asked James to discuss his trip to Washington in 1904. He said that he had gone there on March 14; his wife's sister, Bertha Chinn, had gone to Charleston when he left, and his wife had come to Washington about the middle of April. James stated that he had not been given the chance to object to his sister-in-law's going to Charleston during his absence. "My relations with Miss Bertha Chinn were very pleasant," he commented, "but I objected to her influence on my wife. My wife had a tendency to be with her family, and be governed by them, and it was her idea that when I married her I married all of her family and that everything must be arranged to suit her own happiness." "In fact," James stated dramatically, "I found that I had married the whole Chinn family and this has been at the bottom of all my troubles!" While James went on to testify that Nina had spent most of every summer with her family, Mr. Sheffield interrupted to ask, "At this time, you were not making both ends meet?" "That was not my fault!" retorted James. "I was giving her all I made and more." When Mr. Sheffield asked whether the summer arrangements had helped save him money, James replied that he had sent money to his wife but had never seen her private accounts. Mr. Sheffield continued to question James about his version of the trip to Washington. Nina had written to him there that she had been frightened in the Charleston Navy Yard, yet he had telegraphed her not to come to Washington. James's explanation for this request was that the navy yard had been perfectly safe and that he had already written Miss Cochrane to come. If his wife had also come, it would have interfered with those plans.

Mr. Sheffield turned to a discussion of Nina Walker's health issues. James stated that she had apparently been in good health before their marriage. "In the spring of 1906[,] she complained about her health?" asked Mr. Sheffield. "That was chronic with her," groused the witness; he did not remember "any special complaint at that time." Mr. Sheffield asked whether James had cut off funds for Nina and the children in 1906, after she had refused to join him in Brooklyn. James agreed that he had done so, explaining, "It was evident to me that she would not return to me unless pressure was applied." He said that he personally had not wanted to stay in Brooklyn, due to the expense, but the government had not considered it a temporary appointment, and he might have had to stay there for five years, as far as he knew. Mr. Sheffield raised the topic of the birthday party in Brooklyn, as discussed in James's April 27, 1906, letter to his wife (see Chapter 4). The witness claimed that he did not remember exactly what he had written but commented, "One naturally makes a letter as picturesque as possible."

James disagreed that his wife had responsibility for their children during her married life. "Technically she did," he stated, "but she delegated it to others who were about." Regarding his wife's charge that he had refused to take her to the theater, James claimed to only remember one such incident and explained it by stating that he had a couple of cocktails on an empty stomach and had not wished to go to the theater in that condition. Mr. Sheffield continued cross-examining James about the events of the summer and fall of 1909. James stated that he had gone to see Nina while she had been staying at the Batchelers' to tell her that something must be done about caring for the children, as the current situation was very unsatisfactory. "There was no compulsion in my proposals," James maintained. "I would not agree to my wife's suggestions[,] because she wished to send two of the children to board at the Cloyne School and they were too young." When asked about his alleged threat to put his wife in an insane asylum, James denied that, at the previous trial, he had claimed that statement had been made in jest. This comment prompted Mr. Sheffield to find the transcript of the previous trial and read aloud James's testimony to that effect. Grumpily, James stated, "I do not remember."

When asked about whether he had gonorrhea prior to his marriage, James replied that he had been told he did. He had informed Drs. Whitney and Scott that was the case and then had undergone a "microscopic examination" that had determined that he did not have gonorrhea at that time. Under continued questioning, James testified that he had known Mabel Cochrane for two years as a waitress in North Station before she had asked him whether he could find a position for her brother in the Brooklyn Navy Yard. He had told her there was no vacancy but that he would keep him in mind. Miss Cochrane had given him her photograph, but he had left it on his desk and never thought anything about it. He denied that Nina had forwarded to him a picture of Mabel Cochrane while he was in Washington, at which point Mr. Sheffield read from a letter that James had sent to his wife, thanking her for sending a photograph. James responded, "To the best of my knowledge and belief I am now testifying that it was not a picture of Mabel Cochrane that my wife sent me." He admitted that he had corresponded with Miss Cochrane, saying, "Naturally, I did write her about her brother's appointment. However, I did not give her directions on how to find my house in Charleston." At the end of this testimony, it was 4:30 P.M., and Judge Stearns adjourned the court until Friday morning.

Rhode Island Superior Court Retrial, Friday, November 14, 1913[2]

Superior court opened just before 9:30 A.M., with Mr. Sheffield continuing his cross-examination of James Walker. He returned to the letters purportedly written to the witness by Mabel Cochrane. As he had done in the previous trial, James claimed that the more personal passages in these letters had been inserted into copies of what had been innocent notes. Mr. Sheffield showed James the letter his wife had received from the postman and opened, which had been written in January 1905 and was now marked as "Exhibit B" (see Chapter 4). James denied that he had been excited when asking for the mail, as Nina had testified, and claimed that he had not asked for any particular letter. When he had noticed that a letter was missing, he had asked for it. "Was the postman in the habit of telling you how many letters he left at the house?" Mr. Sheffield inquired. "No, because he usually left all the mail at the office" was the reply. James again claimed that the letter in question was not a true copy. "Well," asked Mr. Sheffield, "can you recognize any phrases in it as Miss Cochrane's expressions?" James answered, "No. I cannot dissect the thing and tell what is true and what is false there." He said he had a vague recollection of receiving a letter that in some ways had resembled the copy he had been shown. He had torn up this letter in front of his wife. A couple of nights later, he had a conversation with his wife, who had been noticeably upset. The letter had made Nina suspect that James had been unfaithful to her. James stated, "I explained to her that I could not have been unfaithful due to my medical condition. My wife cried a little, but on the whole seemed to feel better."

Mr. Sheffield asked James whether he knew that Reese Alsop had written to Nina in January 1905 about Mabel Cochrane's letters to him. The witness replied that he had heard Dr. Alsop read his letter earlier in the current trial. His father and mother had also been sent alleged copies of Mabel Cochrane's letters, about which his father had spoken to him. "After the correspondence of 1904 with Miss Cochrane, did you keep press copies [exact copies made with a "copying press"] of the letters you wrote to your wife?" asked Mr. Sheffield. James stated that he had usually made press copies of letters he had written at the office but he had not done so for letters he had written at home. He might have written letters to Miss Cochrane from the office but had no idea where any copies were now. The witness agreed that he had written to Miss Cochrane in 1905 but stated that he had not had a continuing correspondence with her. "Whenever she changed her apartments[,] you knew of it?" Mr. Sheffield asked. "I had her address," James answered. He continued softly, "Miss Cochrane was brought up without much regard for the conventions and wrote a letter which was not according to them." Mr. Sheffield adeptly interjected, "And you had her for a guest?"

Mr. Sheffield discussed the witness's financial situation. James stated that he had only recently found out what his full situation was. He had investments when he had first married but did not have custody of them. He had never known what the amount was and had not cared; his family had handled them for him. They would cut off coupons and send him a check. "It was about $10,000 or $12,000," Mr. Sheffield commented and then asked doubtfully, "Not enough to take the trouble to find out about it?" James quickly replied, "It was well invested and I received the income. It is now worth $19,500, increased by investment." "I understood you to say that at no time during your married life did your income exceed your expenses?" asked Mr. Sheffield. James agreed that had been so. He went over the financial records for each year and said that he had made two investments, including $1,200 from his father's estate. He had not come out ahead, he stated. Any deficits while living with his wife had been made up by assistance from his mother to him or from Virginia Chinn, Nina's mother, to her. James admitted that he had never paid anything for the support of his wife and children since they had left him, except under court order. "I didn't care to finance the enemy," he commented scathingly.

James said that, at the time of his resignation from the navy, his pay and allowances had totaled about $4,900. He had resigned, effective the previous December, to fight this divorce case. "Had not the government given you assurance that you would not be ordered away until this case was finished?" asked Mr. Sheffield. "Certainly not," James replied. "I was to be ordered to Guam or the Philippines." "You were a civil engineer and what have you done for a living since?" Mr. Sheffield inquired. James admitted that he had done nothing but work on the farm in Brownfield, Maine. He stated that he had bought the farm for $2,900 and had expended another $1,000 on it. He had bought it in the name of his brother-in-law, Richard Y. FitzGerald, and then had sold it to his mother for $3,500. "You are doing nothing, then, except watch[ing] those apple trees grow?" asked Mr. Sheffield. "You wouldn't think so if you followed me; you would be going some. I am farming in earnest," replied James. And, he thought, I wish I were there right now.

Mr. Sheffield asked James, "How much are you in debt to your mother?" James replied that he could not tell because "it ran back a long way." He had transferred his interest in his father's estate to her and was not sure of the amount of the transfer. His farm had been transferred to her to pay part of his debt. James stated that his expenses had been approximately the same since Mrs. Walker and the children had left and that he now had additional legal expenses. "I want to ask you whether you intend to make Maine your permanent home," stated Mr. Sheffield. The response from James was "Yes."

Mr. Sheffield asked James about how he had punished his children. James explained that the "quirt" (riding whip) he had used had been given to him by an American Indian in Montana. James admitted that it probably had left marks, because "they are easily made on persons of light complexion, but I gave no excessive punishment, nor did it lessen [the children's] affection for me." Mr. Sheffield showed James a letter from Nina, admonishing him not to forget that he had a son at the Cloyne House School in Newport and that he should try to see the boy. James replied that, at the time, he had forgotten that his son was there. He explained that, following the previous trial, he had gone on vacation and had not tried to see the children because he had not understood that he was allowed to see them. "You had competent counsel to tell you if you had any doubts?" asked Mr. Sheffield. Before his client could respond, Mr. Burdick interrupted to object, "He doesn't know whether he had competent counsel or not," and the question was withdrawn. This was the end of a very long cross-examination. Mr. Burdick approached the depleted witness for a brief redirect, asking him to clarify why he had paid for Miss Cochrane's board in Charleston. "She had been engaged to stay on—at my wife's request, and I thought it would be cheaper than to pay her passage to Boston and back," James replied. Judge Stearns turned to James and asked him whether he knew what it was about Miss Cochrane's letter that had prompted his wife to think he was unfaithful. James replied that he thought the familiar tone had made her jealous. He repeated that all the loving terms in the copy of the letter had not been in the original.

James Walker quickly left the witness stand as soon as his cross-examination was completed. He looked worn out. Henry Goddard Pickering, his distinguished-looking maternal uncle, took his place. Mr. Pickering testified that the Walker children had been very affectionate toward their father when they had visited him at the training station and at Jamestown the previous summer. He agreed with those who believed that James was an "entirely proper person to have charge of the children." Mr. Pickering repeated his story from the first trial about when he had visited Nina the day after she had left her husband and she had told him that she had been thinking of leaving for more than twelve years. Under cross-examination, he stated that at that time, he had told Nina Walker that James Walker was a good man. Her answer had been that he only thought so because he did not really know him. Mr. Pickering also revealed that he had received a letter from Nina in 1904, while she had been staying at the home of Admiral John Walker, James's father, asking him to come and help her with some family trouble. He said that he would have canceled his appointments to come if he had thought it was important, but he had not.

As in the 1911 trial, Mr. Timothy O'Leary, the pay officer at the training station, and Mrs. O'Leary testified about the affection between James Walker and his children and of his devotion to them. Next, James's sister Mrs. Susan Walker FitzGerald testified about her visit to Newport while Nina had been away and Elizabeth had appendicitis. Nina had written her a note of thanks after that, she said. Mr. Burdick read the note aloud, emphasizing the part where Nina had stated, "James was so noble in his care of her and promptness of action that I feel my absence made little difference" (see Chapter 4). Susan stated that, when she had been at her brother's house on several occasions after his wife had left, the children had visited their father three times a week and had played with him "with great affection." She referred to it as "a jolly crowd, with much comradery between them." Susan said she had been impressed because she and her siblings had been raised in a very undemonstrative way. Mrs. FitzGerald said that when the children had visited their father in Jamestown, the relations between them had been "those of unrestrained affection."

James's eldest sister, Frances (Fanny) Thomas, testified next, confirming that James had a very affectionate relationship with his children. While visiting Washington in 1904, she had been shown the alleged copy of Miss Cochrane's letter sent by Nina to the admiral. The witness was handed Exhibit B and silently read through it. When she was finished reading, Mrs. Thomas stated that it was not an exact copy of the letter she had seen. This one was "foolish and unwise," and the letter she had seen had been shorter. After so long it was hard to tell, but she did not think there was anything about "dreaming" or "love" in the letter she had seen. Under cross-examination, Mrs. Thomas admitted that she had only seen the letter from Miss Cochrane once but claimed that she had read it very carefully. She stated that she was unable to pick out the exact phrases in Exhibit B that were not in the original but thought the entire tone was different.

After Mrs. Thomas left the stand, Mr. Barney returned to submit medical testimony in favor of his client and repeated his request that Judge Stearns admit into evidence a letter that Mr. Walker had written to Dr. Charles M. Whitney regarding his consultation with Dr. Balch. Judge Stearns stated that he would continue to exclude it. Disgruntled, Mr. Barney read the deposition of Dr. Howard T. Swain, a Boston physician who was an instructor in the Harvard Medical School. Mr. Barney had asked Dr. Swain whether a woman with an intact and unstretched hymen would definitely be deemed a virgin. The doctor had stated that the woman in question would be "innocent of any sexual activity." For Judge Stearns, that was enough for one week, and he adjourned court until the following Monday.

Rhode Island Superior Court Retrial, Monday, November 17, 1913[3]

Mr. Barney began the new week by reading a deposition from Dr. Charles Henry Hare, of Boston and the Harvard Medical School, whose testimony agreed with Dr. Swain's testimony of the previous Friday that a woman with an intact hymen would be considered a virgin. Under cross-examination by Nina's attorney during the deposition, he had wavered slightly, stating that he thought that Miss Cochrane was probably a virgin but could not say for a fact that she was. Dr. George W. Kaan, a Brookline physician and graduate of the Harvard Medical School, whose testimony was also presented through deposition, had agreed that "an examination readily gave complete proof" of virginity. In cross-examination, he had acknowledged that Dr. Thomas and Mr. FitzGerald had asked him to testify and that he had heard the case discussed in the presence of Dr. Palmer and about a half dozen other doctors. Several more physicians had been deposed by Mr. Barney, including Dr. Nathaniel R. Mason, Dr. Robert L. DeNormandie, Dr. Franklin S. Newell, and Dr. Ernest B. Young. Predictably, all had agreed with the assessments of Drs. Palmer and Culbertson.

Heads turned in the courtroom as Mrs. Rebecca White Walker regally took the stand. Her snow-white hair contrasted impressively with her fashionable black outfit. James's mother spoke of how she and the admiral had financially helped her son and Nina at the beginning of their marriage. She acknowledged that James had been away during the time his first child was born, but stated that when he had returned from Nicaragua, he had gone straight to see his wife. "He was kind, pleasant, and very fond of Nina," Mrs. Walker said, "and talked constantly of the child."

She commented pointedly, "He would not caress his wife in my presence; he is not very demonstrative." The witness remembered one time when she had stopped to see James and his family on her way to New Hampshire; he had been so concerned about his children that he had consulted her as to whether their clothing was warm enough.

Mrs. Walker repeated her testimony from the previous 1911 trial that she had suggested Nina and James take a smaller house and employ one servant fewer in Brookline to solve their money problems and that she had given them financial help for several months. She also retold the story of how she had explained to her daughter-in-law that the way she treated James was "not the way to manage a husband," but Nina would not listen to her. Mrs. Walker again testified that she had paid for a special nurse to care for baby Serrell at Mrs. Chinn's house in Washington. When she had heard that Nina was going to dismiss the nurse after she had stopped paying for her, James had taken the nurse and child to his sister's house in Boston. "Well, I was very ill at the time," Mrs. Walker explained, "but my husband sent a letter to James. In my opinion, the child could not safely be left without the care of a special nurse." Judge Stearns gently interrupted Mrs. Walker at this point to explain to her, "Many things which are interesting and logical are not admissible under the rules of evidence." Mrs. Walker acknowledged this but continued, "We conferred with James, his wife being at home in Brookline, and thought it best to send the child and nurse to my daughter's home on Beacon Street in Boston. Her husband is a physician and James passed the house daily on his way to work."

In response to further questioning by Mr. Barney, Rebecca Walker reiterated her story that, before the birth of her fourth child, Nina had said that she would leave her husband if she were ever "with child" again. Mrs. Walker had told her that she would have to leave her children behind, but Nina had replied, "I don't know about that." With prompting from Mr. Barney, James's mother repeated other stories unfavorable to Nina's case. Her assessment was that her daughter-in-law "had been with her own mother too much[,] and that was why she had abandoned James."

Rhode Island Superior Court Retrial, Tuesday, November 18, 1913[4]

Mr. Barney briefly recalled Dr. Ernest Cushing to the witness stand to reaffirm that he agreed with Dr. Palmer's findings that Mabel Cochrane was a virgin. Then Rebecca Walker returned to testify. She restated her testimony from the previous trial regarding the lecture Nina had given James at her home in Washington and confirmed that the argument had been not about Miss Cochrane but about where Nina had wished to go for the summer. Rebecca Walker said she had told Nina that she was sorry that she was not allowed to go where she wanted for the summer, but that it was entirely James's decision. She had asked Nina about her second choice for a summer destination, and her daughter-in-law had said that it would be Watch Hill, on the coast of Rhode Island. Mrs. Walker had an old friend who took boarders there and, without telling Nina, had told her son that she would provide $500 toward the expenses for Nina and the children to go to Watch Hill.

Mr. Barney showed Mrs. Walker the alleged copy of the Cochrane letter that Nina had sent to Admiral Walker (see Chapter 3). She stated that, although some things looked familiar, the "whole tone of the letter had been changed from the original and it seem[ed] longer." There had been no terms of endearment in the letter sent to the admiral. In addition, there had been no sentence about Mr. Walker being "jollied" and "bearing inspection." Mr. Barney asked whether Mrs. Walker remembered a reference to the famous adulteress, Nan Patterson, in the original letter. She replied, "Yes, and that struck the Admiral and me as being peculiar." There had also been something about a dream in the original, but it seemed that had been twisted in this alleged copy. Mrs. Walker said that she and her husband had considered the letter very carefully to determine, if possible, the character of the woman who had written it. They had found it to be "free and easy." Admiral and Mrs. Walker had told Nina that they were sorry about the letter, but that if James had said that things were all right, "she could rely entirely on him." Nina had stopped complaining about Mabel Cochrane and had never mentioned the letter again. "My son's treatment of his wife was perfectly kind and as it should be," said Mrs. Walker. When Mr. Barney asked whether Nina had shown even a slight suspicion about her husband after the letter incident, the witness replied, "No, 'suspicion' is too strong a word."

After Nina had left the Newport Naval Training Station, Mrs. Walker had stayed there with James for eight months, she said. The children had come to see him, and there had been "a noticeable comradery; they were very happy together." Mrs. Walker stated that her son had maintained his home at the station, ready to receive his wife and children. He had given it up, she said, only after Judge Baker's decision against him after the 1911 trial. Mr. Barney then discussed financial issues with Mrs. Walker. She testified that the income from her late husband's estate was $24,767. When asked how much James owed her, Mrs. Walker slowly opened a ledger, used her finger to point down the columns, and replied that he owed her $7,513.36. "He did owe me $13,713.36," she stated, "but he paid part of it back." Mr. Barney asked how James would be able to provide for his children, should he receive custody of them. "I am able and willing to provide for their education and give them loving care" was her reply.

During cross-examination, Mr. Sheffield asked Mrs. Walker whether she knew that Nina had been upset by James's absence at the birth of their first child. Mrs. Walker said that she did not remember. Mr. Sheffield produced a telegram, which he showed her, but she said that she did not recognize it. He asked her to read the telegram aloud, and she did so in a quiet voice. It stated, "No response from you. Nina disappointed. Unless letter near, telegraph your pleasure. Daughter charming" (see Chapter 3). Mr. Sheffield asked Mrs. Walker to read the signature on the telegram, which was "R. W. Walker." Then he asked her, "Do you know of any other R. W. Walker in Washington?" "I think there was a real estate agent of that name," Mrs. Walker replied coyly. "And," Mr. Sheffield asked, "would he send that telegram?" Mrs. Walker had to reluctantly admit that she must have sent the telegram to her son.

"You had some ill feeling against the Chinns, after the incident with the nurse?" Mr. Sheffield inquired. Mrs. Walker stated slowly and crisply, "I did not approve of their standards, particularly in Miss Chinn's letter to me." Regarding Exhibit B, the alleged copy of the Cochrane letter that Nina had shown to the witness and her husband, Rebecca Walker said that she did not consider it evidence against her son. "It might be compromising, but a woman may write a letter to any man," she explained. As she had in her direct testimony, Mrs. Walker stated that the alleged copy shown in court was not the same as the letter she had seen originally and that her opinion was that the copy would show that the writer was "an improper person." Mr. Sheffield asked the witness whether she had characterized the letter as "foolish" during the previous trial, and she stated that she would now like to change that description to "injudicious." Mrs. Walker agreed that Nina had evidently been very upset by the letter and thought that a "serious family consultation" was necessary. Rebecca Walker concluded, "I think that women brought up in the South are more naturally suspicious of their husbands than those in the North."

At that point, Mr. Sheffield referred to the letter Mrs. Walker had written to her son prior to his marriage (Chapter 2). "Didn't your son, before his marriage, write to you saying he proposed to 'live as he saw fit' after his marriage, under certain circumstances?" he asked. Mr. Sheffield read from that letter, in which Mrs. Walker complained that her son had written a "discourteous and improper letter" to her and also warned that "there is but one way to live—that is a clean, honest, unselfish life." Mrs. Walker attempted to interrupt him, but he continued to read more of the letter, in which she entreated her son "not to take a step which would ruin Nina's future life." Mrs. Walker explained that she had been speaking about his breaking the engagement. "He could lead a clean, honest life if he had broken the engagement, could he not?" asked Mr. Sheffield. Again the witness had to agree. "Did you not say that your son had a bad temper, but kept it under control?" Mrs. Walker would not admit that James's temper was "noticeable, as compared with other men." "He did have wonderful self-control," she commented. "Did you testify during the previous trial that your son was a 'cold man'?" Mr. Sheffield probed. Mrs. Walker said that she now wished to change that statement and continued, "I might have said 'self-control,' which was misunderstood for 'cold.' He was warm-hearted."

Mr. Sheffield now turned to a different matter. "When did you turn your securities over to your son?" he asked. "I never did," said the witness. "Where were the securities during the last trial?" Mr. Sheffield asked. Mrs. Walker replied that she had discovered that they were not in her safe-deposit box. "Included in the $13,000.00 owed to me by my son is a good deal of money that has gone to my son's wife," she commented. When asked to explain this statement, Mrs. Walker said that she had furnished her son with money to pay the allowance to Nina that the court had ordered. Mr. Sheffield asked whether James Walker had paid anything at all for the support of his family from the time Nina had left in 1909 to the time of Judge Baker's order in 1911. Mrs. Walker said she thought that he had. "For his wife and children?" roared Mr. Sheffield. The witness answered that she could not say; she thought that "family" referred to her and other members of their family.

After this cross-examination, Mr. Barney called the next witness for the defense, Alice P. Mullen. Miss Mullen had come with Mrs. FitzGerald to the Newport Naval Training Station for two weeks to help with the Walker children's visits. She testified that the children and Mr. Walker had been very happy together. Mr. Henry Pickering Walker, of Hudson, Massachusetts, was called to testify next. As James's younger brother, he gave the usual Walker testimony that family relations were good. Mrs. Katherine Alice Walker, his wife, testified that she had seen James and Nina together once at her wedding, once at a funeral, and once at a party. The relations between the two had seemed "perfectly pleasant and natural" to her, but she had the impression that Nina Walker was "extremely selfish." Katherine Walker explained that Nina had talked about her dissatisfaction with Admiral Walker's will and other issues with the Walker family for an entire train trip from New York to Boston.

The defense testimony was interrupted at this point so that yet another medical witness could be called to testify, this time by Nina's attorney,

William R. Harvey. Dr. Edgar B. Smith had practiced medicine in Providence for many years. Mr. Harvey again asked whether a woman with an intact hymen would be considered a virgin. When he pronounced the term "hymen" in a peculiar manner, he was corrected by both the stenographer and Mr. Barney but regained his composure. Dr. Smith answered Mr. Harvey's question by stating that the woman doctors' reports did not necessarily prove that Miss Cochrane was a virgin. He discussed the elasticity of the hymen and explained that it varied from woman to woman. "There are plenty of cases where an intact hymen, which used to be considered proof of virginity, has existed when the facts were known to be directly the opposite," he stated. On cross-examination, Mr. Barney, with an air of self-assurance, asked Dr. Smith whether he was speaking of an "imperforate hymen," a condition in which the hymen lacks an opening and completely obstructs the vagina. Dr. Smith replied patiently that he was talking about a normal variation in hymen elasticity and not about an imperforate hymen, which was rare. Judge Stearns asked the witness whether a medical specialist could tell whether sexual intercourse had occurred, despite an intact hymen. Dr. Smith replied, "A competent examiner could tell a great deal, but not even a competent practitioner could speak solely from examination."

Mr. Harvey called Dr. Charles W. Stewart to testify. This medical expert had studied in Vienna, Berlin, and Heidelberg, and had been a surgeon for seventeen years at the Newport Hospital. Mr. Harvey asked him whether an intact hymen indicated that a woman was a virgin, this time pronouncing the term correctly. The witness stated that an intact hymen was not sufficient evidence of whether the woman had engaged in intimate relations.

Following the interruption for medical testimony, Mr. Barney resumed his client's side of the case. He recalled Mrs. Frances (Fanny) Thomas, James's eldest sister, to testify regarding the identification of Mabel Cochrane. She stated that she had been present when Miss Cochrane had been introduced to Mr. Barney and another attorney, Mr. Henry T. Richardson, at her mother's home. This led directly to the testimony of that Brookline attorney, Mr. Richardson. Mr. Richardson stated that he had been introduced to Miss Cochrane at Mrs. Rebecca Walker's house when Mr. Barney had asked her whether she would come to court and testify in this trial. Mr. Sheffield jumped up and objected to this line of questioning, but Judge Stearns stated that he thought that James Walker's attorneys had the right to show an effort to produce a material witness. Mr. Richardson repeated that Mr. Barney had asked Miss Cochrane to testify but added that she had refused to do so. When asked her reason for refusing, Mr.

Sheffield again objected, and this time the judge sustained his objection. Miss Cochrane had consented to give a deposition in the case, Mr. Richardson stated, but with certain conditions. Judge Stearns affirmed that this response was admissible to show why the defense did not produce the testimony of this witness. Mr. Richardson stated that it was agreed that he would be Miss Cochrane's personal counsel and hold her deposition at a time and place that would avoid newspaper notoriety. "I met with her in my office on October 23 and we set the date for the deposition on the afternoon of Saturday, November 1," Mr. Richardson explained. Mr. Barney asked, "And, what was her condition then, on Saturday[,] November first[,] in the afternoon, when she came to see you?" Mr. Sheffield objected once more but was overruled. Mr. Richardson answered, "She apparently was in a nervous condition, had been crying, in my judgment from her appearance. She refused to go on with the deposition." "It was too late to reach the magistrate," he explained, "but I communicated with Mr. Barney and attempted to have Miss Cochrane reconsider." "Later," he continued, "I received a letter from her giving her address as 'general delivery, Springfield, Massachusetts.' She had left her former apartment in New Castle Court in Boston. I went to Springfield and stood in front of the Springfield Post Office for hours, searched two New York trains and several hotel registers. I even searched in New York for Miss Cochrane, but could not find her." At this point, it was 4:40 P.M., and Judge Stearns wearily stated, "I think work enough has been done for the stenographer." Court was adjourned until the next morning.

Rhode Island Superior Court Retrial, Wednesday, November 19, 1913[5]

Although it was past mid-November, Wednesday was an unexpectedly warm and sunny day. The mild temperature, reaching seventy-six degrees, cut down a bit on the courtroom spectators who wanted to take advantage of the unseasonable weather but did not distract the most devoted followers of the Walker case. Witnesses in the case did not have the option of staying away to enjoy the weather. These included Dr. Edward S. Allen of Providence, who was called as a defense medical expert by Mr. Barney. He seemed somewhat uncomfortable when asked whether a woman with an intact and tight hymen would be considered a virgin but stated that he would do his best to answer the question and was "most certain" that the woman in question would be a virgin. However, to give an accurate answer, he would really rather make his own examination. Then Mr. Barney asked Dr. Allen the long, complicated hypothetical question that he was in the habit of asking physicians with regard to James Walker's medical condition. Dr. Allen responded that the patient described in the question "positively had a chronic type of gonorrhea, of perhaps six, eight, or ten years' standing." The doctor explained, "There are several sorts of 'cocci' which produce results resembling those of gonorrhea. I believe, however, that I would be able to make a diagnosis even without the use of the microscope." He continued, "Disease germs change their character; they will suddenly cease to be virulent, for no apparent reason—in the laboratory—and, it is believed they do so in animals and the human being, as well. Virulence is not the same as infection." Mr. Harvey demonstrated his own understanding of the medical facts while cross-examining the doctor. Dr. Allen finally stated, "Mr. Walker had most likely been subject to certain causes which would have made gonorrhea reappear long before he claimed it did."

Miss Mary F. Bangs, Mrs. Rebecca Walker's secretary, predictably testified that James Walker and his children had "delightful relations" and that he had shown "the keenest interest in their welfare, moral and physical." "They seemed fond of Mrs. Walker, senior," she said, "and she was very fond of them." During her cross-examination, Miss Bangs said that she had been employed by Mrs. Walker for more than four years and had taken a great interest in this case. In response to Mr. Harvey's inquiry, she stated that she could not recollect whether Mr. James Walker had ever gone to the boat to meet his children when they had come to visit. Mr. Harvey's next question was "Did Mr. Walker sometimes go away when the children were expected without telling them he would be gone?" For a moment, Miss Bangs looked as though she was cornered. She answered nervously, "I don't remember it" and then continued timidly, "Did I testify about it at the last trial? If I said so then it was true; I testified truly."

James Walker was recalled to the stand to refute some of his wife's testimony. He denied that he had suggested to his mother that she invite Mabel Cochrane to her home in Washington and denied having ever taken Miss Cochrane to Mount Vernon. "I once walked with her to the Zoo in Washington on a Sunday afternoon, though," James stated helpfully. When asked about the money his mother had testified that he owed her, James answered that he actually owed her more than she had stated. "The expenses of this trial are very heavy," he added. During cross-examination, Mr. Harvey asked James why he had resigned from the navy, and he replied that he had done so to fight this case. "Did you not make an affidavit that you resigned on account of your health?" bellowed Mr. Harvey. "That was one reason," the witness replied, "but the main one was to fight this case." Mr. Harvey roared, "Would not the government allow you opportunity to defend yourself in this case?" "That can't go on forever," James replied. "I was ordered to go to Guam or the Philippines."

Mr. Burdick asked permission to recall Nina Walker to ask her a question regarding James's health condition. Judge Stearns, saying he thought that both sides had "gone about as far in this case as was proper," did not allow this. Mr. Burdick then turned to his interminable stack of depositions and read the one from Mrs. Mary Clark, taken the previous October in Washington, DC. Mrs. Clark was the wife of Mr. Frank Wigglesworth Clark, a noted geologist, and testified that she had known Rebecca Walker for many years. She described an incident when Nina Walker had told her that she was unhappy because her husband was not sociable and did not go out but only sat on the plaza in his shirt-sleeves. Nina Walker had also complained that she was too confined with her four children and had confided that she wanted to get a separation. Mrs. Clark testified that she had advised her, "People do not obtain separations for such things."

Mr. Burdick read the deposition of Mr. Louis B. McBride, who had testified that he had known James Walker well while both had worked at the Brooklyn Navy Yard and that he believed that Mr. Walker had been "very moderate in his use of intoxicating liquors and did not habitually use them at all." In addition, Mr. Walker "did not have women guests, or see women except those who were guests of his fellow officers." Mr. McBride had never heard him use abusive language toward anyone. He joined the chorus of Walker witnesses who considered James a "proper person to have custody of his children," although he admitted that he had never met them. Charles W. Parks, USN, had been deposed as well. He had served as James Walker's assistant at the Boston Navy Yard and at the Portsmouth Navy Yard. Parks stated that he had seen "nothing to indicate that Mr. Walker was unsuitable to have care of his children." When asked what he knew about Mr. Walker's character, Mr. Parks replied that he "was one man about whom he could answer that question to his satisfaction." It took Judge Stearns a few minutes to parse that response, but he ultimately determined that it was a good character reference.

Mr. Burdick then turned to the deposition from Mrs. Eliza Ripley, Nina's eighty-year-old paternal aunt who lived in Brooklyn and had acknowledged in her testimony at the previous trial that she had been asked to testify by "Mrs. Admiral Walker." Avid followers of the Walker case remembered that Judge Baker had ruled out part of Mrs. Ripley's previous deposition because he had seen no relevance to her statements regarding "hereditary divorce" on the maternal side of Nina Walker's family. This deponent's testimony that it was the "universal" opinion that Mrs. Chinn was not known for her truthfulness had also created a legal debate at the previous trial, since she had been unable to identify any particular person who held this opinion. This time, question after question in Mrs. Ripley's deposition was ruled out, with objections noted by Mr. Burdick. Finally, Judge Stearns asked whether there was any other line of questioning in the deposition. When told there was not, the judge wearily stated that he would note an objection to ruling out the "whole lot" of Mrs. Ripley's deposition in case there was a later appeal. However, many courtroom observers thought that the mere fact that James Walker's attorney had raised the issues involved in Mrs. Ripley's deposition was sufficient to make the point that the women in Nina Walker's family were prone to leaving their husbands and possibly being untruthful.

Miss Amelia Hedges, a first cousin of Nina Walker's, had also been asked questions about Mrs. Chinn's truthfulness during her deposition. Judge Stearns ruled out her entire deposition, because he determined that the questions had not been asked properly. Mr. Joseph Noyes, a lawyer from New York, had given testimony in his deposition about the "amicable relations" in the Walker family. The final deposition read that morning was from the civil engineer Frederic R. Harris, USN, who had been James Walker's assistant in Charleston and had lived with him for much of that time. He had testified that Mr. Walker had drunk very little and had never used abusive or profane language; in fact, "his language was very good." During cross-examination, Mr. Harris acknowledged that Nina Walker was "a competent person to care for her children," despite what he called her "inappropriate hysterics" regarding danger in the navy yard.

Following the luncheon recess, Mr. Burdick attempted to introduce a deposition from another woman who had testified about the Chinn family's marital history. Judge Stearns again excluded the entire testimony, with an objection noted. Next came the deposition from William B. Ferguson, USN, the host of the infamous Brooklyn birthday party. He had testified that James Walker had been "very temperate in his drinking" and that his "conversation was always free from bad language." Mr. Ferguson had admitted that he did not know anything about James's family life.

Mr. Barney read Dr. Henry M. Cutts's deposition. Dr. Cutts had been the Walkers' family physician during two of the children's births. He repeated his testimony from the previous trial that Nina had been upset about having another child and that he had given her some pills, even though he had not really thought that they would have any effect on her pregnancy. In his deposition, Professor Edward Charles Pickering, a distinguished astronomer at Harvard University, stated that he had known James Walker's mother and grandfather since he was a boy; they were relatives. Professor Pickering did not know Mr. Walker's wife and children. When Mr. Barney read his question about the general reputation of the Walker family, Mr. Harvey objected. "The Walker family?" Judge Stearns asked skeptically and sustained the objection. Mr. Barney stated that he thought the response was admissible regarding custody of the children. Judge Stearns, however, thought the testimony was "too remote."

Mrs. Alma H. Child had worked as a nurse at the Walker house when their second child was born. Mrs. Child testified that Mr. Walker had not been around much and that "Miss Bertha Chinn had full charge of the house, by her sister's direction." She observed that "Miss Chinn found fault with Mr. Walker about almost everything." The witness stated that, although Mrs. Nina Walker had wanted her to stay, she had left the house "because of unpleasantness," although, in her testimony, Bertha had claimed that Mrs. Child had been fired. Testimony regarding conversations between Mrs. Child and Miss Chinn were ruled out.

Dr. Almon Cooper's deposition indicated that he had attended Nina Walker at the birth of her second child and that she was a "somewhat nervous woman." Mr. George Wigglesworth, a member of the Harvard University Board of Overseers, had again been deposed as a character witness for the Walker family. Judge Stearns ruled out his entire deposition. The judge also excluded the depositions from a husband and his wife regarding an alleged will that Miss Chinn had made for her sister.

Mr. Sheffield thought it was important to rebut some of the testimony given for the defense and recalled his client to do so. He began by asking about Mrs. Rebecca Walker's version of why the baby and nurse had gone to Mrs. Thomas's house. Nina stated that she had hired the nurse, Mrs. Long, to take care of Serrell, who was sickly, and that her husband had agreed that Mrs. Long should go to Washington with him to stay at Mrs. Chinn's house for six weeks. Nina said that she had paid Mrs. Long and had never known that James's mother had furnished the money. While in Washington on Navy business, her husband had written her that "there was some trouble" about the baby nurse, and Nina had replied that he should bring Serrell home to Brookline. "I had everything ready," the witness stated bitterly, "when my husband arrived home—without my baby." She maintained that she had objected strongly and had gone to the Thomases' house the next day, but they had refused to give up her child. They had kept the baby from her, she claimed, from November until January.

Nina Walker also refuted her husband's testimony regarding Mabel Cochrane's photograph. She asserted that the first time she had seen it was when Miss Cochrane had sent it to Charleston and she had forwarded it to her husband, who had written to thank her for it. Nina pointed out that, in the previous trial, James had not denied that the photograph he had written about was of Miss Cochrane; he had done so only during the current trial. She also corroborated Charles Slappy's testimony regarding the arrangement of the rooms in the Charleston house. Nina insisted that, although she had usually been the one who hired the servants, she had never had anything to do with engaging or paying Miss Cochrane and had not even known how much she was paid.

Regarding the Cochrane letter she had received from the postman and opened, Nina asserted that her husband had come on horseback "in hot haste" to retrieve it. She contended that he had not opened, read, and destroyed it in her presence, as he had claimed in his testimony. "He put it in his pocket," she stated, "and rode off." She had written to Admiral Walker about the letter, notifying him that she would be coming to see him about it. "I arrived Sunday morning and was kept waiting until noon, when the Admiral finally appeared," she complained. "I was utterly exhausted by my journey, but it was not until evening that I was given any opportunity to speak with Admiral Walker about the letter. I tried until 11:00 o'clock, but found it was no use to try longer and retired." Later, she said, "I found [that] Admiral Walker thought I was to blame for coming to see him in the matter!" Mr. Sheffield asked Nina, "Did you add, amend, or change the Cochrane letter in any way?" She replied, "No. The copy is an exact copy." Judge Stearns asked her how much time she had had to make the copy. "About a half an hour or a little less" was her answer.

Nina Walker's testimony differed from her husband's regarding his medical condition. She asserted that her husband had told her that he had gonorrhea and had said that he had also told Dr. Scott that he had it; he had not said that he had oxaluria. Mr. Sheffield showed Nina a letter that she had written to her husband that stated, "I really have been very much troubled for you over this move and the horrid mixup with the [d]ry dock people, and so much injustice shown in the matter, but I am proud of the stand you have taken all the way through and very glad you are my husband[;] I have not seen a better yet[;] are you not surprised?"[6] (see Chapter 4). Nina blushed slightly and explained that she had written to express her good opinion of her husband with the hope that it would encourage him to break off with Mabel Cochrane and come back to her. Judge Stearns asked her whether she had been suspicious of her husband at that time, and Nina confirmed that she had.

Mr. Sheffield read aloud the letter from Mabel Cochrane to her sister, undated but presumed to be from the summer of 1903 (see Chapter 3). In it, Mabel discussed her preparations for the Fourth of July, including her plans "to make Eddie and Mr. Walker buy a string of Chinese lanterns to string along the piazza and a bundle of firecrackers." Mabel had also written, "I may have a little *pink lemonade* [Mr. Sheffield made sure to indicate that this was underscored] on the side with a *stick* [also underscored] in it." The most provocative parts of the letter were the last lines, which read, "For there is a full quart of Club Whiskey in the wine closet, and I hold the key. I guess I will be able to make things hum for a little while."[7] The letter was admitted into evidence.

During re-cross-examination, Mr. Burdick showed Nina Walker the photograph of her husband in uniform that had been allegedly found at the Crapo house and asked her whether she had removed that picture from the training station when she had left. She denied this, stating that she had only taken two photographs of James: one that she had given to Mr. Harvey to use for the case and another that she still had. Mr. Burdick asked Nina about her previous response to Judge Stearns that she had been "suspicious" of her husband at the time that she had written him a loving letter on July 4, 1905. Nina was suddenly mindful of her attorney's caution that she should not appear to have condoned her husband's infidelity by reconciling with him after finding out about it. She replied that she would like to modify her answer to state that she had not been "suspicious" but "anxious." Mr. Burdick asked why she had been anxious, and Nina replied, "Admiral Walker was not willing to give me any assurance that he would act to stop such letters coming from Miss Cochrane." "Were there any more such letters?" inquired Mr. Burdick, to which Nina answered there had not been. "Then why were you suspicious?" he shot back. With some hesitation, Nina responded, "My husband's attitude towards myself and the children made me suspicious." "When you wrote that he was a perfect husband, etc., was it your desire, in spite of Mr. Walker's relations with Miss Cochrane[,] to retain his affection?" Mr. Burdick asked. "I have all along tried to retain his affection. It has never been my wish to sever relations" was Nina's rejoinder.

Judge Stearns took his prerogative to ask Nina about the letter she had written to Susan FitzGerald on May 5, 1909, in which she had thanked Susan for coming after Elizabeth's emergency surgery for appendicitis while Nina was away. It had also stated, "James was so noble in his care of her and promptness of action that I feel my absence made little difference[;] it was a great shock to me, but seeing Elizabeth so comfortable the night of my arrival, I was saved the greater anxiety that James passed through"[8] (see Chapter 4). Nina turned toward the judge. She explained with a wavering voice that when she had returned from her trip, James had told her that Elizabeth was not at home and had broken the news that their daughter had undergone emergency surgery. In an emotional tone,

Nina stated, "I feared that my child had been carried away from us." When she had learned that Elizabeth was doing well in the hospital, "I was so glad to find it was all right about the child that I expressed myself thus in that letter." Judge Stearns accepted this answer and only later realized that the letter in question was dated sixteen days after Nina's return and therefore had not been prompted by her immediate reaction.

To complete the medical testimonies for the day, Mr. Harvey called Dr. Rufus E. Darrah to the stand. Dr. Darrah had practiced medicine in Newport since 1896, was a member of the State Board of Health, and was the chairman of the Newport Board of Health. Mr. Harvey asked him whether an intact hymen was medical evidence of virginity. Dr. Darrah replied, "Even giving full credence to the statements and ability of the women doctors," he could not make a determination of whether Miss Cochrane was a virgin. The physical examinations performed on her were not sufficient, and he "would want to learn some other points before venturing any opinion as to the status of the patient." Court was adjourned until yet another day of trial.

Rhode Island Superior Court Retrial, Thursday, November 20, 1913[9]

Overnight there had been a heavy downpour, but the unseasonable weather continued. In fact, it was declared the warmest November 20 since 1879.[10] Nina Walker's attorney, Mr. Harvey, read a deposition given by Dr. James Foster Scott. At the previous trial, Nina had stated that she had visited her physician in Washington with her husband to discuss his health problem. In his deposition for the current trial, Dr. Scott had testified that, although he had never treated Mr. Walker, he had a "strong impression" that Mr. Walker had confided in him that he had contracted gonorrhea recently. When he had seen Mr. Walker at a later date, James had "contradicted all this, saying that I had done him a gross injustice and was mistaken at almost every point." However, Dr. Scott had stated that he must go by his own recollection. When asked where he had first met with Mr. Walker, Dr. Scott had replied, "It was on the street, in the gloaming [at dusk]." The doctor had maintained, "I am not unfriendly to either side. I tried all I could to bring them together, but they did not thank me for it!"

Dr. Scott had been alarmed that James Walker had told him that he had contracted gonorrhea, he explained, because Nina Walker had been his patient, and it had involved her health and well-being. Nina Walker had later written to him, stating that her husband had confessed to her what he had told the doctor and asking him to confirm it. Mr. Harvey had shown

Dr. Scott the letter he had written in response to Nina, affirming that Mr. Walker had told him that he had recently contracted gonorrhea. The doctor stated in his deposition that subsequently, Mr. Walker had come to see him in Washington, saying that his wife was upset and that Dr. Scott was the only one who could reconcile them. "I wracked my brain to do what I could," Dr. Scott had testified. "I then wrote a 'joint letter' to Mr. and Mrs. Walker saying I was not infallible, and could have been wrong about what Mr. Walker told me." Dr. Scott had commented, "Mr. Walker seemed to emphatically love his wife and desire reconciliation. I did what I thought was right, and did not care one rap about it."

At this point, Judge Stearns called attention to the fact that Dr. Scott's previous deposition did not appear with the court documents for the current case. Mr. Barney objected that his side was unable to be present at the taking of the earlier deposition. Despite Mr. Sheffield's assurance that they were represented by "the ablest lawyer in Washington," the previous deposition was excluded.

Mr. Sheffield read another deposition, this one from Miss Jennie Collins, of Roxbury, Massachusetts, who had been a boarder at the Crapo house for three years while Mabel Cochrane had also lived there. She had testified that on three occasions, she had seen three different men in or leaving Miss Cochrane's room in the early-morning hours. Miss Collins had not been certain whether Mabel had been in her room at the time, but she had spoken to Mrs. Crapo about this. When asked whether Miss Cochrane's sister had been living with her at the time, Miss Collins had replied that she had not been. She also believed that Mabel Cochrane had not been employed at the time. Mr. Harvey also read the deposition of Miss Margaret E. Crawford, who had helped Mrs. Crapo do general cleaning for four or five years during the time Mabel Cochrane had resided in the back parlor of her house. Miss Crawford had also seen male callers in or leaving Miss Cochrane's room in the early morning. This was the final deposition. A recess was called to allow time for the attorneys for both sides to review the trial exhibits, after which the evidence was declared closed.

Mr. Barney began the closing arguments for James Walker. He claimed that testimony alleging his client's adultery was all circumstantial. "As to Slappy's evidence, no one would hang a dog on it. Like the rest of the testimony," Mr. Barney insisted, "it is unbelievable!" He entreated, "There was the presence of young Mr. Cochrane. There is no duenna [chaperone] like a younger brother!" Mr. Barney continued to argue that there was no trouble until Bertha Chinn had appeared in Charleston. Nina Walker had gone to Washington not to complain about Miss Cochrane but to avoid staying in the navy yard. "Miss Chinn seems to have been the evil genius in this case!" Mr. Barney exclaimed. He maintained that Nina Walker, "a younger daughter who was perhaps babied, [had come] to Washington because she was accustomed to getting her own 'way.' That is the keynote of her character." He continued, "She claims she implored her mother-in-law that she and Mr. Walker should be together in Charleston the coming summer, rather than having Mabel Cochrane there, but this is clearly contradicted by other evidence." It was 12:40 P.M., and Judge Stearns called a recess. As people stepped out of the courtroom, they blinked into sunlight that was unexpectedly bright for a November afternoon in Newport. No one, with the possible exception of the principals in the case and their attorneys, really wanted to return to the courtroom after lunch.

That afternoon, Mr. Barney continued the closing arguments for his client. Referring to "the alleged copy of the alleged Cochrane letter," he maintained that Mr. Walker had shown "a high sense of honor in calling on Miss Cochrane in Boston." Mr. Barney insisted, "There was no evidence that it was Mr. Walker who was referred to as 'the doctor.' Even the Crapo people have not dared go very far in giving their evidence." Mr. Barney praised Drs. Palmer and Culbertson for their ability and integrity. "Our side has produced such an array of experts as I have never known to be gathered on one side of a case," he declared. "Their evidence shows that Mabel Cochrane could not have been of such a character as the allegations against her would indicate. The only thing which can be done is to attack the ability or truthfulness of the two who made the examination," Mr. Barney claimed. He commented contemptuously on testimony by medical experts for the other side, who had stated that it was possible that Mabel Cochrane had engaged in intimate relations with James Walker, despite an intact hymen. "It was contrary to the testimony of these eminent and truthful women," Mr. Barney implored. "It is not possibility, but high probability, which is to be considered in a case like this."

Aware that the shadow of Mabel Cochrane loomed heavily over this case, Mr. Barney admitted that her absence might be seen as highly significant. "That may be true," he stated, "but the fact that she submitted to an examination shows that she knew she was innocent. Having done this, it is not surprising if she felt she had done all she should, and avoided any more notoriety." Mr. Barney added, "Had I thought she would not give her deposition, I would have put her under summons. I would have been glad for the court to see her." He called Judge Stearns's attention to the fact that, after the "Charleston affair," Nina Walker had continued to live with her husband. Therefore, he claimed, she could not ask the court to consider any evidence founded on what had purportedly happened in

Charleston, or before that. "She cannot now change her mind," he argued. "Even if he was guilty, she has condoned it, and there is no evidence of guilt after that time."

The "real reason" Nina Walker had left her husband, according to Mr. Barney, was that she could not have her way regarding the children. "I do not believe that the court would think she was actually afraid of being incarcerated in a lunatic asylum," he stated. "Before Nina Walker left her husband, she arranged to deprive him of his children, she prevaricated, she forged his name, and he returned home to find his home ransacked and all the papers which could be used in this case gone." "It is wonderful that his sanity has not left him!" Mr. Barney declared and then continued, "Should this trumped-up case be decided against Mr. Walker, he would be branded as a man unfit to ever have a home." Everyone took a long breath and a recess.

Mr. Sheffield began the closing arguments for Nina Chinn Walker by making it clear, lest anyone still doubted it, that "there is now no possibility of reconciliation." Mr. Sheffield asserted, "Had Mr. Walker tried, when Nina Walker telephoned after leaving, it might have been considered. This case must now be determined either here on the issue of separate maintenance or as an absolute divorce in due time. Mr. Walker brought on himself whatever there is." "Strange and unusual defenses, developed at great length, have been introduced," Mr. Sheffield stated. "Otherwise the case is a simple one." Miss Mabel Cochrane had been with Mr. Walker in Charleston for an indefinite period of time as a guest, not as a housekeeper. "After her arrival," he claimed, "the Slappys were given a vacation and soon after they returned, Mabel Cochrane disappeared. The next summer this was repeated and, from August to the following February, Mr. Walker kept Miss Cochrane at a boarding house in Charleston. Not until she returned to Charleston did Mrs. Nina Walker first see her." Mr. Sheffield continued, "Then her husband went to Washington and sent for Miss Cochrane. Mrs. Walker, alarmed, followed them to Washington. What was she to think?"

The strongest evidence that James Walker had to defend himself against his wife's charge of adultery with Mabel Cochrane was the expert medical testimony stating that she was a virgin. Therefore, Mr. Sheffield had to make a strong case that Miss Cochrane had engaged in extramarital relations with his client's husband, despite the evaluations of a long list of physicians. He determined that, rather than impugn the medical experts, he would attack a weaker link. That weaker link was testimony by Sallie Walker and Helen Kellogg (formerly Helen Hull), who had identified Miss Cochrane for the doctors. "Why, neither of these young women ever met this governess except one week in the spring of 1904 at the residence of Admiral Walker in Washington!" Mr. Sheffield exclaimed. "It was in the midst of the social season, and is it likely that these young society women paid much attention to the governess?" He continued, "Yet . . . they introduced her to the women physicians as being the woman they had seen but a few times five years earlier!" "Furthermore," Mr. Sheffield stated, "in the hypothetical question concerning her virginity, which was framed by Mr. Walker's attorneys themselves, this person examined was described as thirty years old, while according to the testimony of their own witness, Miss Cochrane's brother, she is thirty-eight." "In view of all these considerations," Mr. Sheffield concluded, "I ask your honor to weigh carefully the statements that the woman examined in Boston was in fact Mabel Cochrane." Mistaken identity was a bombshell accusation exploded too late to be defused by James Walker's attorneys.

Mr. Sheffield closed his arguments by stating, "A principal interest in this case is that of the children. Two are of the age when by law they may choose their own guardian." He suggested that the Walker children have a private interview with Judge Stearns. There was no objection to this. Judge Stearns stated that he would reserve his decision until he had the opportunity to deliberate on the case. With a sigh, he collected all the letters, surgical instruments, depositions, and other forms of evidence to examine more thoroughly. Nina and James Walker separately resigned themselves to spending yet more time waiting for a resolution.

11

"Gross Misbehavior and Wickedness"

December 4, 1913, to December 4, 1916

On Thursday, December 4, 1913, Sydney Harvey, the clerk of the Newport Superior Court, was at his desk early. There had been talk that Judge Charles Falconer Stearns would announce his opinion in the Walker divorce case today. At 9:13 A.M., the written opinion was delivered to the clerk's office by registry post. James Walker's attorneys and a newspaper reporter were present when Mr. Harvey opened the envelope. Nina Walker and her attorneys would hear the news later.

In his ruling, Judge Stearns first reviewed the history of Nina Walker's divorce petition, stating that she had been granted a divorce on the ground of adultery until the Rhode Island Supreme Court had ruled that her husband could have a new trial based on additional evidence. Judge Stearns went on to state that the new trial had provided circumstantial evidence that James Walker had committed adultery, particularly in Mr. Charles Slappy's testimony. If Mr. Slappy's statements were true, the judge asserted, they would be important evidence, but he noted that Slappy's story should be considered with caution, because it was given by a discharged employee who had disputes with both Mr. Walker and with Miss Cochrane. Furthermore, Judge Stearns concluded, the suggestive behavior that Mr. Slappy had reported was "hardly consistent with probabilities that the parties acted with such total disregard of secrecy and the danger of discovery."[1] The judge implied the possibility that Mr. Slappy had lied in his testimony. He did not point out that Mr. Slappy was a "colored man," but the prevalent racism of the time might have influenced the judge's opinion about the accuracy of his testimony.

Judge Stearns stated that "circumstances merely suspicious are inadequate" to determine adultery and that "the burden of proof is on the accuser, not the accused." Consequently, he did not believe that Nina Walker had thoroughly proven that her husband was guilty of adultery. Taking into consideration the testimony of the twenty-five doctors who had given medical opinions during the trial, Judge Stearns was impressed that there was "less difference of opinion among the experts than might be expected." He understood that a physician could only determine the probability that a woman was a virgin, but all the medical witnesses had agreed that a physician who actually performed an examination would be much more accurate than one who was "simply asked to give his opinion in answer to a hypothetical question." The judge was "much influenced by the opinions of Dr. Palmer and Dr. Culbertson, who have had a long and varied professional experience in the diseases of women and kindred subjects." His confidence rested in "not only their professional attainments, but also in their integrity." Both of these physicians had determined that Miss Cochrane's hymen showed no signs of dilation or rupture, and there was no scar from any former rupture. To Judge Stearns, this evidence confirmed that Miss Cochrane was in all probability a virgin. Additional medical evidence proved that she had not contracted a venereal disease. Judge Stearns believed that none of the medical testimony proved otherwise. Furthermore, according to him, Miss Cochrane had demonstrated her innocence by submitting voluntarily to "an examination which no court had the power to order." "Certainly," Judge Stearns concluded, "if she is a common woman, her conduct in submitting to the physical examination and the result thereof presents a case unique both in medicine and the law."[2]

The judge admitted that there were "suspicious circumstances surrounding the relations of the respondent and Mabel Cochrane" and that he did not accept Mr. Walker's statement that his relationship with Mabel Cochrane "[had been] quite as innocent as he claims." James Walker, in Judge Stearns's opinion, "can not with fairness complain of his wife for drawing the conclusion of his infidelity that she did from the facts which were in her possession." The judge stated that, despite this opinion, he believed that Nina Walker had continued to engage in marital relations with her husband after she had first discovered the purported infidelity and that if adultery had occurred, she had condoned it.[3]

Walter Barney and Clark Burdick broke into wide smiles as they read the lengthy final sentence in the decision: "Taking the view that I do as to the weight of the evidence and in view of the fact that no infidelity was claimed with any other than Mabel Cochrane, I find that the petitioner has failed to prove her case and, accordingly, the prayer of the petitioner is denied."[4] In other words, James Walker was found not guilty based on the new evidence, and the previous superior court decision to award his wife a divorce was overturned. James Walker's attorneys agreed that this decision called for a visit to the tavern, despite the early hour. But first, they sent a telegram to their client at his farm in Maine to tell him the good news.

William Harvey invited his clients, Nina Walker; her mother, Virginia Chinn, and her sister, Bertha Chinn, to come to his Newport office to hear Judge Stearns's decision. As Mr. Harvey read the opinion aloud, Mrs. Chinn scowled and clicked her tongue loudly in a "tut-tut" sound. Bertha looked as though she might explode, while poor Nina simply looked bereft. Mr. Harvey quietly read the final sentence of the judge's opinion. When he got to "the prayer of the petitioner is denied," Mrs. Chinn growled, "Oh, my!" while Bertha turned her head to look out the window. Nina timidly asked, "Not proved infidelity?" "I don't understand, . . ." she murmured, "all those inappropriate letters and the witnesses at the boarding house . . . and in Charleston." Mr. Harvey was not certain how to approach this delicate topic and began hesitantly, "There are ways in which a woman can be with a man that doesn't. . . ." Six female eyes were suddenly focused on him, and he flushed and tried to begin again. "I mean," he stammered, "there are activities that men and women can engage in, regardless of how licentious they may be, that don't leave evidence." How could he explain what he meant to say—that certain acts, although sexual in nature and certainly "lewd and lascivious," did not meet the definition of adultery? After all, he was a man of the world and had learned a thing or two from ladies of the night in his bachelor days. He finally gave up trying to illuminate the matter for the three ladies, two of whom probably had very limited carnal experience and the third of whom was presumably as chaste as the day she was born. Mr. Harvey simply stated, "We will immediately file notice with the Rhode Island Supreme Court that we intend to prosecute a bill of exceptions objecting to Judge Stearns's decision."[5]

Meanwhile, Sarah Palmer, recognizing that it would be some time until the Walker divorce was finally settled, requested that the Rhode Island Superior Court return one of the defense's exhibits that belonged to her. It was her speculum, which Dr. Palmer stated was "of special make and cannot be obtained in the market."[6] Attorneys for both sides agreed to withdraw Exhibit Z and "restore it to Dr. Palmer for her use, with the understanding that i[t] is to be returned for use in the court at any time it is desired, on reasonable notice."[7]

Nina and her family moved a few more times in Newport, first to a spacious house on Rhode Island Avenue, which was difficult to keep warm in winter. Then they then rented a cottage from Mrs. Dalgreen for two years, "before moving again to a more comfortable, although less pretentious home two squares away at the corner of Kay and Catherine Streets." Nina remembered that, during that time, "We were very much absorbed in my individual legal battle and the common affairs of life."[8]

On Monday night, January 12, 1914, there was a bit of excitement. Nina and the rest of the household were awakened suddenly in the middle of the night by the servant girl, who had discovered a small fire in the kitchen. Someone quickly took charge of the situation and phoned the fire department. Fortunately, the fire was soon extinguished, and, because it was confined to a small area in the kitchen, little damage was done. Due to the notoriety of the Walker case, even that small event was reported in a newspaper as far away as New York City.[9]

James's divorce petition charging Nina with desertion and cruelty was still pending in Maine, and newspapers throughout the Northeast speculated that she could lose custody of her children if that case went to trial.[10] On January 24, 1914, the Supreme Judicial Court of Maine announced its opinion regarding Nina's charge that her husband's divorce petition had no standing in that state. The justices determined that state law only required that Mr. Walker reside in Maine in good faith for one year prior to filing for divorce, regardless of when or where the cause of divorce had occurred. According to Maine law, both charges that James Walker had made against his wife, including desertion for more than three consecutive years and cruel and abusive treatment, could be valid grounds for divorce. Nina must either fight James's motion for divorce on those grounds or be divorced by him in the state of Maine.[11] Given how long and hard she had fought to obtain a divorce from her husband in Rhode Island, neither Nina nor her family were willing to accept a divorce in Maine that named her as the guilty party, especially if she could lose her children. They determined to continue litigating her case in Rhode Island. James, obviously delighted by the most recent decision there, decided that things were starting to go his way in the Plantation State, so the case in Maine could wait.

After receiving the court's permission to extend their deadline, on March 12, 1914, Nina Walker's attorneys filed their bill of exceptions to the December 1913 Rhode Island Superior Court decision overturning her divorce. They argued that several errors had been made in Judge Stearns's rulings throughout the trial, including allowing James to state that his illness was oxaluria, allowing a medical witness to state that James's condition was chronic, and allowing Mabel Cochrane's attorney to testify about her emotional state. Furthermore, Nina Walker's attorneys claimed that the judge should have allowed Sarah Crapo to testify more fully about Mabel Cochrane's male callers. Nina's attorneys also claimed that Judge Stearns had erred in overruling a courtroom reading of Dr. James Foster Scott's deposition statement retracting his testimony from the previous trial and admitting that James Walker had told him that he had gonorrhea.[12] The Rhode Island Supreme Court heard the bill of exceptions shortly afterward, on April 6, 1914.

On May 13 of that year, James asked the court to allow him temporary custody of his children from June 15 to October 1 every year.[13] Before this petition could be heard, Nina and her attorneys filed their own petition charging that James had abandoned his paternal duties by not paying for the education, maintenance, and support of his wife and children since November 14, 1913. This was despite the fact that the Rhode Island Superior Court had reduced his support obligation from the original $350 per month to $250, and then to only $150 per month.[14] Although James's temporary custody hearing was to begin on May 24, it was postponed because Nina's attorneys reported that their client was too ill to testify.[15] In June, James filed a motion with the superior court asking that the order for the support of his wife and children be either vacated or reduced to a more reasonable amount. He claimed that his financial circumstances had "greatly changed owing to the heavy expenses" he faced due to fighting his wife's divorce actions.[16] The charge that James Walker was delinquent in paying support to his family was not a trivial matter. He could be held in contempt of court for neglecting his children. In his defense, James's attorneys had to show that the court-ordered support was beyond his means. Nina's attorneys sought to prove that James and his family were hiding financial resources that should have been used to support Nina and the children.

The most important witness called to testify in the matter of financial support was James's mother, Mrs. Rebecca White Walker. Her deposition was taken in Boston on July 3, 1914, with William Harvey representing Nina and Clark Burdick and Richard Y. FitzGerald representing his brother-in-law James. At Mr. Burdick's request, Mrs. Walker produced a number of cancelled checks that she had written to James since the beginning of the divorce proceedings. According to Mrs. Walker, her son was currently so destitute that she had loaned him a total of $24,652.59, of which he had repaid $7,000. Part of this repayment had included transferring ownership to her of the farm in Brownfield in June 1912, valued at $3,500. Mrs. Walker stated that, while she now owned the farm and paid all its expenses, James still lived on it and directed the farm work, sending her detailed reports. She agreed that she was losing money on the farm and expected to do so for several years. Mrs. Walker explained, "It brings in very much less than it costs, which was one reason for my taking it over, because my son could not afford to carry it." Mrs. Walker said she hoped that would change.[17]

Under cross-examination, Mr. Harvey led Mrs. Walker through a series of questions to ascertain who had originally held the title to the farm she had taken from James to partially repay his debt. Mrs. Walker was uncertain whether it had originally been deeded to James or to her son-in-law, Mr. FitzGerald. Through his questions, Mr. Harvey pressed Mrs. Walker to confirm that the farm had originally been bought with her own money and transferred to James, who had later given it back to her, supposedly to repay debts. During her testimony, Mrs. Walker admitted that she regarded all the funds she had given to James prior to the divorce proceedings (including his monthly allowance) as "gifts," whereas all the money she had given him since then she regarded as "debts."[18]

To demonstrate that James had access to other sources of income, Mr. Harvey asked Mrs. Walker what had happened to some valuable bonds in James's name that had been stored in her safe-deposit box. At first she claimed that she did not know what had happened to them but thought they might be "in the hands of a friend." Following further questions, Mrs. Walker grudgingly admitted that she thought the "friend" might be her son-in-law, Dr. John Jenks Thomas.[19]

Mr. Harvey asked Mrs. Walker about the $100 monthly allowance James was allotted from her husband's will, of which she was the executor. Mrs. Walker stated that she now kept those funds as partial payment for James's debt to her. James Mudge, the court stenographer, had to stifle a chuckle at the point in the deposition when Mr. Harvey asked Mrs. Walker on what principal the $100 was founded, and she retorted, "The *moral principle,* do you mean, so to speak, or the p-r-i-n-c-i-p-a-l?" After Mr. Harvey confirmed he meant the latter, Mrs. Walker corroborated that the value of the total estate at the time of her husband's death had been $600,000 but stated that she had no idea what it was currently worth. She thought for a moment and then clarified that legacies of $30,000 apiece had been invested for each of her four other children, which had been deducted from the principal amount and were not under her control. James had been allotted the monthly allowance in place of the legacy given to his siblings, she explained.[20]

Mr. Harvey pressured Mrs. Walker to admit that James would share in the entire amount of the remaining estate after her death, but she persisted in claiming that she did not know how much the estate was currently worth. She justified this ignorance by saying that, due to her poor eyesight, the accounting was now handled by a bookkeeper. Although the bookkeeper reported to her, she was "not quite as familiar with the details of the financial end as I otherwise should be." To some of those present at the deposition, it seemed dubious that a woman like Mrs. Walker would not know her own financial status down to the penny.[21]

On July 11, 1914, the superior court heard James Walker's petition for temporary custody of his children from June 15 to October 1 each year. A poignant scenario emerged when two of the Walker children testified against their father. First Serrell, then thirteen years of age and a pupil at the Cloyne House School, told Justice John Doran that his father "had never manifested any interest in him or any of the other children." He also testified that he detested his paternal grandmother, Rebecca Walker. Tears rolled down James's face as his only daughter, Elizabeth, testified. Now a very pretty girl, sixteen years of age, she stated haltingly and with downcast eyes, "No, I don't love my father. I don't want anything to do with him. I love my mother, and want to be with her. I don't care for my [Walker] grandmother, and have no wish to see her or have anything to do with her." James Walker's response was that his wife had "poisoned" his children's minds against him.[22]

Unfortunately, on the very same date as James Walker's custody hearing, other American fathers took more drastic action when denied custody of their children. In Saint Louis, Edward Ellenbreck was separated from his wife, who had custody of their two-year-old daughter. He went to her parents' house and tried to snatch his daughter while the family was sitting on the porch. When his wife and her relatives stopped him from fleeing with the little girl, Ellenbreck dropped her and drew a revolver. He then shot and killed his mother-in-law, shot his wife and father-in-law, and also shot a visitor at their home. He missed while firing at his sister-in-law and ran out of bullets before attempting to shoot his brother-in-law.[23] On the same day, in New York, the dead body of Frank Mueller, separated from his wife and children, was found in his apartment next to the body of his six-year-old son. It was determined that he had killed the boy with a razor and then committed suicide.[24] By comparison, James Walker showed great restraint in confining himself to a war of words.

Not until March 1, 1915, did the Rhode Island Supreme Court rule on Nina Walker's objections to Judge Stearns's December 1913 opinion in her husband's favor, which had overturned her divorce. In its ruling, the supreme court stated, "The case was very fully tried, and the transcript of testimony is voluminous."²⁵ While evidence in the first trial had indicated that adultery might have occurred, new evidence in the second trial had cast this into doubt. All of Nina's objections to the decision in the second trial were overruled, and the court found no support for the other alleged grounds for divorce. Judge Stearns's decision in James Walker's favor was sustained, and the case was remitted once again to the superior court for further proceedings.²⁶

Nina Walker's attorneys had an alternative strategy in case they were unable to prove adultery. On March 10, 1915, they filed a motion for reargument of the divorce suit based on her husband's "gross misbehavior and wickedness repugnant to and in violation of the marriage covenant." The motion claimed that this charge was clearly supported by evidence presented at the previous trials. "Gross misbehavior and wickedness," a ground for divorce legal only in Rhode Island, was the perfect standby to substitute for adultery and had been included in Nina Walker's original suit. Although James Walker's attorneys had disproven adultery in the second trial, they had not disproven this other unique ground. William Sheffield and William Harvey cited Rhode Island law to argue that the specifics for gross misbehavior and wickedness did not have to be included in their new motion, since they were obvious from other evidence, but they would amend the motion if ordered to do so by the court.²⁷

Yet again, on May 26, 1915, Nina Walker and her attorneys petitioned the superior court to enforce support payments due from her husband. James had sent Nina funds following the support hearing held the previous year, but his last payment had been on February 6. The timing suggested that James had stopped paying support when the supreme court had sustained Judge Stearns's decision overturning the divorce.²⁸

On July 1, 1915, the Rhode Island Supreme Court determined that if Nina Walker were to amend her petition with specific details supporting the charges of gross misbehavior and wickedness, they would hear arguments as to whether a divorce could be granted on those grounds.²⁹ The next day, Nina's attorneys formally informed the supreme court that they would amend their petition to include specifics.³⁰ Also on that day, Nina's attorneys called for a superior court hearing on the charge that James Walker should "be held in contempt of court for failure to comply with the order of the court in regard to allowances to be paid as ordered by the court."³¹

Nina Walker presented specifics for her charges of gross misbehavior and wickedness repugnant to and in violation of the marriage contract on August 2, 1915, including the following seven allegations against James Walker:

1. That for a period of time from 1901 and continuing thereafter, he has kept up and continued an undue, improper, indecorous[,] and licentious association and intimacy with a woman, named Mabel Cochrane, many years his junior, and of questionable character and immoral habits.
2. That for said period and while your petitioner was in delicate health, he has, while bestowing his affections upon the said Mabel Cochrane, shown an utter indifference towards your petitioner[,]part of the time entirely ignoring her, to the detriment of her health and has, when your petitioner was in delicate health, demanded the separation of the children from her and from each other and threatened to put her in an insane asylum, if she did not consent to said arrangement, and has otherwise cruelly treated your petitioner to such an extent that she was obliged to live apart from respondent.
3. That in the fall of 1901, and from that time forward, so long as the petitioner lived with him, the respondent was suffering from a venereal disease and from the sequelae of a venereal disease, which condition was infectious or contagious, and he was unable during said period to perform the ordinary marital relations, and that your petitioner was ignorant of the cause and nature of the disease up to the time she left him.
4. That sometime in the fall of 1901, or thereabouts, the respondent contracted from some person to the petitioner unknown, the venereal disease of gonnorrhea [*sic*] and continued to suffer from it or its affects [*sic*] for a period of years thereafter.
5. That during the period beginning in the fall of 1901, and continuing thereafter, the respondent has bestowed upon and received from a woman named Mabel Cochrane, marked and improper attention, has indulged in undue and improper familiarity and intimacy with her; has part of the time, in the absence of his wife, and without her knowledge (and all of the time without her knowing who Mabel Cochrane was), had said Mabel Cochrane stay in his home for long periods of time and had her occupy a room or rooms adjoining or connecting with his so that they were constantly in each other's company, and improperly familiar and unduly intimate; that at other times while respondent was in the City of Charleston, South Carolina, he has boarded the said Mabel Cochrane in a hotel in said city; that during said period from 1901 the respondent has carried on a correspondence with said Mabel Cochrane, has received from

her a letter or letters reflecting upon your petitioner, as well as letters of an improper and lascivious nature, and which show improper and lascivious relations between the said respondent and said Mabel Cochrane, and said respondent has continued to correspond with said Mabel Cochrane, and has from time to time visited her clandestinely in her apartments in Boston and elsewhere, and has been received by her alone, and with locked doors, when she was immodestly and improperly clad and has been guilty of other gross misbehavior and wickedness with same Mabel Cochrane.
6. That the said Respondent has been guilty of licentious and lascivious conduct with one Mabel Cochrane and other persons to your petitioner unknown, repugnant to and in violation of his marriage contract.
7. That the said respondent has been guilty of cruel and brutal conduct towards your petitioner, repugnant to and in violation of his marriage contract.[32]

Thus, Nina's attorneys gathered most of the previous charges against her husband and neatly tied them together with the label "gross misbehavior and wickedness repugnant to and in violation of the marriage contract."

The Rhode Island Supreme Court heard Nina Walker's amended petition on October 25, 1915. The justices' decision, announced on December 10, stated that they had reviewed the specific allegations of gross misbehavior and wickedness and found that if the first allegation, the fifth allegation, and the part of the sixth allegation relating to Mabel Cochrane were supported by evidence in the most recent trial, the charge of gross misbehavior and wickedness would be proven. The supreme court justices cited Judge Stearns's decision from that trial, in which he had stated, "I do not accept the statement of the respondent that his relations with Mabel Cochrane were quite as innocent as he claims." From this, they concluded that although adultery had not been supported by the medical evidence, it did not mean that "improper, licentious and lascivious relations did not exist."[33]

Despite James Walker's objections to presenting Mabel Cochrane's letters as evidence at trial, the supreme court found that it had been "established that the letters were all written by Mabel Cochrane and received by the respondent." Those letters, written by Miss Cochrane while she was a servant to the Walkers, "contained expressions of hostility to his wife and great affection towards him, and contained references to improper conduct between the writer and himself; nevertheless the respondent did not repudiate the matter contained in the letters but continued to write to Mabel Cochrane." Furthermore, James Walker had "had her at his house for a considerable time while his wife was away, and on a number of occasions visited her alone at her lodgings, which consisted of a single bed room." Because of Mr. Walker's conduct after receiving the letters, the supreme court determined that they were "admissible as competent evidence against him [of gross misbehavior and wickedness]."[34]

The Rhode Island Supreme Court further ruled that to be considered "gross misbehavior and wickedness," the respondent's conduct "should have some character of licentiousness or brutality allying it in its moral attributes with adultery or extreme cruelty," the other grounds for divorce in the state. When considering the Walker case, the justices concluded, "In our opinion the conduct of the respondent with Mabel Cochrane, continuing over a long period, although not amounting to acts of adultery, had such a character of licentiousness as allied it to that offence and was like it in kind." Therefore, Nina Walker had the right to prosecute her amended petition, including her specific allegations of gross misbehavior and wickedness. If she could prove the allegations, the superior court should grant her "a divorce from bed, board[,] and future cohabitation with the respondent until the parties be reconciled, and assigning to her a separate maintenance out of the estate of the respondent." However, the respondent, James Walker, had the right to contest the charges made in Nina Walker's petition.[35]

A "Statement of Causes," filed by James Walker's attorneys on January 3, 1916, set forth twenty-four objections to the supreme court's most recent decision in the case. First, it maintained that, since no errors had been shown in the superior court's decision, the supreme court could not reverse that decision and did not have the authority or power to allow Nina Walker to amend her petition by specifying a new ground for divorce. The allegation of gross misbehavior and wickedness was "mere surplusage," James's attorneys claimed, and had not been a ground originally considered by the superior court in its decision. They further asserted that there was conflicting evidence regarding the allegation of gross misbehavior and wickedness, which the defense did not have the opportunity to respond to because the charge had not been raised during the trial. Furthermore, James Walker's attorneys argued that if the supreme court were to order the superior court to decide the case in favor of his wife, it would usurp the jurisdiction of that court and "would deprive the respondent of the equal protection of the law and of liberty and property without due process of law," in violation of both the U.S. Constitution and the Constitution of Rhode Island. James's attorneys maintained that the supreme court must instead send the case back to the superior court to decide on its own, because that court had exclusive original jurisdiction of petitions for divorce, separate maintenance, alimony, and custody of children under Rhode Island law since 1909.[36]

On June 1, 1916, the Rhode Island Supreme Court confirmed that it had considered Mr. Walker's contention that he had never had an opportunity to answer the charges of gross misbehavior and wickedness, which they found to be "strictly true," even though evidence presented during the previous trial did fully support those charges. Nevertheless, the supreme court agreed with the defense that the relevance of previous testimony to the charges of gross misbehavior and wickedness had not been "passed upon by a justice of the Superior Court who has seen and heard the witnesses." Therefore, the case should be returned to the superior court for a new trial based on Nina Walker's charges of gross misbehavior and wickedness.[37] James Walker then filed objections that the Rhode Island Supreme Court did not have the appropriate powers either to grant his wife permission to amend her divorce petition or to order a new trial. However, on July 6, that court announced that it had already considered those objections and determined that it had "ample jurisdiction to permit the amendments in question and to direct a new trial."[38]

The financial support that James owed to Nina and their children remained a problem. On May 26, Nina Walker once again filed a motion in the superior court to hold her husband in contempt for failure to pay for the education, maintenance, and support of her children and her since February 6, 1915.[39] A ruling on August 5 by Judge Elmer J. Rathbun stated that the order for allowance payment had been in effect during the entire time the Walker case had been under consideration by the Rhode Island Supreme Court, "although petitioner had good reason to believe it was abrogated by the decision of the Supreme Court." He therefore determined that "the respondent is technically, at least, in contempt." Even though James offered to prove that he was "wholly without means and unable to make any payment for the support of his wife and children," he was not allowed to provide evidence to that effect. Judge Rathbun stated that either party could now apply to the court for a hearing on whether Mr. Walker was able to contribute toward the support of his wife and children and what further action should be taken by the court.[40]

Unable to wait any longer for the divorce suit to be settled, Bertha persuaded her mother to return to their home in Washington, after six years away. They brought Elizabeth with them so she could attend the National Cathedral School as a day student. Nina "was glad to have her at a private school where she might form lasting friendships." An old friend, General M. Wilson, a trustee of the school, made it possible for Elizabeth to get a scholarship, since Nina was still not receiving the court-ordered support payments from her husband. Nina explained how she supported her family: "My mother gave me an allowance to augment my small income and with that I had to provide as best I could for the children and myself." Dr. Huntington, the headmaster of the Cloyne House School, and his wife "came to my assistance as they did many times, for my sons' tuition and board never equaled the requirements stated in the school catalogue, and offered to let us occupy the resident section of Cloyne School." In those "spacious surroundings," and with their "excellent Irish cook," Nina maintained "the atmosphere of home" that "made that summer a memorable one."[41]

Summer and fall passed quietly for the Walkers. On Monday, December 4, 1916, Sydney Harvey, the clerk of the Newport Superior Court, was at his desk, as usual. Judge Rathbun asked Mr. Harvey to forgo his lunch hour and report to his courtroom at noon that day. This was something Judge Rathbun rarely required of him, so Mr. Harvey knew it was important and was pleased to comply. His wife, Irene, had fixed him an especially good breakfast, and he had a sack containing the remains of last night's dinner to nibble when he could. Above and beyond his dedication to the legal system, Mr. Harvey knew that something was up regarding the infamous Walker case, and Irene would be impressed if she heard the news directly from him. It had been almost exactly three years since Judge Stearns had ruled that James Walker was not guilty of adultery. Although Mr. Harvey knew that a new petition charged Mr. Walker with "gross misbehavior and wickedness repugnant to and in violation of the marriage covenant," he had not heard anything about it lately.

The Walker hearing was scheduled for noon based on the excuse that Walter Barney, the senior counsel for James Walker, was in poor health. Sydney guessed that the scheduling, at a time when the courtroom was cleared, was also planned to avoid unwanted spectators. Both the petitioner, Mrs. Nina Chinn Walker, and the respondent, Mr. James Wilson Grimes Walker, were in court. Mr. Barney and Clark Burdick were present to represent James Walker; William Harvey was there for Nina Walker. The only others present were Virginia Chinn, Bertha Chinn, and a reporter for the *Newport Daily News*, who discreetly stood in the back with a notepad and no camera.

As Sydney Harvey took his seat, it became clear that the parties had at long last come to an agreement. In contrast to the mass of witnesses who had testified at the previous Walker trials, no oral testimony was given. The hearing was brief, offered entirely based on depositions from Mrs. Nina Walker, her mother, her sister, Mr. William Harvey, Mr. Alexander O'D Taylor, and Dr. Huntington in which they had all presented evidence about James Walker's failure to support his wife and children. Mr. Walker's side presented no evidence or comment. Finally, Judge Rathbun banged his gavel and stated, "I hereby rule in favor of the petitioner, Mrs. Nina Walker, and grant her an absolute divorce, on the ground that her husband, James Wilson Grimes Walker, has neglected to provide for his wife and children. Mrs. Nina Walker is awarded custody of the four Walker children." No support payments were ordered.[42]

Mrs. Chinn's lips were set in a firm line, her daughter Bertha pursed hers, and Sydney Harvey thought he could detect a look halfway between a smile and a frown on Nina Walker's face. It was difficult to observe James Walker's expression, since his head was down until the very end, when he abruptly walked out of the courtroom. Judge Rathbun turned to Sydney and asked, "Please seal the record of this hearing."[43] When he was back at his desk, Sydney took out his ink pad and the large stamp with the words "Filed Under Seal" carved into the rubber and imprinted a nearly perfect image of this warning on the bottom of each page of the final hearing record. This mark would prevent anyone from ever reviewing it without a court order. In due course, the record would be destroyed.

Court Clerk Sydney Harvey marveled that, after all the lawyers and witnesses, the hearings, and motion after motion for more than seven years, this was how the Walkers' marriage finally ended. James Walker would go home to his farm and Nina Walker would go home to her children. Sydney was not alone in recognizing the paradox. The *Newport Daily News* reporter at the back of the courtroom wrote, "The Walker case has been one of the most remarkable tried in any court."[44]

Nina Chinn and James Wilson Grimes Walker married during the transitional time of the Progressive Period, when values and norms were evolving. The long-held view that wives should be dominated by their husbands was disrupted in the early twentieth century by the dawning recognition that women had the right to determine their own lives. In this new social environment, marriages were founded on emotional attachment rather than on duty. Nina wanted a marriage that would more closely approximate the contemporary ideal. She expected what most people currently require in a spouse: a loving partner who does not carry on affairs and is a caring parent, willing to share in decision making, eager to talk things over, and respectful. When she realized that her marriage would never reach that ideal, she determined to end it. Many years after her divorce, Nina would write, "I have never regretted the stand I took[;] it was the only way I saw it then and the only way I see it now."[45]

Nina's husband, James, preferred more traditional Victorian standards for upper-middle-class marriage. He did not understand why he was required to demonstrate his affection for his wife and children, be accountable for his actions, give up his complete authority, discuss problems, or value his wife's opinions. Previous generations of wealthy men had extramarital relationships that were accepted by their wives—why could he not do the same?

Nina would write in her unpublished autobiography, "I look from my bedroom windows and see a lovely vista of Rock Creek Park. . . . Below me flows the sparkling little stream of the Creek[;] by its side as a girl of twenty-two I confided my love and dreams of our future to the father of my children."[46] Although they may have loved each other at the time, Nina and James's individual visions of what married life would entail were incompatible. Could their marriage have been "saved"? Might they have resolved their differences and lived together peacefully? The gulf between them had probably grown too wide.

It is debatable whether the Walker children would have been better off if their parents had stayed together; the divorce alleviated everyday tension from their lives but separated them forever from their father and his family. Regarding the husband and wife, it seems that each found a more satisfying life when their marriage finally ended. The following Epilogue reveals how the lives of the main characters continued.

Epilogue
The Rest of Their Lives

WHEN THEIR DIVORCE WAS FINAL, Nina Chinn Walker and James Wilson Grimes Walker were free to live separate lives. As Nina would later eloquently describe, "My husband's and my life was similar to two currants [sic] in a stream, one flowing east and the other flowing west[;] having started in unison[,] a rock divided them and the soil shapes their destiny."[1] Marriages are not fairy tales, and neither are divorces. As in most cases, neither party got exactly what he or she hoped for. James did not gain custody of his children or full restoration of his reputation, but he did get to live quietly in Maine and keep his inheritance. Nina did not receive support payments or full vindication, but she did retain custody of her children and the legal right to live apart from her husband. For many readers, what happens to the characters after the main story ends is almost as interesting as what came before. This Epilogue updates the principal characters' stories.

The Petitioner, Nina Chinn Walker

Many years after the final judge's decision, Nina wrote the following in her unpublished autobiography:

> There are times when one goes through the motions of living and life seems unreal[;] such I experienced through the eight years of our legal battle. . . . There is a safety valve in human nature that

keeps us poised both in trials and in supreme happiness, without which we could not survive . . . "hope."[2]

Nina had considered leaving her husband before she filed suit in 1909, but she was afraid to do so without losing her children. Her fears were not unfounded. Wives and children were historically viewed as property, and, even in the early twentieth century, judges cited common law stating that fathers had a "natural right" to their children unless they were unfit. Fathers usually received custody after a separation or divorce despite committing adultery or other offenses. In the late nineteenth century through the early twentieth century, there was a growing recognition that children had rights of their own, and judges began to consider their best interests. Mothers were increasingly able to gain custody, because the "cult of motherhood" ideology promoted the ideal that children needed their nurturing. At the time when Nina filed for divorce, however, mothers had legal guardianship rights only in nine states and the District of Columbia. Legislators in other states feared that giving women custody rights would encourage mothers to leave their husbands.[3] Nina Walker was fortunate that enlightened judges awarded her custody of all four children throughout the divorce proceedings and permanent custody at the conclusion. Nina would later write:

> After eight long years of court proceedings my divorce was granted in December 1916 and the custody of my children given to me with no strings tied to us. A trifling money settlement was made, my husband giving me eight thousand dollars and covering some of the court fees. My lawyers['] fee I paid each year of the trials, from the allowance the courts granted me from my husband, that ceased at the final settlement.

Nina was grateful that "the community of Newport had been with me during eight years of harrowing experience" and "the Navy supported me also—friends and acquaintances in the service and out, had been most kind and considerate, making it hard for me to leave." "Yet," she believed, "I needed to break away, leaving the past to weave into my heart a deeper appreciation of the true values of life, and to turn my thoughts to the future and my children's more mature requirements."[4]

Nina took Elizabeth with her to get Grahame settled at Amherst College in the fall of 1917 before moving the rest of the family to Washington, DC, "where," she said, "we hoped to have a settled home." Nina explained, "Our moves were so constant that my little girl's answer years before to the question 'Where is your home?' was 'where my mother is,' [which] was still apropos." Sons Serrell and Herbert wanted to join the military, and the best training schools were in the Washington area. Nina also "desired a broader social life" for Elizabeth. Although Nina's mother, Virginia Chinn, wanted them to live with her and Nina's sister, Bertha Chinn, Nina decided that "my children had grown to the age of greater independence, and the restrictions my sister demanded of them left us to look for a place by ourselves, be it ever so humble." By October, Nina and her children were living in a small apartment in the home of an old schoolmate, close to Dupont Circle. Serrell and Herbert attended Western High School, and Elizabeth prepared to enter formal society.[5]

Nina undoubtedly sought an escape from the notoriety that had surrounded her divorce proceedings. She gradually became involved in Washington social activities, which was required if Elizabeth was to make a successful marriage. Nina chaperoned her daughter to private and public events. They spent a couple of months at the beginning of 1919 in New Orleans as guests of her good friends Colonel James C. Sanford, of the Army Corps of Engineers, and his wife.

On Saturday, January 24, 1920, Nina and her mother gave a "coming out tea" for Elizabeth at the Washington Club, "the most exclusive club in the city," to formally introduce her to society. Tea was served due to the Volstead Act and the Eighteenth Amendment to the Constitution, which prohibited alcohol.[6] After a summer spent deciding between two suitors, Elizabeth Grimes Walker married John Williams Davis in October 1921. Nina said of her daughter's wedding:

> I was happy to have Elizabeth share the fuller life of marriage[;] it is necessary to our completeness, [for] when combined with congeniality life is enriched beyond expression[;] but if what is termed "an unfortunate marriage" is made, tragidies [sic] follow that in its wake often bring a keener understanding, and a helping hand to our fellow creatures, and no greater blessing can come to a woman than the adoration and love of her children.[7]

Nina was active in the laity of the Episcopal Church.[8] She moved to Annapolis for a while to cut down on expenses, boarding at a large two-story house while Serrell boarded at a military coaching school and Herbert lived at the Naval Academy. By the summer of 1922, Nina and her oldest son, Grahame, had found a "tiny apartment" where "memories of illness, suffering, and distress crowd[ed] themselves upon me during the year and eight months we were there."[9] Grahame had surgery to remove a kidney stone, and Nina was not well herself and had lost a lot of weight, so her mother provided the funds for her and Grahame to stay at a nursing home. During this time, Nina's mother suffered a mild attack of the flu and then a stroke, which left her speechless and with a limp arm.

Although she knew that her mother, Virginia, was very sick, Nina did not let herself think that she might die. Then, while leaving Virginia's house after a visit, she passed her sister sewing black mourning material. This image shocked Nina into realizing that she could lose her mother soon, and she was grateful that she had the opportunity to thank her for all the love and support that she had given her and her children over the years. Nina wrote that, after returning to the nursing home from her visit with her mother, "the strain was very great both emotionally and physically and upon my return that night I suffered a heart attack, the first of several that followed through the years to come."[10]

Virginia Serrellina Wood Chinn died, at age eighty, on Friday, February 16, 1923, at her home. She was buried in Rock Creek Cemetery, with her maternal relatives in the Wood family plot. Perhaps comparing her mother's life to her own, Nina believed that Virginia "was tenderly protected from the ordinary womanly duties that fall to the lot of most of us." She had lived most of her adult life with either her mother or her older daughter, who, according to Nina, had shielded her from the troubles of life.[11]

After her mother's death and three weeks in the nursing home, Nina and Grahame went to Atlantic City to recover and then to an old friend's home on Mount Desert Island, in Maine. When her sons Serrell and Herbert were again forced to resign from the military due to failing their mathematics exams, they came home. Elizabeth Walker Davis, the daughter of Nina's daughter, Elizabeth, said of her grandmother's life at this time:

> She moved to 2222 Q Street, in Washington's fashionable Georgetown, into a long, narrow townhouse of two stories and a tiny back garden. There she quietly entertained, read her books, and was catered to by one presumably devoted Negro [sic] servant who cooked and cleaned and did every physical thing the house needed. Or else a man was hired-in temporarily, for those things men do best. There she lived a quiet life, for remember she had life-long heart problems.[12]

Nina's daughter, Elizabeth, who now lived with her husband, Jack, in Syracuse, New York, became pregnant. She spent most of her pregnancy in Washington, in an apartment in the same building with her mother and brothers. Nina's first grandchild, John Williams Davis Jr., called "Jackie," was born on October 28, 1926. Nina became a doting grandmother. Elizabeth and the baby stayed in Washington through the New Year, reminiscent of when Nina lived with her own mother following her children's births. After returning to Syracuse with her husband, Elizabeth and her family visited her mother frequently.[13]

Nina's writing was finally published. A poem by "Nina Walker" appeared in the April 3, 1929, edition of the *Christian Monitor*. It is not officially documented as a poem by Nina Chinn Walker, and her granddaughter, Elizabeth Walker Davis, did not know about its existence. However, when it sent to her, Dr. Davis verified that it was most likely written about her mother, Elizabeth, Nina's daughter, whose eyes were blue and who "avoided gloom lifelong."[14] The poem follows:

On Rainy Days
*When days seem dark and dreary
And skies above are gray;
My blue-eyed daughter fancies
A game that's fun to play.
Pretending she's the sunshine
That drives away the gloom,
Her cheery little presence
Soon brightens up the room.
The rain is quite forgotten,
Her smile so bright,
Sometimes keeps right on shining
Way into the night.*[15]

In June 1935, Nina's eldest son Grahame married Marion Caroline Boss, whom Nina described as "a sweet young woman and a good wife for Grahame."[16] A year later, her youngest child Herbert married Adaline Peter Cox. Nina said, "The smile and kiss that Herbert gave me before taking the bride away assured me of their happy future, for as a rule it is the man's attitude in the home that makes for contentment."[17] On the way home from the wedding, Nina stopped in Lexington, Kentucky, where she connected with members of her father's family and visited his grave.

Although Nina Chinn Walker was only fifty-seven by the time her granddaughter Elizabeth Walker Davis was born in 1930, Dr. Davis thinks of her as "in elderly ill health"[18] and wishes that she had known her grandmother as a young woman. She wonders whether Nina was "as sternly controlled" as she looks in a photograph of her younger self. "For certainly," Dr. Davis comments, "she was austerely self-contained and controlled by the time I knew her."[19]

Dr. Davis remembers Nina as "distant and respectful." One incident from her childhood particularly calls this impression to mind. At the time, Elizabeth was nine years old, and her brother Tim was five years old. Their mother was hospitalized for several nights, and the children were supposed to stay at their grandmother's house. As her granddaughter recalls, "Instead I righteously took Tim's hand, walked the three blocks back to our apartment, stating that was where we belonged." Dr. Davis was impressed with how Nina handled the situation. She recalls, "[My grandmother] sent her servant over to our apartment to negotiate with me. An agreement was reached: Tim and I would spend the days in our home, but walk over to Grandmother's house for supper and bed." Dr. Davis believes that Nina respected her granddaughter's wish for independence because it is a personality trait they shared. "Back across the decades," she reminisced, "I realize how much I loved her, as well as how important she was to my life choices."[20]

Nina never lost her interest in writing or in her family history. In 1934, she began what would become a 699-page handwritten autobiography, completed in 1937. It appears that different sections of this manuscript were passed down to various family members. Only parts of the autobiography were found, including pages 1–299 (identified here as unpublished autobiography A)[21] and pages 420–699 (identified here as unpublished autobiography B).[22] All pages are in Nina's handwriting, and the autobiography was never published. From my reading of her work, it seems that Nina had talent as a writer, with a keen eye for detail and an understanding of human relationships, from her own perspective. It is thought-provoking to wonder what Nina might have accomplished if she had greater educational and career opportunities.

Nina's unpublished autobiography begins with excerpts from her mother's autobiography (also unpublished), continues through recounting Nina's own childhood, and then chronicles the events of her life up until February 24, 1937, when she signed and dated it, ten years before her death. Nina mentions only brief details about her divorce but indicates that it had a profound effect on her life and the lives of her children. She generally refers to James as "my husband" rather than by his first name and never mentions Mabel Cochrane by name, instead calling her "the young woman" or her husband's "inamorata." In addition to personal events, the autobiography contains abundant references to world events and Nina's personal opinions about them. She abhorred the loss of life during World War I, during which she and Elizabeth rolled bandages for the Red Cross. She survived the Great Depression, worried about the rise of fascism and communism, and adored President Franklin Delano Roosevelt. Several pages toward the end of her autobiography concern Nina's fascination with the abdication of King Edward VIII. She had strong religious and moral standards not only concerning her husband's conduct but also that of the former king. Nina asserts, "Even more strange and sad it is that [Edward] should have sought happiness in a manner inconsistent with Christian principles of marriage, and within a social circle whose standards and ways of life are alien to all the best instincts and traditions of his people."[23]

It is surprising to read Nina's opinions about women's suffrage and feminism, to which she was opposed. An example is the following:

> I emphatically disapproved of suffrage for women in 1910 and in this day [the 1930s] my opinion remains as it did then. I have lived to see demonstrated the results I predicted. The humiliation of our men and the charm of woman hood [have been] reduced to a low standard. . . . The women in their forcefulness have driven our men to their lowest ebb of efficiency, taking from them their self-pride and sense of protection towards those they love. The good Lord made us different, with inate [sic] difference in our desires and ambitions, but united in the fundamentals of life . . . [l]ife in its fullness, its richness, its entirety which[,] when interpreted for a woman, means home, husband, and children.[24]

Nina, who had suffered under the Victorian model of upper-middle-class family life, and who had fought hard to release herself from it, still approved of the gender system that had suppressed countless women like her. She even went so far as to blame feminists for causing the Great Depression. This stance demonstrates how intransigent the ideology of separate spheres can be.

Nina Chinn Walker died on January 4, 1947, at Doctors Hospital in Washington, DC, at age seventy-three. She was buried in the family plot at Rock Creek Cemetery,[25] near the church where she had married fifty years before. As far as anyone knows, Nina never saw nor spoke with her husband, James, after the divorce was settled.

The Petitioner's Sister, Elizabeth Bertha Chinn

Nina's sister Elizabeth, called Bertha, never married and lived with her mother until Virginia Chinn died. She had testified with expert skill at her sister's divorce hearings. Bertha claimed that she and her sister's husband had been on friendly terms, but James asserted that there had always been problems when she had visited. Certainly, the angry letter she wrote to Mrs. Walker in November 1900 ignited tensions between James's and Nina's families (see Chapter 3). During closing arguments in the superior court retrial on November 20, 1913, James's lawyer Walter H. Barney argued that there had been no trouble between Nina and James "until Miss Bertha Chinn appeared in Charleston." "Miss Chinn seems to have been the evil genius in this case!" he declared (see Chapter 10). Regardless of whether this claim was true, Bertha does appear to have played some role in encouraging Nina's anger toward her husband and her ultimate decision to leave him. She was visiting her sister in Charleston when Nina took an urgent trip to Washington to discuss Mabel Cochrane in the spring of 1904 (see Chapter 3), and she and her mother lived in close proximity to Nina at the time when Nina made her final decision to leave her husband (see Chapter 5).

Nina's granddaughter Elizabeth Walker Davis claims that a "triangle of quiet, gentle female intrigues and power plays" between Virginia, Bertha, and Nina "continued as long as they lived."[26] She bases this impression on what she knows of the lifelong rivalry she saw between her grandmother Nina and her great-aunt Bertha.[27]

Shortly before the final verdict, Bertha and her mother returned to Washington, DC, and the house they had left six years before. Dr. Davis, Nina's granddaughter, suspects that, when her grandmother moved back to Washington with the children, "there was a quiet, gentlewomanly battle of entitlement between my grandmother Nina and my great-aunt Bertha, who always lived [at] home with her mother and apparently felt most entitled to her mother's property." "But," Dr. Davis believes, "my grandmother Nina Chinn Walker must also have known a deep sense of entitlement—for she alone had created the next generation of the family."[28]

Since her maternal uncle Serrell Wood had no children, Bertha had long expected that his hereditary English estate, Osmington, would be left to her, as his oldest heir. Although he had reportedly made a verbal request about this bequest to his widow near the time of his death in 1907, all of his property was eventually divided among her own relatives. Despite several trips to England by Bertha and her mother to consult with attorneys about breaking the will, the efforts were to no avail. According to Nina, this disappointment destroyed the plan Bertha had long envisioned for her life and precipitated a series of struggles between Bertha and her. Nina remarked, "As time passed and my sister recognized there was little prospect of my receiving any adequate means from my husband, her attitude towards me and my children changed perceptibly[;] she constituted herself the head of the family and the arbiter of our mother's purse." She commented, "'When to a natural imperious nature there is joined a neurotic, hysterical temperament, the consequences can be disastrous'[;] so wrote one who was a student of human nature and so it was with my sister."[29]

Nina implicated her sister in a series of events that she believed harmed her children and her. Bertha had a strong influence on their mother and had coerced her to insist that Nina's son Grahame would live at her home while attending St. Albans (a prestigious boy's school in Washington), although Nina had obtained a full tuition-and-board scholarship for him. Since the goal had been for Grahame to participate fully in the life at St. Albans, Nina and he decided that attending as a day student would make him "an outsider and detached from the intrinsic life of the school." Instead, Grahame returned to Cloyne House School in Newport, and Elizabeth rejoined her class at the local high school instead of returning to the Cathedral School, in Washington. According to Nina, "Grahame's naturally sweet disposition accepted the disappointment better than I, who envisaged the years to come when the affiliation with St. Albans and the Cathedral would not only be a pleasure but a lasting benefit."[30]

In 1919, Bertha persuaded her mother to sell her home, announcing it to Nina only after the deal was done, although Virginia had said many times that she would never sell the family estate. "I felt mother had made a grievous mistake," Nina said.[31] While her mother and sister were in England in April 1920, Nina and her children moved into Mrs. Chinn's large new house from their small apartment. When Mrs. Chinn returned, she wanted Nina and her children to stay in her home, but Bertha prevented them from doing so. According to Nina, it was difficult to find an apartment she could afford, and, although she finally did, she wondered why Bertha had been so coldhearted to the wishes of her sister and her nieces and nephews as well as her mother.[32]

Nina recalled another incident at the time her daughter was planning to get married: when, she wrote, "Again my sister's domination over our frail little mother had an unhappy effect." She explained, "My mother was proud of her granddaughter and pleased with Jack [Elizabeth's fiancé] and sincerely desired to give them a lovely wedding, with a reception afterward." However, according to Nina, "my sister's unfortunate qualities of 'initiative that unbridled became arrogance, resourcefulness that turned to cunning, efficiency to greed, tenacity to obstinacy and willingness to take authority and responsibility to pride and lust for power' led her to deny my mother that pleasure." Bertha required that the wedding invitations be in her mother's name and that Bertha herself "be given authority to make all the arrangements without consulting Elizabeth's taste." These conditions were not acceptable to Elizabeth and Nina, so Nina instead used her own limited funds to pay for the wedding. Nina's mother was very upset that she could not provide for her granddaughter's wedding, but she "was compelled to submit to her older daughter, to avoid a prolonged display of temper."[33]

Granddaughter Elizabeth Walker Davis believes that Nina and her sister maintained a "stability of sorts" until their mother died, but "when great-grandmother [Virginia Chinn] died[,] then stability also died, with outrage and lifelong anger."[34] The story Dr. Davis heard many times was that, during the funeral of the family matriarch, on February 16, 1923, "while Great-Aunt Bertha was in church, gently grieving behind her black veils, her hired moving van had pulled up in front of the family home and her hired men had removed all the most valuable paintings, furniture, memorabilia, and belongings of all sorts. Bertha obviously felt entitled."[35] This is not what actually happened, according to Nina, but it is not far from the truth in spirit.

According to Nina, after her mother's death, "My sister moved into my mother's bedroom immediately after the funeral and by word and deed made it abundantly clear that all was in her hands." Five weeks after their mother's will was read to Nina, her sister produced a codicil that had been dated, drawn, and executed while Nina and her daughter had been in Madison, Wisconsin. This codicil left everything to Bertha, after payment of bequests. Nina believed that "the codicil was distinctly by my sister's dictation, and characteristic of her unfortunate inborn vindictive and jealous nature." Nina wrote, "It cut me completely off from an inheritance that had come to my mother from her mother, and therefore from my sister's and my grandmother."[36]

Nina, although "profoundly shocked," realized that her mother had not intended to leave her "practically penniless" but had been trying to avoid her sister's "uncontrollable temper by yealding [sic] to her demands." Nina remembered that, shortly before her grandmother's death, the old woman had signed a codicil to her will that Bertha had dictated, revoking "the legacy she had left her son to pay off the mortgage of his Osmington property . . . leaving the remainder of her estate to our mother, with the exception of five hundred dollars to my sister and me."[37] Nina wondered whether this was the reason that Bertha later did not inherit her uncle Serrell's English property.

Nina found "it was an imperative and most painful duty that forced me to consult a lawyer to obtain a partial share of my rightful inheritance—to bring suit against my only sister—one who I worshiped as a child—made life seem topsy, turvy, and the hurt remains." After delaying for a year, Bertha finally agreed to compromise and make an out-of-court settlement.[38] Nina claimed that, following their mother's death and at least up until the time she would write her autobiography in 1937, "letters of abuse, newspaper clippings with unpleasant subtle intimations continue to reach me through the mail, my sins of commission and omission as she [Bertha] views them she tries to impress upon me." Nina determined, "Our advances toward a mutual understanding are completely misunderstood and only increase her arrogance[;] therefore we have taken the one course open to us for peace, absolute silence."[39]

Granddaughter Elizabeth Walker Davis believed that Nina and Bertha never spoke to each other again,[40] but there is evidence of warm written correspondence between them in 1942, five years before the sisters died.[41] A genial letter from Bertha to Nina, dated February 16, 1942, was recently found folded up in an old scrapbook.[42] Near the end of the letter, Bertha mentions having seen their father's relatives when she visited California. She signs it, "With much love Affectionately, Bertha." So, Nina and her sister did reconcile, at least in writing, at the end of their lives.

Elizabeth Bertha Chinn died later in the same year as her sister, on November 22, 1947, at age seventy-six, and was buried at Rock Creek Cemetery.[43] Elizabeth Walker Davis has fond memories of her great-aunt Bertha, although she says that she only knew her as "an old, old lady." About her, she comments, "One thing Bertha never did—she never married. She chose one side of my family's female dilemma—do we want to marry and have children, or do we want to live lives totally under our own control? Or do we want to do both, in succession?" Although Nina and her sister may have been estranged for a while, "Bertha stayed in routine contact with all her sister's children," Dr. Davis remembers. "And to my knowledge, grandmother Nina never objected, probably because there was considerable money to be inherited. My mother took me to visit Bertha periodically throughout my childhood in Washington. Undoubtedly Aunt Marion [John Grahame Walker's wife] did the same with her children."[44]

Elizabeth Walker Davis believes that Bertha remembered her own mother's death and "its lifelong resulting animosities" when she ordered "all possessions to be sold at auction, no exceptions, and the resulting money estate to be divided in complicated ways which seemed fair to her." Everyone in her extended family was included in the will, according to Dr. Davis, "even including English cousins I had never known existed." She says, "My mother's share was doled out monthly, a wise provision given my mother's immense spending talents. My own share was fifty dollars a month until I was thirty, then a lump sum, a thousand I think." The stipend from Great-Aunt Bertha helped put Dr. Davis through college.[45] Her cousin Herbert

Wood Walker Jr. also remembers the terms of Great-Aunt Bertha's will and how helpful it was to have those funds.[46]

The Respondent, James Wilson Grimes Walker

James's father, the venerated Admiral John Grimes Walker, began his life in a small rural town, Hillsborough, New Hampshire, from where he rose to the upper echelon of the U.S. Navy. His disgraced son, James Wilson Grimes Walker, retreated to the small rural town of Brownfield, Maine, just over the New Hampshire border, where he resided for the rest of his life. James had not lived up to his uncle's distinguished name, did not have his father's illustrious career, and had failed at marriage. One of James's problems was generational, because American culture had changed during the Progressive Era, and it was difficult for young men to adapt to new cultural expectations for masculinity.[47] Another problem for James was more individual, since he had a very different personality from his father. He was more introverted and was probably comfortable devoting his life to farming and writing rather than engaging in the politics required to advance a naval career. Perhaps James's biggest problem was his marriage to a woman who demanded his full attention and sympathy, which were beyond his capacity to give.

With funds from his mother and the legal maneuvering of his brother-in-law, Richard Y. FitzGerald, James acquired a large Brownfield farm, which included the biggest barn in Maine at the time (see the photographs on page 163). It had originally been a breeding barn for Jersey cows in 1908 and at one end had twin four-story silos.[48] According to a longtime resident of Brownfield who visited it in her childhood, the barn had fancy hardwood floors, very unusual for the time.[49] It had been built as "a show place with all the cutting edge technology," and people came from far away to take tours of the building.[50]

Despite the hard work of running a farm, Brownfield must have been a pleasant haven for James following his very public naval career and divorce. The little town is located in Oxford County, Maine, in the valley of Mount Washington in the White Mountains, and features several ponds. While Admiral Walker may have had grander plans for his oldest son, James seemed to enjoy small-town life. He boarded workers on his property who helped run the farm, and his constant companions were German shepherds. James buried two dogs on the front lawn, and the base of their stone marker still stands under a maple tree.[51]

Interviews with Brownfield residents who were children when James was an older man reveal that everyone in town called him "Colonel Walker." He was often seen in military uniform, sometimes on horseback (see the top and middle photographs on page 162).⁵² As the owner of Meadow Mountain Farms, James became involved in town affairs. In 1918, the Brownfield selectmen were directed to research the construction of a continuous highway from Portland to Fryeburg, Maine. James met with a judge in Portland, wrote letters, and convened a meeting to secure this benefit for the surrounding towns. The road was eventually constructed and became Maine Route 113 (originally called the Pequawhet Trail).⁵³

After James's mother died on March 24, 1925, her only brother, Henry Goddard Pickering, died on July 16, 1926. He had been a prominent attorney in Boston, had provided funds to furnish James and Nina's home in Brookline, and had testified for James in the divorce trials. Henry Pickering was buried in the family plot in Mount Auburn Cemetery in Cambridge, Massachusetts. In his will, he made bequests to Boston Children's Hospital and various other charities totaling $22,000. To his sister Rebecca's children, including Frances, Susan, Sarah, Henry, and James, he left $10,000 each and an equal share in the residue of his estate. Susan Walker FitzGerald, James's younger sister, was the executor.⁵⁴

James's most notable foray into public life post-divorce was to give a speech about the U.S. Constitution in Brownfield on Memorial Day 1927. Citing previous commentary and quoting poetry to support his own views, James argued that the concurrent movement to rewrite the U.S. Constitution would destroy its integrity and was a particularly dangerous threat to states' rights. The following excerpt represents the essence of his message:

> For we are the executors of heroes, we are trustees of the great estate of liberty, built up by centuries of suffering and toil, cemented with the blood of countless patriots. Upon us devolves the responsibility of conserving this estate, of transmitting it unimpaired to generations yet unborn. Let us remember that the Constitution of our fathers was never in greater danger than it is today.⁵⁵

James Walker forcefully called for citizens to involve themselves personally:

> For we, each one of us, must help direct our country's destinies. Unless we qualify ourselves for thought; unless we take a constant and unselfish part in the civic and political life of our community; unless we earnestly strive to preserve and to apply the basic principles of the Constitution, we are traitors alike to posterity and to those who fought and bled and died that the government of the people, by the people[,] and for the people should not perish from the earth.⁵⁶

James's Memorial Day address in Brownfield appeared in the *Lewiston* (Maine) *Journal*, whose editors commented that they did not ordinarily print Memorial Day addresses except by the president of the United States.⁵⁷ Many other newspapers around the United States then reprinted the speech and commented favorably on it. An article in the *Washington Post*, for example, states, "Sometimes a spark struck from the anvil of patriotism grows into a great blaze[,] and an address made by a naval officer in a small Maine town last Memorial Day on the Constitution has gained remarkable renown since then."⁵⁸

Walter Neale, a New York publisher, printed James's speech in 1928, with the title *Trustees of Liberty: An Appeal for the Preservation of the Constitution of the United States as Handed Down by the Fathers*. Kenneth C. M. Sills, the president of Bowdoin College, states in the introduction, "To have presented on a moving occasion in sensible speech the basic principles of the Constitution is indeed a service to liberty. Commander Walker's address on Memorial Day is therefore worthy of attention far beyond the borders of the little Maine village in which it was originally delivered."⁵⁹ Perhaps if he had still been alive, Admiral John Grimes Walker might have taken pride in his son for this accomplishment.

James did some traveling and also entertained old friends at his farm. A local couple, Albin and Ethel Hill, lived with James for a number of years as his servants. By 1940, James had taken in lodgers, Nelson and Doris Hall and Ralph E. Hill,⁶⁰ who may have also been hired help.

In 1937, Nina, his former wife, stated in her unpublished autobiography that James "has no contact with his children, with the exception of meeting our daughter and her husband when they staid [*sic*] overnight with his mother in Hamilton, Mass. Since the birth of my daughter's children[,] she has made efforts to arouse his interest in the three lovely grandchildren, but he is concerned singly with his immediate surroundings."⁶¹ Although her mother, Nina's daughter Elizabeth, seldom mentioned him, Elizabeth Walker Davis had a romantic childhood image of her grandfather, including that he traveled a lot, becoming "a member of some Indian tribe in Wisconsin or Minnesota or the Dakotas."⁶² She and her brother Tim visited their grandfather in Maine for a month during the summer she was twelve and Tim was eight years old. Her mother sent them alone by train from Washington to Maine, which Dr. Davis maintains was "a common occurrence back in the 1940's."⁶³ This would probably have been in 1942, when James was seventy-four years old. Dr. Davis remembers that he had "a large, comfortable, sprawling Victorian house at the wooded edge of a small Maine town" that was full of American Indian and Western "oddities and curiosities and memory-holders." She recalls her visit with her grandfather James Walker:

> I remember leisurely days of rambling through New England woods just outside grandfather's house at the edge of a tiny New England town. I remember the mouth-elating wild blackberry cobblers cooked by his New England housekeeper. I remember an Indian warrior's feather-laden headdress hanging on the wall, taken down momentarily so I could try it on and admire myself in the mirror. I remember two immense gray dogs always close to Grandfather, bonelessly stretched near his chair or leaping through the grasses as he walked tall across a field.[64]

This is the one time that Elizabeth Walker Davis recalls seeing her maternal grandfather. She claims that her mother, Elizabeth, only mentioned him "to complain that his two German Shepherd dogs would inherit his money."[65] The idea of an inheritance from the Walker estate may have been the primary reason that his daughter sent her children to visit him. The other Walker grandchildren have no memory of ever having a personal connection with James.

Later in life, probably when farming became too much for him, James sold his property and moved into Isabel Stickney's rooming house (also known as "Stickney Tavern"), east of the railroad tracks in Brownfield. One current local resident lived across the street from the tavern when she was a child in the early 1940s and helped out there. She remembers dusting "Colonel" Walker's room and making his bed when she was about eleven years old and also waiting on him at the tavern. She "couldn't believe how dark and cluttered with things his room was" and recalls that he had a big dog she was afraid of. She also notes that "the Colonel" ate a special diet and describes one time when she served him a New England boiled dinner by mistake. He did not care but just "got a big portion and gobbled it down."[66] The rooming house was destroyed in the October 1947 fire that devastated 85 percent of Brownfield, and it is not known where James Walker resided after that, although he did stay in the town.

James Wilson Grimes Walker died in Brownfield on November 2, 1950. He was eighty-two and had lived apart from his wife and children for many more years than he had lived with them. James was buried in the Pickering family plot in historic Mount Auburn Cemetery in Cambridge, Massachusetts (see the photograph on page 164). After his divorce from Nina, he never remarried, and no later romantic attachment was recorded.

His granddaughter, Elizabeth Walker Davis, claims that his beloved dogs did "theoretically inherit" his legacy, but "somehow his money got diverted to and divided among his human descendants," to his daughter and three sons.[67] James's grandson Herbert Wood Walker Jr. recalls that his maternal grandfather left his estate to his children (possibly $35,000), but with the stipulation that it would pass to them only after the last of his dogs had died. Therefore, the kennel took very good care of the dogs for as long as they could. Herbert Jr. and his sister, Anne Cox Walker, share a childhood memory that one evening their father received a long-distance phone call, which was an important event in those days. When their father, James's youngest son, got off the phone, he announced cheerfully, "The last dog died!" The inheritance money significantly improved their lives.[68]

The Respondent's Mother, Rebecca White Pickering Walker

From the beginning, the battle between Nina and James was a family feud. As with Nina's sister, opposing attorneys often implicated James's mother as the source of Nina and James's marital problems. Nina recognized that "many times the principals in the case appeared to be overlooked and the issue waged between my mother-in-law and my sister[;] there lay the lasting bitterness."[69]

In her unpublished autobiography, Nina gave some insight into Rebecca Walker's character. According to her, "the unfortunate lady suffered many humiliating indignities during her married life." Her husband's word was law, with no deviations allowed, and he rarely bestowed gifts or affection. The admiral was "sociable and agreeable to outsiders," but "his wife was at all times the butt of his ill temper that fell with the persistency of water from a leaking faucet."[70]

Nina revealed that she had been told "by one who knew" that at one point in the past, Mrs. Walker had come back from a trip to Europe with her children and learned of her husband's "infatuation" with a woman named Mrs. Boyd Smith. Rebecca had left him, gone to her father's home in Boston, and remained there until her father had persuaded her that it was "financially advisable" for her to go back to her husband "and continue her life with him."[71] Many years later, Mrs. Walker would be callously unsympathetic to her daughter-in-law's complaints about her own son's infidelity.

Nina hinted that there were "uncertainties" about Mrs. Smith's oldest son, Boyd, who "idealized his 'godfather,'" John Grimes Walker. As a young boy, Boyd often stayed with the Walker family, and the admiral gave him special attention and "supervised his education." Boyd Smith died in his early thirties, and, according to Nina, "At the death of Mrs. Smith the admiral suddenly became an old man[;] his years weighed heavily upon him as the zest of life was burnt out. Within two years he followed her into the shadow of death." Nina concluded, "Mrs. Walker endeavored to council her humiliation in her home life by a colossal conceit in her [Pickering] ancestry."[72] She also believed that Rebecca Walker poured all of her bitterness into her attempts to control her children, particularly Sallie, the youngest daughter she purposely kept at home, and James, her oldest son. Nina placed a large part of the blame for what she considered James's "weak character" on his mother.[73]

The divorce hearings made public a lot of incriminating evidence against James that Mrs. Walker must already have known about, but "her Boston pride and determination blinded her better judgment and led her to believe 'affirmed boldness and money could overcome legality.' No point of technicality was overlooked by her lawyers. I advisedly say 'her[,]' for it was she who fought the case to the bitter end. My husband neither had the will nor the means to do so." To Nina, Rebecca Walker was "a woman of iron will sadly misdirected."[74]

Mrs. Walker's eyesight was failing, due to cataracts in both eyes, until she had successful surgery at the age of eighty. In later years, James's mother became feeble and developed palsy. Rebecca White Pickering Walker died on Tuesday, March 24, 1925, in Brookline, Massachusetts. She was almost ninety years old. Nina wrote, "Many years had passed since the old lady had communicated with my children, but the Christmas before her death[,] as a gesture of thoughtful acknowledgement of their existence, she sent each one a book inscribed by her trembling hand."[75]

James and Nina's children joined their father and the Walker aunts and uncle at Rebecca's funeral on March 28 at All Souls Unitarian Church in Washington and at Arlington National Cemetery, where her remains were buried next to the admiral's. Nina reported that Mrs. Walker's "heart was embittered towards [Nina's children] to the very last, and they were not mentioned in her will, wherein her oldest son was denied his inheritance ostensibly 'because of his unfortunate marriage' so worded in the will, but to translate into the vernacular, to repay the debt of the heavy divorce expenses that she herself [had] induced him to incur."[76] Nonetheless, according to the second codicil of her will, James's mother left him some sentimental items. Nina believed "the habit of years was too strong[;] her policy of simultaneously admonishing and protecting her son was carried on even in her will."[77]

The Respondent's Sister Susan Grimes Walker FitzGerald and Brother-in-Law Richard Yancey FitzGerald

At a time when many educated women believed they had to choose between domestic life and a career, Susan Walker FitzGerald was a woman who had it all. Fifty-three percent of women who graduated from her alma mater, Bryn Mawr, between 1889 and 1908 did not marry, and among those who did, a significant percentage never had children.[78] In contrast, Susan had four children as well as a career. She gave birth to Anne FitzGerald in 1902 and Rebecca Pickering FitzGerald in 1906. The family lived in California for two years during that time, seeking treatment for their second daughter's illness. When Richard contracted typhoid fever in 1906, the FitzGerald family moved to the admiral's home in Washington, DC, while he recuperated. A third daughter, Susan FitzGerald, was born in 1908.[79] Having previously worked at Barnard College, as the head of a settlement house, and as a member of the first New York Child Labor Committee, Susan became a supervisor of social work in Boston, where Richard would later establish his law practice.

By the time of her brother's divorce trial, Susan had become a well-known women's rights advocate (see Chapter 5). She was very active in the campaign for women's suffrage, taking leadership roles in local and national organizations, and wrote a newspaper column and several pamphlets promoting women's rights. Although women had not yet won the right to vote, Susan Walker FitzGerald launched a political career by running, unsuccessfully, for the Boston School Board in 1911.[80] Susan spoke before a Joint Committee of Congress urging votes for women's suffrage and campaigned in Colorado and Utah for Woodrow Wilson.[81] Her son, Richard Leigh FitzGerald, was born in 1914.

Susan Walker FitzGerald came to Newport when her niece Elizabeth had an emergency appendectomy while Nina was away on a cruise (see Chapter 4). Several months later, Nina filed for divorce. Despite her feminist credentials, Susan completely allied herself with her brother James during the divorce proceedings, particularly praising him as a good father. She was most likely the person who persuaded Mabel Cochrane to have a medical examination, and she accompanied her to Dr. Sarah Ellen Palmer's office.

Susan Walker FitzGerald was instrumental in helping American women finally gain the right to vote on August 26, 1920. She served as the National Committeewoman of the Women's Division of the Democratic State Committee in Massachusetts that year and became the first woman to make a presidential nominating speech.[82] In 1922, Susan was elected the first female Democratic member of the Massachusetts House of Representatives (a Republican woman was elected the same year). She served one term as a congresswoman, was a delegate to the Democratic National Convention in 1924, and remained politically active later in life. On January 20, 1943, Susan Walker FitzGerald died suddenly, following surgery at Massachusetts Memorial Hospital for injuries she had suffered in an accident. Susan was seventy-one; in addition to her children and grandchildren, she was survived by both of her sisters and her older brother James.[83]

Susan's husband, Richard Yancey FitzGerald, had died a few months before she did. As an attorney, he was very active in Susan's brother's divorce case. Richard helped secure Rhode Island attorneys for James and was instrumental in mounting his defense. He also held some of James's securities for him during the course of the divorce and was involved with Mrs. Walker in conveying the Maine farm property to him. After working for a Boston legal firm, Richard became the secretary and legal counsel for the New England Power Association in 1914, a position he held until his retirement in 1927. Richard died at his home in Jamaica Plain on June 28, 1942, at age sixty-nine.[84] Unlike Nina and James Walker, Susan and Richard FitzGerald had an unusually loving and egalitarian relationship. Their correspondence, both before and during their marriage, was warm and respectful.[85]

The Respondent's Sister Frances Pickering Walker and Brother-in-Law John Jenks Thomas

Frances Pickering Walker (known as Fanny), and her husband, Dr. John Jenks Thomas, were the couple who Nina charged had kept the infant Serrell away from her for several months. Dr. Thomas, a well-known neurologist at Boston City Hospital, had been very helpful in finding medical experts to testify for James, and he had also testified on family matters. A 1910 article in the *New York Times* quotes Dr. Thomas's claim that women were "by nature" unfit to appreciate art due to their lack of "poise and balance." What did his feminist sister-in-law, Susan Walker FitzGerald, think about that?

Dr. Thomas wrote a number of medical papers on nervous and mental diseases and contributed his medical service during the First World War. He worked at Boston City Hospital for more than forty years, later as a consulting physician on nervous diseases, and taught for several years at Tufts College Medical School. He was also an associate in neurology at the Harvard Medical School, and, beginning in 1929, he was a consulting neurologist at Boston Children's Hospital as well.[86]

John Jenks Thomas died on July 18, 1935. Fanny and he had lived all their married life in Boston, raising their children there, including John Grimes Walker Thomas, Henry Pickering Thomas, Alfred Thomas, and Rebecca Pickering Thomas. Fanny had testified for James during the divorce hearings. Following her husband's death, she moved to Newsome Park, in a Boston area called Jamaica Plain, where her sister Susan lived. She went on a trip to France for several months in 1939.[87] Fanny wrote a manuscript titled *Career of John Grimes Walker, U.S.N.: 1835–1907*, in which she refers to her father's personal papers. This work was photocopied and copyrighted by her son John G. W. Thomas in 1959.[88]

Frances Pickering Walker died on May 19, 1947, at age seventy-nine and was buried in the Pickering family plot in Mount Auburn Cemetery. The headstone designating the grave for Frances and John Thomas is next to the tiny graves of her deceased little sisters, Alice Pickering Walker, who had died a few days after she was born, and Elizabeth Grimes Walker, who had died at four years old (see the photograph on page 164).

The Respondent's Brother, Henry Pickering Walker

James's only brother, Henry Pickering Walker (called "Hal" by some and "Harry" by others), died a few months before his sister Susan. After graduating from Harvard University, he was employed by Lord Electric Company and then by National Contracting Company of New York, working on subway and sewer construction in the Boston area. In June 1898, Henry volunteered for the First Engineer Regiment, U.S. Volunteers, and was commissioned as a second lieutenant. He served in Puerto Rico, repairing roads and bridges during the Spanish-American War. He was sent back to New York, sick with malaria and typhoid fever. Henry recuperated and then was discharged from the U.S. Army in January 1899. He worked for engineering firms in New York City; Washington, DC; and Philadelphia.[89]

Beginning in 1902, Henry Pickering Walker was an engineer for the General Electric Company in Schenectady, New York. In 1907, he married Katherine Alice Sanman, a young widow, in Salem, Massachusetts, where many of the Pickering relatives also lived. The wedding occurred shortly before his father, Admiral John Walker, died, and their first son was named John Grimes Walker in his memory. Unfortunately, the baby died a couple of days after he was born, in October 1909, the same month in which Nina filed for divorce. Another son, Henry Pickering Walker, was born in 1911.[90]

Henry had been the best man at his brother's wedding. Like the rest of the Walker family, he took James's side in the divorce case. In both the March 1911 trial and the November 1913 trial, Henry testified that his brother had treated Nina well and that he was a good father. His wife, Katherine, also testified in 1913, stating that the relations between James and Nina Walker had seemed fine when she met them but that she thought that Nina was very selfish. During the 1913 trial, Henry Pickering Walker made his own headlines when Richard W. Sears, a news photographer, accused him of kicking his camera. Henry was charged with assault and ordered to pay damages, and the case eventually concluded in a precedent-setting decision that guaranteed the rights of future American press photographers (see Chapter 10).

According to Nina, "Hal was never physically robust[;] with increasing poor health[,] he later bought a farm in Massachusetts and retired to live an outdoor life."[91] Henry and Katherine Walker moved to Hudson and then to Cambridge, Massachusetts, where he was listed in 1920 as a proprietor of farms.[92] They later lived in Brookline, Massachusetts.[93] When his wife, Katherine, died in December 1937, Henry moved to Boston to live with his son.[94] He died of coronary sclerosis on February 11, 1942, at age sixty-nine,[95] and was buried in his wife's family plot in Harmony Grove Cemetery, in Salem, Massachusetts.[96]

Katherine and Henry Pickering Walker's son, Henry Pickering Walker Jr., nicknamed "Pick," grew up in Massachusetts and graduated from Harvard University. He married Joanna Dziecioloski in 1946, and they had two sons and a daughter.[97] Pick had a twenty-year career in the U.S. Army, serving in World War II and the Korean War. After he retired as a lieutenant colonel in 1960, he earned a doctorate in history from the University of Colorado and for eleven years was assistant editor of a history journal. He wrote a well-reviewed book, *The Wagonmasters*, was a co-author of *The Arizona Atlas*, and was at work on a biography of Admiral Walker when he died in 1984. Henry's oldest child, also named Henry Pickering Walker and called "Bud," comments, "Since reading my father's manuscript on the admiral and the correspondence between him and Betty [Rebecca], I have this nagging feeling that James and my grandfather, Henry Pickering Walker I (nicknamed Harry), did not develop into the men that the admiral had hoped." He wonders whether "the Admiral's long absences from his family may have had an effect upon his sons and their development as men."[98] Bud believes that the relationship between his father and grandfather was also distant.

The Respondent's Sister Sarah Cochrane Walker

Sarah Cochrane Walker (called Sallie) never married and lived with her mother until Rebecca Walker's death in 1925. She continued to live in Brookline, Massachusetts, for several years[99] and then moved to nearby Boston.[100] She traveled, including a voyage to England in 1931, apparently accompanied by her sister Frances (Fanny),[101] and to Switzerland in the 1950s. The last surviving of her siblings, she died on December 5, 1953, in Neuchâtel, Switzerland, at age seventy-five.[102] Her headstone in the Pickering family plot in Mount Auburn cemetery is between that of her brother James and the one for her sister Frances and her husband (see the photograph on page 164).

Nina and James Walker's Children

The Walkers' First Child and Only Daughter,
Elizabeth Grimes Walker

Elizabeth Grimes Walker, the eldest of the Walker children, was nineteen years old by the time her parents' divorce was settled. Her father had been absent at her birth, shortly before he had left for many months in Nicaragua, and he had angered her mother by not communicating frequently while he was away (see Chapter 3). Through the years of their parents' separation, the Walker children visited their father at his home and at their grandmother Walker's home, and they went on vacation with their Walker relatives.

During the divorce trials, several judges asked Elizabeth which parent should have custody of her and her brothers. This must have been a difficult responsibility for a young girl. When Elizabeth testified at the July 1914 custody hearing, as her father shed tears, she stated hesitantly that she did not love him and did not want anything to do with him, and she also disavowed her paternal grandmother (see Chapter 11).

Elizabeth lived with her maternal grandmother and her aunt Bertha in Washington for her junior year of high school at the Cathedral School, a prestigious girl's academy that she attended on scholarship. She returned to Newport to live with her mother and brothers during the following summer and later finished high school there. During the spring vacation of her senior year, while she and her brother Grahame were visiting friends in New Jersey, she had a bicycle accident and suffered a serious brain concussion. Elizabeth and her mother stayed with friends in Brookline, Massachusetts, during her recovery, and a young lieutenant who had been Elizabeth's companion in Newport got temporary duty in nearby Boston so that he could be helpful. According to Nina, "Although a tacit engagement followed, by mutual consent the attachment died a natural death."[103]

Elizabeth and Grahame "entered wholeheartedly into the social life." In February 1918, the *Washington Times* reported that Elizabeth Grimes Walker and some other rebellious pre-debutantes "slipped out" prior to "coming out" by holding a costume party. The article was accompanied by a large photograph of Elizabeth in the costume she wore.[104] Nina wrote that at her "coming out" tea at the exclusive Washington Club on January 24, 1920, "my daughter was the prettiest rose in the garden of flowers that surrounded her." At another social event, even President Woodrow Wilson remarked to his wife that Elizabeth was "a beauty."[105]

Elizabeth joined the Junior League and volunteered with the Red Cross.[106] In the autumn of 1921, she was a teacher at Gunston Hall, "a fashionable boarding and day school."[107] Nina noted that her daughter Elizabeth was not only beautiful but also fashionable and "always drew attention by many compliments, often from strangers . . . not flattery but sincere [praise], and she knew it."[108]

Nina wrote in her unpublished autobiography that, as the summer of 1922 approached, Elizabeth had an important decision to make about her future, since "two admirers were pressing their suits and daughter was not sure of herself."[109] The top two contenders for Elizabeth's hand in marriage were war veteran Jack Davis, who worked for the federal government, and Ben Potter, whom she had met when she was a student at the Cathedral School and he was at St. Albans. To help her daughter choose between them, Nina suggested that she and Elizabeth travel first to Virginia, to see Jack's family, and then up to Wisconsin, where they would be near Ben.

In Petersburg, Virginia, Elizabeth and her mother were "pleasantly entertained" by Jack Davis's mother and sister, with the southern hospitality that Nina admired. In Madison, Wisconsin, Elizabeth and Nina entered summer school at the University of Wisconsin; Elizabeth took classes in editorial and newspaper reporting, and Nina "listened in" to classes on present-day politics and music appreciation. A letter sent to Elizabeth from a friend implies that Elizabeth was considering a career in journalism, at which the writer claims she would be successful but asks, "Don't you think it is a bit too masculine for a woman?"[110]

Ben Potter took Elizabeth and her mother on a trip to the beautiful Wisconsin lake area. According to Nina, the "trip was thoroughly enjoyable to me, but spelled the parting of the ways for my daughter and Ben."[111] She described what happened next:

> My daughter struggled with that age old conflict searching of the heart, through her days of study, intense heat, and social gayeties. With continued doubts and misgivings Elizabeth asked my advice. Possibly a word from me helped her final decision. I do not know. A telegram was sent to Jack late one evening.[112]

In mid-September 1921, Nina announced Elizabeth's engagement to Jack in Newport. The newspaper announcements reported Elizabeth's paternal Pickering and Walker pedigrees but did not mention her father. Jack, whose full name was John Williams Davis, was ten years older than Elizabeth and descended from a distinguished pre-Revolutionary Virginia family. His father, Richard Beale Davis, fought in the Confederate Army and served in the General Assembly of Virginia. Jack earned a graduate degree from Cornell University in mechanical engineering and taught at Harvard, Vanderbilt, Stanford, and the University of Illinois. He enlisted as a private first class and served as a flight instructor during World War I, rising to captain before he left the service in 1919.[113] At the time of his marriage to Elizabeth, Jack worked in the Department of the Bureau of Mines, where he designed and supervised the operation of helium plants to produce the lighter-than-air gas used for dirigibles.[114] He was employed there until 1925 and became widely known for inventing a process to separate helium from natural gas.[115]

Elizabeth Grimes Walker and John Williams Davis married on October 22, 1921. Due to Bertha's purported influence over their mother, Nina paid for the wedding herself, which was held at the National Cathedral's Bethlehem Chapel instead of Rock Creek Church, where Elizabeth's mother's and grandmother's weddings had been, with a reception at the Washington Club. One of those officiating at the ceremony was Nina's cousin the Reverend Reese F. Alsop, who had also presided at Nina's and Virginia Chinn's weddings and had provided advice to Nina about her divorce. James Wilson Grimes Walker, the bride's father, was not present. The newlyweds made their home in Washington, DC, after returning from their wedding trip.[116]

An unsigned letter was sent to Elizabeth during the early years of her marriage. Although the writer calls Elizabeth "daughter" and refers to himself as "daddy," the consensus from people who have read the letter, including Elizabeth's daughter, is that, considering the subject matter and tone, it is not actually from her father but from a much younger man, who discusses studying the law, living in the South, and flirting with women. The handwriting does not appear to be the same as James Walker's in his letters to Nina. The letter may actually have been sent by a close friend, a brother, or one of her former beaux.[117]

Elizabeth and Jack moved to Fort Worth, Texas, where Jack continued working for the U.S. government. Later, they moved to Syracuse, New York, where Jack was a consulting engineer for the Allied Chemical Company. Elizabeth had a "painful breast tumor" surgically removed at a hospital in Washington, and for the last few months of her first pregnancy, she rented an apartment in the same building where her mother and brothers lived. Elizabeth gave birth to John Williams Davis Jr. on October 28, 1926.[118]

A daughter, also named Elizabeth Walker Davis, was born to Elizabeth in 1930. She was called "Bettina" as a young child, and her grandmother Nina described her as "fair haired, fairy like."[119] She is now Dr. Elizabeth Walker Davis, and she provided a great deal of information for this book. A second son, Timothy Pickering Davis, was born in 1934. Beginning in 1929, Jack was a consulting engineer for the Atmospheric Nitrogen Corporation and the Solvay Process Company, in Hopewell, Virginia. On October 5, 1938, at fifty-one years of age, he died of a heart attack at his mother's home in Petersburg, Virginia, and was buried in Blandford Cemetery there.[120] His gravestone states that he was the son of Richard Beale and Nannie Hall Davis. No mention is made of his wife.[121] Elizabeth later moved to California and worked for thirteen years as a clerk at the U.S. Naval Supply in Oakland. She died of cardiac arrest at Presbyterian Hospital in San Francisco on August 1, 1968, at sixty-nine years of age.[122] Elizabeth Grimes Walker Davis was cremated, and her ashes were placed at Olivet Memorial Park in Colma, California.[123]

Elizabeth and John William Davis's daughter, Elizabeth Walker Davis, describes her parents' marriage as "made in hell." Her mother, she says,

> loved huge parties and spending lots-and-lots of money; he [her father] loved peace, quiet, letters back and forth with Einstein-and-others. My mother told me that about three years into their marriage he suggested divorce, so she punctured all the condoms in the drawer and got pregnant. This pattern repeated itself twice more (me and my youngest brother). The final time my father just left and filed for divorce. My mother was content with the idea of divorce, but lastingly furious when instead my father died just before the divorce was final—and so there was no alimony. There went her dream of finally returning to the wealthy party-life.[124]

Dr. Davis, who has two doctorates, including one in family studies, believes that "a social butterfly and a serious research scientist should never marry."[125]

A divorce would not have been alarming to this family. Not only did Elizabeth's parents go through a highly visible divorce; it was well-known that her grandmother Virginia Serrellina Wood Chinn was separated from her grandfather Richard Henry Chinn for many years. This arrangement was by mutual agreement, since Virginia detested life on her husband's plantation in Cuba and moved back to her family's estate in Washington when her daughters were very young. When Richard Chinn finally sold the plantation, instead of joining his wife and daughters in Washington, he moved to California. According to Nina, "a legal divorce was never considered by my mother nor father[;] the arrangement as it stood seemed satisfactory to both and they remained apart." Her father, unlike her husband, regularly sent money to support his children.[126]

James Walker's attorneys attempted to prove that Nina's maternal grandmother, Elizabeth Davis Wood, had also been estranged from her husband, Robert Serrell Wood, at the time of his death. According to Nina, "Grandfather loved his home and family, yet his restless spirit with the lure of travel took him back to England for visits and to the West Indies."[127] So it is probably true that the Woods were physically separated at times. Although he was buried at sea, the large memorial marker where his wife was buried in Rock Creek Cemetery in 1906 includes an engraved inscription in memory of them both.[128] It does not appear that Nina's grandparents, Robert and Elizabeth Wood, were either legally or emotionally separated.

In summary, the facts are that Nina's mother lived apart from her husband by mutual agreement; Nina divorced; and Nina's only daughter, Elizabeth Grimes Walker Davis, was separated from her husband and narrowly escaped divorce when he died. Her daughter's only daughter, Elizabeth Walker Davis, also divorced her husband, in what she refers to as a "friendly divorce."[129] James Walker's attorneys claimed that the women in Nina's family had a "hereditary impulse to desert their husbands" and that if Nina were granted a divorce, the pattern would continue with her daughter and future generations (see Chapter 10). Although many behavioral characteristics were routinely attributed to genetics in the early twentieth century, scientific knowledge has progressed beyond that stage. Many contemporary studies show strong evidence that children of divorced parents are more likely to divorce themselves.[130] "Intergenerational transmission of divorce" may occur for several possible reasons, but none of these is attributed to genetic factors. Current social science research indicates that family and cultural norms, as opposed to heredity, affect whether people divorce.[131] Some of their descendants believe that Nina and James's traumatic divorce might be the reason for the high divorce rate among their grandchildren. This point is interesting but difficult to prove. Regardless, it seems logical that a child raised in a family that condones ending a bad marriage would be more likely to accept divorce as a feasible solution than would a child raised by a family that condemns marital breakups. As divorce became more attainable and acceptable in the early twentieth century, it offered a legal remedy for many unhappy spouses, not just those in the Walker family.

The Walkers' Second Child, John Grahame Walker

John Grahame Walker (called Grahame) was Nina and James Walker's oldest son. He was ten years old when the divorce began in 1909 and was raised without a father from that point on. Nina struggled over how to protect him while at the same time respecting his masculinity. "My oldest was an obedient boy," she said. "I instinctively felt his deep affection for me, which I now know must have imposed upon him undue advantage and hurt his manly spirits."[132]

Grahame was left-handed, and Nina thought her son looked "awkward and uncouth" when he threw the ball with his left hand, so she tied it close to his body in a misguided attempt to "correct" him. She later lamented this practice and wrote, "I did not know then, that the months of stuttering that followed was the direct result of my endeavors to controle [sic] what to him was natural. The present day books on child psychology would have prevented my error and make me less regretful."[133]

Grahame was a good athlete and particularly loved football. According to Nina, "his light build gave me much concern when I saw him matched against the heavy weight of more robust boys."[134] She consulted a physician the summer before Grahame's senior year of high school, when he was to become the team captain. The physician told her that there was no danger and that football would "develop both body and mind." Unfortunately, when the Cloyne House School played the town team, Grahame was tackled by a larger boy, tearing his collar [sic] from the shoulder. He underwent "a then unusual and delicate operation of tying the bones together with a silver cord." His mother believed that "the most poignant ache was in his young heart, for he knew his ambitions for taking part in college sports were frustrated, as the injury was in his right shoulder that would effect [*sic*] even his game of tennis. Thereafter, there was a perceptible slope to his shoulder and a slight limp in his walk that has somewhat diminished with the years."[135]

Since "Grahame showed no special bent for his life work," and there was no man around to advise him, Nina decided that her oldest son could use some guidance. She took a particularly bold approach to finding it for him. During the Christmas holidays of their senior year of high school, Nina took Grahame and Elizabeth to New York City. She sent her son to J. P. Morgan with a letter of introduction asking that Grahame be given a position in his bank. Mr. Morgan told him, "Go to college [and] then come back to me."[136]

As she had done in the past, Nina consulted with her cousin the Reverend Reese Alsop regarding college for Grahame, and he recommended Amherst College. Since no support came from Grahame's father, his mother was overjoyed when her close friend Sarah visited in the spring of 1917 and later asked "in the sweetest and most tackful [*sic*] way if she could have the privilege of defraying Grahame's expenses through college . . . having gathered that my financial status was far from adequate to educate my three sons as I would wish."[137] Sarah's husband also happened to be a trustee of Amherst.

In the spring of 1917, Grahame was not yet eighteen, the required age for enlistment, but he could not wait to join the war effort. Although the military board knew his age, "they also were carried away in the heat of enthusiasm and accepted him with no embarrassing questions asked, as second class seaman in the U.S. Naval Reserves."[138]

After he spent the summer washing dishes for the navy, Grahame entered Amherst in the fall of 1917 and joined a fraternity. His mother supplemented his income, but his social life took him away from his studies and proved to be expensive, putting him in debt. By spring vacation, Grahame decided to pay off his debts and leave college to work in Washington to earn his own living as a "runner" in the Washington Loan and Trust Company Bank. In 1918, he was detailed to the naval unit at Brown University to continue his studies for a promotion to ensign. His mother always regretted that "when the Armistice was signed[,] Grahame at once asked for his release and received his discharge [on] December 18, 1918, two weeks before his examinations for an officer's commission." She later wrote, "There followed twelve years of groping in the dark" trying to find his calling, until "a girl came into my son's life as a lodestar pointing the way. It was she who led him to his life's work, the study and practice of law, and eventually to the alter [*sic*]."[139]

At twenty years of age, Grahame worked as a real estate salesman,[140] and he became an aviator.[141] In the early 1930s, he worked for the Census Bureau while attending Washington College of Law at night.[142] In June 1935, at age thirty-six, John Grahame Walker married Marion Caroline Boss, who was twenty-seven and the daughter of Mr. and Mrs. William Albert Boss, of Chevy Chase, Maryland.[143] They moved into an apartment in Washington, DC, where Marion worked as a clerk for the Works Progress Administration (WPA) and Grahame was an attorney.[144] Grahame and Marion later relocated to Maryland and raised their children, Sarah Walker and Priscilla Grahame Walker. Priscilla remembers only that she knew that the divorce between her grandparents was considered a family scandal and that her father never talked about his own father.[145]

Grahame Walker became involved in politics, serving on his county council and as its president. He was elected to the Maryland House of Delegates, and later he became a People's Court judge, a position he held through 1963. In 1965, John Grahame Walker became nationally known as the defense attorney in a landmark case in the Maryland Court of Appeals. The decision in this case reversed a murder conviction by ruling that jurors cannot be required to swear to a belief in God. John Grahame Walker died of a heart attack in Bethesda, Maryland, on February 11, 1968, at the age of sixty-seven, and was buried in Rock Creek Cemetery, where his mother and maternal grandparents were buried.[146] His wife, Marion, died many years later in Silver Spring, Maryland, on September 30, 1990, and was buried with her husband.[147]

The Walkers' Third Child, Robert Serrell Wood Walker

Robert Serrell Wood Walker was called Serrell from the time he was young. As an infant, he was sickly and cared for by a nurse at Virginia Chinn's home in Washington, DC, for several months. When Rebecca Walker stopped sending money for the nurse, Bertha Chinn wrote an irate letter in which she purportedly accused James of financial incompetence and bad behavior toward Nina. She also insinuated that Nina became pregnant with Serrell because her husband had threatened to have an affair if she did not give in to his demands for sex. Following this letter, James brought baby Serrell and his nurse to stay with his sister Fanny and her husband in Boston. Nina claimed that she had begged to get Serrell back, but he was not returned to her until months later (see Chapter 3).

As a fourteen-year-old student at the Cloyne House School, Serrell testified against his father in a custody hearing, stating that James had never shown interest in him or the other children and that he hated his grandmother Rebecca Walker (see Chapter 11). Serrell graduated from the Severn School in Maryland and tried for years to get an appointment to West Point, without success. Then, in 1920, a U.S. senator from South Paris, Maine (his father's locale), appointed him to the Naval Academy. When Serrell failed the mathematics exam during his first year at the academy, he was forced to resign from the navy. Nina sent him to a coaching school, and he was admitted to West Point in 1922. After again failing a mathematics exam, he resigned in 1924. He moved home with his mother and brothers and worked in the Washington office of the telephone company.[148]

Still pursuing a military career, in July 1928, Serrell became a first lieutenant in the Coast Artillery Reserve Corps at Fort Monroe, Virginia.[149] In the early 1930s, living with his mother and two brothers in Washington, he started a general insurance business and became an associate member of the Insurance Institute of America.[150] He was fond of writing letters to the editor and sent letters on a variety of topics to the *Washington Post*, including one to urge that the Army-Navy football game be moved to Washington, DC;[151] another to defend the high price of workmen's compensation insurance;[152] and another to call for a religious revival to help end the Great Depression.[153]

During World War II, Serrell was a captain in the army. He lived in Washington for many years and worked at a variety of occupations, including as a teacher, a playground director, a salesman, a radio announcer, and a newscaster. He later retired from the Federal Aviation Administration.[154] Serrell was also active in community and church activities and was a member of the Sons of the American Revolution and the Academy of Political and Social Sciences.[155]

Serrell remained a bachelor until after his mother's death. At the age of fifty-two, he married Mary Ella Carper Blamey on July 10, 1953, in Arlington, Virginia.[156] Mary Ella was fifty-one at the time and had been widowed by her first husband, Albert Blamey.

Like his mother, Serrell enjoyed writing poetry. In 1950, a few years after her death, he published his first collection of poems, *A Star Still Shines: Poems of Love and Faith*, with Exposition Press. This publication was followed in 1951 by *Farewell, Dear Heart! Poems of Devotion*, dedicated "To My Mother," and *Love Lyrics* in 1952. These books are infused with religious imagery and piety and several poems praising mothers. In 1953, Serrell published *Oh Mother Mine! Happy Times with Little Rhymes*, also with Exposition Press. The poems in this book extoll the many facets of motherhood, with such tributes as "A Mother's Faith," "The Guiding Light," and "My Mother's Eyes." An example of his verse is the following:

> My Mother[157]
> *Never within her watchful eyes*
> *Was I not all-supreme;*
> *Guarded by love that ever lies*
> *Within a mother's dream*
> *For never was a dream too small,*
> *Whose manner was so rare,*
> *In doing did not, after all,*
> *Show Mother's hand was there.*
> *A house is not a home, I know,*
> *Unless there dwells inside*
> *Someone to whom your footsteps go—*
> *Whose heart is open wide!*
> *If ever I should want a nook*
> *Within this world of space,*
> *Give me again that precious look*
> *Upon my mother's face!*

Although Serrell wrote many poems celebrating a heavenly father, only one poem in all of his four books speaks of an earthly father. This poem is found in *Farewell, Dear Heart! Poems of Devotion*, a book dedicated to his mother:

> Father[158]
> *You owe your best to Mother—yes,*
> *'Tis absolutely true;*
> *Yet without Father, you must know,*
> *There wouldn't have been you.*
> *Remember him therefore some way,*
> *Be it ever so small.*
> *And don't forget to honor, too,*
> *The Father of us all.*

It is not known whether Serrell ever saw his own father after becoming an adult. He died on August 3, 1970, at age sixty-nine, in Arkansas.[159] Like many in his maternal family, he was buried in Rock Creek Cemetery.[160] His wife, Mary Ella Carper Blamey Walker, died in Arkansas on December 27, 1994, at the age of ninety-three.[161]

The Walkers' Youngest Child, Herbert Wood Walker

Herbert, the youngest of Nina and James's children, was hospitalized in the fall of 1905 at three years of age for surgical correction of the hernia he was born with. This was most likely the reason Nina delayed her return to Charleston that year (see Chapter 4). He was almost eight years old when his mother took him and his older brothers and sister away from his father. After his parents' separation, he visited his father with his siblings and spent some vacation time with his father's family. During the 1913 divorce trial, James claimed that, on those visits, Herbert "stuck to [him] like a burr."

Like his brother Serrell, Herbert sought an appointment to a military academy for years. In 1919, he entered the Naval Academy in Annapolis. He and his brother Serrell were midshipmen at the same time. Like his brother, Herbert failed the mathematics examination and was forced to resign from the navy in March 1920. After a government investigation into the high failure rate at the Naval Academy, he was eligible for reinstatement, received a second appointment, and reentered Annapolis as a plebe in May 1921. As happened with Serrell, Herbert failed to pass the mathematics examination the second time around and was again forced to resign in February 1923. He went back to Washington to live with his mother and brothers and worked as a bank teller at a branch office of the Washington Loan and Trust Company Bank, where Grahame had also worked.[162] In July 1927, Herbert sailed to France. Upon his return to Washington, DC, he took finance courses with the American Institute of Banking and later served as an officer of that organization.[163]

On June 6, 1936, at age thirty-four, Herbert married Adaline Peter Cox, the daughter of Mr. and Mrs. William Nettleton Cox, of Louisville, Kentucky.[164] Adaline lived in Washington, had completed three years at Vassar College, and was a member of the Junior League.[165] Although her parents gave the young couple a lavish wedding in Kentucky, Adaline's mother reportedly never forgave her for leaving home and marrying.[166] Herbert and Adaline rented an apartment in Washington. He continued to work at the Washington Loan and Trust Company Bank and later worked at the Morris Plan Bank,[167] while Adaline was a secretary for the Federal Housing Administration (FHA).[168] They had two children, Anne Cox Walker in 1942 and Herbert Wood Walker Jr. in 1944.

Nina's son Herbert and his family lived in Virginia and then in North Carolina for several years, while he worked as a bank examiner for the Federal Home Loan Bank. Herbert Jr. says that his father traveled quite a bit for his job and was home only one week a month, which did not sit well with Adaline. Since her parents were fairly wealthy, they were able to convince Herbert to move his wife and children down to Kentucky and work at his father-in-law's distillery warehouse. The plan, according to Herbert Jr., was for his father to become vice president and eventually take over the business. Unfortunately, when Mr. Cox died, another company bought the distillery and fired his son-in-law. Herbert went back to his former profession as a bank examiner, this time in Cincinnati, but lived with his wife and children in Cleveland, near Lake Erie, where his son remembers that he loved watching the big boats. Herbert Jr. says his father always had pictures of seascapes in his homes. Finally, Herbert Sr. and Adaline retired to a home on the ocean in Atlantic, North Carolina, and often walked on the beach. They also took a tramp steamer on a voyage through the Panama Canal,[169] perhaps remembering his grandfather's and father's involvement in that venture.

According to his children, Herbert Sr. had no further contact with his father after the divorce and "felt abandoned." He told his son that he was brought up by "strong women." His daughter Anne says that her father did not talk about his own father or his father's family, but she heard from her mother that it was "a very sad and unfortunate situation." Herbert Jr. and Anne remember their mother telling them that she had tried to make contact with their grandfather, James Walker, when they were born, but he rebuffed her efforts. Anne wonders why Rebecca Walker, who did not die until 1925, never contacted her grandchildren after they became adults.[170]

Anne Cox Walker saw her grandmother Nina only two times. The first was when Anne was a baby, and the second was shortly before Nina died, when she visited her son Herbert in Fredericksburg. She stayed at the Francis Scott Key Hotel and took the family to dinner there. Anne remembers Nina as a figure in a long black coat holding two orange balloons for her and her younger brother. She explains that a few months later, her father received a message that his mother was ill, took a bus to the hospital, and stopped to buy her flowers. When he arrived at her hospital room, he was told that he was too late—Nina had just died.[171] Herbert Sr.'s aunt Bertha came to visit once; Anne thinks it was after the death of her grandmother. A news article in late November 1947 reported that the District of Columbia zoning board gave Herbert and his aunt Bertha permission to open a private language school on NW Eighteenth Street, but Bertha died very shortly afterward.[172]

Herbert Wood Walker Jr. believes that his mother also came from a troubled family and that his parents had an unhappy marriage. Adaline was a "socialite," he explains, and liked to go to parties, while his father was quiet and did not like to socialize, so they fought a lot about that. This is reminiscent of Nina's complaints about Herbert's father, James, whose mother had earlier warned her son that he kept too much to himself (see Chapter 2).[173]

Herbert Jr. did not have a close relationship with his father, who he believes did not really know how to be a good father due to the broken relationship with his own father. Later in life, Herbert Jr. discovered that he has Asperger's syndrome, a neurological disorder on the mild end of the autism spectrum,[174] and he suspects that his father may have had it as well. It is possible that his grandfather James Walker's difficulties with sociability also may have resulted from this disorder. Herbert Jr. also believes that, in addition to difficulty with social interaction, a tendency to depression was passed down in his paternal family. That is one of the reasons Herbert Jr. decided not to have children and did not marry until he was fifty-four years old. He is aware that his uncle Serrell married in his fifties as well. Herbert Jr.'s sister Anne did not have biological children either but both siblings are stepparents.[175]

Anne Cox Walker is glad that she and her brother have some of Nina's furniture, and she cherishes Bertha's wooden sewing box, but she believes that she missed an opportunity to have other sentimental items from her father's family. Once, when her father was in his seventies, he came to visit Anne and told her that he had been in an antiques shop where he had seen his aunt Bertha's dresser set, including a comb, mirror, and brush. He knew that it was his aunt's, because he remembered the design and the engraving "EBC" from seeing it a child. Anne was very excited about obtaining this heirloom, but, when she checked with the store, she was disappointed to hear that it had been sold.[176] Her father had not cared enough to buy it when he had the chance.

Herbert Wood Walker was the youngest and last to survive of the principal participants in the Walker divorce. He died in Morehead City, North Carolina, on May 13, 1982, at age eighty. His wife, Adaline Cox Walker, died in Asheville, North Carolina, on February 4, 1997.

The Alleged Co-respondent, Mabel Cochrane

Mabel Cochrane is the biggest enigma in the Walker divorce story. No details can be found about her life before she met James Walker in 1901 or after she escaped from testifying in November 1913.

Like many poor single women working in America's northeastern cities at the turn of the twentieth century, Mabel lived in inexpensive rooming houses without supervision. Peers became a support system for these young women, and together "they established their own urban subculture with its own definitions of femininity and standards of behavior that often stood in stark contrast to middle class women of the time."[177] Attitudes regarding sex were more relaxed in this subculture, and these women felt freer to associate with men who were strangers. Because they worked at such jobs as waitressing, which paid poorly, young women sought out men who could provide them with meals, entertainment, and some indulgences. Often the men were compensated with a range of sexual favors. Poor urban young women were sometimes referred to as "charity girls," who, unlike prostitutes, did not accept cash from men but did rely on them for material support. Their peers considered it quite respectable to "pick up" men they met at work or on the street, as Mabel did, and young women often competed as to who was more successful at doing this.[178] As a waitress, Mabel had to be pleasant to her customers to earn good tips, but she learned to go beyond this, distributing copies of her photograph to possible benefactors. She chatted about her "gentlemen friends" with other women, including Sarah Crapo, her landlord's daughter. Mabel's inappropriate letters reflect the more open and intimate communication style used by urban working girls, in contrast to what was expected from upper- and middle-class women (see Chapters 3 and 11).[179]

When her private relationship with James Walker became public, Mabel panicked. She was willing to undergo a medical examination to prove her virginity but balked at testifying in a deposition. As a poor single young woman, Mabel was very vulnerable, and she must have known that she was no match for the two powerful families fighting in court, with her as a pawn. Even Henry T. Richardson, the attorney James Walker provided for her, could not completely protect her from risk, particularly since his main interest was helping James. The last time that anyone involved with the Walker case heard from Mabel was via the letter she sent to Mr. Richardson in November 1913 with the address "General Delivery, Springfield Massachusetts." Despite fervent attempts to find her, she "disappeared."

A Mabel Cochrane is listed in the 1915 Boston City Directory. Did she return quietly to Boston and live at 599 Columbus Avenue?[180] Was she the Mabel B. Cochrane who married in Boston in 1925?[181] Did she sail on the ship *Evangeline* from Nova Scotia in 1937?[182] There are possible clues, but none is definitive. If "well-behaved women seldom make history,"[183] this is particularly true for poor women. Frightened following her brief encounter with fame for not behaving well, Mabel probably returned to a well-behaved, mundane life, possibly marrying and changing her name. Unlike for the other principals in the Walker divorce case, members of prominent wealthy families, there is no documented trace of Mabel Cochrane's later life.

Author's Notes

THE QUESTION PEOPLE ASK ME most often about this book is "How did you get the idea?" My best answer is "By accident." As most researchers know, a project does not always end up where it started; the blind alleys are frustrating, but the surprises along the way are exhilarating. At first, I planned to write about a woman, Sarah Ellen Palmer, who was a physician before the turn of the twentieth century. While researching my original subject online, I discovered that she, along with other physicians, had provided courtroom testimony in a divorce case between Nina and James Walker. I was fascinated that medical evidence of the purported lover's virginity was offered as proof that extramarital sex could not have occurred.

The more I read about the Walker case, the more it captivated me. The supporting characters involved members of two historically important and powerful families who battled for years, including a distinguished admiral and a prominent suffragist. This divorce drama was particularly interesting because it unfolded at a time when social rules and values were transitioning from the very rigid Victorian period to the Progressive Era. It was clear that the story of the Walkers' divorce might appeal to a wide audience.

As a professional sociologist in the fields of gender, sexual behavior, and family, I had the appropriate tools to tell this story. I have studied, written, and taught about these subjects for many years, including in my doctoral program at Brandeis University, in my previous book (*Am I Still a*

Woman? Hysterectomy and Gender Identity), and as a faculty member at the University of New Hampshire. A book project about the Walker divorce was therefore irresistible.

After consuming online articles about the Walker case, I set out to obtain records of the case from the Rhode Island court system. I spoke by telephone with a very helpful court clerk in Newport—Ray Beretta—but was not optimistic that he would be able to retrieve records that were more than one hundred years old. Several weeks later, I called Mr. Beretta back to thank him for what I assumed had been a futile effort. To my amazement, he responded, "I have stacks of records waiting for you." I asked my husband, Tom, whether he would like to take a day trip to Newport, Rhode Island, and he replied, "Pack an overnight bag." We arrived at the courthouse later that day, and the court clerk handed me all the documents for the Walker divorce hearings, including correspondence between the principals that had been used as evidence. As it turned out, we did need to stay overnight in order to go through all the paperwork, since we could not take the documents out of the courthouse. I am extremely grateful to Ray Beretta for all his help.

I also found Walker family ancestral information that Lynne Thomas Guidetti had posted online. We e-mailed back and forth, and she was extremely helpful and encouraging. Via e-mail, Lynne introduced me to Nina and James Walker's granddaughter—their only daughter's only daughter, Elizabeth Walker Davis (also known as Elizabeth Socha Davis). Dr. Davis, who has been an exceptionally rich source of information about her family, generously shared photographs and part of her unpublished autobiography, "Stories My Mother Told Me." Among other achievements, she holds two doctorates—one in zoology and the other in family studies—which she earned two decades apart, and she provides a unique perspective on the Walker family personalities and relationships. Lynne Guidetti also introduced me through e-mail to the grandson of James Walker's only brother, Henry Pickering Walker, who, like his grandfather and father, is also named Henry Pickering Walker but goes by the name "Bud." Bud Walker provided outstanding assistance by making available relevant information from his father's unpublished manuscript on Admiral Walker and by providing access to the Walker Family Tree on Ancestry.com. He offered important insights into the relationship between the admiral and his sons. My gratitude to Elizabeth Walker Davis and Bud Walker is boundless, as it is to Lynne Guidetti Thomas for introducing them to me.

In 2013, Cindy Iverson was doing family history research for a friend in California, when she happened to come across an old scrapbook in the collection of her friend's deceased mother and generously made the contents available online. The scrapbook, which appears to have belonged to Elizabeth Grimes Walker Davis, Nina and James Walker's daughter, contains not only family photographs but also such memorabilia as calling cards and wedding announcements for Elizabeth and her friends. I am very grateful to Cindy for understanding the importance of this find and for making it available to Bud Walker and me.

Tom and I made yet another field trip to Newport, Rhode Island, so that I could comb through the microfilm version of the local papers, the *Newport Daily News* and the *Newport Mercury*. I thank the library staff and the supporters of the Newport Library for enabling me to fill in many of the story's details. On this trip, I also visited Naval Station Newport (the former Naval Training Station), where Nina Walker finally left her husband.

We also traveled to Brownfield, Maine, where James Walker lived out his years after the divorce. I spoke with Nat Peirce, co-owner with Aaron Anker of GrandyOats, a company that produced organic granola in the huge barn that James Walker once owned. At the time we visited Brownfield, the company was just about to move to new quarters. Nat graciously gave us a tour of the barn, even gifting me a small piece of the structure as a memento. Thank you, Nat. The volunteers at the Brownfield Historical Society were generous with informative printed, photographic, and verbal data. I heartily thank Joanna Thurston and Norma Pandora Hopkins, two volunteers who remembered James Walker from their childhoods and agreed to be interviewed. They also told me about Jeff Solter, who took time out from his automotive repair business to give us a tour of his house next door, which James Walker had originally owned and used to house his farmworkers. This led to a telephone interview with a previous owner of the house, Carol Brooks, who provided such information as where James's dogs were buried. I am grateful to both. I also thank the clerks at the Registry of Deeds in nearby Fryeburg, Maine, who helped me find the original deeds to James Walker's farm, which, as I suspected, were in the names of his mother and his brother-in-law. I thank Marianne Hansen, the curator and academic liaison for rare book and manuscript collections at Bryn Mawr College, and her staff for scanning correspondence between James Walker's sister Susan Walker FitzGerald and other family members and e-mailing the scans to me.

Nearing the end of my book, I thought my information was complete. Then, a few weeks before my manuscript deadline, I heard from Priscilla Walker Shows—the daughter of Nina and James's oldest son, John Grahame Walker—whom I had tried to contact several months earlier.

Priscilla provided information in a telephone interview and generously supplied the first part of Nina's unpublished autobiography (her descendants referred to it as a "diary"), which her cousin Anne Cox Walker had given to her. This took me completely by surprise, since I had no idea that Nina's autobiography existed. Although Priscilla had not been in contact with her Walker cousins for many years, she had enough information about them for me to locate Herbert Wood Walker Jr. and Anne Cox Walker, the son and daughter of James and Nina Walker's youngest son, Herbert Wood Walker. Both of them kindly agreed to be interviewed by telephone and provided much information about their family. Herbert also sent me a photograph of Nina and her children, a biography of Admiral Walker written by his daughter Frances, and a family will. Thus, I was able to interview children of all of the Walker offspring (Serrell Walker, who married late in life, had no children). Perhaps the biggest revelation came when Herbert Wood Walker Jr. provided a document that had been stored for many years at the back of a file cabinet, which turned out to be the last 280 pages of Nina Walker's unpublished autobiography. His sister, Anne Cox Walker, then supplied additional pages for the first part of the autobiography (the middle 121 pages have not been located). Nothing is more valuable than hearing from a subject in the first person. Taking notes from the faded handwritten pages of that document was certainly well worth the effort. Nina's personal account not only added more flavor to the story; it also enabled me to better understand her. I owe a thousand thanks to Herbert, Anne, and Priscilla for that treasure!

Thanks so much to Micah B. Kleit, former editor-in-chief of Temple University Press (TUP), for shepherding my manuscript through the initial approval process. I greatly appreciate the wonderful support and attentiveness of my editor, Sara Jo Cohen. I owe a great debt of gratitude to Joan Vidal, senior production editor at TUP, and to Heather Wilcox, my copy editor, who helped considerably to make my manuscript coherent, correct, and complete. I also thank other staff members at TUP, including editorial assistant Nikki Miller, marketing director Ann-Marie Anderson, advertising manager Irene Imperio Kull, and publicity manager Gary Kramer. Additional thanks go to Susan Thomas for her work on the index.

Additional gratitude goes to Kathy Hart, my dear friend, who read early drafts of the manuscript and gave me the encouragement that only a book lover can. She also has an eagle's eye for typos and misspellings. My wonderful husband, C. Thomas Arrington, was my fieldwork companion, my site photographer, my technical support, and the best photocopier, collator, and cheerleader ever. He graciously accepted my long-term relationship with the Walker project. I might have allowed myself to go hungry on some of my more intense research and writing days if he had not come to my rescue with his tasty meals.

My children, Dr. G. David Poznik and Jessica Elson Poznik, have become remarkable adults. I am so proud of their intelligence, accomplishments, and compassion for other people, and I thank them for supporting my work. Special gratitude goes to my mother, Edith Wiener Elson, who, with my late father, Matthew Elson, has always encouraged my work. She read through every draft of my manuscript and is an insightful editor. My mother defies all expectations about older women and provides me and my peers with great optimism about our own later years. I offer love and gratitude to the rest of my wonderful family and friends who sustained me through this book project!

Notes

PROLOGUE

1. William L. O'Neill, *Divorce in the Progressive Era* (New Haven, CT: Yale University Press, 1967), ix.
2. Ibid.
3. Ibid., x.
4. Paul H. Jacobsen, *American Marriage and Divorce* (New York: Rhinehart, 1999), 90, qtd. in O'Neill, *Divorce in the Progressive Era*, 20. Although both authors admit that data on marriage and divorce gathered before 1890 can be unreliable, particularly due to misreporting, they still claim that the figures demonstrate a drastic increase in the divorce rate following the Civil War.
5. Marilyn Coleman, Lawrence H. Ganong, and Kelly Warzinik, *Family Life in the 20th Century* (Westport, CT: Greenwood Press, 2007).
6. Glenda Riley, *Divorce: An American Tradition* (New York: Oxford University Press, 1991), 124.
7. Elaine Tyler May, *Great Expectations: Marriage and Divorce in Post-Victorian America* (Chicago: University of Chicago Press, 1980), 2.
8. Riley, *Divorce*, 122.
9. O'Neill, *Divorce in the Progressive Era*, 190.
10. J. Herbie DiFonzo, *Beneath the Fault Line: The Popular and Legal Culture of Divorce in Twentieth-Century America* (Charlottesville: University Press of Virginia, 1997), 14.
11. John D'Emilio and Esther B. Freedman, *Intimate Matters: A History of Sexuality in America* (New York: Harper and Row, 1988), 80.
12. Ibid., 81.
13. Qtd. in ibid., 204.
14. Riley, *Divorce*, 124.
15. O'Neill, *Divorce in the Progressive Era*, 79.

16. For more about how private troubles and public issues are inextricably connected, see C. Wright Mills, *The Sociological Imagination* (New York: Oxford University Press, 1959).

17. "Mrs. N. C. Walker to Appeal," *New York Herald*, December 9, 1913, Chronicling America: Historic American Newspapers, http://chroniclingamerica.loc.gov/.

18. "President Denies Women's Request for Suffrage Message," *New York Herald*, December 9, 1913, Chronicling America: Historic American Newspapers, http://chroniclingamerica.loc.gov/.

19. "Says Dr. Griffin Refused Her $40 a Week Out of $80,000 Income," *New York Herald*, December 9, 1913, Chronicling America: Historic American Newspapers, http://chroniclingamerica.loc.gov/.

20. "Said She Had to Wash Automobile," *New York Herald*, December 9, 1913, Chronicling America: Historic American Newspapers, http://chroniclingamerica.loc.gov/.

21. "Wife Hysterical in Divorce Court," *New York Herald*, December 9, 1913, Chronicling America: Historic American Newspapers, http://chroniclingamerica.loc.gov/.

22. May, *Great Expectations*, 4.

23. Riley, *Divorce*, 45–46; Roderick Philips, *Untying the Knot: A Short History of Divorce* (Cambridge, UK: Cambridge University Press, 1991), 141.

CHAPTER 1

1. "Pretty Wedding at Rock Creek," *Washington Post*, February 25, 1897, ProQuest Historical Newspapers, *Washington Post* Archives (1877–1995); "The World of Society—A Picturesque Wedding Event at Old Rock Creek," *Evening Star*, February 24, 1897, Chronicling America: Historic American Newspaper, http://chroniclingamerica.loc.gov/.

2. Elizabeth Walker Davis, "Stories My Mother Told Me" (unpublished manuscript), 6.

3. "The World of Society."

4. "Pretty Wedding at Rock Creek."

5. *Morning Times*, February 25, 1897, Chronicling America: Historic American Newspapers, http://chroniclingamerica.loc.gov/.

6. "Pretty Wedding at Rock Creek"; *Evening Star*, February 25, 1897.

7. *Evening Star*, February 25, 1897.

8. "Pretty Wedding at Rock Creek"; "The World of Society"; *Morning Times*, February 25, 1897; *Evening Star*, February 25, 1897.

9. *Morning Times*, February 25, 1897.

10. "Pretty Wedding at Rock Creek"; "The World of Society."

11. *Morning Times*, February 25, 1897.

12. "Pretty Wedding at Rock Creek."

13. *Morning Times*, February 25, 1897.

14. *Evening Times*, February 25, 1897.

15. "Weather Conditions," *Washington Post*, February 25, 1897, ProQuest Historical Newspapers, *Washington Post* Archives (1877–1995); "The Weather Today," *Morning Times*, February 24, 1897, Chronicling America: Historic American Newspapers, http://chroniclingamerica.loc.gov/.

16. *Old Farmer's Almanac 2002*, https://www.almanac.com/.

17. Edward C. Stiness, *Reports of Cases Argued and Determined in the Supreme Court of Rhode Island* (Providence: Oxford Press, 1911), 32:29.

CHAPTER 2

1. Aaron Walker (1728–1775) was a lieutenant in the colonial army who married Esther Carpenter. Their great-grandson, Alden Walker (1793–1858), married Susan Grimes, the sister of James Wilson Grimes (1816–1872), the governor of Iowa from 1854 to 1858 and a U.S. senator from 1859 to 1869. Alden and Susan Walker had three children. Their middle child was John Grimes Walker, James's father. Frederick A. Virkus, *The Abridged Compendium of American Genealogy: First Families of America. A Genealogical Encyclopedia of the United States* (Chicago: A. N. Marquis, 1925), 1:483, http://wc.rootsweb.ancestry.com/cgibin/igm.cgi?op=AHN&db=seththomasfam12&id=I03512, courtesy of Lynn Thomas Guidetti (accessed February 10, 2013).

2. John Pickering (1615–1657) was the first in his family to emigrate from England and settle in North America. He married Elizabeth Alderman (1615–1662), and they had a son, John Pickering II (1637–1694), who distinguished himself in King Philip's War and later married Alice (Flint) Bullock. Their great-grandson, Timothy Pickering (1745–1829), received his A.B. from Harvard University in 1763 and went on to become a jurist and member of George Washington's staff; he served as a quartermaster general during the American Revolution. Timothy Pickering was later the postmaster general of the United States from 1791 to 1794, the secretary of war in 1794, the secretary of state from 1795 to 1800, a U.S. senator from 1803 to 1811, and a member of the 13th and 14th Congresses from 1813 to 1817. On July 17, 1745, he married Rebecca White (1777–1846), a native of England. Timothy and Rebecca's son, John (1777–1846), held a law degree and was an eminent philologist. John Pickering and his wife, Sarah White (1777–1846), had three children, including Henry White Pickering (1811–1898), who eventually became the president of the Old Boston Bank. Ibid.

3. Ibid.

4. In the seventeenth century, John Chinn (Chynn) had boarded a ship called the *James* and settled in Lancaster County, Virginia. His son, Raleigh Chinn (1684–1741), married Esther Ball (1685–1751), who was the half-sister of Mary Ball Washington, the mother of President Washington. Nina's ancestors had yet another connection to President Washington through Raleigh's younger brother, John Chinn II (1691–1737). His wife was Margaret Ball, who shared a grandfather, Colonel William Ball, with Mary Ball Washington. Colonel Ball had emigrated from England to North America in approximately 1650. A few generations after the Chinn brothers married Esther and Margaret Ball, Nina's forebear Richard Henry Chinn was born, on November 14, 1795, in Harrison County, Kentucky. He became the law partner of Henry Clay and served as a member of the Kentucky House of Representatives in 1831 and in the U.S. Senate, from 1833 to 1837. Richard Henry Chinn married his third cousin, Elizabeth, who had been born on May 8, 1798, to Robert Holmes and Susanna Chinn. Henry and Elizabeth Holmes Chinn had fourteen offspring. Nina's father, Richard Henry Chinn, became the seventh of these in Scott County, Kentucky, on December 26, 1826. Ibid.

5. Virkus, *Abridged Compendium of American Genealogy*, 1:483.

6. Nina Chinn Walker, unpublished autobiography A, 1934, 8.

7. Virginia Serrellina Wood, unpublished journal, included in ibid.

8. Nina Chinn Walker, unpublished autobiography A, 1934, 46.

9. Virkus, *Abridged Compendium of American Genealogy*, 1:483.

10. Dumas Malone and the American Council of Learned Societies, "John Grimes Walker," in *Dictionary of American Biography* (New York: Charles Scribner's Sons, 1936).

11. George Waldo Browne, "John Grimes Walker," in *The History of Hillsborough, New Hampshire, 1892–1921* (Manchester, NH: John B. Clarke, 1921), 281.
12. Ibid.
13. Ibid.
14. Henry Goddard Pickering to John Grimes Walker, telegram, September 22, 1868. John Grimes Walker Papers. Special Collections, Wichita State University Library.
15. Henry Pickering Walker Sr., unpublished manuscript, courtesy of Henry Pickering Walker Jr.
16. Virkus, *Abridged Compendium of American Genealogy*, 1:483.
17. John Grimes Walker took the *Sabine* on a training mission to Europe from 1869 to 1870. Walker was appointed to other prominent naval positions, including the secretary of the Lighthouse Board from 1873 to 1878. He served as the chief of the Bureau of Navigation from 1881 to 1889, where he received reports from the newly created Office of Naval Intelligence and reported directly to the secretary of the navy. Browne, "John Grimes Walker," 281.
18. Henry Pickering Walker Sr., unpublished manuscript, courtesy of Henry Pickering Walker Jr.
19. Henry White Pickering to John Grimes Walker, January 29, 1877, qtd. in Henry Pickering Walker Sr., unpublished manuscript, courtesy of Henry Pickering Walker Jr.
20. Henry Pickering Walker Sr., unpublished manuscript, courtesy of Henry Pickering Walker Jr.
21. John Grimes Walker to Henry F. Woodman, March 31, 1878, Henry Pickering Walker, qtd. in Henry Pickering Walker Sr., unpublished manuscript, courtesy of Henry Pickering Walker Jr.
22. Admiral Albert Gleaves, *Life and Letters of Rear Admiral Stephen B. Luce* (1925), 172, qtd. in Malone, "John Grimes Walker."
23. Browne, "John Grimes Walker," 281.
24. Jessie Combs, Communications Coordinator, MIT Office of the Registrar, e-mail message to the author, August 14, 2013.
25. Nina Chinn Walker, unpublished autobiography B, 1937, 457.
26. *Harvard College Class of 1895 Third Report* (Cambridge, MA: Harvard University), 182.
27. *Nina Walker v. James W. G. Walker*, "Deposition of Rebecca W. P. Walker," Superior Court of R.I., January 3, 1910, 20.
28. Ibid., 12.
29. Ibid.
30. David McCullough, *The Path between the Seas: The Creation of the Panama Canal* (New York: Simon and Schuster, 1977), 305.
31. Henry Walker Jr., grandson of Henry Pickering Walker, believes that neither of the admiral's sons may have developed into the men their father hoped they would be. He wonders whether the admiral's long absences may have affected their development as men. Henry Pickering Walker Jr., e-mail message to the author, August 17, 2013.
32. Virkus, *Abridged Compendium of American Genealogy*, 1,483.
33. Nina Chinn Walker, unpublished autobiography A, 1934, 46.
34. Ibid., 293–295.
35. Ibid., 287–295.
36. "Richard Henry Chinn," Kentucky, Death Records, 1852–1953, Ancestry.com. Original Source: Certificate and Record of Death, registered no. 183, City of Lexington, Bureau of Vital Statistics, Fayette County, Kentucky.

37. Nina Chinn Walker, unpublished autobiography A, 1934, 1–2, 58.
38. Ibid., 280.
39. Ibid., 281.
40. Ibid., 251.
41. "Pretty Wedding at Rock Creek," *Washington Post*, February 25, 1897, ProQuest Historical Newspapers, *Washington Post* Archives (1877–1995).
42. Ibid., 58.
43. *Nina Walker v. James W. G. Walker*, "Deposition of Nina C. Walker," Superior Court of R.I., January 3, 1910, 32.
44. Nina Chinn Walker, unpublished autobiography A, 1934, 280.
45. Ibid., 274.
46. "Social and Personal," *Washington Post*, December 31, 1890, ProQuest Historical Newspapers, *Washington Post* Archives (1877–1995).
47. Ibid.
48. *Evening Star*, December 30, 1892, Chronicling America: Historic American Newspapers, http://chroniclingamerica.loc.gov/.
49. *Evening Star*, October 21, 1893, Chronicling America: Historic American Newspapers, http://chroniclingamerica.loc.gov/.
50. In fact, either Nina Chinn or her sister, Bertha, may have attended this party, since only one "Miss Chinn" is listed. It seems probable that Nina was there. "Her Public Reception," *Washington Post*, January 21, 1894, ProQuest Historical Newspapers, *Washington Post* Archives (1877–1995).
51. "In Hospitable Homes," *Washington Post*, February 13, 1895, ProQuest Historical Newspapers, *Washington Post* Archives (1877–1995).
52. *Washington Times*, May 30, 1895, Chronicling America: Historic American Newspapers, http://chroniclingamerica.loc.gov/.
53. Nina Chinn Walker, unpublished autobiography A, 1934, 57.
54. Rebecca W. P. Walker to James W. G. Walker, November 13, 1896, 1–2, photocopy in the author's possession.
55. Ibid., 2.
56. Ibid., 2–3.
57. Ibid., 3; emphasis original.
58. Ibid.
59. Ibid., 4.
60. Ibid., 4–5; emphasis in original.
61. Ibid., 5–7; emphasis in original.
62. Ibid., 7–8; emphasis in original.
63. Ibid., 8–9.
64. Ibid., 9.
65. Ibid., 9–10.
66. Ibid., 10.

CHAPTER 3

1. *Nina Walker v. James W. G. Walker*, Superior Court of R.I., January 3, 1910, 12–13.
2. David McCullough, *The Path between the Seas: The Creation of the Panama Canal, 1870–1914* (New York: Simon and Schuster, 1977), 305.
3. Ibid., 264.

4. Ibid.

5. "Walker Denies 'Mushy' Part," *Boston Daily Globe*, November 12, 1913, ProQuest Historical Newspapers, *Boston Globe* (1877–1995).

6. Rebecca W. P. Walker to James W. G. Walker, telegram, December 2, 1897.

7. James W. G. Walker, *Ocean to Ocean: An Account, Personal and Historical, of Nicaragua and Its People* (Chicago: A. C. McClurg, 1902), 26.

8. Ibid.

9. Ibid., 27.

10. Ibid., 28–34.

11. John G. Walker to Rebecca W. P. Walker, December 17, 1897, 1, photocopy in the author's possession.

12. Ibid., 2.

13. Rebecca W. P. Walker to Nina C. Walker, n.d., photocopy in the author's possession.

14. Walker, *Ocean to Ocean*.

15. Ibid., 280.

16. *Nina Walker v. James W. G. Walker*, Superior Court of R.I., January 3, 1910, 6.

17. "The American Navy," *Evening Telegram* (New York), April 19, 1899, Chronicling America: Historic American Newspapers, http://chroniclingamerica.loc.gov/.

18. Henry Pickering Walker Sr., unpublished manuscript, 25, courtesy of Henry Pickering Walker Jr.

19. *Nina Walker v. James W. G. Walker*, Superior Court of R.I., January 3, 1910, 16. However, James W. G. Walker is also listed by the 1900 federal census as being at the naval base: 1900 U.S. Census, Navy Yard, Suffolk, Massachusetts, Ancestry.com, roll 697, p. 1A, enumeration district 1841, FHL microfilm 1240676.

20. Rebecca W. P. Walker to Nina C. Walker, April 28, 1899, 1–3; emphasis in original.

21. Ibid., 3–4.

22. Henry Pickering Walker Sr., unpublished manuscript, 25, courtesy of Henry Pickering Walker Jr.

23. "Walker-Thomas Wedding," *New York Times*, October 22, 1899, ProQuest Historical Newspapers, *New York Times* Archives.

24. Ibid.

25. "The World of Society—The Walker-Thomas Wedding at All Souls' Church Today," *Evening Star*, October 21, 1899, Chronicling America: Historic American Newspapers, http://chroniclingamerica.loc.gov/.

26. "Personal," *Sun*, October 22, 1900, Chronicling America: Historic American Newspapers, http://chroniclingamerica.loc.gov/.

27. Elizabeth Walker Davis, "Stories My Mother Told Me" (unpublished manuscript), 9.

28. Bertha Chinn to Rebecca W. P. Walker, 2, photocopy in the author's possession.

29. Ibid., 2–3.

30. Ibid., 3; emphasis in original.

31. Ibid., 3–4.

32. *Nina Walker vs. James W. G. Walker*, "Deposition taken before William F. Poole, Esq., Commissioner, in the matter of a motion on Petition for Separate Maintenance," Superior Court of R.I., July 3, 1914.

33. "Mrs. Walker Testifies Again," *Newport Daily News*, November 20, 1913.

34. Ibid.

35. "Said She Would Leave Him," *Newport Daily News*, November 18, 1913.
36. *Nina Walker v. James W. G. Walker*, Superior Court of R.I., January 3, 1910, 24.
37. "Mrs. Walker on Stand," *Washington Herald*, March 9, 1911, Chronicling America: Historic American Newspapers, http://chroniclingamerica.loc.gov/.
38. *Nina Walker v. James W. G. Walker*, "Bill of Particulars," Superior Court of R.I., February 18, 1911.
39. Ibid.
40. "Mrs. Walker on Stand," *Washington Herald*, March 9, 1911.
41. "Walker Denies 'Mushy' Part," *Boston Daily Globe*, November 12, 1913.
42. *Nina Walker v. James W. G. Walker*, "Amended Petition," Superior Court of R.I., January 12, 1911, 2.
43. Ibid.
44. "Mr. Walker Weeps in Divorce Trial," *New York Herald*, March 11, 1911, Chronicling America: Historic American Newspapers, http://chroniclingamerica.loc.gov/.
45. "Navy Officer Blames 'In-Laws' for Troubles," *Washington Herald*, November 14, 1913, Chronicling America: Historic American Newspapers, http://chroniclingamerica.loc.gov/.
46. According to http://thecostofliving.com/index.php?id=170, the average annual wage in 1900 was $432; according to http://www.westegg.com/inflation/infl.cgi, what cost $2,400 in 1900 would cost $68,927.08 in 2015.
47. "Walker Denies 'Mushy' Part," *Boston Daily Globe*, November 12, 1913.
48. John Grimes Walker to James Wilson Grimes Walker, October 29, 1900, qtd. in Henry P. Walker Sr., unpublished manuscript, 27, courtesy of Henry P. Walker Jr.
49. "The Nicaragua Canal," *Outlook*, April 12, 1902, 925–926.
50. Walker, *Ocean to Ocean*, 20.
51. "The Nicaragua Canal," *Buffalo Express*, March 29, 1902, 10.
52. "The Nicaragua Canal," *Outlook*, April 12, 1902, 925.
53. Walker, *Ocean to Ocean*, 128.
54. Ibid., 139.
55. Ibid., 144.
56. Ibid., 177.
57. Ibid., 181.
58. Ibid., 136.
59. James W. G. Walker, "Reading Journey in the Borderlands of the United States, Central America," *Chautauquan*, 38 (1904): 544–556.
60. Ibid., 547.
61. "Goes to Charleston." *Boston Daily Globe*, March 2, 1902, ProQuest Historical Newspapers, *Boston Globe* Archives (1877–1995).
62. *Nina Walker v. James W. G. Walker*, Superior Court of R.I., January 3, 1910, 2.
63. Nina Chinn Walker, unpublished autobiography B, 1937, 421.
64. Ibid., 422.
65. *Nina Walker v. James W. G. Walker*, Superior Court of R.I., January 3, 1910, 24.
66. *Nina Walker v. James W. G. Walker*, "Amended Petition," Superior Court of R.I., January 12, 1911, 2.
67. "Walker Denies 'Mushy' Part," *Boston Daily Globe*, November 12, 1913.
68. *Nina Walker v. James W. G. Walker*, "Amended Petition," Superior Court of R.I., January 12, 1911, 2.
69. Mabel Cochrane to sister, July 1903, photocopy in the author's possession; emphasis in original.

70. James W. G. Walker to Nina C. Walker, August 22, 1903, 1–2, photocopy in the author's possession.
71. Ibid., 2–3.
72. Ibid., 3.
73. Nina Chinn Walker, unpublished autobiography B, 1937, 422–423.
74. Ibid., 434.
75. Ibid., 427.
76. "Mrs. Walker Shows Letters," *New York Press*, March 9, 1911, Chronicling America: Historic American Newspapers, http://chroniclingamerica.loc.gov/.
77. "Denies Wife's Charges," *Boston Daily Globe*, November 6, 1913, 18, ProQuest Historical Newspapers, *Boston Globe* Archives (1877–1995).
78. Mabel Cochrane to James W. G. Walker, Spring 1904, photocopy in the author's possession.
79. Ibid.
80. Nina Chinn Walker, unpublished autobiography B, 1937, 437.
81. "Denies Wife's Charges," *Boston Daily Globe*, November 6, 1913.
82. "Tone of Letters Changed," *Newport Daily News*, November 18, 1913.
83. Nina Chinn Walker, unpublished autobiography B, 1937, 437.
84. "Married the Chinn Family," *Boston Daily Globe*, November 14, 1913, ProQuest Historical Newspapers, *Boston Globe* Archives (1877–1995).
85. *Nina Walker v. James W. G. Walker*, "Amended Petition," Superior Court of R.I., January 12, 1911, 2.
86. Mabel Cochrane to James W. G. Walker, n.d., 1904 #2, photocopy in the author's possession.
87. Mabel Cochrane to James W. G. Walker, May 7, 1904, photocopy in the author's possession.
88. Mabel Cochrane to James W. G. Walker, January 9, 1905, photocopy in the author's possession.
89. Shannon Peterson, "Yellow Justice: Media Portrayal of Criminal Trials in the Progressive Era," *Stanford Journal of Legal Studies* 1, no. 1 (1999): 18–26. After a mistrial and a second trial with a hung jury, the case against Nan Patterson was dropped, and Nan tried but failed to capitalize on her infamy by becoming an actress.
90. "Seeks to Divorce Engineer in Navy," *New York Herald*, March 8, 1911, Chronicling America: Historic American Newspapers, http://chroniclingamerica.loc.gov/.
91. "Mrs. Walker Shows Letters," *New York Press*, March 9, 1911.
92. "Mr. Walker Weeps in Divorce Trial," *New York Herald*, March 11, 1911, Chronicling America: Historic American Newspapers, http://chroniclingamerica.loc.gov/.
93. "Walker Denies 'Mushy' Part," *Boston Daily Globe*, November 12, 1913.
94. "Sent from Navy Yard," *Boston Daily Globe*, June 17, 1905, ProQuest Historical Newspapers, *Boston Globe* Archives (1877–1995).
95. "Naval Officer Too Keen," *New York Times*, June 17, 1905, ProQuest Historical Newspapers, *New York Times* Archives.
96. "Sent from Navy Yard," *Boston Daily Globe*, June 17, 1905.
97. Ibid.
98. Ibid.
99. "Naval Officer Too Keen," *New York Times*, June 17, 1905.
100. "The Charleston Dry Dock Row Statements from Contractors Who Are Interested in the Matter," *State*, no. 5105 (June 20, 1905): 20.

101. Ibid.

102. "South Anxious for Square Deal," *Syracuse Journal*, June 21, 1905, Chronicling America: Historic American Newspapers, http://chroniclingamerica.loc.gov/.

103. "Various News Items." *Evening Post*, June 21, 1905, Chronicling America: Historic American Newspapers, http://chroniclingamerica.loc.gov/.

104. "Transfers Revoked," *Boston Evening Transcript*, July 13, 1905, Chronicling America: Historic American Newspapers, http://chroniclingamerica.loc.gov/.

105. "South Anxious for Square Deal," *Syracuse Journal*, June 21, 1905.

106. "Naval Officer Too Keen," *New York Times*, June 17, 1905.

107. "Heading Off a Scandal," *State*, no. 5132 (July 17, 1905): 4.

CHAPTER 4

1. Nina C. Walker to James W. G. Walker, July 4, 1905, 1, photocopy in the author's possession.

2. Ibid., 1–2.

3. The couple would have a daughter, Rebecca, two years later.

4. Nina C. Walker to James W. G. Walker, July 4, 1905, 2, photocopy in the author's possession.

5. Ibid., 3.

6. See http://flyingdreams.home.mindspring.com/nick.htm.

7. Ibid.; http://youthscompanion.com/.

8. Nina C. Walker to James W. G. Walker, July 4, 1905, 4, photocopy in the author's possession; emphasis in original.

9. Ibid., 4–5.

10. Ibid., 5; emphasis in original.

11. Ibid.

12. "The Cochranes in Charleston," *Newport Daily News*, November 6, 1913.

13. James W. G. Walker to Nina C. Walker, October 5, 1905, 1, photocopy in the author's possession.

14. Ibid., 1–2.

15. James W. G. Walker to Nina C. Walker, October 7, 1905, photocopy in the author's possession.

16. James W. G. Walker to Nina C. Walker, October 9, 1905, 1, photocopy in the author's possession.

17. *Nina Walker vs. James W. G. Walker*, "Motion to Amend Petition and Amended Petition," Superior Court of R.I., August 2, 1915.

18. *Nina Walker vs. James W. G. Walker*, "Bill of Exceptions," Superior Court of R.I., March 12, 1914.

19. *Oxaluria* is the buildup of oxalate in the body, causing the increased excretion of oxalate, which in turn results in renal and bladder stones, possibly causing urinary obstruction (often with severe and acute pain), secondary infection of the urine, and eventually kidney damage.

20. James W. G. Walker to Nina C. Walker, October 9, 1905, 1.

21. Ibid.; emphasis in original.

22. Ibid., 2.

23. Ibid.

24. Nina C. Walker to James W. G. Walker, October 10, 1905, 1–2, photocopy in the author's possession.

25. Nina Chinn Walker, unpublished autobiography B, 1937, 421.
26. Nina C. Walker to James W. G. Walker, October 10, 1905, 2–3, photocopy in the author's possession.
27. Ibid., 3–4.
28. Ibid., 4.
29. Nina C. Walker to James W. G. Walker, October 13, 1905, 1, photocopy in the author's possession.
30. Ibid., 2.
31. Elizabeth Walker Davis, "Stories My Mother Told Me," unpublished manuscript, 10.
32. "Seeks to Divorce Engineer in Navy." *New York Herald*, March 8, 1911, Chronicling America: Historic American Newspapers, http://chroniclingamerica.loc.gov/.
33. Nina Chinn Walker, unpublished autobiography B, 1937, 427.
34. Ibid., 428; emphasis in original.
35. Ibid., 433.
36. Ibid., 429.
37. "Promotions in the Navy," *Evening Post*, April 14, 1906, Chronicling America: Historic American Newspapers, http://chroniclingamerica.loc.gov/.
38. *Nina Walker v. James W. G. Walker*, Superior Court of R.I., January 3, 1910, 9. "Navy Yard News," *Brooklyn Daily Eagle*, March 28, 1910, Chronicling America: Historic American Newspapers, http://chroniclingamerica.loc.gov/.
39. James W. G. Walker to Nina C. Walker, April 27, 1906, 1, photocopy in the author's possession.
40. Ibid., 2.
41. Ibid.
42. Nina Chinn Walker, unpublished autobiography B, 1937, 437–438.
43. Rebecca W. Walker to Nina C. Walker, September 22, 1906, 2, photocopy in the author's possession.
44. Ibid., 2–3.
45. Ibid., 3.
46. Nina Chinn Walker, unpublished autobiography B, 1937, 438.
47. John G. Walker to James W. G. Walker, October 16, 1906, 1–2, photocopy in the author's possession.
48. Ibid., 2–3.
49. Ibid., 3–4.
50. Ibid., 4.
51. Nina Chinn Walker, unpublished autobiography B, 1937, 439–440.
52. Ibid., 440.
53. W. Gerry Morgan to James W. G. Walker, November 27, 1906, photocopy in the author's possession.
54. "Central America during a Revolution." *Brooklyn Daily Eagle*, February 14, 1907, Chronicling America: Historic American Newspapers, http://chroniclingamerica.loc.gov/.
55. "Navy Yard News." *Brooklyn Daily Eagle*, March 28, 1907, Chronicling America: Historic American Newspapers, http://chroniclingamerica.loc.gov/.
56. Nina Chinn Walker, unpublished autobiography B, 1937, 441–443.
57. Ibid., 445.
58. Ibid.
59. Ibid., 448.

60. Ibid., 449–450.
61. Ibid., 455.
62. Ibid., 456.
63. "Walker Funeral Saturday," *Washington Post*, September 18, 1907, ProQuest Historical Newspapers, *Washington Post* Archive.
64. "Will of Admiral Walker," *Washington Post*, September 25, 1907, ProQuest Historical Newspapers, *Washington Post* Archive.
65. "Cannot Be Located," *Newport Daily News*, November 19, 1913.
66. Nina Chinn Walker, unpublished autobiography B, 1937, 460.
67. Ibid., 462.
68. *Nina Walker v. James W. G. Walker*, Superior Court of R.I., January 3, 1910, 2.
69. Nina Chinn Walker, unpublished autobiography B, 1937, 465.
70. "Wife Leaves Naval Officer," *New York Times*, October 23, 1909, ProQuest Historical Newspapers, *New York Times* Archive.
71. "Bound for Insular Ports," *New York Herald*, April 3, 1909, Chronicling America: Historic American Newspapers, http://chroniclingamerica.loc.gov/.
72. Nina Chinn Walker, unpublished autobiography B, 1937, 473.
73. The couple would have a son, Richard Leigh, in 1914.
74. Susan Walker FitzGerald Papers, Special Collections Department, Bryn Mawr College Library.
75. Susan W. FitzGerald to Richard Y. FitzGerald, April 17, 1909, 1–2, Susan Walker FitzGerald Papers, Special Collections Department, Bryn Mawr College Library.
76. Ibid., 2.
77. Susan W. FitzGerald to Richard Y. FitzGerald, April 18, 1909, 2, Susan Walker FitzGerald Papers, Special Collections Department, Bryn Mawr College Library.
78. Ibid., 3.
79. Nina Chinn Walker, unpublished autobiography B, 1937, 473–474.
80. Susan W. FitzGerald to Richard Y. FitzGerald, April 18, 1909, 3.
81. Elizabeth G. Walker to Susan W. FitzGerald, April 30, 1909, 1, Susan Walker FitzGerald Papers, Special Collections, Bryn Mawr College Library.
82. Nina C. Walker to Susan W. FitzGerald, May 5, 1909, 2, Susan Walker FitzGerald Papers, Special Collections, Bryn Mawr College Library.
83. *Nina Walker v. James W. G. Walker*, Superior Court of R.I., January 3, 1910, 28.
84. Nina Chinn Walker, unpublished autobiography B, 1937, 480.
85. *Nina Walker v. James W. G. Walker*, Superior Court of R.I., January 3, 1910, 6.
86. Ibid., 3, 26.
87. Ibid., 3.
88. Ibid., 12.
89. Nina Chinn Walker, unpublished autobiography B, 1937, 427–428.

CHAPTER 5

1. The description of Nina and James's meeting at the house on Washington Street is an imagined scenario based on details given in *Nina Walker v. James W. G. Walker*, Superior Court of R.I., January 3, 1910, 27–28, and Nina Chinn Walker, unpublished autobiography B, 1937, 480.
2. *Nina Walker v. James W. G. Walker*, Superior Court of R.I., January 3, 1910, 28.
3. Ibid., 30.
4. Nina Chinn Walker, unpublished autobiography B, 1937, 483.

5. Ibid.
6. Ibid., 484.
7. "Tells of Leaving Walker." *New York Press*, March 10, 1911, Chronicling America: Historic American Newspapers, http://chroniclingamerica.loc.gov/.
8. Nina Chinn Walker, unpublished autobiography B, 1937, 484.
9. See http://www.brynmawr.edu/library/speccoll/guides/fitzgerald.
10. William Sheffield Jr. would be an unsuccessful candidate for reelection in 1912, although he would become a member of the Republican National Committee in 1913. He died in 1919 and was buried in the Island Cemetery in Newport, having served that city throughout his life; See http://bioguide.congress.gov/scripts/biodisplay.pl?index=S000318.
11. William R. Harvey would become one of the founders and vice president of the Newport Historical Society. Holly Collins, *The Preservation Society of Newport County 1945–1965: The Founding Years* (Newport, RI: Newport Historical Society, 2006), 56.
12. After leaving the firm in 1913, Max Levy served in the Rhode Island House of Representatives and Senate and was elected for several terms as a judge in the First Judicial District Court of Rhode Island. "Max Levy Reelected," *Newport Daily News*, January 2, 1953, http://www.jta.org/1923/01/19/archive/judge-max-levy-reelected (accessed January 23, 2014).
13. Nelson Manfred Blake, *The Road to Reno: A History of Divorce in the United States* (Westport, CT: Greenwood Press, 1962), 234.
14. U.S. Bureau of the Census, *Marriage and Divorce: Summary, Laws, Foreign Statistics* (Washington DC: U.S. Government Printing Office, 1909).
15. Blake, *Road to Reno*, 233.
16. Glenda Riley, *Divorce: An American Tradition* (New York: Oxford University Press, 1991), 82.
17. Ibid., 45–46; Roderick Philips, *Untying the Knot: A Short History of Divorce* (Cambridge, UK: Cambridge University Press, 1991), 141.
18. *Judicial and Statutory Definitions of Words and Phrases* (St. Paul, MN: West Publishing, 1904), 4:3168.
19. Edward C. Stiness, *Reports of Cases Argued and Determined in the Supreme Court of Rhode Island* (Providence: Oxford Press, 1911), 32:28.
20. Ibid., 32:29.
21. Riley, *Divorce*, 45–46; Philips, *Untying the Knot*, 50–51.
22. Stiness, *Reports of Cases Argued and Determined in the Supreme Court of Rhode Island*, 32:29.
23. Ibid.
24. Ibid., 32:29–30.
25. Ibid., 32:30.
26. She may have been a distant Walker relative.
27. Thomas Williams Bicknell, *History of the State of Rhode Island and Providence Plantations: Biographical* (New York: American Historical Society, 1920); Providence School Committee, *Report of the School Committee for the Year 1899–1900; Centennial* (Providence: Snow and Farnham City Printers, 1901).
28. John William Leonard, *Woman's Who's Who of America: A Biographical Dictionary of Contemporary Women of the United States and Canada* (New York: American Commonwealth, 1916), 77.
29. Photograph in Providence School Committee, *Report of the School Committee for the Year 1899–1900*.

30. In addition, Clark Burdick was a member of the Newport Representative Council from 1906 to 1916 and in later years would go on to serve as the mayor of Newport in 1917 and 1918. He was elected as a U.S. congressman from 1919 to 1933; see U.S. Congress, *Biographical Directory of the United States Congress 1774–Present*, http://bioguide.congress.gov/scripts/biodisplay.pl?index=S000318.

31. Photograph in ibid.

32. *Newport Mercury* 152, no. 22 (November 6, 1909): 1.

33. Richard Y. FitzGerald to Susan W. FitzGerald, December 6, 1909, 1, Susan Walker FitzGerald Papers, Special Collections, Bryn Mawr College Library.

34. Ibid., 5.

35. Ibid., 1–2.

36. Ibid., 4–5.

37. See http://www.brynmawr.edu/library/speccoll/guides/fitzgerald.shtml.

38. Ibid.

39. Susan W. FitzGerald, *What Is a Democracy?* (Washington, DC: National American Woman Suffrage Association, 1910); emphasis in original.

40. Elizabeth Cady Stanton, "Are Homogeneous Divorce Laws in All the States Desirable?" *North American Review* 170, no. 520 (1900): 405.

41. Stiness, *Reports of Cases Argued and Determined in the Supreme Court of Rhode Island*, 32:30.

42. Ibid., 32:31.

43. Ibid.

44. Patrick T. Conley, *Liberty and Justice: A History of Law and Lawyers in Rhode Island, 1636–1998* (Riverside: Rhode Island Publications Society, 1998).

45. "Alumni Notes," *Boston University Law Review* 2, no. 1 (1922): 136.

46. "Wife Charges Cruelty," *Washington Herald*, October 23, 1909, Chronicling America: Historic American Newspapers, http://chroniclingamerica.loc.gov/; "Wife Leaves Naval Officer," *New York Times*, October 22, 1909, ProQuest Historical Newspapers, *New York Times* Archives; "Navy Woman Asks Divorce," *Sun New York*, October 23, 1909, Chronicling America: Historic American Newspapers, http://chroniclingamerica.loc.gov/.

47. "Case Not Heard in Full," *Newport Daily News*, January 3, 1910.

48. Ibid.

49. *Nina Walker v. James W. G. Walker*, Superior Court of R.I., January 3, 1910, 3.

50. Ibid., 4.

51. Ibid.

52. Ibid., 5.

53. Ibid., 8.

54. Ibid., 10.

55. Ibid., 11.

56. Ibid., 13–15.

57. Ibid., 16–18.

58. Ibid., 19.

59. Ibid., 21.

60. Ibid.

61. Ibid., 22.

62. Ibid., 23–25.

63. Ibid., 25–28.

64. Ibid., 29.

65. Ibid., 30.
66. Ibid., 31.
67. Ibid., 34.
68. Ibid., 44.
69. Ibid., 34.
70. Ibid., 35.
71. Ibid., 36.
72. Ibid., 39.
73. Ibid., 39–40.
74. Ibid., 40.
75. Ibid., 41.
76. Ibid., 41–42.
77. "Case Not Heard in Full." *Newport Daily News*, January 3, 1910, 5.
78. Ibid.
79. Ibid.
80. "A Naval Shake-Up," *New York Tribune*, January 9, 1910, Chronicling America: Historic American Newspapers, http://chroniclingamerica.loc.gov/.
81. Based on information in "Judge Rathbun Declines to Admit the Walker Case," *Newport Daily News*, February 7, 1910.
82. Ibid.; "Divorce Case Halted," *Washington Herald*, February 8, 1910, Chronicling America: Historic American Newspapers, http://chroniclingamerica.loc.gov/; "Rejects Mrs. Walker's Suit," *Washington Post*, February 8, 1910, ProQuest Historical Newspapers, *Washington Post* Archives; "Divorce Case Thrown Out," *New-York Daily Tribune*, February 8, 1910, Chronicling America: Historic American Newspapers, http://chroniclingamerica.loc.gov/; "Mrs. Walker Denied Decree," *Boston Daily Globe*, December 31, 1910, Proquest Historical Newspapers, *Boston Globe* (1872–1981).
83. "Judge Rathbun Declines to Admit the Walker Case," *Newport Daily News*, February 7, 1910; "Divorce Case Halted," *Washington Herald*, February 8, 1910.
84. "Storage Tanks for Navy," *Christian Science Monitor*, February 11, 1910, Chronicling America: Historic American Newspapers, http://chroniclingamerica.loc.gov/.
85. "Sues His Mother-In-Law," *New York Times*, February 23, 1910, ProQuest Historical Newspapers, *New York Times* Archives; "Sues for Loss of Wife's Love," *Washington Post*, February 23, 1910, ProQuest Historical Newspapers, *Washington Post* Archives.
86. Henry Campbell Black, *Black's Law Dictionary*, rev. 4th ed. (St. Paul, MN: West Publishing, 1968).
87. Alienation of affection is currently a legal ground in only a few states and is no longer a legal ground in Rhode Island.
88. No information was found beyond the filing of this case in either court records or newspaper reports.
89. "James W. G. Walker," 1910 U.S. Census, Ancestry.com.
90. "Naval War College," *Evening Post*, June 4, 1910, Chronicling America: Historic American Newspapers, http://chroniclingamerica.loc.gov/.
91. Susan W. FitzGerald to Richard Y. FitzGerald, June 11, 1910, 1, Susan Walker FitzGerald Papers, Special Collections, Bryn Mawr College Library.
92. Ibid., 2.
93. Ibid.
94. "Before the Supreme Court," *Newport Daily News*, November 10, 1910.
95. Stiness, *Reports of Cases Argued and Determined in the Supreme Court of Rhode Island*, 32:32–33.

96. Ibid., 32:33.
97. Nina Chinn Walker, unpublished autobiography B, 1937, 486.
98. Ibid., 521.
99. *Nina Walker v. James W. G. Walker*, "Petition for Separate Maintenance," Superior Court of R.I., January 12, 1911; "Mrs. Walker Brings Suit," *Washington Herald*, January 13, 1911, Chronicling America: Historic American Newspapers, http://chroniclingamerica.loc.gov/.
100. *Nina Walker v. James W. G. Walker*, "Petition," Superior Court of R.I., January 12, 1911.
101. *Nina Walker v. James W. G. Walker*, "Notice of Hearing," Superior Court of R.I., delivered to Clark Burdick and notarized January 26, 1911.
102. *Nina Walker v. James W. G. Walker*, "Bill of Particulars," Superior Court of R.I., February 18, 1911.
103. *Nina Walker v. James W. G. Walker*, "Amended Petition," Superior Court of R.I., n.d., 1.
104. Ibid., 1–2.
105. Ibid., 2.
106. "Petitions for Dedimus Potestatem," Superior Court of R.I., February 21 and 25, 1911.
107. Conley, *Liberty and Justice*, 377; *Representative Men and Old Families of Rhode Island* (Chicago: J. H. Beers, 1908), 1:394–395; Judge Baker would serve as an associate justice of the superior court until his appointment as an associate justice of the Rhode Island Supreme Court, on which he served from 1913 to 1919. Judge Darius Baker died in 1926.
108. "RI Facts and Trivia," http://www.quahog.org/factsfolklore/index.php?id=14.

CHAPTER 6

1. The account of the *Walker v. Walker* hearing on Tuesday, March 7, 1911, is based on the following sources: "Mrs. Walker's Case," *Newport Daily News*, March 8, 1911; "Mrs. Walker Again Sues," *Washington Post*, March 8, 1911, ProQuest Historical Newspapers, *Washington Post* Archives. It is also based on the following sources: "Seeks to Divorce Engineer in Navy," *New York Herald*, March 8, 1911; "Mrs. Walker Seeks Divorce," *New-York Daily Tribune*, March 8, 1911; "Wife Suing Naval Officer, March 8, 1911; "Mrs. Walker Asks Divorce," *Washington Herald*, March 8, 1911; "Mrs. Walker on Stand," *New York Press*, March 9, 1911; "Mrs. Walker Shows Letters," *New York Press*, March 9, 1911, all available at Chronicling America: Historic American Newspapers, http://chroniclingamerica.loc.gov/.
2. "Mrs. Walker Again Sues," *Washington Post*, March 2, 1911.
3. "Wife Suing Naval Officer," *New York Press*, March 8, 1911.
4. From *de bene esse*, meaning conditionally or provisionally.
5. "Mrs. Walker's Case," *Newport Daily News*, March 8, 1911.
6. The account of the *Walker v. Walker* hearing on Thursday morning, March 9, 1911, is based on the following source: "Mother and Nurse," *Newport Daily News*, March 9, 1911.
7. The account of the *Walker v. Walker* hearing on the afternoon of Thursday, March 9, 1911, is based on the following sources: "Visited Her in Boston," *Newport Daily News*, March 10, 1911; "Walker Divorce Case," *Oswego Daily Times*, March 10, 1911, Chronicling America: Historic American Newspapers, http://chroniclingamerica.loc.gov/; and

"Tells of Leaving Walker, *New York Press*, March 10, 1911, Chronicling America: Historic American Newspapers, http://chroniclingamerica.loc.gov/.

8. The year Mabel Cochrane first resided in his boardinghouse is blurred in the reporting of Mr. Crapo's testimony, but this is the best estimate of what it states.

9. *Nina Walker v. James W. G. Walker*, "Bill of Exceptions," Superior Court of R.I., December 15, 1911, 2.

10. The account of the *Walker v. Walker* hearing on Friday, March 10, 1911, is based on the following sources: "Mr. Walker's Defense," *Newport Daily News* March 11, 1911; "Walker Weeps on Stand," *Washington Post*, March 11, 1911, ProQuest Historical Newspapers, *Washington Post* Archives; and "Mr. Walker Weeps in Divorce Trial," *New York Herald*, March 11, 1911, Chronicling America: Historic American Newspapers, http://chroniclingamerica.loc.gov/.

11. "An Imposing Funeral," *Newport Daily News*, March 11, 1911.

12. The account of the *Walker v. Walker* hearing on the morning of Monday, March 13, 1911, is based on the following source: "Treated Mr. Walker," *Newport Daily News*, March 13, 1911.

13. The account of the *Walker v. Walker* hearing on the afternoon of Monday, March 13, 1911, is based on the following sources: "Repudiates Letters," *Newport Daily News*, March 14, 1911; "Naval Engineer on Stand," *Washington Herald*, March 14, 1911, Chronicling America: Historic American Newspapers, http://chroniclingamerica.loc.gov/; and "Love Letter to Navy Man," *Washington Post*, March 14, 1911, ProQuest Historical Newspapers, *Washington Post* Archives.

CHAPTER 7

1. The account of the *Walker v. Walker* hearing on the morning of Tuesday, March 14, 1911, is based on the following sources: "Testifies for Her Son," *Newport Daily News*, March 14, 1911; "Walker a Good Father," *New York Times*, March 15, 1911, ProQuest Historical Newspapers, *New York Times* Archives.

2. This reference was to a character, "Mrs. Caudle," created by Douglas William Jerrold. He wrote about this woman and her husband in the British humor magazine *Punch* in the 1840s as well as in a book titled *Mrs. Caudle's Curtain Lectures*. Apparently "Mrs. Caudle" scolded her poor husband incessantly, and the term "Caudle lecture" became popular to describe that type of behavior.

3. Letter from Rebecca W. Walker to Nina C. Walker, April 28, 1899, photocopy in the author's possession.

4. The account of the *Walker v. Walker* hearing on the afternoon of Tuesday, March 14, 1911, is based on the following sources: "Relatives and Friends," *Newport Daily News*, March 15, 1911; "Walker a Good Father," *New York Times*, March 15, 1911.

5. Marilyn Coleman, Lawrence H. Ganong, and Kelly Warzinik, *Family Life in the 20th Century* (Westport, CT: Greenwood Press, 2007), 163.

6. Information based on "Newspaper Man in Trouble," *Newport Daily News*, March 15, 1911.

7. The account of the *Walker v. Walker* hearing on the morning of Wednesday, March 15, 1911, is based on the following sources: "Heredity in Divorce Cases," *Newport Daily News*, March 15, 1911; "Newspaper Man in Trouble," *Newport Daily News*, March 15, 1911.

8. The implication was that the pills might cause a miscarriage.

9. The account of the *Walker v. Walker* hearing on the afternoon of Wednesday,

March 15, 1911, is based on the following sources: "End of the Walker Case," *Newport Daily News*, March 16, 1911; "Walker Testimony Completed," *Washington Herald*, March 16, 1911, Chronicling America: Historic American Newspapers, http://chroniclingamerica.loc.gov/.

10. Information regarding the *Sears v. Walker* case was obtained from the following sources: "Newspaper Man in Trouble," *Newport Daily News*, March 15, 1911; "Protection for Newspaper Photographers," *Bulletin of Photography* 10 (January 3–June 26, 1912): x; "Henry P. Walker to Pay Damages," *Schenectady Gazette*, June 24, 1911, Chronicling America: Historic American Newspapers, http://chroniclingamerica.loc.gov/.

11. "Protection for Newspaper Photographers," *Bulletin of Photography* 10 (January 3–June 26, 1912): x.

12. "Lowers Divorce Bars," *Newport Daily News*, March 17, 1911.

13. The account of the March 18, 1911, hearing in *Walker v. Walker* is based on the following sources: "Walker Decision Held," *Newport Daily News*," March 20, 1911; "Judge Suggests Reconciliation," *Boston Daily Globe*, March 19, 1911, ProQuest Historical Newspapers, *Boston Globe* Archives (1877–1995). It is also based on the following sources: "Walker Case Near End," *Washington Herald*, March 19, 1911; "Would Reconcile Walkers," *New-York Daily Tribune*, March 19, 1911, both available at Chronicling America: Historic American Newspapers, http://chroniclingamerica.loc.gov/.

14. "Walker Case Near End," *Washington Herald*, March 19, 1911.

15. "Judge Suggests Reconciliation," *Boston Daily Globe*, March 19, 1911.

16. "Walker Decision Held," *Newport Daily News*, March 20, 1911.

17. Ibid.

18. Ibid.

19. Ibid.

20. "Judge Suggests Reconciliation," *Boston Daily Globe*, March 19, 1911.

21. Ibid.

22. Susan W. FitzGerald to Richard Y. FitzGerald, April 4, 1911, Susan Walker FitzGerald Papers, Special Collections Department, Bryn Mawr College Library.

23. Margaret Deland, "The Change in the Feminine Ideal," *Atlantic Monthly* 105 (1910): 296.

24. William L. O'Neill, *Divorce in the Progressive Era* (New Haven, CT: Yale University Press, 1967), 179.

CHAPTER 8

1. "Decision for Mrs. Walker," *Newport Daily News*, April 26, 1912.
2. Ibid.
3. Ibid.
4. Ibid.
5. Ibid.
6. Ibid.
7. Ibid.
8. Ibid.
9. Ibid.
10. Ibid.
11. Ibid. In a previous case, *Stevens v. Stevens* (S R.I. 557,561), the court found that "gross misbehavior and wickedness did not justify a divorce on the ground that the respondent husband, for a period shorter than the period required by the statute in cases

of desertion, [although he] has lived in the same home with, or previously been the daily companion of, another woman, each avowing for the other entire affection, though no criminal relation has existed between them." *Judicial and Statutory Definitions of Words and Phrases* (St. Paul, MN: West Publishing, 1904), 4:3168.

12. "Decision for Mrs. Walker," *Newport Daily News*, April 26, 1912.

13. Ibid.

14. "Mrs. Walker Divorced," *New York Times*, April 26, 1911, ProQuest Historical Newspapers, *New York Times* Archives; "Mrs. Walker Wins Divorce," *Boston Daily Globe*, April 26, 1911, ProQuest Historical Newspapers, *Boston Globe* Archives (1877–1995); "Mrs. Walker Wins in Divorce Case," *New York Herald*, April 26, 1911, Chronicling America: Historic American Newspapers, http://chroniclingamerica.loc.gov/.

15. "Divorced Father Loses Right to Son," *New York Herald*, April 26, 1911, Chronicling America: Historic American Newspapers, http://chroniclingamerica.loc.gov/.

16. Mary Ann Mason, *From Father's Property to Children's Rights: The History of Child Custody in the United States* (New York: Columbia University Press, 1994), 50.

17. Ibid., 58.

18. *Nina Walker v. James W. G. Walker*, "Motion," filed with Superior Court of R.I., May 8, 1911.

19. "Pleads Social Needs to Escape Paying Alimony," *Washington Times*, June 10, 1911; "Navy's 'Unwritten Law,'" *The Sun*, June 11, 1911, both available at Chronicling America: Historic American Newspapers, http://chroniclingamerica.loc.gov/.

20. *Nina Walker v. James W. G. Walker*, "Support Order," Superior Court of R.I., June 10, 1911.

21. Biographical information on Sarah Ellen Palmer from Olive Tardiff, *They Paved the Way: A History of New Hampshire Women* (Exeter, NH: Women Weekly Publishing, 1980); "Deaths and Funerals: Dr. Sarah E. Palmer." *Boston Daily Globe*, August 24, 1945, ProQuest Historical Newspapers, *Boston Globe* Archives (1877–1995); "Dr. Sarah Ellen Palmer," *New York Times*, August 24, 1945, ProQuest Historical Newspapers, *New York Times* Archives; "Obituaries: Sarah Ellen Palmer," *Exeter News-Letter*, August 30, 1945, Exeter Historical Society Archives; American Council of Learned Societies, ed., "Palmer, Sarah Ellen," *Dictionary of American Biography* (repr., 1936; New York: C. Scribner's Sons, 1928); John William Leonard, ed., "Palmer, Sarah Ellen," *Woman's Who's Who of America: A Biographical Dictionary of Contemporary Women of the United States and Canada, 1914–1915* (Detroit: Gale Research, 1914); "Dr. Sarah Ellen Palmer," *Boston Globe*, August 24, 1945, ProQuest Historical Newspapers, *Boston Globe* (1872–1979).

22. Lillian Faderman, *To Believe in Women: What Lesbians Have Done for America—a History* (New York: Houghton Mifflin, 1999), 255, 271, 395.

23. Emma B. Culbertson, "The Best Preparation for a Woman Physician," *Vassar Miscellany* 25 (1896): 321.

24. Physical description of Sarah Ellen Palmer from "Seacoast Women: Sarah Ellen Palmer," http:seacoastnh.com/women/pal.

25. *Nina C. Walker v. James W. G. Walker*, "Bill of Exceptions," Superior Court of R.I., December 15, 1911.

26. Ibid.

27. Charles Henry Huberich, "Venereal Diseases, in the Law of Marriage and Divorce," *American Law Review* 37 (1902): 226–236.

28. *Nina C. Walker v. James W. G. Walker*, "Bill of Exceptions," Superior Court of R.I., December 15, 1911.

29. "Naval Officer in Court," *Boston Daily Globe*, March 14, 1912, ProQuest Historical Newspapers, *Boston Globe* Archives (1877–1995).

30. *Nina Walker v. James W. G. Walker*, "Respondent's Motion for a New Trial on the Ground of Newly Discovered Evidence," Supreme Court of R.I., March 21, 1912.

31. *Nina C. Walker v. James W. G. Walker*, "Notice and Service," May 6, 1912.

32. *Nina C. Walker v. James W. G. Walker*, "Rescript," Supreme Court of R.I., May 29, 1912, 1.

33. "Navy Orders," *The Sun*, April 16, 1912, Chronicling America: Historic American Newspapers, http://chroniclingamerica.loc.gov/.

34. "Fights Walker Decree," *New York Herald*, May 11, 1912, Chronicling America: Historic American Newspapers, http://chroniclingamerica.loc.gov/.

35. *Nina C. Walker v. James W. G. Walker*, "Rescript," Supreme Court of R.I., May 29, 1912, 1.

36. Ibid.

37. Ibid.

38. Ibid.

39. *Nina C. Walker v. James W. G. Walker*, "Exception and Notice of Intention to Prosecute Bill of Exceptions, Etc.," Supreme Court of R.I., June 5, 1912.

40. *Nina C. Walker v. James W. G. Walker*, "Bill of Exceptions," Supreme Court of R.I., July 15, 1912, 1.

41. Ibid.

42. Ibid., 2.

43. Handwritten note, signed by Darius Baker Jr. on text of court's copy of *Nina C. Walker v. James W. G. Walker*, "Bill of Exceptions," Supreme Court of R.I., July 15, 1912.

44. *Nina C. Walker v. James W. G. Walker*, "Motion for Reduction of Allowance," Superior Court of R.I., June 27, 1912.

45. Ibid.

46. *Nina C. Walker v. James W. G. Walker*, "Support Order," Superior Court of R.I., August 3, 1912.

47. Nina Chinn Walker, unpublished autobiography B, 1937, 510.

48. "To Rehear Divorce Case," *Boston Daily Globe*, November 30, 1912, ProQuest Historical Newspapers, *Boston Globe* Archives (1877–1995).

49. "Disliked Assignment," *New York Times*, December 8, 1913, ProQuest Historical Newspapers, *New York Times* Archives.

50. "Navy," *Washington Times*, December 4, 1912, Chronicling America: Historic American Newspapers, http://chroniclingamerica.loc.gov/.

CHAPTER 9

1. Nina Chinn Walker, unpublished autobiography B, 1937, 427.

2. Moulton, Sampson, and Fernald, *Maine Reports: Cases Argued and Determined in the Supreme Judicial Court of Maine* (Waterville: Supreme Judicial Court of Maine, 1914), 111:404; Alphonso Moulton, Howard L. Sampson, and Granville Fernald, eds., *Centennial History of Harrison, Maine* (Harrison, ME: Southworth Publishing, 1909), 444.

3. "Walker Now Asks Divorce," *New York Times*, February 12, 1913, ProQuest Historical Newspapers, *New York Times* Archives; "Walker's Marital Troubles Again Aired," *Washington Herald*, February 13, 1913, Chronicling America: Historic American Newspapers, http://chroniclingamerica.loc.gov/.

4. See http://grandyoats.com/index.php/our-story; Nat Pierce, owner of Grandy Oats, interview by the author, October 22, 2014.

5. State of Maine, Oxford County Registry of Deeds, Western District, Fryeburg, ME, bk. 100, p. 293.

6. Ibid., bk. 102, pp. 153, 154.

7. Ibid., bk. 95, p. 471.

8. Ibid., bk. 103, p. 32.

9. Ibid.

10. Ibid., bk. 112, pp. 140–142.

11. Nina Chinn Walker, unpublished autobiography B, 1937, 532.

12. Moulton, Sampson, and Fernald, *Maine Reports*, 111:404; "Harry Rust Virgin," *Lewiston Evening Journal*, April 12, 1932, Chronicling America: Historic American Newspapers, http://chroniclingamerica.loc.gov/; Ernest Constant Bowler, ed., *An Album of the Attorneys of Maine* (Bethel, ME: News Publishing, 1902), 93.

13. Moulton, Sampson, and Fernald, *Maine Reports*, 111:404.

14. *Nina C. Walker v. James W. G. Walker*, "Motion for Reduction of Allowance," Superior Court of R.I., March 20, 1913; "Walker Divorce Case Up Again," *Newport Daily News*, March 21, 1913; "Sues to Have Alimony Cut," *Boston Globe*, March 21, 1913, ProQuest Historical Newspapers, *Boston Globe* Archives (1877–1995).

15. *Nina C. Walker v. James W. G. Walker*, "Motion for Reduction of Allowance," Superior Court of R.I., March 20, 1913; "Walker Divorce Case Up Again," *Newport Daily News*, March 21, 1913; "Sues to Have Alimony Cut," *Boston Globe*, March 21, 1913.

16. *Nina C. Walker v. James W. G. Walker*, "Motion for Commission to Take Deposition," Superior Court of R.I., March 25, 1913.

17. *Nina Walker v. James W. G. Walker*, "Rescript," Superior Court of R.I., May 8, 1913.

18. Ibid.; "Walker Allowance Less," *Newport Daily News*, May 8, 1913.

19. Judge Baker served as an associate justice of the superior court until his appointment as an associate justice of the Rhode Island Supreme Court, on which he served from 1913 to 1919.

20. *Nina Walker v. James W. G. Walker*, "Rescript," Superior Court of R.I., June 2, 1913.

21. Ibid., July 7, 1913.

22. *Nina Walker v. James W. G. Walker*, "Motion," Superior Court of R.I., August 13, 1913.

23. *Nina Walker v. James W. G. Walker*, "Order," Superior Court of R.I., August 21, 1913.

24. Standard Certificate of Death, Registered No. 5501, filed June 13, 1912, Commonwealth of Massachusetts.

25. *Nina Walker v. James W. G. Walker*, "Motion for Commission to Take Deposition," Superior Court of R.I., October 20, 1913.

26. Judge Stearns's ancestor Isaac Stearns came to Massachusetts with Governor John Winthrop and Sir Richard Saltonstall in 1630. A later ancestor was a commander in the Battle of Concord in 1775: http://www.rootsweb.ancestry.com/~rigenweb/articles/208.html. Charles Falconer Stearns would serve as a justice for many years, including as the chief justice of the Rhode Island Supreme Court from 1929 to 1935. Justice Stearns died in 1945.

27. The account of the *Walker v. Walker* hearing on Tuesday, November 11, 1913, is based on the following sources: "Miss Cochrane's Letters," *Newport Daily News*, November 11, 1913; "Walker Tells His Story" *Newport Daily News*, November 11, 1913, 5; "Differed over Children," *Newport Daily News*, November 12, 1913; "Love Notes in

Court," *Washington Post*, November 11, 1913, ProQuest Historical Newspapers, *Washington Post* Archives; "Walker Denies 'Mushy' Part," *Boston Daily Globe*, November 12, 1913, ProQuest Historical Newspapers, *Boston Globe* Archives (1877–1995).

28. Photographs of Judge Henry Stearns available at http://search.ancestry.com/cgibin/sse.dll?gl=ROOT_CATEGORY&rank=1&new=1&so=3&MSAV=1&msT=1&gss=seorecords&gsfn=AmyNewton&gsln=Stearns&msbdy=1867&msbpn__ftp=Rhode+Island%2C+USA&msddy=&msdpn__ftp=&cpxt=0&catBucket=p&uidh=000&cp=0.

29. The account of the *Walker v. Walker* hearing on Wednesday, November 5, 1913, is based on the following sources: *Nina C. Walker v. James W. G. Walker*, "Rescript," Superior Court of R.I., December 4, 1913; "Denies Wife's Charges," *Boston Daily Globe*, November 6, 1913, ProQuest Historical Newspapers, *Boston Globe* Archives (1877–1995); "Physicians Testify," *Newport Daily News*, November 6, 1913; "Women Doctors Testify," *New York Times*, November 6, 1913, ProQuest Historical Newspapers, *New York Times* Archives.

30. Since a transcript was not available, Dr. Palmer's testimony was synthesized from the following: "Physicians Testify," *Newport Daily News*, November 6, 1913, 6; *Nina C. Walker v. James W. G. Walker*, "Rescript," Superior Court of R.I., December 4, 1913.

31. Since a transcript of Dr. Culbertson's testimony was not available, her testimony was synthesized from the following: "Physicians Testify," *Newport Daily News*, November 6, 1913, 6; *Nina C. Walker v. James W. G. Walker*, "Rescript," Superior Court of R.I., December 4, 1913.

32. The account of the *Walker v. Walker* hearing on Thursday, November 6, 1913 is based on the following sources: "The Letters in the Case," *Newport Daily News*, November 6, 1913; "The Cochranes in Charleston," *Newport Daily News*, November 6, 1913; "More Medical Testimony," *Newport Daily News*, November 7, 1913.

33. The account of the *Walker v. Walker* hearing on Friday, November 7, 1913, is based on the following sources: "Cross-Examination Ended," *Newport Daily News*, November 7, 1913; "Mother and Sister Heard," *Newport Daily News*, November 8, 1913.

34. The account of the *Walker v. Walker* hearing on Monday, November 10, 1913, is based on the following source: "Depositions Read," *Newport Daily News*, November 10, 1913.

35. The account of the *Walker v. Walker* hearing on Tuesday, November 11, 1913, is based on the following sources: "Miss Cochrane's Letters," *Newport Daily News*, November 11, 1913, 8, 3; "Walker Tells His Story," *Newport Daily News*, November 11, 1913, 5; "Differed over Children," *Newport Daily News*, November 12, 1913, 10, 8; "Love Notes in Court," *Washington Post*, November 11, 1913; "Walker Denies 'Mushy' Part," *Boston Daily Globe*, November 12, 1913.

36. William Gerry Morgan to James W. G. Walker, November 27, 1906, photocopy in the author's possession.

37. The account of the *Walker v. Walker* hearing on Wednesday, November 12, 1913, is based on the following sources: "Medical Experts Testify," *Newport Daily News*, November 12, 1913, 5; "More Medical Evidence," *Newport Daily News*, November 12, 1913; "Doctors Testify at Walker Hearing," *Boston Daily Globe*, November 13, 1913, ProQuest Historical Newspapers, *Boston Globe* Archives (1877–1995).

CHAPTER 10

1. The account of the *Nina C. Walker v. James W. G. Walker* hearing on Thursday, November 13, 1913, is based on the following sources: "Evidence of Experts," *Newport News*, November 13, 1913, 5; "Makes General Denial," *Newport News*, November 14,

1913; "Married the Chinn Family," *Boston Daily Globe*, November 14, 1913; "Walker Denies 'Mushy' Part," *Boston Daily Globe*, November 12, 1913, both available at ProQuest Historical Newspapers, *Boston Globe* Archives (1877–1995); *Washington Herald*, "Navy Officer Blames In-Laws for Troubles," *Washington Herald*, November 14, 1913, Chronicling America: Historic American Newspapers, http://chroniclingamerica.loc.gov/.

2. The account of the *Nina C. Walker v. James W. G. Walker* hearing on Friday, November 14, 1913, is based on the following sources: "Letters Have Been Changed," *Newport Daily News*, November 14, 1913, 3, 5; "Family Relations Pleasant," *Newport Daily News*, November 15, 1913.

3. The account of the *Nina C. Walker v. James W. G. Walker* hearing on Monday, November 17, 1913, is based on the following sources: "Said She Would Leave Him," *Newport Daily News*, November 18, 1913; "Glances through Lorgnette at Passing Masks and Faces," *Washington Post*, November 19, 1913, ProQuest Historical Newspapers, *Washington Post* Archives.

4. The account of the *Nina C. Walker v. James W. G. Walker* hearing on Tuesday, November 18, 1913, is based on the following sources: "Tone of Letters Changed," *Newport Daily News*, November 18, 1913; "Cannot Be Located," *Newport Daily News*, November 19, 1913; "Miss Cochrane Flees Walker Court Case," *Washington Times*, November 23, 1913, image 1, Chronicling America: Historic American Newspapers, http://chroniclingamerica.loc.gov/.

5. The account of the *Nina C. Walker v. James W. G. Walker* hearing on the morning of Wednesday, November 19, 1913, is based on the following sources: "Talked of a Separation," *Newport Daily News*, November 19, 1913, 5; "Straw Hats and Indian Summer," *Newport Daily News*, November 19, 1913; "Claim Hereditary Impulse to Desert," *Boston Daily Globe*, November 20, 1913, ProQuest Historical Newspapers, *Boston Globe* Archives (1877–1995). The account of the *Nina C. Walker v. James W. G. Walker* hearing on the afternoon of Wednesday, November 19, 1913, is based on the following source: "Mrs. Walker Testifies Again," *Newport Daily News*, November 20, 1913.

6. Nina C. Walker to James W. G. Walker, July 4, 1905, 4–5, photocopy in the author's possession.

7. Mabel Cochrane to sister, July 1903, photocopy in the author's possession.

8. Nina C. Walker to Susan W. FitzGerald, May 5, 1909, Susan Walker FitzGerald Papers, Special Collections Department, Bryn Mawr College Library.

9. The account of the *Nina C. Walker v. James W. G. Walker* hearing on Thursday, November 20, 1913, is based on the following sources: "Evidence Finally All In," *Newport Daily News*, November 20, 1913; "Close of Walker Case," *Newport Daily News*, November 21, 1913; "Wife's Counsel Charges Fraud," *Boston Daily Globe*, November 21, 1913, ProQuest Historical Newspapers, *Boston Globe* Archives (1877–1995).

10. "Real Indian Summer," *Newport Daily News*, November 20, 1913; "Fine Weather Continues," *Newport Daily News*, November 21, 1913.

CHAPTER 11

1. "Petition Is Denied," *Newport Daily News*, December 6, 1913.

2. *Nina Walker v. James W. G. Walker*, "Rescript," Superior Court of R.I., December 4, 1913, 5–6.

3. Ibid., 6–7.

4. Ibid., 7.

5. *Nina Walker v. James W. G. Walker*, "Notice of Intention to Prosecute Bill of Exceptions," Superior Court of R.I., December 6, 1913.

6. *Nina Walker v. James W. G. Walker*, "Deposition of Dr. Sarah E. Palmer," Superior Court of R.I., December 19, 1913.

7. *Nina Walker v. James W. G. Walker*, "Stipulation," Superior Court of R.I., December 29, 1913.

8. Nina Chinn Walker, unpublished autobiography B, 1937, 533.

9. "Fire in Newport Soon Extinguished," *New York Herald*, January 13, 1914. Chronicling America: Historic American Newspapers, http://chroniclingamerica.loc.gov/.

10. These included the *Boston Daily Globe*, the *Washington Post*, the *New York Herald*, the *Sun* (New York), the *North Tonowanda Evening News* (New York), the *Geneva Daily Times* (New York), and the *Sunday Times* (Batavia, New York).

11. William P. Thompson, reporter, *Maine Reports: Cases Argued and Determined by the Supreme Judicial Court of Maine* (Waterville, ME: Sentinel Publishing, 1914), 111:405–408.

12. *Nina Walker v. James W. G. Walker*, "Bill of Exceptions," Superior Court of R.I., March 12, 1914.

13. "Fight over Walker Children," *New York Times*, May 13, 1914, ProQuest Historical Newspapers, *New York Times* Archives.

14. *Nina Walker v. James W. G. Walker*, "Petition," Superior Court of R.I., May 21, 1914.

15. "Navy Man's Suit for His Four Children Is Halted," *Washington Times*, May 24, 1914, Chronicling America: Historic American Newspapers, http://chroniclingamerica.loc.gov/.

16. *Nina Walker v. James W. G. Walker*, "Court Motion," Superior Court of R.I., June 26, 1914.

17. *Nina Walker v. James W. G. Walker*, "Deposition of Rebecca W. Walker, Petition for Separate Maintenance," Superior Court of R.I., July 3, 1914.

18. Ibid.

19. Ibid.

20. Ibid.

21. Ibid.

22. "Walker Weeps as His Children Deny Their Love for Him . . . ," *Evening News*, July 11, 1914, http://infoweb.newsbank.com.libproxy.unh.edu/iw-search/we/.

23. "Man Shoots Four When He Calls at Home of Wife's Parents . . . ," *Evening News*, July 11, 1914, http://infoweb.newsbank.com.libproxy.unh.edu/iw-search/we/.

24. "After a Series of Financial Losses Man Kills Himself and 6 Year Old Son with Razor," *Evening News*, July 11, 1914, http://infoweb.newsbank.com.libproxy.unh.edu/iw-search/we/.

25. *Atlantic Reporter* 93 (March 18–June 3), permanent ed. (St. Paul, MN: West Publishing, 1915), 36.

26. "Divorce Petition of Mrs. Walker Reversed," *Newport Daily News*, March 1, 1915; "Mrs. Walker's Suit Denied," *Washington Post*, March 7, 1915, ProQuest Historical Newspapers, *Washington Post* Archives; "Nina Chinn Walker Fails to Prove Divorce Charges," *Washington Times*, March 8, 1915, image 5, Chronicling America: Historic American Newspapers, http://chroniclingamerica.loc.gov/.

27. *Nina C. Walker v. James W. G. Walker*, "Motion for Reargument," Supreme Court of R.I., March 10, 1915.

28. *Nina C. Walker v. James W. G. Walker*, "Motion," Superior Court of R.I., May 26, 1915.

29. *Nina C. Walker v. James W. G. Walker*, "Rescript," Supreme Court of R.I., July 1, 1915.
30. William Paine Sheffield and William R. Harvey to Bertram S. Blaisdell, Esq., Clerk, Supreme Court of R.I., July 2, 1915, photocopy in the author's possession.
31. William Paine Sheffield and William R. Harvey to Clark Burdick and William McLeod, July 2, 1915, photocopy in the author's possession.
32. *Nina C. Walker v. James W. G. Walker*, "Amended Petition," Supreme Court of R.I., August 2, 1915.
33. *Nina C. Walker v. James W. G. Walker*, "Opinion," Supreme Court of R.I., December 10, 1915, 4.
34. Ibid., 6.
35. Ibid., 7.
36. *Nina C. Walker v. James W. G. Walker*, "Statement of Causes," Supreme Court of R.I., January 3, 1916; *Nina C. Walker v. James W. G. Walker*, "Motion to Remand Cause to the Superior Court," Supreme Court of R.I., January 3, 1916.
37. *Nina C. Walker v. James W. G. Walker*, "Rescript," Supreme Court of R.I., June 1, 1916.
38. *Nina C. Walker v. James W. G. Walker*, "Rescript," Supreme Court of R.I., July 6, 1916.
39. *Nina C. Walker v. James W. G. Walker*, "Motion to Adjudge Respondent in Contempt," Superior Court of R.I., May 26, 1916.
40. *Nina C. Walker v. James W. G. Walker*, "Rescript," Superior Court of R.I., August 5, 1916.
41. Nina Chinn Walker, unpublished autobiography B, 1937, 535.
42. "Divorce for Mrs. Walker," *Newport Daily News*, December 5, 1916; "Divorces J. W. G. Walker," *Boston Globe*, December 5, 1916, and "Absolute Divorce Given Mrs. Nina Walker," *Boston Daily Globe*, June 8, 1917, both available at ProQuest Historical Newspapers, *Boston Globe* Archives (1877–1995); "Mrs. Nina Walker Divorced," *Washington Post*, December 5, 1916, ProQuest Historical Newspapers, *Washington Post* Archives; "Mrs. Walker Wins Divorce," *The Sun*, December 5, 1916, and "Divorce Granted to Mrs. Nina C. Walker," *New York Herald*, December 18, 1916, both available at Chronicling America: Historic American Newspapers, http://chroniclingamerica.loc.gov/.
43. "Divorce for Mrs. Walker," *Newport Daily News*, December 5, 1916.
44. Ibid.
45. Nina Chinn Walker, unpublished autobiography B, 1937, 485–486.
46. Ibid., 696–698.

EPILOGUE

1. Nina Chinn Walker, unpublished autobiography B, 1937, 428.
2. Ibid., 484–485.
3. Mary Ann Mason, *From Father's Property to Children's Rights: The History of Child Custody in the United States* (New York: Columbia University Press, 1994), 49–64.
4. Nina Chinn Walker, unpublished autobiography B, 1937, 561.
5. Ibid., 562.
6. Ibid., 563.
7. Ibid., 616.
8. "Clergy and Laity Plan Attendance at Synod," *Washington Post*, November 15, 1924, ProQuest Historical Newspapers, *Washington Post* Archives.

9. Nina Chinn Walker, unpublished autobiography B, 1937, 618.

10. Ibid., 619.

11. Ibid., 621.

12. Elizabeth Walker Davis, "Stories My Mother Told Me" (unpublished manuscript), 16.

13. "Capital Society Events," *Washington Post*, October 1, 1928, ProQuest Historical Newspapers, *Washington Post* Archives.

14. Elizabeth Walker Davis to the author, e-mail, March 5, 2013.

15. Nina Walker, "On Rainy Days," *Christian Science Monitor*, April 3, 1929.

16. Nina Chinn Walker, unpublished autobiography B, 1937, 575.

17. Ibid., 678–679.

18. Elizabeth Walker Davis, "Stories My Mother Told Me" (unpublished manuscript), 6.

19. Ibid., 7–8.

20. Ibid., 8.

21. I thank Anne Cox Walker and Priscilla Grahame Walker Shows for generously making this part of the manuscript available to me.

22. I thank Herbert Wood Walker Jr. for discovering this part of the manuscript and for generously making it available to me.

23. Ibid., 692–693.

24. Ibid., 514–515.

25. "Nina Chinn Walker," http://www.findagrave.com/cgi.bin/fg.cgi?page=gr&GSln=WA&GSpartial=1&GSbyrel=all&GSst=9&GScntry=4&GSsr=481&GRid=37193791&.

26. Elizabeth Walker Davis, "Stories My Mother Told Me" (unpublished manuscript), 6.

27. Ibid., 11.

28. Ibid., 13–14.

29. Nina Chinn Walker, unpublished autobiography B, 1937, 534.

30. Ibid., 536–569.

31. Ibid., 595.

32. Ibid., 601.

33. Ibid., 611.

34. Elizabeth Walker Davis, "Stories My Mother Told Me" (unpublished manuscript), 13–14.

35. Ibid., 14.

36. Nina Chinn Walker, unpublished autobiography B, 1937, 623.

37. Ibid.

38. Ibid., 624.

39. Ibid., 624–625.

40. Elizabeth Walker Davis, "Stories My Mother Told Me" (unpublished manuscript), 14.

41. See http://trees.ancestry.com/tree/58343568/photo/10?pgnum=1& (accessed July 18, 2013).

42. I thank Cindy Iverson for recognizing the importance of this scrapbook, transcribing the notes and letter, and alerting Bud Walker, who then generously notified me and made the information available to me.

43. "Obituary 1," *Washington Post*, November 25, 1947, ProQuest Historical Newspapers, *Washington Post* Archives.

44. Elizabeth Walker Davis, "Stories My Mother Told Me" (unpublished manuscript), 16.
45. Ibid.
46. Herbert Wood Walker Jr., telephone interview by the author, June 30, 2016.
47. Sylvia D. Hoffert, *A History of Gender in America* (Upper Saddle River, NJ: Prentice Hall, 2003), 461.
48. Nat Pierce, owner of Grandy Oats, interview by the author, October 22, 2014.
49. Joanna Thurston, Brownfield Historical Society, interview by the author, October 22, 2014.
50. See www.grandyoats.com (accessed October 15, 2014).
51. Carol Brooks, telephone interview by the author, October 22, 2014.
52. Joanna Thurston, Brownfield (ME) Historical Society, interview by the author, October 22, 2014; Norma Pandora Hopkins, Brownfield (ME) Historical Society, interview by the author, October 22, 2014; photographs from Brownfield Historical Society.
53. Handwritten note accompanying letter from James W. G. Walker, Brownfield (ME) Historical Society.
54. "Pickering Bequests to Charity $22,000," *Boston Daily Globe*, July 22, 1926, ProQuest Historical Newspapers, *Boston Globe* Archives (1877–1995).
55. James W. G. Walker, *Trustees of Liberty* (New York: Walter Neale, 1928), 13–14.
56. Ibid., 17.
57. Ibid., v.
58. "V.P.W." and "Patriotism Note Struck by Treatise," *Washington Post*, April 22, 1928, ProQuest Historical Newspapers, *Washington Post* Archives.
59. Kenneth C. M. Sills, "Introduction," in Walker, *Trustees of Liberty*, vii.
60. 1940 U.S. Federal Census, Ancestry.com. Original data: U.S. Bureau of the Census, Sixteenth Census of the United States, 1940 (Washington, DC: National Archives and Records Administration, 1940), T627, 4,643 rolls.
61. Nina Chinn Walker, unpublished autobiography B, 1937, 561.
62. Elizabeth Walker Davis, "Stories My Mother Told Me" (unpublished manuscript), 11.
63. Ibid., 11–12.
64. Ibid., 12–13.
65. Ibid., 13.
66. Norma Pandora Hopkins, Brownfield Historical Society, interview by the author, October 22, 2014.
67. Elizabeth Walker Davis, "Stories My Mother Told Me" (unpublished manuscript), 13.
68. Herbert Wood Walker Jr., interview by the author, June 30, 2016; Anne Cox Walker, interview by the author, July 5, 2016.
69. Nina Chinn Walker, unpublished autobiography B, 1937, 485.
70. Ibid., 658.
71. Ibid.
72. Ibid., 659.
73. Ibid., 658.
74. Ibid., 484–485.
75. Ibid., 657.
76. Ibid.
77. Ibid., 658.

78. John D'Emilio and Estelle B. Freedman, *Intimate Matters: A History of Sexuality in America* (New York: Harper and Row, 1988), 190.
79. See http://www.brynmawr.edu/library/speccoll/guides/fitzgerald.
80. Ibid.
81. "Finds G.O.P. Unfriendly," *Boston Daily Globe*, October 21, 1916, ProQuest Historical Newspapers, *Boston Globe* Archives (1877–1995).
82. "Susan Fitzgerald: Educator and Social Worker Dies . . . ," *New York Times*, January 21, 1943, ProQuest Historical Newspapers, *New York Times* Archives.
83. Ibid.; "Susan Fitzgerald, Suffragette, Dies," *Daily Boston Globe*, January 21, 1943, ProQuest Historical Newspapers, *Boston Globe* Archives (1877–1995).
84. "R. Y. FitzGerald, Ex–Power Group Executive, Dead," *Daily Boston Globe*, July 29, 1942, ProQuest Historical Newspapers, *Boston Globe* Archives (1877–1995); "Richard Y. Fitzgerald Ex-Secretary, Counsel of New England Power Group Dies," *New York Times*, June 29, 1942, ProQuest Historical Newspapers, *New York Times* Archives.
85. Susan Walker FitzGerald Papers, Special Collections Department, Bryn Mawr College Library.
86. "Dr. John Thomas, Neurologist, Dies," *New York Times*, July 18, 1935, ProQuest Historical Newspapers, *New York Times* Archives; "Dr. John J. Thomas, Neurologist, Dead," *Boston Globe*, July 18, 1935, ProQuest Historical Newspapers, *Boston Globe* Archives (1877–1995).
87. "Many Bostonians Leave for July and Aug Travels . . . ," *Boston Globe*, July 2, 1939, ProQuest Historical Newspapers, *Boston Globe* Archives (1877–1995).
88. I thank Herbert Wood Walker Jr. for making this manuscript available to me.
89. Henry Pickering Walker Sr., unpublished manuscript, courtesy of Henry Pickering Walker Jr.
90. "Henry Pickering Walker," http://person.ancestry.com/tree/21327721/person/1067084164/facts.
91. Nina Chinn Walker, unpublished autobiography B, 1937, 454.
92. 1920 U.S. Federal Census, Ancestry.com (images reproduced by FamilySearch). Original data: U.S. Bureau of the Census, Fourteenth Census of the United States, 1920 (Washington, DC: National Archives and Records Administration, 1920), NARA microfilm publication T625, 2076 rolls, record group 29.
93. 1930 U.S. Federal Census, Ancestry.com. Original data: U.S. Bureau of the Census, Fifteenth Census of the United States, 1930 (Washington, DC: National Archives and Records Administration, 1930), T626, 2,667 rolls.
94. See http://interactive.ancestrylibrary.com/2442/m-t0627-01679-00382/95872021?backurl=http%3a%2f%2fsearch.ancestrylibrary.com%2fcgi-bin%2fsse.dll%3fgst%3d-6&ssrc=&backlabel=ReturnSearchResults.
95. Massachusetts Death Index, 1901–1980, 8:274, Index Vol. 121, Reference #F63.M362 v.121.
96. "Henry Pickering Walker," Find a Grave, http://www.findagrave.com/cgi-bin/fg.cgi.
97. "Historian-writer Henry P. Walker Dies," *Arizona Daily Star*, August 24, 1984, Chronicling America: Historic American Newspapers, http://chroniclingamerica.loc.gov/; "Henry Pickering Walker," *Harvard Magazine* 87, no. 3 (1985).
98. Henry Pickering Walker Jr. to the author, August 16, 2013.
99. See http://search.ancestry.com/cgi-bin/sse.dll?db=1930usfedcen&h=328906&ti=0&indiv=try&gss=pt; Original data: U.S. Bureau of the Census, Fifteenth Census

of the United States, 1930 (Washington, DC: National Archives and Records Administration, 1930), T626.

100. See http://search.ancestry.com/cgi-bin/sse.dll?db=canadianbc&h=4173205&ti=0&indiv=try&gss=pt; Original data: Records of the Immigration and Naturalization Service, RG 85 (Washington, DC: National Archives and Records Administration).

101. See http://search.ancestry.com/cgi-bin/sse.dll?db=nypl&h=2014132991&ti=0&indiv=try&gss=pt; Original data: Passenger Lists of Vessels Arriving at New York, New York, 1820–1897, Records of the U.S. Customs Service (Washington, DC: National Archives and Records Administration), National Archives microfilm publication M237, 675 rolls.

102. See http://person.ancestry.com/tree/21327721/person/1067125641/facts. Original Source: General Records of the Department of State (Washington, DC: National Archives and Records Administration), record group RG59-Entry 205, 1950–1954 Switzerland K–Z, box 1015.

103. Nina Chinn Walker, unpublished autobiography B, 1937, 546.

104. *Washington Times*, February 10, 1918, Chronicling America: Historic American Newspapers, http://chroniclingamerica.loc.gov/.

105. Nina Chinn Walker, unpublished autobiography B, 1937, 563.

106. Ibid., 569–570.

107. Ibid., 606–607.

108. Ibid., 592.

109. Ibid., 607.

110. A. Jaquelin Todd to Elizabeth G. Walker, September 19, 1921, included in an old scrapbook discovered by Cindy Iverson.

111. Nina Chinn Walker, unpublished autobiography B, 1937, 608.

112. Ibid., 609.

113. "Elizabeth Walker to Wed," *Washington Post*, September 14, 1921, ProQuest Historical Newspapers, *Washington Post* Archives; *Washington Times*, September 12, 1921, and *New York Tribune*, September 18, 1921, both available at Chronicling America: Historic American Newspapers, http://chroniclingamerica.loc.gov/.

114. Nina Chinn Walker, unpublished autobiography B, 1937, 610.

115. "Davis, Who Got Helium from Gas, Dies," *Washington Post*, October 5, 1938, ProQuest Historical Newspapers, *Washington Post* Archives.

116. *Washington Times*, October 6, 1921, Chronicling America: Historic American Newspapers, http://chroniclingamerica.loc.gov/; Nina Chinn Walker, unpublished autobiography B, 1937, 613–614.

117. Unsigned to Elizabeth G. Walker Davis, included in an old scrapbook discovered by Cindy Iverson.

118. Nina Chinn Walker, unpublished autobiography B, 1937, 654.

119. Ibid., 676.

120. "Davis, Who Got Helium from Gas, Dies," *Washington Post*, October 5, 1938, ProQuest Historical Newspapers, *Washington Post* Archives.

121. "John Davis Williams," Find a Grave, Memorial #18768036, http://www.findagrave.com/cgi-bin/fg.cgi (accessed February 15, 2013).

122. "Elizabeth W. Davis, Sister of Judge," *Washington Post*, August 4, 1968, ProQuest Historical Newspapers, *Washington Post* Archives.

123. California, San Francisco Area Funeral Home Records, 1895–1985, Ancestry.com. Original data: San Francisco Area Funeral Home Records, 1895–1985, Researchity.com, microfilm publication, 1129 rolls.

124. Elizabeth Walker Davis to the author, e-mail, August 7, 2013.

125. Elizabeth Walker Davis to the author, e-mail, August 11, 2013.
126. Nina Chinn Walker, unpublished autobiography A, 1934, 53.
127. Ibid., 10–11.
128. District of Columbia, Find a Grave Index, 1790–2012, Ancestry.com. Original data: Find a Grave, http://www.findagrave.com/cgi-bin/fg.cgi (accessed February 15, 2013).
129. Elizabeth Walker Davis to the author, e-mail, August 11, 2013.
130. B. M. D'Onofrio et al., "A Genetically Informed Study of the Intergenerational Transmission of Marital Instability," *Journal of Marriage and Family* 69 (2007): 793–809; P. R. Amato, "Explaining the Intergenerational Transmission of Divorce," *Journal of Marriage and the Family* 58 (1996): 628–640; P. R. Amato and A. Booth, "Consequences of Parental Divorce and Marital Unhappiness for Adult Well-Being," *Social Forces* 69 (1991): 895–914; L. Bumpass, T. C. Martin, and J. A. Sweet, "The Impact of Family Background and Early Marital Factors on Marital Disruption," *Journal of Family Issues* 12 (1991): 22–42; A. Diekmann and K. Schmidheiny "The Intergenerational Transmission of Divorce: A Fifteen-Country Study with the Fertility and Family Survey," *Comparative Sociology* 12 (2013): 211–235; J. D. Teachman, "Stability across Cohorts in Divorce Risk Factors," *Demography* 39 (2002): 331–351.
131. C. T. Gager, S. T. Yabiku, and M. R. Linver, "Conflict or Divorce? Does Parental Conflict and/or Divorce Increase Likelihood of Adult Children's Cohabiting and Marital Dissolution?" *Marriage and Family Review* 52 (2016): 243–261; S. E. Jacquet and C. A. Surra, "Parental Divorce and Premarital Couples: Commitment and Other Relationship Characteristics," *Journal of Marriage and Family* 63 (2001): 627–638; S. G. Johnston and A. M. Thomas, "Divorce versus Intact Parental Marriage and Perceived Risk and Dyadic Trust in Present Heterosexual Relationships," *Psychology Reports* 78 (1996): 387–390; P. R. Amato and D. D. DeBoer, "The Transmission of Marital Instability across Generations: Relationship Skills or Commitment to Marriage?" *Journal of Marriage and Family* 63, no. 4 (2001): 1038, 1046.
132. Nina Chinn Walker, unpublished autobiography B, 1937, 453.
133. Ibid., 453–454.
134. Ibid., 522.
135. Ibid., 539–540.
136. Ibid., 540.
137. Ibid., 542.
138. Ibid., 551.
139. Ibid., 575.
140. 1920 U.S. Census, Washington, DC, Ancestry.com, roll T625_206, p. 11A, enumeration district 67, image 842 (images reproduced by FamilySearch). Original data: U.S. Bureau of the Census, Fourteenth Census of the United States, 1920 (Washington, DC: National Archives and Records Administration, 1920), NARA microfilm publication T625, 2076 rolls.
141. 1930 U.S. Census Place, Washington, DC, Ancestry.com, roll 293, p. 3B, enumeration district 0051, image 488.0, FHL microfilm 2340028. Original data: U.S. Bureau of the Census, Fifteenth Census of the United States, 1930 (Washington, DC: National Archives and Records Administration, 1930), T626.
142. "G.A. Finch Named Professor in Law," *Washington Post*, October 4, 1931, and "Schools and Colleges," *Washington Post*, December 4, 1932, both available from ProQuest Historical Newspapers, *Washington Post* Archives.
143. "Chevy Chase Tea Is Told of Engagement," *Washington Post*, March 22, 1931, ProQuest Historical Newspapers, *Washington Post* Archives.

144. Year: 1940; Census Place: Washington, District of Columbia, District of Columbia; Roll: T627_571; Page 3A; Enumeration District: 1–535; online publication (Provo, UT: Ancstry.com Operations, 2012). Original data: U.S. Bureau of the Census. Sixteenth Census of the United States, 1940 (Washington, DC: National Archives and Records Administration, 1940), T627.

145. Priscilla Grahame Walker Shows, telephone interview by the author, June 27, 2016.

146. "J. Grahame Walker, Judge, County Council President," *Washington Post*, February 12, 1968, ProQuest Historical Newspapers, *Washington Post* Archives.

147. "Marion Boss Walker," U.S., Find a Grave Index, 1600s–Current, http://www.findagrave.com/cgi-bin/fg.cgi (accessed February 15, 2013).

148. Nina Chinn Walker, unpublished autobiography B, 1937, 600–638.

149. "Society: Entertainment keep Society Busy," *Washington Post*, July 15, 1928, ProQuest Historical Newspapers, *Washington Post* Archives.

150. "Insurance Body Honors R. Serrell W. Walker," *Washington Post*, August 29, 1932, ProQuest Historical Newspapers, *Washington Post* Archives.

151. "Exploiting Army-Navy Men," *Washington Post*, January 13, 1929, ProQuest Historical Newspapers, *Washington Post* Archives.

152. "Why Workmen's Compensation Insurance Costs More," *Washington Post*, August 24, 1932, ProQuest Historical Newspapers, *Washington Post* Archives.

153. "For a Religious Revival," *Washington Post*, March 12, 1934, ProQuest Historical Newspapers, *Washington Post* Archives.

154. "R. S. Walker, 69, Former FAA Employee," *Washington Post*, August 5, 1970, ProQuest Historical Newspapers, *Washington Post* Archives.

155. R. Serrell W. Walker, *O Mother Mine! Happy Times with Little Rhymes* (New York: Exposition Press, 1953), front and back flaps.

156. See http://interactive.ancestrylibrary.com/9279/43067_172028004349_0584-00161/27934343?backurl=http%3a%2f%2fsearch.anc estrylibrary.com%2fcgi-bin%2fsse.dll%3fgst%3d-6&ssrc=&backlabel=ReturnSearchResults.

157. R. Serrell W. Walker, *O, Mother Mine!*, 53.

158. R. Serrell W. Walker, *Farewell, Dear Heart! Poems of Devotion* (New York: Exposition Press, 1952).

159. "R. S. Walker, 69, Former FAA Employee," *Washington Post*, August 5, 1970.

160. "Robert Serrell W. Walker," U.S., Find a Grave Index, 1600s–Current, Ancestry.com. Original data: Find a Grave, http://www.findagrave.com/cgi-bin/fg.cgi.

161. Social Security Death Index, Ancestry.com. Original data: Social Security Administration, Social Security Death Index, master file.

162. Nina Chinn Walker, unpublished autobiography B, 1937, 605–606, 622, 638.

163. "Banking Graduates Given Certificates," *Washington Post*, September 20, 1928; "Banking Students End First Semester," *Washington Post*, April 13, 1929; and "Realty Bonds Deposit Rises to $11,500,000," *Washington Post*, September 12, 1933, all available from ProQuest Historical Newspapers, *Washington Post* Archives.

164. "Miss Cox to Be Wed to Herbert Walker," *New York Times*, April 12, 1936, N5, ProQuest Historical Newspapers, *New York Times* Archives; Social Security Death Index, Ancestry.com. Original data: Social Security Administration, Social Security Death Index, master file.

165. "Adaline P. Cox, Herbert Walker Plan Marriage," *Washington Post*, April 12, 1936, and "Herbert Walker and Miss Cox Are Married," *Washington Post*, June 7, 1936, both available from ProQuest Historical Newspapers, *Washington Post* Archives.

166. Herbert Wood Walker Jr., interview by the author, June 30, 2016.

167. "A. I. B. Delegates to Convention Are Nominated," *Washington Post*, April 15, 1938, ProQuest Historical Newspapers, *Washington Post* Archives.

168. See http://search.ancestry.com/cgi-bin/sse.dll?db=1940usfedcen&h=650399&ti=0&indv=try&gss=pt.

169. Herbert Wood Walker Jr., interview by the author, June 30, 2016.

170. Ibid.; Anne Cox Walker, interview by the author, July 5, 2016.

171. Anne Cox Walker, interview by the author, July 5, 2016.

172. "Phone Annex Can't Exceed Height Limit," *Washington Post*, November 27, 1947, ProQuest Historical Newspapers, *Washington Post* Archives.

173. Rebecca W. P. Walker to James W. G. Walker, November 13, 1896, 7–8, photocopy in the author's possession.

174. According to www.healthline.com, Asperger's syndrome (AS) is one of a group of neurological disorders known as autism spectrum disorders (ASDs). AS is considered to be on the mild end of the spectrum. People with AS have difficulty with social interaction and exhibit repetitive behavior, rigidity in thinking, and a focus on rules and routines.

175. Herbert Wood Walker Jr., interview by the author, June 30, 2016.

176. Anne Cox Walker, interview by the author, July 5, 2016.

177. Hoffert, *A History of Gender in America*, 294.

178. Kathy Peiss, "Charity Girls and City Pleasures: Historical Notes on Working Class Sexuality, 1880–1920," in *Feminist Frontiers III*, ed. Laurel Richardson and Verta Taylor (New York: McGraw Hill College, 1993).

179. Ibid.

180. U.S. City Directories, 1822–1995, Ancestry.com.

181. U.S. City Massachusetts, Marriage Index, 1901–1955 and 1966–1970, Ancestry.com.

182. U.S. Passenger and Crew Lists, 1820–1963, Ancestry.com.

183. Laurel Thatcher Ulrich, "Vertuous Women Found: New England Ministerial Literature, 1668–1735," *American Quarterly* (online) 28 (1976): 20–40.

Index

Note: Page numbers in *italics* refer to illustrations.

adultery: circumstantial evidence of, 143–146; condonation of, 147–148, 219, 226; as grounds for divorce, 75–76; sexually transmitted disease and, 2–3; in *Walker v. Walker*, 12, 33–34, 94, 143–146, 149
alienation of affection, 91–92, 296n87
alimony, 3, 77, 149, 155, 167–169, 211, 229–231, 232, 236
Allen, Dr. Edward S., 213–214
Alsop, Rev. Reese F., 7, 57, 103, 174–175, 203
American Sociological Society (now American Sociological Association), 2
Amherst College, 268
Anthony, Susan B., 3
Asperger's syndrome, 274

Baker, Darius, 95–96, 132, 140–141, 154–155, 168, 169; children of, 142
Balch, Dr. Alfred W., 196
Bangs, Mary F., 127–128, 214
Barney, Walter Hammond, 77–78
Barney, Walter Howard, 78
Barrows, Chester W., 167–168
Bartlett, Ida R., 126
Belmont, (Mrs.) Alva, 155
Belmont, Oliver Hazard Perry, 155

Bessie W. Manchester v. Jonathan G. Manchester, 97
Blamey, Mary Ella Carper, 270
Bonaparte, Charles Joseph, 47–48
Boss, Marion Caroline, 245, 269
Boston, James Walker's experiences in, 33–35, 39, 108–109, 113, 114, 119, 181–182, 185, 199–200, 202
Boston Navy Yard, James Walker's assignment to, 29
Bromwell, Dr. Joseph R., 8, 20
Brookline, Massachusetts, Walker family in, 29–30, 85, 98, 122, 125, 185
Brooklyn, New York: James Walker's experiences in, 58–59, 100, 112, 117, 131, 202, 215, 216; James Walker's seizure of his children for, 60–62, 102, 104, 107, 124; Walker family in, 188–189
Brooklyn Navy Yard, 58, 188, 201–202
Brown, George J., 155
Brownfield, Maine: James Walker in, *162, 163*, 165–167, 204–205, 252–256; James Walker's farm in, *163*, 166, 204–205; Rebecca White Walker's farm ownership in, 229–230; Stickney Tavern in, 255
Burdick, Clark, 78, 295n30

INDEX

Cabot, Dr. Hugh, 176–177
Caudle lecture, 123, 298n2
charity girls, 275
Charleston Navy Yard: John E. W. Cochran at, 175, 176, 182–183; Mabel Cochrane at, 37–40, 99, 102–103, 113–114, 118, 123, 175–176, 181, 185–187, 199, 200–201, 205, 218–219; Jewell Filtration Company at, 45–48, 50–51; Walker family at, 36–37, 38–40, 56–58, 98–99, 102–103, 112, 113–114, 201; James Walker's assignment to, 36–37, 45–48
Charmian, Pennsylvania, 59
Chautauquan Magazine, 35–36
Child, Alma H., 132, 217
child custody: historical practice of, 242; in *Walker v. Walker*, 77, 78–79, 93–94, 148–149, 169–170, 229–231, 242
child punishment: by James Walker, 100, 103–104, 107, 111, 189, 205; by Rebecca White Pickering Walker, 60, 124, 127
Chinn, Elizabeth Bertha, 8, 20, *157;* birth of, 18; death of, 251; estate of, 251–252; letter to Rebecca White Pickering Walker from, 31–33, 122, 129–130, 134, 248; in Newport, Rhode Island, 73; post-trial life of, 247–252; retrial testimony of, 179, 180; trial testimony of, 106–108, 134; James Walker's alienation of affection lawsuit against, 91–92; on James Walker's behavior, 107, 179; James Walker's view of, 201; Nina Walker's rivalry with, 248–251
Chinn, Elizabeth Holmes, 14
Chinn, Nina. *See* Walker, Nina Chinn
Chinn, Richard Henry (father of Nina Chinn), 14, 15, 18–19
Chinn, Richard Henry (grandfather of Nina Chinn), 14, 266
Chinn, Virginia Serrellina (née Wood), 7, 8, 14; Nina Chinn's tea held by, 20–21; Richard Chinn's separation from, 18–19; estate of, 251–252; Richard FitzGerald's suspicion of, 79; marriage of, 15; in Newport, Rhode Island, 73–74, 88–90; retrial testimony of, 178–179; stroke and death of, 244, 250; trial testimony of, 104–106; veracity of, 130–131, 215–216; James Walker's alienation of affection lawsuit against, 91–92; on James Walker's behavior, 104–106; in Washington, DC, 18, 88–90
Clark, Frank Wigglesworth, 215

Clark, (Mrs.) Mary, 215
Cloyne House School, 69–70, 93, 202, 205, 237, 249, 269–270, 280
Cochran, John (Jack) E. W., 37; in Charleston, 175, 176, 182–183, 185; retrial testimony of, 182–183
Cochrane, Mabel, 33–34; Jennie Collins's deposition on, 221; Sarah R. Crapo's retrial testimony about, 181–182, 200; William H. Crapo's testimony about, 108–109, 147; in divorce petition by Nina Walker, 94, 95; Susan Grimes Walker FitzGerald's meetings with, 149–151; housekeeper position of, 37; Drs. Palmer and Culbertson's examinations of, 150–151, 153, 171–173, 226, 227; photograph of, 102–103, 117–118, 134, 202–203, 217–218; post-trial life of, 274–275; refusal to testify by, 212–213, 222–223; Charles Slappy's testimony about, 175–176; vaginal smear from, 198; as Walker children's governess, 103, 184; Walkers' invitation to Washington to, 40–41, 113, 118, 123, 184, 186–187, 201; James Walker's photograph in possession of, 181–182, 200, 219. *See also* virginity (Mabel Cochrane's); Walker–Cochrane correspondence; Walker–Cochrane relationship
Collins, Jennie, 221
Colwell, Francis, 78
Cooley, Charles, 8
Cooper, Dr. Almon, 131–132, 217
Cox, Adaline Peter, 245, 272
Crapo, Sarah R., 170, 181–182, 200, 229
Crapo, William H., 108–109, 147; death of, 170
Crawford, Margaret E., 221
Culbertson, Dr. Emma B., 150–151; affidavit from, 153; Mabel Cochrane's examination by, 151, 153, 154, 173; retrial testimony of, 173, 226
Cushing, Dr. Ernest, 193–194, 208
Cutts, Dr. Henry M., 131, 216

Darrah, Dr. Rufus E., 220
Davis, Elizabeth (Nina's maternal grandmother, aka Elizabeth Davis Wood), 14, 19, 57, 266
Davis, Elizabeth Grimes Walker (Mrs. John Williams Davis). *See* Walker, Elizabeth Grimes (Mrs. John Williams Davis)

Davis, Elizabeth Walker (daughter of Elizabeth Grimes Walker Davis), 244, 245–246; on Chinn sisters' rivalry, 248, 250; on her parents' marriage, 265; on James Walker, 254–255
Davis, John (Jack) Williams, 243, 263–266
Davis, John Williams, Jr., 245
Davis, Richard Beale, 264
de bene evidence, 100, 103, 182, 297n4
Deland, Margaret, 142
delphiniums, 71–72
DeNormandie, Dr. Robert L., 207
Dewey, George W., 31, 132
divorce: Margaret Deland on, 142; high-society, 3–4; historical rates of, 1–2, 3, 283n4; intergenerational, 130, 215–216, 266–267; legal grounds for, 4–5, 75–76; newspaper coverage of, 3–4, 82–83, 97, 128–129, 136–137; in Rhode Island, 4–5, 76–77; sociological theories about, 2, 142, 266–267; in South Carolina, 75; state-related differences in, 4–5, 75–76; in Washington, DC, 75. *See also Walker v. Walker* (divorce petition by Nina Walker); *Walker v. Walker* (Maine); *Walker v. Walker* (Rhode Island, first trial); *Walker v. Walker* (Rhode Island, second trial); *Walker v. Walker* (Rhode Island, Motion for Reargument of divorce suit); *Walker v. Walker* (Rhode Island, final Divorce Hearing for absolute divorce)
Dougherty, John, 45, 46, 48
Dubois, Edward C., 93
Dziecioloski, Joanna (Mrs. Henry Pickering Walker Jr.), 261

Ellenbreck, Edward, 231
Epting, C. D., 181
extramarital relationships. *See* adultery

FitzGerald, Anne, 67
FitzGerald, Rebecca, 67
FitzGerald, Richard Yancey, 67; death of, 259; post-trial life of, 257–258; Rebecca White Pickering Walker's advice from, 74; in *Walker v. Walker*, 79, 80, 259
FitzGerald, Susan (daughter of Susan G. W. FitzGerald and Richard Y. FitzGerald), 67
FitzGerald, Susan Grimes Walker, 8, 30, 157; birth of, 16; children of, 67; Mabel Cochrane's meetings with, 149–151; death of, 259; in Newport, Rhode Island, 92; political career of, 258–259; post-trial life of, 257–258; trial testimony of, 79, 80–81, 120; Walker children's care by, 66–67, 68, 92, 141, 206, 219–220; Nina Walker's thank-you letter to, 68–69, 79, 219–220; women's suffrage activity of, 80–81, 155, 258–259; working life of, 67
Frazier, John, 181
Freeman, Eben Winthrop, 167
Fremont, John C., 115

Giddings, Franklin, 142
Gilman, Charlotte Perkins, 3
Goddard, Frances Dana (Mrs. Henry White Pickering), 14
gonorrhea (James Walker's), 2–3, 33; acute, 196; Dr. Edward S. Allen's testimony about, 213–214; Dr. Alfred W. Balch's deposition about, 196; Dr. Hugh Cabot's testimony about, 176–177; chronic, 52–53, 116, 190–192, 196–198, 213–214; Dr. Charles H. Gwynn's testimony about, 116–117, 190–193; knowing communication of, 152; list of remedies (prescription) for, 100, 109–110, 112, 115–116, 176–177, 190, 193; pelvic inflammatory disease and, 63; Dr. Henry Joseph Perry's testimony about, 133, 196–197; physicians' retrial testimony about, 176–177, 190–193, 196–198, 214, 220–221; physicians' testimony about, 109–110, 115–117, 133–134, 152; Dr. George Douglas Ramsay's testimony about, 109–110, 133; Dr. James Foster Scott's deposition about, 220–221; Dr. William A. Sherman's testimony about, 177; smear for, 198; Dr. Paul Thorndike's testimony about, 197–198; James Walker's letters about, 51–52, 100, 176; James Walker's symptoms of, 51–53; James Walker's testimony about, 112, 119, 190; Nina Walker's testimony about, 100, 103, 218; Dr. Charles M. Whitney's testimony about, 115–116, 192–193; wives' infection with, 2–3, 33
Gray, Justine Sutton, 4
Green, Edward W., 8
Gregory, L. E., 45

Greytown (San Juan del Norte), Nicaragua, 28
Griffin, Dr. Edward Harrison, 3–4
Grimes, James Wilson, 13, 15, 16
Grimes, Susan, 13
"gross misbehavior and wickedness," 4–5, 76–77, 95; petition for new trial by, 232–236
Grove, Dr. W. D., 106
Gwynn, Dr. Charles H., 116–117, 190–192

Hare, Dr. Charles Henry, 207
Harris, Frederic R., 45–47, 216
Harvard University, 17, 75, 132, 216
Harvey, Sydney, 225, 237, 238
Harvey, William R., 75, 294n11
Hedges, Amelia, 216
Hollyday, R. C., 58
Holmes, Oliver Wendell, 132
Howard, George E., 2, 142
Hubbard, Dr. Joshua C., 195
Hull, Helen (Mrs. Helen Kellogg), 126, 151, 183–184
Huntington, Oliver W., 69–70, 93, 237
Hyde, Charles Cheney, 30

Isthmian Canal Commission, 34

Jewell Filtration Company, 45–48, 50–51
"Journey through Central America" (Walker), 35–36

Kaan, Dr. George W., 207
Kellog, Helen (née Hull), 126, 151, 183–184

Lee, Thomas Z., 78
Legaré, George Swinton, 47
Levy, Max, 75, 294n12
Little, William McCarty, 180
Loeb, William, 47
Long, John Davis, 31

Mahon, Mary A., 92
Malloy, William P., 117
Mason, Dr. Nathaniel R., 207
Massachusetts: divorce in, 75; Walker family residence in, 29–33, 85, 98, 122, 125, 185
Massachusetts Institute of Technology (MIT), 17
Mawin, Clara W., 92

May, Elaine Tyler, 2
McBride, Louis B., 215
McCann, Francis I., 78
McCullough, David, 18
McKinley, William, 25, 27, 29
Moore, W. O., 181
Morgan, Dr. William Gerry, 62–63, 188
Morton, Paul, 45, 47
Mueller, Frank, 231
Mullen, Alice P., 126, 211

National Cathedral School, 236–237
National Woman Suffrage Association, 3, 81
Newell, Dr. Franklin S., 207
Newport, 28
Newport, Rhode Island: Catherine and Kay Streets Walker family residence in, 228; Virginia Chinn in, 70, 73–74, 88–90, 179; cottage, Walker family residence in, 228; Henry Goddard Pickering's visit to, 128, 205–206; Rhode Island Avenue Walker family residence in, 73–74, 88–90, 94, 228; Nina Walker's boardinghouse stay in, 71–73, 88, 104, 110, 189, 202; Nina Walker's Washington St. boardinghouse stay in, 70, 99, 178
Newport Naval Training Station, 66–70, 189; Virginia Serrellina Chinn and Elizabeth Bertha Chinn's stay at, 70, 104, 105, 107, 109; Susan Grimes Walker FitzGerald at, 66–68, 92, 141–142, 183, 206, 211, 219; Frances Pickering Walker Thomas at, 92, 141–142; Nina Walker's departure from, 9–12, 73–74, 84, 87–88, 101, 103, 110–111, 189; Rebecca White Pickering Walker at, 93–94, 127–128, 209, 214; Walker family's residence at, 66, 73, 81–82, 83–84, 87, 99, 189
Newport Water Works v. William N. McVicker, 91
Nicaragua Canal Commission, 27–28
Noyes, Joseph, 216

Ocean to Ocean: An Account, Personal and Historical, of Nicaragua and Its People (Walker), 29, 34–35, 63
Oleary, Julia, 92
O'Leary, Timothy C., 126

O'Neill, William L., 1
Owens, Robert Dale, 142
oxaluria, 52–53, 133–134, 177, 291n19

Palmer, Dr. Sarah Ellen, 150–151, 227; affidavit from, 153; Mabel Cochrane's examination by, 151, 153, 154, 172–173; retrial testimony of, 171–173, 226
Parker, John, 8
Parks, Charles W., 215
Patterson, Nan, 44, 123, 209, 290n89
pelvic inflammatory disease, 63
Perry, Dr. Henry Joseph, 133, 196–197, 198
Pickering, Edward C., 132, 216–217
Pickering, Henry, 31
Pickering, Henry Goddard, 8, 16; death of, 253; estate of, 253; retrial testimony of, 205–206; trial testimony of, 128; Nina Walker's divorce petition testimony of, 85–86; Nina Walker's letter to, 60, 206; on *Walker v. Walker*, 79
Pickering, Henry White, 14
Pickering, John, 13
Pickering, Timothy, 13
Picking, H. F., 29
Pollock, Virginia S., 82
Portsmouth, New Hampshire, Walker family at, 63–65, 167, 189
Portsmouth Navy Yard, James Walker's assignment to, 63–64, 167
Potter, Ben, 263–264
press, *Walker v. Walker* coverage by, 82–83, 97, 128–129, 136–137
Progressive Period: divorce in, 1–5, 142; father-child relations in, 126; marital expectations during, 238–239; political and industrial scandals in, 45–48; urban working girls in, 274–275

Ramsay, Dr. George Douglas, 109–110, 133, 152
Rathbun, Elmer J., 82, 83, 84, 90, 91, 236, 237
Razor v. Razor, 100
Reynolds, Dr. Edward, 179–180
Rhode Island: Court and Practice Act (1905) of, 82; divorce in, 4–5, 76–77 (*see also Walker v. Walker* [Rhode Island, first trial]; *Walker v. Walker* [Rhode Island, second trial]; *Walker v. Walker* [Rhode Island, Motion for Reargument of divorce suit]; *Walker v. Walker* [Rhode Island, final Divorce Hearing for absolute divorce])
Rhode Island Bar Association, 82
Richardson, Henry T., 212–213
Riley, Andrew J., 46
Ripley, Eliza, 19; retrial deposition of, 215–216; trial deposition of, 130–131, 134, 152
Ripley, Elsie, 8
Roosevelt, Theodore, 47

Sanford, James C., 243
Sanman, Katherine Alice (Mrs. Henry Pickering Walker), 65, 211, 260–261
Scott, Dr. James Foster, 85, 90, 190, 199, 220–221, 229
Sears, Richard W., 128–129, 135–136, 171, 261
Sears v. Walker, 135–136, 171, 261
sexually transmitted infections, 2–3, 33. *See also* gonorrhea (James Walker's)
Sheffield, William Paine, Jr., 73, 75, 294n10
Sherman, Dr. William A., 152, 177
Slappy, Charles, 175–176, 199, 218, 225–226
Slocum, Annetta, 4
Slocum, Dr. William H., 4
Smith, Boyd, 256–257
Smith, (Mrs.) Boyd, 256
Smith, Dr. Edgar B., 212
South Carolina, divorce in, 75
Spencer, Herbert, 2
St. Albans School, 249
Stanton, Elizabeth Cady, 3, 81
Stearns, Charles Falconer, 78–79, 136, 170, 225–227, 302n26
Stevens v. Stevens, 299–300n11
Stewart, Dr. Charles W., 212
Storer, Dr. Malcolm, 194
suffragist movement. *See* women's suffrage
Sullivan, Mortimer, 136
Summers, (Mrs.) Charles G., 31
Sumner, William Graham, 2
syphilis, 2–3

Taft, Theodore M., 30
Taylor, Alexander O'D, 180–181
third-party correspondence, 100, 103, 182, 297n4

Thomas, Alfred, 50
Thomas, Frances (Fanny) Pickering Walker, 49–50, *157;* birth of, 15–16; burial site of, *164;* death of, 260; marriage of, 30–31; post-trial life of, 259–260; retrial testimony of, 206, 212; trial testimony of, 129–130; Walker children's care by, 32–33, 102, 122, 141, 208, 217
Thomas, John Jenks, 116; burial site of, *164;* death of, 260; marriage of, 30–31; post-trial life of, 259–260; retrial testimony of, 198–199; trial testimony of, 127; Serrell Walker's care by, 32–33, 102, 122, 208, 217
Thompson, Robert H. P., 180
Thorndike, Dr. Paul, 197–198
Topham, James G., 91
Townsend, Annie, 66
Treaty of Portsmouth, 64

University of Wisconsin, 263
U.S. Naval Academy, 15, 17, 243, 244, 270, 272

venereal diseases, 2–3, 33; knowing communication of, 152. *See also* gonorrhea (James Walker's)
virginity (Mabel Cochrane's), 195–224; Dr. Edward S. Allen's testimony about, 213; Judge Darius Baker's retrial conditions and, 155–156; Dr. Emma Culbertson's testimony about, 173; Dr. Ernest Cushing's testimony about, 193–194, 208; Dr. Rufus E. Darrah's testimony about, 220; Dr. Charles M. Green's deposition about, 195; Dr. Charles Henry Hare's deposition about, 207; Dr. Joshua C. Hubbard's deposition about, 195; Dr. Sarah Palmer's testimony about, 171–173; Dr. Sarah Palmer's and Dr. Emma Culbertson's examinations of, 150–151, 153, 154; Dr. Edward Reynolds's testimony about, 179–180; Dr. Edgar B. Smith's testimony about, 212; Judge Charles Falconer Stearns on, 226; Dr. Charles W. Stewart's testimony about, 212

Walker, Adaline Cox, 272–274
Walker, Alice Pickering, 16, *164*
Walker, Anne Cox, 272, 273, 274
Walker, Elizabeth (Bessie) Grimes, 16, *164*
Walker, Elizabeth Grimes (Mrs. John Williams Davis), 10, *161;* appendicitis of, 66–69, 206, 219–220; birth of, 28; Charleston experiences of, 56; "coming out" tea for, 243, 263; death of, 265; education of, 236–237, 262–263; marriage of, 243, 249–250, 263–264; post-trial life of, 262–267; pregnancies of, 244–245, 265; testimony against father by, 231, 262; Rebecca White Pickering Walker's care for, 59–60; Wilton, New Hampshire, experiences of, 60, 124, 127
Walker, Henry (Bud) Pickering, 261–262, 286n31
Walker, Henry (Hal, Harry) Pickering, 8, 16, 17, 30; appearance of, 18, *157;* death of, 260; marriage of, 260; post-trial life of, 260–262; retrial testimony of, 211; Richard W. Sears dispute with, 128–129, 135–136, 171, 261; trial testimony of, 127
Walker, Henry (Pick) Pickering, Jr., 261–262
Walker, Herbert Wood, 10, *161;* birth of, 33; death of, 274; hospitalization of, 54, 272; marriage of, 272; military education of, 243, 244, 272; post-trial life of, 272–274
Walker, Herbert Wood, Jr., 272–274
Walker, James Wilson Grimes: adultery of, 12, 33–34, 94, 143–146, 149; alienation of affection lawsuits by, 91–92; ancestry of, 13–14, 285nn1–2; appearance of, 18, *157, 159;* birth of, 15–16; Boston experiences of, 33–35, 39, 108–109, 113, 114, 119, 181–182, 185, 199–200, 202; Boston Navy Yard assignment of, 29; Brooklyn experiences of, 58–59, 100, 112, 117, 131, 202, 215, 216; Brooklyn Navy Yard assignment of, 58, 201–202; in Brownfield, Maine, *162, 163,* 165–167, 204–205, 252–256; burial site of, *164;* character of, 16–17, 21–26, 98, 105–107, 124–125, 210–211, 215; Charleston Navy Yard assignment of, 36–37, 45–48; Charleston Navy Yard scandal and, 45–48; childbirth absences of, 28, 30, 98, 113, 125, 184, 185, 200, 207, 210; childhood of, 16–17; chil-

dren's relationship with, 100, 102–104, 108, 120, 126–128, 135, 169–170, 178, 179, 180, 189, 205–206, 214; children's testimony against, 231, 262, 269–270; Mabel Cochrane's correspondence with (*see* Walker–Cochrane correspondence); Mabel Cochrane's photograph of, 181–182, 200, 219; Mabel Cochrane's relationship with (*see* Walker–Cochrane relationship); death of, 255–256; divorce petition delivery to, 12, 74; education of, 16–17; estate of, 256; father's relationship with, 17, 18, 60–61, 117; finances of (*see* Walker family finances); flirtations of, 33, 58–59, 100, 111–112, 114, 117, 131, 185 (*see also* Walker–Cochrane relationship); gift of jewelry for, 55; gonorrhea of (*see* gonorrhea [James Walker's]); inheritance of, 65; invitation to Mabel Cochrane to Washington by, 40–41, 113, 118, 123, 184, 186–187, 201; in Jamestown, Rhode Island, 169–170; Memorial Day 1927 address by, 253–254; naval commission resignation of, 156, 168, 204, 214–215; Navy leave for, 153–154, 156; Navy promotions of, 29, 58; New Hampshire trip of, 51; Newport Naval Training Station assignment of, 66–70; on Nicaragua Canal Commission, 27–28; Nicaragua memoir by, 29, 34–36, 63; on Nicaraguan women, 35, 36; Pensacola Naval Station assignment of, 90–91; Portsmouth Navy Yard assignment of, 63–64, 167; post-divorce life of, 252–256; premarital employment of, 17–18, 24–25; Miss Radcliffe matter and, 53, 56; retrial testimony of, 184–190, 199–205, 214–215; seizure of his children from Washington by, 60–62, 102, 104, 107, 124; siblings of, 15–16 (*see also* FitzGerald, Susan Grimes Walker; Thomas, Frances [Fanny] Pickering Walker; Walker, Alice Pickering; Walker, Elizabeth [Bessie] Grimes; Walker, Henry [Hal, Harry] Pickering; Walker, Sarah [Sallie] Cochrane); testimony of, 110–115, 117–119, 133; Nina Walker's correspondence with, 38, 49–56, 79, 100, 114, 176, 202; Nina Walker's telephone call to, 74; Rebecca White Pickering Walker's opposition to marriage of, 21–26, 210–211; wedding of, 7–9. *See also Walker v. Walker* (divorce petition by Nina Walker)

Walker, John Grahame, 10, *161;* athletic interests of, 267–268; birth of, 30; death of, 269; education of, 69–70, 93, 249, 268; marriage of, 245, 269; in Naval Reserves, 268; political career of, 269; post-trial life of, 267–269; renal surgery on, 243–244; Rebecca White Pickering Walker's care for, 59–60; Wilton, New Hampshire, experiences of, 60

Walker, John Grimes, 7, 13; appearance of, 18, *157, 160;* Charleston Navy Yard crisis and, 48; in Civil War, 15; death of, 64–66; estate of, 65, 125–126, 230–231; naval career of, 15, 16, 17, 86, 261–262, 286n17, 286n31; on Nicaragua Canal Commission, 27–28; personality of, 31; on James Walker's letters to Nina Walker, 60–61, 114; James Walker's seizure of his children and, 61–62, 102, 104, 107, 124; on Walker–Cochrane correspondence, 57, 102, 123–124, 209, 210, 218

Walker, (Mrs.) Katherine Alice Sanman, 65, 211, 260–261

Walker, Nina Chinn, *157, 158, 161;* adolescence of, 20–21; Rev. Reese F. Alsop's letter of advice to, 103, 175, 203; ancestry of, 14–15, 285n4; autobiography (unpublished) of, 239, 241–242, 246–247; in Brookline, Massachusetts, 29–30, 98, 122, 125, 185; Brooklyn move of, 61–62; in Charleston, South Carolina, 36–37, 38–39, 56–58, 98–99, 102–103, 112, 113–114, 201; at Charmian, Pennsylvania, 59; childbirth experiences of, 28, 30, 31, 33, 113, 122–123, 131–132, 134–135, 179, 200, 207–208, 210; childhood of, 18, 19–21; cruise vacation for, 66–67; death of mother of, 244, 247, 250; declaration of separation by, 72–73, 74; departure from Newport Naval Training Station by, 9–12, 73–74, 84, 87–88, 101, 103, 110–111, 189; estate of mother of, 250–251; fire in house of, 228; Susan FitzGerald's letter from, 68–69, 79, 219–220; on gift of jewelry, 51; New Hampshire trip of, 51; at Newport, Rhode Island, 65–66,

Walker, Nina Chinn *(continued)*
69–70, 71–74, 88–90, 93–94, 99, 101, 103, 110, 189, 202, 228, 242; Henry Goddard Pickering's letter from, 60, 206; Henry Goddard Pickering's visit to, 128, 205–206; ill health of, 59, 62–63, 66, 85, 106, 188, 201; poetry by, 245; at Portsmouth, New Hampshire, 63–65; post-divorce life of, 241–247; probable pelvic inflammatory disease of, 63; Miss Radcliffe matter and, 53, 56; retrial testimony of, 171, 173–174, 177–178; sexual abstinence of, 33; short story writing by, 50; sister's rivalry with, 248–251; social activities of, 21; social debut of, 20–21; tea for, 20–21; trial testimony of, 98–103, 134–135; on Elizabeth Walker's appendicitis, 67–69, 79, 219–220; James Walker's correspondence with, 49–56, 58–59, 79, 100, 114, 176, 202; John Grimes Walker's death and, 65–66; Rebecca White Pickering Walker's correspondence with, 29–30, 59–60; Washington, DC, post-trial residence of, 242–245; in Watch Hill, Rhode Island, 49–51, 99; wedding of, 7–9. *See also Walker v. Walker* (divorce petition by Nina Walker); *Walker v. Walker* (Maine); *Walker v. Walker* (Rhode Island, first trial); *Walker v. Walker* (Rhode Island, second trial); *Walker v. Walker* (Rhode Island, Motion for Reargument of divorce suit); *Walker v. Walker* (Rhode Island, final Divorce Hearing for absolute divorce)

Walker, Priscilla Grahame, 269

Walker, Rebecca White (née Pickering), 7, *157, 160;* ancestry of, 13–14; Bertha Chinn's letter to, 31–33, 129–130, 134, 248; death of, 257; divorce petition testimony of, 86; estate of, 257; finances of, 29–30, 31–32, 34, 166, 209–210, 211, 229–231; husband's abuse of, 31, 256; husband's Nicaraguan correspondence with, 28–29; marriage of, 15; post-trial life of, 256–257; premarriage letter to James Walker from, 21–26, 124–125, 210–211; retrial testimony of, 208–211; trial testimony of, 121–126; Elizabeth and Grahame Walker's stay with, 59, 60, 124, 127; on Elizabeth Grimes Walker's birth, 28, 121, 210; James Walker's seizure of his children and, 61–62, 102, 107, 124; on Nina and James Walker's Brookline home furnishings, 29–30, 122, 125; on Nina and James Walker's relationship, 61–62, 122–124, 207–208; on Nina Walker's letter to Henry Goddard Pickering, 60; on Walker–Cochrane correspondence, 57, 123–124, 209, 210

Walker, Robert Serrell Wood, 10, *161;* birth of, 31, 122; death of, 271; education of, 269–270; marriage of, 270; military education and career of, 243, 244, 270; nurse for, 31–32, 208, 217; poetry of, 270–271; post-trial life of, 269–271; testimony against father by, 231, 269–270; Frances and John Jenks Thomas's care of, 32–33, 102, 122, 208, 217

Walker, Sarah (daughter of John Grahame Walker), 269

Walker, Sarah (Sallie) Cochrane, 16, 151, *157;* burial site of, *164;* death of, 262; post-trial life of, 262; retrial testimony of, 184; trial testimony of, 127

Walker, Sarah Lydia, 78

Walker, Susan Grimes. *See* FitzGerald, Susan Grimes Walker

Walker, William, 34–35, 63

Walker–Cochrane correspondence, 40–45; Rev. Reese F. Alsop's view on, 103, 174–175, 203; Judge Darius Baker's appraisal of, 146; Mabel Cochrane's photograph with, 102–103, 117–118, 134, 202–203, 217–218; about Mabel Cochrane's Washington, DC, invitation, 40, 42, 113, 123, 186–187; Bertha Chinn's testimony about, 108; Virginia Chinn's testimony about, 105; "gross misbehavior and wickedness" ruling and, 234–235; inappropriate content of, 41–45, 118–119, 123; retrial admittance of, 182; Frances Walker Thomas's testimony about, 129, 206; James Walker's retrial testimony about, 187, 203–204; James Walker's testimony about, 115, 117–118; John Grimes Walker's views on, 57, 102, 123, 209, 210, 218; Nina Walker's copies of, 57, 99, 101–102, 103, 119, 187; Nina Walker's possession of, 44–45, 56–57; Nina Walker's retrial testimony about, 177–178, 218; Rebecca White Pickering

Walker's retrial testimony about, 209, 210; Rebecca White Pickering Walker's testimony about, 123

Walker–Cochrane relationship: in Boston, 33–35, 108–109, 113, 114, 119, 181–182, 199–200, 202; in Charleston, 37–40, 95, 99, 102–103, 113–114, 118, 123, 134, 175–176, 181, 185–187, 199–201, 205, 218–219; in Washington, DC, 40–41, 42, 103, 113, 118, 123, 186–187, 214

Walker Commission: first, 27–28; second, 34

Walker family finances: alimony and child support and, 77, 149, 155, 166, 167–169, 211, 229–230, 232, 236; Judge Chester W. Barrows's appraisal of, 168–169; Brownfield farm and, 166, 229–230; Bertha Chinn's letter about, 31–32; expenses vs. income and, 34, 200; in final Divorce Hearing for absolute divorce, 237–239; in first trial, 100–101, 112, 114, 117, 125–126; in retrial, 200, 204–205, 209–210, 211, 229–231; James Walker's retrial testimony about, 200, 204–205; James Walker's trial testimony about, 112, 114, 117; John Grimes Walker's legacies and, 65, 125–126, 168, 230–231; Nina Walker's letter to Henry Goddard Pickering about, 60; Nina Walker's testimony about, 100–101; Rebecca White Pickering Walker's contributions to, 29–30, 31–32, 34, 122, 209–210, 211, 229–231

Walker v. Walker (divorce petition by Nina Walker): alimony and, 77; ". . . from bed, board, and future cohabitation," 77; bill of particulars for, 81, 94–95; Virginia Chinn's cross-examination for, 88–90; Virginia Chinn's testimony for, 88–89; custody of Walker children and, 77, 78–79, 93–94, 170–171; dismissal of, 91, 93; jurisdictional issue in, 80, 81–82, 83–91; Henry Goddard Pickering's testimony for, 85–86; press coverage of, 82–83; Judge Elmer Rathbun for, 82, 83, 84, 90, 91; Dr. James Foster Scott's deposition for, 90; second filing of, 94–95 (*see also Walker v. Walker* [Rhode Island, first trial]); Walker children's welfare and, 88; James Walker's attorneys for, 77–78, 83–84; James Walker's cross-examination for, 85; James Walker's motion to dismiss, 81–82; James Walker's testimony for, 34, 84–85; Nina Walker's attorneys for, 83; Nina Walker's cross-examination for, 87–88; Nina Walker's testimony for, 33–34, 86–88; Rebecca White Pickering Walker's testimony for, 86. *See also Walker v. Walker* (Rhode Island, first trial)

Walker v. Walker (Maine), 165–167, 228

Walker v. Walker (Rhode Island, first trial), 97–149; alimony rulings in, 149, 155, 167–169; attorneys for James Walker in, 77–78; attorneys for Nina Walker in, 75; Judge Darius Baker for, 95–96; Judge Darius Baker on reconciliation for, 140–141; Mary F. Bangs's testimony for, 127–128; Ida R. Bartlett's testimony for, 126; bill of exceptions to ruling in, 152–153; child custody ruling in, 148–149; Alma Child's deposition for, 132; Bertha Chinn–Rebecca Walker correspondence in, 129–130; Bertha Chinn's cross-examination for, 108; Bertha Chinn's testimony for, 106–108, 134; Virginia Chinn's cross-examination for, 105–106; Virginia Chinn's testimony for, 104–105; closing argument for James Walker for, 137–139; closing argument for Nina Walker for, 139–140; Dr. Almon Cooper's deposition for, 131–132; William H. Crapo's testimony for, 108–109, 170; Henry M. Cutts's deposition for, 131; William B. Ferguson's deposition for, 131; finding of adultery in, 143–146, 149; Richard FitzGerald's interest in, 79; Susan Walker FitzGerald's testimony for, 120; Dr. W. D. Grove's deposition for, 106; Dr. Charles H. Gwynn's testimony for, 116–117; Helen E. Hull's testimony for, 126; Alice P. Mullen's testimony for, 126; nurse Latham's testimony for, 103–104; Timothy C. O'Leary's testimony for, 126; Dr. Henry Joseph Perry's testimony for, 133; petition to reopen after, 152–155; Edward C. Pickering's deposition for, 132; Henry Goddard Pickering's testimony for, 128; press coverage of, 82–83, 97, 128–129, 136–137; Dr. George Ramsay's testimony for, 109–110, 133–134, 152;

Walker v. Walker (Rhode Island, first trial) *(continued)*
residency requirement in, 76–77; Eliza Ripley's deposition for, 130–131, 134, 152; ruling in, 143–149; third-party correspondence in, 100, 103; Frances Walker Thomas's testimony for, 129–130; John Jenks Thomas's testimony for, 127; Walker children's relationship to father in, 100, 102, 107, 108, 111, 126–128, 135; Walker children's welfare in, 100, 102, 103–104, 104–105, 106, 107–108, 111, 126, 134–135; Henry Pickering Walker's testimony for, 127; James Walker–Mabel Cochrane correspondence in, 40–45, 99–100, 101–103, 105, 108, 115, 117–119, 123, 129, 134, 146 (*see also* Walker–Cochrane correspondence); James Walker–Mabel Cochrane relationship in, 33–34, 37–38, 39–41, 99, 102–103, 108–109, 113–114, 119 (*see also* Walker–Cochrane relationship); James Walker's character in, 98, 124–125; James Walker's cross-examination for, 113–115, 117–119; James Walker's finances in, 100–101, 112, 114, 117, 125–126; James Walker's gonorrhea in, 52–53, 100, 109–110, 115–117, 119, 133–134; James Walker's testimony for, 110–113, 117–119, 133; Nina Walker's cross-examination for, 101–102; Nina Walker's redirect examination for, 102–104; Nina Walker's testimony for, 98–101, 134–135; Rebecca White Pickering Walker's cross-examination for, 124–126; Rebecca White Pickering Walker's testimony for, 121–124; Sarah Cochrane Walker's testimony for, 127; Dr. Charles M. Whitney's testimony for, 115–116; George Wigglesworth's deposition for, 132

Walker v. Walker (Rhode Island, second trial), 165–232; Dr. Edward S. Allen's testimony for, 213–214; Rev. Reese F. Alsop's testimony for, 174–175, 203; Judge Darius Baker's preconditions for, 154–156, 168, 169; Dr. Alfred W. Balch's deposition for, 196; Mary F. Bangs's testimony for, 214; bill of exceptions to ruling in, 228–229, 231–232; Dr. Hugh Cabot's testimony for, 176–177; chief ground for, 152–153; child custody hearing after, 229–231; children's care in, 223, 224; Alma H. Child's testimony for, 217; Bertha Chinn's testimony for, 179, 180; Virginia Chinn's testimony for, 178–179; Mary Clark's deposition for, 215; closing arguments in, 221–224; John E. W. Cochran's testimony for, 182–183; Mabel Cochrane's photograph in, 202–203, 217–218; Mabel Cochrane's refusal to testify in, 212–213, 222–223; Mabel Cochrane's virginity in (*see* virginity [Mabel Cochrane's]); Jennie Collins's deposition for, 221; Dr. Almon Cooper's deposition for, 217; Sarah R. Crapo's testimony for, 181–182, 200; Margaret E. Crawford's deposition for, 221; Emma B. Culbertson's affidavit for, 153; Dr. Emma B. Culbertson's testimony for, 173, 226; Dr. Ernest Cushing's testimony for, 193–194, 208; Dr. Henry M. Cutts's deposition for, 216; Dr. Rufus E. Darrah's testimony for, 220; C. D. Epting's deposition for, 181; William B. Ferguson's deposition for, 216; Susan Walker FitzGerald's testimony for, 206; John Frazier's deposition for, 181; Dr. Charles M. Green's deposition for, 195; Dr. Charles H. Gwynn's testimony for, 190–192; Dr. Charles Henry Hare's deposition for, 207; Frederic R. Harris's deposition for, 216; Amelia Hedges's deposition for, 216; Dr. Joshua C. Hubbard's deposition for, 195; Dr. George W. Kaan's deposition for, 207; Helen Hull Kellogg's testimony for, 183–184; Louis B. McBride's deposition for, 215; William McCarty Little's testimony for, 180; W. O. Moore's deposition for, 181; motion to oppose for, 153; Alice P. Mullen's testimony for, 211; Joseph Noyes's deposition for, 216; Sarah E. Palmer's affidavit for, 153; Dr. Sarah Ellen Palmer's testimony for, 171–173, 226; Charles W. Parks's deposition for, 215; Dr. Henry Joseph Perry's testimony for, 196–197, 198; petition for, 152–155, 165; Edward Charles Pickering's deposition for, 216–217; Henry Goddard Pickering's testimony for, 205–206; Dr. Edward Reynolds's testimony for, 179–

180; Rhode Island Supreme Court ruling on Nina Walker's objection to decision in, 231–232; Henry T. Richardson's testimony for, 212–213; Eliza Ripley's deposition for, 215–216; ruling in, 225–227; Dr. James Foster Scott's testimony for, 220–221; Dr. William A. Sherman's testimony for, 177; Charles Slappy's testimony for, 175–176, 225–226; Dr. Edgar B. Smith's testimony for, 212; Judge Charles Falconer Stearns for, 170; Judge Charles Falconer Stearns's decision in, 226–227; Dr. Charles W. Stewart's testimony for, 212; Dr. Malcolm Storer's testimony for, 194; Dr. Howard T. Swain's deposition for, 207; Alexander O'D Taylor's testimony for, 180–181; Frances Walker Thomas's testimony for, 206, 212; John Jenks Thomas's testimony for, 198–199; Robert H. P. Thompson's testimony for, 180; Dr. Paul Thorndike's testimony for, 197–198; Walker children's care in, 178–179, 202, 205; Walker children's relationship to father in, 178, 179, 180, 189, 205–206, 214; Henry Pickering Walker's testimony for, 211; James Walker–Mabel Cochrane correspondence in, 174–175, 177–178, 182, 187, 203–204, 206, 209, 210, 218 (*see also* Walker–Cochrane correspondence); James Walker–Mabel Cochrane relationship in, 199–201, 202, 205, 214, 218–219 (*see also* Walker–Cochrane relationship); James Walker's cross-examination for, 190, 200–205; James Walker's finances in, 200, 204–205, 209–210, 211; James Walker's gonorrhea in, 176–177, 190–193, 196–198, 202, 213–214, 218, 220–221 (*see also* gonorrhea [James Walker's]); James Walker's personality in, 210–211; James Walker's testimony for, 184–190, 199–205, 214–215; Katherine Alice Walker's testimony for, 211; Nina Walker's cross-examination for, 174, 178; Nina Walker's testimony for, 171, 173–174, 177–178, 217–220; Rebecca White Pickering Walker's testimony for, 207–211; Sarah Cochrane Walker's testimony for, 184; Dr. Charles M. Whitney's testimony for, 192–193; George Wigglesworth's deposition for, 217

Walker v. Walker (Rhode Island, Motion for Reargument of divorce suit): "gross misbehavior and wickedness" petition for, 232–236; Rhode Island Supreme Court ruling in, 236; "Statement of Causes" filing and, 235–236

Walker v. Walker (Rhode Island, final Divorce Hearing for absolute divorce), 237–238; Judge Elmer Rathbun's decision in, 238; sealing of record in, 238

Ward, Lester, 2

Washington, DC: Virginia Chinn's residence in, 18, 88–90, 249; Mabel Cochrane's invitation to, 40–41, 113, 118, 123, 184, 186–187, 201; divorce in, 75; James Walker's seizure of his children from, 60–62, 102, 104, 107, 124; Nina Walker's post-divorce residence in, 242–247

Watch Hill, Rhode Island, Walker family at, 49–51, 99, 134, 187–188, 209

Whitney, Dr. Charles M., 115–116, 192–193, 207

Wigglesworth, George, 132, 217

Willard, Frances, 3

Wilson, Woodrow, 3, 263

women's suffrage, 3; Susan FitzGerald's activity on, 80–81, 155, 257–258; Nina Walker on, 247

Wood, Elizabeth Davis, 14, 19, 57, 266

Wood, Jefferson Serrell, 15

Wood, Robert Serrell, 14, 266

Young, Dr. Ernest B., 207
Young, Francis Thomas ("Caesar"), 44

JEAN ELSON is Senior Lecturer Emerita in the Department of Sociology at the University of New Hampshire and the author of *Am I Still a Woman? Hysterectomy and Gender Identity* (Temple).